D0259138

The
Rise and Decline
of
English Modernism

By the same author and published by SPCK

The First Lambeth Conference (1967)

Anglicanism and the Lambeth Conferences (1978)

The
Rise and Decline
of
English Modernism

THE HULSEAN LECTURES 1979–80

Alan M. G. Stephenson

First published in Great Britain 1984
SPCK
Holy Trinity Church
Marylebone Road
London NW1 4DU

British Library Cataloguing in Publication Data

Stephenson, Alan M. G.
    The rise and decline of English modernism.
    1. Church of England—History—20th century
    I. Title
    283'.42'0904   BX5101

    ISBN 0-281-04124-5

    Photoset and printed in Great Britain by
        Photobooks (Bristol) Ltd

These Hulsean Lectures are dedicated to
The Reverend Percival Gardner-Smith M.A., B.D.,
now in his ninety-seventh year;
distinguished Anglican Modernist, Life Fellow
of Jesus College, Cambridge, Dean 1922–56,
President 1948–58, University Lecturer in
Theology at Cambridge 1926–53, enthusiastic
student of theology who taught the author from
1950 to 1954

Contents

Bibliographies

Preface

My interest in the English Modernist Movement began when I arrived at Ripon Hall, Oxford, in 1954 for my ministerial training under Bishop Geoffrey Allen. I was intrigued by the portraits in the magnificent dining hall of prominent English Modernists of the past – Hastings Rashdall, M. G. Glazebrook, H. D. A. Major, Bishop Boyd Carpenter, R. H. Charles. I began learning all I could about them. Dr Henry Major, in advanced old age, was still living at Merton vicarage, near Bicester, Oxfordshire (and his wife too), and I was able to meet and talk to him on several occasions. There could be no better place than Ripon Hall at which to study the subject, as the amount of Modernist literature in the library there was vast. Of course at that time Modernism was considered to be already dead and I cannot recall any fellow student who was interested in the subject.

After a curacy at Knaresborough in Yorkshire and then four years as tutor of Lichfield Theological College, I returned in 1962 as vice-principal of Ripon Hall and began the study of English Modernism and the history of Ripon Hall in earnest. Major had died in 1961 and all his letters and papers had now been deposited at Ripon Hall. This was a unique collection.

These Hulsean Lectures are part of the fruit of that research. No one has published any study of the Movement before. I am glad that SPCK has agreed to publish all the appendices which I added to the original lectures, since these give a great deal of information about English Modernism and its personalities. There is also a comprehensive list of all the Hulsean Lectures since the foundation of the Lectureship.

I have entitled the book *The Rise and Decline of English Modernism*; this was the title of the original lectures. It was suggested by the title of H. D. A. Major's *English Modernism: Its Origin, Methods, Aims*, the William Belden Noble Lectures of 1925–6, which were published by Harvard University Press in 1927. However, I agree that a more accurate title would be 'The Rise and Decline of Anglican Modernism'.

While the lectures were being delivered I was kindly entertained by many members of the theological faculty at their colleges and I am most grateful for their generous hospitality. Dr John Robinson, the Dean of Trinity College, attended all the lectures and gave me a great deal of encouragement. I am sorry he has not lived to see them published. He alluded to them in his book *The Roots of a Radical* (1980):

> I have recently been sitting at Cambridge through a fascinating course of Hulsean Lectures on the English Modernists – the story of the Modern Churchmen's Union, Bishop Barnes, and all that. My sympathies have been with their intellectual courage, but on the whole (there were great exceptions like Charles Raven) they do not seem to have had much fire in their belly. They were accused by their opponents of presenting 'the gospel of negativity', and a more bloodless expression of it 'sickled o'er with the pale cast of thought' one could often hardly imagine. It was said of them, unfairly, that the question from which they started was 'What will Jones swallow?' When similarly charged myself, I used to reply with William Temple, 'No. I am Jones asking what there is to eat.' And a genuine concern for what of the old fare was edible, for what in it really was good news, did underlie the work of the liberals and of the radicals after them (p.83).

The theology of the great Modernists of the past has been superseded and no longer has its protagonists. Nevertheless the Modern Churchmen's Conference, started by Major in 1914, continues to meet successfully every year. Also *The Modern Churchman*, founded by Major in 1911, has recently taken on a new lease of life and is gaining an increasing membership. Ripon Hall was sold to the Open University, but all the Modernist portraits, relics and archives are carefully preserved at Ripon College, Cuddesdon, which is in a flourishing state.

In conclusion I should like to thank the Electors to the Hulsean Lectureship for electing me to this office for 1979 and 1980. It was a great honour, and I note that I am the first incumbent of a parish to be elected since the 1920s. I would also thank my elder son, David, who attended all the lectures, for his help in seeing the book through the press.

Acknowledgements

The publication of these Lectures has been made possible by grants from the following sources: The Most Rev. Robert Runcie, the Archbishop of Canterbury (Davidson Fund); Christ Church, Oxford; The Modern Churchmen's Union; Ripon College, Cuddesdon; The Rt. Rev. Patrick Rodger, Bishop of Oxford.

Extracts from *The Modern Churchman*, extracts from *Return to the Roots* by John Wren Lewis, and official documents and memoranda of The Modern Churchmen's Union, are all reprinted by kind permission The Modern Churchmen's Union.

Extracts from *Decline and Fall* by Evelyn Waugh, published by Chapman & Hall, are reprinted by permission of A. D. Peters & Co. Ltd.

Extracts from *The Retrospect of an Unimportant Life* by H. H. Henson are reprinted by permission of Oxford University Press.

1

English Modernism and Hulseans

The reader of Evelyn Waugh's novel *Decline and Fall* will remember how the story ends with the hero, Paul Pennyfeather, studying at Scone College, Oxford, with a view to regaining respectability by ordination. The seventh chapter of Part III ends with the words:

> Then the lecturer came in, arranged his papers, and began a lucid exposition of the heresies of the second century. There was a bishop in Bithynia, Paul learned, who had denied the Divinity of Christ, the immortality of the soul, the existence of good, the legality of marriage, and the validity of the Sacrament of Extreme Unction! How right they had been to condemn him!

As he pursues his theological studies, Paul Pennyfeather exhibits no sympathy with any form of modernism, and in the last paragraph of the book we find him gladly accepting the suppression of the Ebionites because 'they used to turn towards Jerusalem when they prayed'. In this respect he is unlike the Rev. Mr Prendergast, a master at that notorious school, Llanabba Castle, who in Chapter Four introduces himself to Paul Pennyfeather with these words:

> 'Ten years ago I was a clergyman of the Church of England. I had just been presented to a living in Worthing. It was such an attractive church, not old, but *very* beautifully decorated, six candles on the altar, Reservation in the Lady Chapel, and an excellent heating apparatus which burned coke in a little shed by the sacristy door, no graveyard, just a hedge of golden privet between the church and the rectory.
> 'As soon as I moved in my mother came to keep house for me. She bought some chintz, out of her own money, for the

1

drawing-room curtains. She used to be "at home" once a week
to the ladies of the congregation. One of them, the dentist's
wife, gave me a set of *Encyclopaedia Britannica* for my study. It
was all very pleasant until my *Doubts* began.'

'Were they as bad as all that?' asked Paul.

'They were insuperable,' said Mr Prendergast; 'that is why I
am here now . . .'

'Yes, I've not known an hour's real happiness since. You see,
it wasn't the ordinary sort of Doubt about Cain's wife or the
Old Testament miracles or the consecration of Archbishop
Parker. I'd been taught how to explain all those while I
was at college. No, it was something deeper than all that. *I
couldn't understand why God had made the world at all . . .* You see
how fundamental that is. Once granted the first step, I can see
that everything else follows – Tower of Babel, Babylonian
captivity, Incarnation, Church, bishops, incense, everything –
but what I couldn't see, and what I can't see now, is *why* did it all
begin?

'I asked my bishop; he didn't know. He said that he didn't
think the point really arose as far as my practical duties as a
parish priest were concerned. I discussed it with my mother. At
first she was inclined to regard it as a passing phase. But it didn't
pass, so finally she agreed with me that the only honourable
thing to do was to resign my living; she never really recovered
from the shock, poor old lady. It was a great blow after she had
bought the chintz . . .'[1]

That, however, was not in fact the end of Mr Prendergast's career
in the ministry. Later in the book, in the first of the two chapters
entitled 'Resurrection', Paul Pennyfeather received a letter from
Dr Augustus Fagan, the Headmaster of Llanabba Castle, in which
he announced to him that Prendergast was resigning his position at
the school. 'Apparently', he wrote, 'he has been reading a series of
articles by a popular bishop and has discovered that there is a
species of person called a "Modern Churchman" who draws the
full salary of a beneficed clergyman and need not commit himself
to any religious belief. This seems to be a comfort to him, but it
adds greatly to my own inconvenience.'[2]

Paul Pennyfeather once again encounters Prendergast in person when he lands in gaol. Prendergast appears as the prison chaplain and announces to Paul the prisoner: 'I've only been at the job a week. I was very lucky to get it. My bishop thought there was more opening for a Modern Churchman in this kind of work than in the parishes. The Governor is very modern too.'[3] However, Mr Prendergast who was already very unpopular, not for his modernism, but because he had seen that some of the prisoners who were singing the wrong words to one of the hymn tunes, were put on No. I diet, did not last very long. Sir Wilfred Lucas-Dockery, the Governor, imagining that one prisoner, a mad, Bible-thumping apocalypticist, was frustrated, because in prison he was unable to pursue his trade as a carpenter, provided him with a bench of tools in his own cell. This prisoner, as we are told in the chapter 'The Death of a Modern Churchman', decided that the chaplain was not an orthodox Christian, and that an angel, clothed in flame, with a crown of flame on his head, had cried, 'Kill and spare not'. So Prendergast, the Modern Churchman, is done to death with one of the tools in accordance with the angel's instructions. At morning chapel the next day Mr Prendergast is nowhere to be seen. His violent death is announced to Paul Pennyfeather by a fellow prisoner under the cover of the hymn, 'O God, our help in ages past'.

Evelyn Waugh's *Decline and Fall* came out in 1928. That year English Modernism was very much in the news because of the Church Congress at Cheltenham in the diocese of Gloucester. The Congress was presided over by the unquestionably orthodox A. C. Headlam, the diocesan Bishop; but two leading Modernists, H. D. A. Major and Bishop Barnes, took part and spoke on a platform which also saw the presence of notable Anglo-Catholic leaders. An open letter of protest against the Modernist position was signed by nearly a thousand signatories, led by Lord Halifax, though there does not seem to be any allusion to this in Lockhart's life.[4] In fact, Modernism had been in the news since 1921. One might even say that the 'twenties were its Golden Decade. Modernists were then being satirized in Ronald Knox's 'Modernist's Prayer'.

> O God, forasmuch as without thee,
> We are not able to doubt thee,

> Help us all by thy grace,
> To teach the whole race,
> We know nothing whatever about thee.

During the same decade, Harold Anson, later Master of the Temple,[5] penned an article in the *Hibbert Journal*, in which he related how a correspondent wrote to him after one of his lectures: 'I hear you are a Modernist'. He wrote back, 'What is a Modernist?' The answer came: 'I cannot find out exactly, but I'm told it is worse than anything.'[6]

The English words 'Modernism' and 'Modernist' go well back into the past. They were originally used, unrelated to religion, to denote a preference for modern ways of thinking and modern styles of expression. The words can still be so used. Thus Gordon Fallows in his *Mandell Creighton and the English Church* (1963) uses the word of wallpaper and remarks of this former Hulsean Lecturer: 'The new wallpapers in modernistic vein for the Vicarage [at Embleton] and Creighton's liberal political views resulted in an element of self-restraint in the brotherly welcome accorded to him by the neighbouring clergy. . .'[7]

However, in the nineteenth century the word begins on rare occasions to be used in a somewhat more theological and religious sense. Thus F. J. A. Hort, in a letter to John Ellerton in 1852, writes: 'Maurice (whom I saw in passing through London) told me that Kingsley prefaced *Hypatia* by stating that all the seeming modernisms were literal translations from the Greek; I have seen no such preface. Maurice said, significantly, that he was sure Kingsley would not intentionally misrepresent old circumstances.'[8] On 25 April 1885, Archbishop Benson, who has been brought back to our attention by a recent book,[9] wrote in his diary, 'Consecrated at St Paul's, with a mighty congregation, Edward King to be Bishop of Lincoln, and E. H. Bickersteth to be Bishop of Exeter. Canon Liddon preached a Manifesto concerning the power and authority of the Episcopate, and condemning all 'Modernismus', not only the courts and the Public Worship Regulation Act, but declaring the Education Act of 1870 to be the root of all evil, and Board Schools its evil fruit.'[10] In these two instances we begin to see 'Modernism' and 'Modernismus' used in a vaguely religious sense. However, the words did not really begin to be used in the

4

full theological sense until after the Roman Catholic Modernist Movement.

Turning, then, to religious modernism, I find the word used in at least six different ways.

1. It was used of Modernism in the Roman Catholic Church, that movement which we associate with the names of Alfred Loisy, George Tyrrell and Friedrich von Hügel, though there are a great number of other men connected with it, as Alec Vidler has shown in his *A Variety of Catholic Modernists* (1970). The movement was condemned in 1907 by Pope Pius X in the decree *Lamentabili* and by the Encyclical *Pascendi*. Michele Ranchetti in his work *The Catholic Modernists* (1969) dates the use of the word 'Modernism' of this Romish movement in 1904, when it was adopted by U. Benigni in the *Miscellanea*. From that time it was used by polemical writers and then taken up by the Pope in *Pascendi*.[11] It would seem that it was only after its use by Roman Catholics that it was widely used of other non-Roman manifestations of theological liberalism.

2. Thus it eventually began to be used in a wide sense of a large movement of religious thought embracing Anglicans, British Nonconformists and American and Continental Protestants. This larger Modernist movement would include men like the English Unitarian, L. P. Jacks, Principal of Manchester College, Oxford, Samuel Angus, the Australian Presbyterian,[12] C. J. Cadoux, the Congregationalist, author of *The Case for Evangelical Modernism* (1938),[13] and his brother A. T. Cadoux, Leslie Weatherhead, author of *The Christian Agnostic* (1965), H. E. Fosdick, the American, and R. J. Campbell, author of *The New Theology* (1907).[14] All of these would not, I think, have turned up their noses if they had been called 'Modernists', even though they might not have written a book with the word 'Modernism' in the title.[15]

3. Within this wider Modernist movement there is the specifically Anglican or English Modernism, with which we are dealing in this book, a movement influenced both by Roman Catholic Modernism and the wider Modernism to which I have just alluded. I date the commencement of English Modernism in 1898, the year when the Modern Churchmen's Union began, though that is not my only reason for dating it then. In this book I am confining myself to

5

English Modernism, i.e. Anglican Modernism as it manifested itself in this country. There will not be space to write about Anglican Modernism in other parts of the Anglican Communion.

4. There is a rather eccentric use of the word modernism by C. van Til of the theology of Karl Barth and Emil Brunner in his book *The New Modernism. An Appraisal of the Theology of Barth and Brunner* (1946). This is an odd and unusual use of the word, to which we shall not have need to refer again. I have in the University of Cambridge heard Barth and Brunner referred to as 'Neo-fundamentalists' rather than as Modernists.

5. Since the Second World War the word 'modernist' has been indiscriminately used of a number of more recent manifestations of theological liberalism. Journalists and more conservative churchmen would label Paul Tillich, Dietrich Bonhoeffer, Hans Küng, John Knox, John Robinson, Paul van Buren, Dennis Nineham, Maurice Wiles, John Fenton, Leslie Houlden, Don Cupitt and Christopher Evans as 'Modernists'. This is all very confusing. A reader of John Robinson's book, *But that I can't believe* (1967), will find a great deal indeed that echoes English Modernism but Dr Robinson has never been associated with the movement. Amand de Mendieta in his *Anglican Vision* (1971) writes: 'Many theologians and responsible laymen of a traditional cast of mind suspect, quite wrongly, that the former Bishop of Woolwich, Dr Robinson, is a Modernist of a peculiar type. This is, I know, quite untrue; the Bishop is certainly not a member of the Modern Churchmen's Union, and he has been strongly attacked in *The Modern Churchman*. But many people remain doubtful about the Bishop's position, and Dr Robinson's name is still often associated with the English Modernists.'[16] Perhaps it would be better to call this group – if group they are – 'Neo-Modernists' or 'Radicals'. What makes confusion worse confounded is that two of them, Dennis Nineham and Maurice Wiles, have spoken at Modern Churchmen's Conferences.[17]

6. Then there is the use of the word 'modernist' anachronistically. People go back into the past and call liberal theologians of bygone centuries 'modernists', from Clement of Alexandria and Origen onwards. This is how H. L. Stewart uses the word in *Modernism Past*

and Present (1932). In this sense the writers of *Essays and Reviews* and *Lux Mundi* could be designated 'modernists'.

In this book we are concerned with English Modernism, which is, admittedly, a very limited part of Modernism in general. But to my mind it is a very important part of the history of the Church of England in the twentieth century. After all, looking at the Church of England, if the eighteenth century is important for the rise of the Evangelical Movement, and the nineteenth century for the Oxford Movement, then the correspondingly important movement in the twentieth century is English Modernism. Hence it deserves some study. No one, however, has yet written at length about it. When, for example, Dr Vidler gave his Robertson Lectures in 1964, he dealt with Roman Catholic Modernism (on which, of course, he was a leading authority) and wrote on English Liberal Catholicism (in which group he included Neville Figgis, Sir Will Spens, A. E. J. Rawlinson and Oliver Quick), but 'Anglican Modern Churchmanship' he relegated to an appended note, though he agreed that they 'certainly formed a distinguishable and distinguished group within the Church of England'.[18]

The purpose, then, of this book is to make good the existing deficiency of some historical survey of the English Modernists, or Modern Churchmen, for they did not openly espouse the name 'Modernists' until after a Conference they held at Girton in 1919. One of the first uses of the term 'Modernist' by an English writer was in William Scott Palmer's *The Diary of a Modernist* (1910). William Scott Palmer was the pseudonym of Mary Emily Dowson, who evidently in those days thought that a man would be more readily listened to than a woman!

Can I now give a sort of thumbnail sketch of the beliefs of the typical English modernist? He was totally convinced of the existence of God. The 'Death of God' school of the 'sixties would have filled him with horror. He believed in a God who was in everything and that everything was in God, but a God who worked only through the evolutionary process. In other words he was a panentheist. He believed in a God who could be known, to a certain extent, in other religions, but who was supremely revealed in the Logos. He had no doubt about the existence of Jesus Christ, though he was prepared to admit that if it were proved that Jesus had never existed, that would not mean the end of his religious faith.[19] His Christology was a degree Christology and adoptionist. His Jesus was not an eschatological figure but rather 'The Lord of Thought'[20] who proclaimed the Fatherhood of God and the Brotherhood of Man. His doctrine of the atonement was Abelardian or exemplarist. He had no hesitation in accepting all that biblical criticism had to say, as far as it had advanced by the death of B. H. Streeter in 1937. He maintained that he believed in the supernatural, but not in the miraculous. His Jesus, therefore, did not perform miracles. He was not born of a Virgin and his resurrection was a spiritual one. The tomb was not empty. He had a strong belief in the life after death and was a universalist. He was not so naive as to think one could exist without dogma, but he wished dogmatic definition to be kept to the minimum. He thought that there was such a thing as essential Christianity. For the English Modernist ethics were more important than doctrine. Life was more important than belief. He did not relish ecclesiasticism or see a great divide between the secular and the sacred. For the English Modernist the Church was a necessary evil.[21] He accepted episcopacy as the best form of church government, but treated the idea of apostolic succession with contempt. He had little interest in ritual. He did not, like the Parish and People Movement, press for the Holy Communion to supersede Mattins and Evensong as the main weekly worship of the Church. He was keen on clerical subscription being relaxed beyond the Act of Archbishop Longley's primacy and less importance attached to the Thirty-nine Articles. For the most part he was a liberal Protestant, and, Vidler would maintain, more Protestant than liberal. He believed in the reform and revision of the 1662 Book of Common Prayer but he was not very renowned as a liturgiologist. He was on friendly terms with the Nonconformists and was favourably inclined to reunion with them but fought shy of Roman Catholics and members of the Eastern Orthodox Church. He was an advocate of the ordination of women and of the marriage of the divorced in church. On sexual matters he was in advance of his contemporaries, advocating contraception when many churchmen were still rigorously opposed to it. On homosexuality he was, I think, rather silent until the 'sixties. Some have criticized the Modernist for being too intent on building the Kingdom of God on earth, but that is a mistake. It was true of the preacher of the Social Gospel but not

of the English Modernist. He did not believe in a this-worldly
Utopia. His vision was clearly set on the life of the world to come.
Indeed, he would be constantly and heavily criticized for being
insufficiently interested in social questions. He was very much an
Erastian and in danger of being over-academic. But on the other
hand the literature he wrote at least had the virtue of being lucid
and intelligible. He was found in the universities, in the parishes,
and in the schools and in the episcopate, but not, I think, often in
the prison service, in spite of *Decline and Fall*, though one Modernist,
W. D. Morrison, had at an earlier date been a notable prison
chaplain and reformer.

Now in any picture of English Modernism allusion must needs
be made to a number of items and persons.

a. First, much will obviously be said about the Modern
Churchmen's Union, which still continues, though these days with
a somewhat uncertain existence. It was founded in 1898 as 'The
Churchmen's Union for the Advancement of Liberal Religious
Thought', and became the Modern Churchmen's Union in 1928.

b. Secondly, there will be frequent reference to the magazine
The Modern Churchman, founded in 1911 and still continuing, though
a bit precariously, today. Its editor is a former Cambridge don,
William Frend. Its contemporary ethos is somewhat different
from traditional English Modernism. It changed when its cover
changed from yellow to white.

c. Then reference will be made to the series of Conferences of
Modern Churchmen, the first of which was held at the Spa Hotel,
Ripon, in 1914, and which have continued most years ever since,
though, at the moment, their future seems uncertain. There
have been sixty-two of them. In the 'twenties and 'thirties
these conferences received a great deal of publicity in the newspapers.

d. Special mention will be made of the most famous of these
conferences, that held at Girton College in 1921, about which
Roger Lloyd says much in his *The Church of England 1900–1960*
(1966), though Bishop Michael Ramsey writes more accurately
about this in his *From Gore to Temple* (1960). References to this
famous conference are not infrequent in contemporary theological

literature. Thus Stephen Sykes in his *The Integrity of Anglicanism* (1978), which all the Lambeth Fathers were reading in 1978, has something to say about it; and Bishop Stephen Neill in *The Truth of God Incarnate* (1977) compares its heresies with those of *The Myth of God Incarnate* (1977).

e.   There will need to be a good deal of reference to Henry D. A. Major, whom his disciple, R. D. Richardson, called 'The Apostle of English Modernism'.[22] That designation is very apt. If one wants a summary of the English Modernist position one can do little better than read Major's William Belden Noble Lectures, *English Modernism. Its Origins, Methods, Aims,* published in 1927.

f.   Three other leading names of men whom one would account giants of Modernism will also come into the picture – Hastings Rashdall, W. R. Inge and Percy Gardner. These all at some time or other held the office of President of the Modern Churchmen's Union.

g.   Allusion must also be made to Ripon Hall, that famous – some would say 'notorious' – theological college founded by Bishop Boyd Carpenter in 1897, and now enjoying respectability through a union with Cuddesdon, though Henry Major would have regarded them as odd bedfellows. That institution which has been depicted in at least two novels,[23] was a breeding ground of English Modernism and hence constantly under attack in the pages of the *Church Times.* Bishop Frank Weston of Zanzibar in his *The Christ and his Critics* (1919) remarks in disgust: 'It is published far and wide that in theological and missionary colleges ordinands are taught by "superior" dons to criticize the Christ as boldly as the best of his critics', and then states that this is proved to be so 'by the very mention of such a college as Ripon Hall, Oxford . . .'[24] In 1947, the retired Bishop Hensley Henson wrote to Dean Selwyn of Winchester: 'I never quite understand what the position of Ripon Hall is in the system of the National Church. Is it a recognised Training College for the clergy, and do the Bishops sanction the training of candidates there? I can hardly imagine Bishop Kirk sending young men for their preparation to it . . .'[25]

h.   There will be some reference to the Church of England Doctrine Report of 1938, which English Modernists have always been keen to regard as giving them the right to exist in the Church of England and which was, to a certain extent, an outcome of Girton 1921. When it came out it was both praised and criticized and now has fallen into oblivion, though there was an amusing allusion to it in Penelope Fitzgerald's chapter on Wilfred Knox (a member of the commission) in *The Knox Brothers* (1977). 'As a matter of fact', she writes, 'the Committee's summing-up, when it eventually appeared in 1938, was greeted in the daily press as CHURCH SAYS SEX NOT EVIL. The report, in consequence, sold surprisingly well, and the Committee had to school themselves to patience and hope that their painstaking summary of the faith would make its way in time.'[26] Needless to say Wilfred's brother Ronald did not think much of it! Yet it is worth noting what an uncompromising Anglo-Catholic, Bishop William Wand, wrote about it in 1961.

> It was typically Anglican in that it did not endeavour to rest its findings in profound philosophical principles, about which no one would ever agree. It was content to point out what was the general consensus among scholars on the subjects discussed – which ranged, in point of fact, over the whole creed – and revealed how wide a range of opinion on controversial matters was consonant with Anglican loyalty. The volume did a vast amount of good in providing a *vade mecum* for the clergy and in assuring the laity that there was an Anglican mind on these matters. Unfortunately, the outbreak of war in the year following its publication diverted attention; and by the time the war was over it had been forgotten by the majority. It is probable, however, that those who have retained their copies and have reason to refer to them in recent years have been surprised to find how good and useful a book it is . . .[27]

i.   The story would not be complete without some time devoted to Bishop E. W. Barnes and his notorious book *The Rise of Christianity* which came out in 1947, and which many regarded, wrongly, as the position upheld by the majority of English Modernists. The book was heavily criticized in Cambridge by C. H. Dodd[28] and J. N. Sanders.[29] Today Bishop Barnes is very much in the news. A few weeks ago I was attending a conference at Christ Church, Oxford, when he was mentioned by Dr Paul Kent, Master of Van

11

Mildert College, Durham, and then by the then Bishop of St Albans, now Archbishop of Canterbury. Archbishop Runcie told us that on his recent travels in Eastern Orthodox countries he found one of the Archbishops troubled about the writings of the Bishop of Birmingham. He thought the prelate was referring to Hugh Montefiore, but discovered it was a reference to Bishop Barnes. Since that Christ Church Conference, there has appeared Sir John Barnes' life of his father. It is ironical that two extracts from this were given in the *Church Times* which continually attacked Bishop Barnes in the 'twenties, 'thirties and 'forties!

If you look at Alec Vidler's Appended Note in his *20th Century Defenders of the Faith*, you will see that all these aspects of the subject are mentioned there, except Ripon Hall; and though he mentions Bishop Barnes and accuses him of pursuing 'a most illiberal and intolerant ecclesiastical policy in the diocese of Birmingham', he strangely does not refer to *The Rise of Christianity* episode. Vidler refers quite rightly to the 'twenties as the 'palmy days of English Modernism'. I would suggest that the flourishing period of the movement was between 1920 and 1940. It was during those decades that the men and women who espoused its cause were glorying in the name 'Modernist' and writing a whole series of books with the words 'Modernist' or 'Modernism' in them. Major's *English Modernism* came out in 1927 and remains the standard compendium of Modernist beliefs. In the same year one of the most distinguished of Cambridge Modernists, J. F. Bethune-Baker, brought out *The Way of Modernism*, published by the Cambridge University Press. Percy Gardner's *Modernism in the English Church* was published by Methuen in 1926. Heffers in Cambridge brought out *Modernism as a Working Faith* by W. Maurice Pryke, Rector of Risby, in 1925. Walter Grierson, writing under the *nom de plume* 'The Enquiring Layman', brought out *Modernism and What it did for Me* in 1929. There were several books published in the U.S.A., like J. Macbride Sterrett's *Modernism in Religion* (1922), Leighton Parks' *What is Modernism?* (1924) and Shailer Mathews' *The Faith of Modernism* (1925). These three American books were widely read by English Modernists.

This sort of literature continued into the 'thirties. Alan Richardson wrote *The Redemption of Modernism* after leaving Ripon Hall for a Northumberland Vicarage, in 1935. R. D. Richardson's

The Gospel of Modernism came out in 1933 with a Foreword by Bishop Barnes and went into a second edition in 1935. I notice that Norman Pittenger has a word of praise for it in his *The Word Incarnate* (1959). R. Gladstone Griffith wrote *The Necessity of Modernism* in 1932 and T. Wigley *The Necessity of Christian Modernism*, with a preface by Major, in 1939. I note the existence of a pamphlet *Modernism and Youth an attempt at Interpretation*, published in 1943. Then protagonism of Modernism came to an end. Glorying in the name 'Modernist' ceased. When did the English Modernist Movement finally come to an end? I should put its demise either in 1961, the year when Major died, which was also the year before *Soundings* appeared, to which three of his pupils contributed, or perhaps better 1968, when Gordon Fallows left Ripon Hall for the bishopric of Pontefract. That would bring in the Conference 'Christ for us Today', held at Somerville in 1967, under the chairmanship of Norman Pittenger. So perhaps 1968 is the more satisfactory date.

As the 'twenties were Modernism's palmy days, so that was the period of a great deal of anti-Modernist literature. Francis J. Hall, the American High Churchman, penned *Christianity and Modernism* in 1924. The Jesuit Father Woodlock wrote *Modernism and the Christian Church*, with a preface by G. K. Chesterton, in 1925. The bulkiest attack upon Modernism came in Charles Harris' *Creeds or No Creeds. A Critical Examination of the Basis of Modernism*, which had no less than two Forewords, one by J. Wells, the Warden of Wadham (who apologized to Dr Major for writing it!) and J. A. Kempthorne, Bishop of Lichfield. A similar attack came in Arthur C. Champneys, *A Different Gospel which is not another Gospel*, written in 1922. H. P. V. Nunn, famous for his introduction to New Testament Greek, until it was revised by Wenham, wrote *What is Modernism?* (1932).

Much of Modernist literature and indeed the anti-Modernist literature is decidedly unpalatable today. So I should not be thought of as trying to persuade anyone to read these books. They are ephemeral and repetitious. A reading of Major's *English Modernism* will suffice for most people. Nevertheless, I do feel that this movement is worthy of the historian's pen. Hence I have come forward to sketch it.

I would suggest that it is not, perhaps, inappropriate to lecture on this subject of English Modernism in Cambridge. It is true that Major was an Oxford man, as also was Rashdall; but Inge and Gardner were students at Cambridge and taught at both Cambridge and Oxford. It is true, too, that Ripon Hall was an Oxford theological college, though Major did think of Cambridge as a possible site for it when he moved it from Yorkshire in 1919. Cambridge was, at any rate, the place where the most famous of Modern Churchmen's Conferences took place in 1921. Indeed no less than sixteen of these conferences were held at Cambridge, the last in 1968. Moreover, there have been many famous Cambridge Modernists. I have already mentioned J. F. Bethune-Baker, the authority on Nestorius, whose book on Early Christian Doctrines was for years a standard text-book. F. C. Burkitt, in spite of his lecture 'The Failure of Liberal Christianity' delivered to the Cambridge Branch of the English Church Union, became a Vice-President of the Modern Churchmen's Union and spoke at its conferences. Alexander Nairne, Hulsean Lecturer 1919–20, spoke at one of its conferences.[30] Then there was John Martin Creed, Hulsean Lecturer in 1936,[31] who married the daughter of A. L. Lilley, an English Modernist, sympathetic towards Catholic Modernism.[32] There are others, Joseph Wellington Hunkin, whose life has recently been written by Alan Dunstan and John Peart-Binns; F. J. Foakes-Jackson, Hulsean Lecturer 1902–3,[33] the famous Dean of Jesus College, Cambridge, who left Cambridge for a Professorship in the U.S.A.; Charles Raven, Hulsean Lecturer in 1926–7, whose life has been written by F. W. Dillistone, though he did not know that once Major tried to persuade Raven to become Vice-Principal of Ripon Hall.[34] We have already mentioned W. R. Inge, Hulsean Lecturer 1925–6 and Lady Margaret Professor of Divinity,[35] Bishop Barnes, a one-time Fellow of Trinity, and Percy Gardner, once Dixie Professor of Archaeology. We can add the name of Gardner's sister Alice, who was a Fellow of Newnham College.[36] To complete our list – though not to exhaust it – we can add the names of Alan Bouquet, Hulsean Lecturer 1924–5,[37] Norman Sykes, Disney Professor of Ecclesiastical History, Percival Gardner-Smith, my old Tutor, who now a nonagenarian is still very much alive in Cambridge, George F. Woods, Hulsean Lecturer in 1962,[38] Ian Ramsey, J. S. Bezzant and J. S. Boys Smith.[39]

You will have noticed how many of these Modern Churchmen

were Hulsean Lecturers. That would seem to suggest that it is not, perhaps, inappropriate to be delivering these Lectures upon the Hulsean Foundation. Indeed, the late Bishop Barnes used to contend that it was one of the most celebrated Hulsean Lecturers, Fenton John Anthony Hort who in his lecture, *The Way, the Truth, the Life*, was in fact the Father of English Modernism. I cannot myself agree with Barnes as I will show in my second lecture. However, Barnes' suggestion and the discovery that many of the Hulsean Lecturers of the twentieth century had been Modernists encouraged me to look back at all the Hulsean Lectures that have been delivered. Indeed, there was a danger of my becoming more fascinated by Hulseanism than by Modernism!

The founder of these Lectures, John Hulse, was certainly no modernist or liberal. This *alumnus* of St John's College, who lived from 1708 to 1790, was a very retiring individual, who held two curacies, one at Yoxall in Staffordshire, the other at Goostry in Cheshire, and then took over the management of the estates he had inherited at Elworth Hall, Sandbach. He married and had a son but both wife and son predeceased him. He was musical, playing violin and flute, and drank nothing but water, owing to poor health. His biographer, Richard Parkinson, remarks: 'He was of delicate frame of body, of a contemplative turn of mind, of diminutive stature, and of an irritable temperament.'[40] He lies buried in the parish church of Middlewich. In his will, which was so important for Cambridge University, he speaks of himself as 'in a very infirm state of health, and for many years afflicted with the stone, and the most acute and extreme pain, yet of sound mind, memory and understanding.'[41] He was also somewhat eccentric and left instructions that when he was buried his body should be left uncovered and carefully watched for several days in case he might not be dead at all![42] He is most famous for his benefactions. These were two divinity scholarships at St John's College; the Hulsean Prize; and the institution of the office of Christian Advocate, later made into the Hulsean Professorship. The fourth part of the benefaction was the office of Christian Preacher or Hulsean Lecturer which I account it a great honour to hold. The first lecturer was Christopher Benson in 1820 and the second J. C. Franks, Vicar of Huddersfield, who is chiefly remembered today in the Brontë saga, as the husband of Elizabeth Firth, the lady who

15

had rejected Patrick Brontë. The Hulsean Lectures were initially sermons, delivered in the University pulpit by (and here I quote the words of the will) 'some learned and ingenious clergyman of Cambridge University under the age of 40'. The task assigned the lecturer was outlined in the will, dated 21 July, 1977, and conveniently quoted in Christopher Benson's second lecture:

> To shew the evidence for revealed religion, and to demonstrate, in the most convincing and persuasive manner, the truth and excellence of Christianity, so as to include, not only the prophecies and miracles, general and particular, but also any other proper or useful arguments, whether the same be direct or collateral proofs of the Christian religion, which he may think fittest to discourse upon, either in general or particular, especially the collateral arguments, or else any particular article or branch thereof; and chiefly against notorious infidels, whether atheists or deists, not descending to any particular sects or controversies, so much to be lamented amongst Christians themselves, except some new or dangerous error, either of superstition or enthusiasm, as of Popery or Methodism, shall arise; in which case, only, it may be necessary for that time, to write and preach against the same.[43]

Having quoted the will thus far, Christopher Benson remarks, 'Such are the liberal and comprehensive terms in which the Founder has described one portion of the duties of the Christian Preacher. With regard to the other, he is equally judicious and directs that he "shall take for his subject, some of the most difficult and obscure parts of Holy Scripture, such, I mean, as may appear to be more generally useful or necessary to be explained, and which may best admit of such comment or explanation, without presuming to pry too far into the profound secrets or awful mysteries of the Almighty".'[44]

No doubt the early lecturers tried to follow this to the letter.[45] But I shall not be expounding any difficulties of Scripture, nor will I be denouncing any notorious infidels, whether atheists or deists, though probably some Modernists have been described by all three designations! As regards the miracles, at any rate, John Hulse will find that I myself feel there is more to be said for them than have some of the Modernists.

The number of lectures was originally twenty. But in 1830, by which time it was being found difficult to find lecturers who could deliver so many, it was reduced to eight. In 1860 they were further reduced to four, for those who could not manage eight. I am afraid the subject of English Modernism will necessitate no less than eight. At some point in the history of Hulseans the age limit was altered; otherwise I should not be here today!

From reading about John Hulse and his pious intentions, I looked through the past lectures, of which there have been 121 series and 107 lecturers. A great number of them have been decidedly apologetic and that was the founder's intention and that was why Hort showed reluctance in taking on the office. What has struck me is the patently liberal flavour of so many of the lectures. Here there is a contrast with the Oxford Bampton Lectures. I do not want to bore you with too many names but listen to the large army of liberal theologians who up to the Great War delivered these Lectures – Henry Alford,[46] Harvey Goodwin,[47] James Moorhouse,[48] Fenton John Anthony Hort,[49] Edwin Abbott,[50] William Boyd Carpenter,[51] Frederic William Farrar,[52] Thomas George Bonney,[53] John Llewelyn Davies,[54] Mandell Creighton,[55] J. M. Wilson,[56] F. R. Tennant,[57] C. W. Stubbs,[58] E. A. Edghill,[59] William Leighton Grane.[60]

Since the Great War there have been a considerable number of men connected with the Modernist Movement who have been Hulsean Lecturers – F. E. Hutchinson,[61] L. E. Elliott-Binns,[62] C. F. Russell, [63] Alan C. Bouquet, W. R. Inge, C. E. Raven, J. M. Creed, E. C. Dewick,[64] G. F. Woods, Kathleen L. Wood-Legh.[65] Others, though not Modern Churchmen, have been noted for their liberal theology, like J. O. F. Murray,[66] R. H. Thouless,[67] Peter Baelz,[68] J. A. T. Robinson,[69] and Maurice Wiles.[70]

In my expedition into past Hulsean Lectures I made some interesting discoveries. All the lecturers until 1956 were Cambridge men. In contrast Oxford appointed one or two Cambridge men as Bampton Lecturers, like F. W. Farrar and William Boyd Carpenter. The vast majority of the Lectures have been delivered by Anglicans. The first Nonconformist lecturer was Anderson Scott in 1929 on Christian ethics. The first lay lecturer was a Quaker and member of Jesus College, H. G. Wood.[71] The first and only lady lecturer was Kathleen Wood-Legh in 1970. The

17

first non-Britisher to lecture was Hendrick Kraemer in 1958.[72]

My Lectures are an historical excursion rather than apologetic. However, many of the Modernists about whom I shall speak have been not inconsiderable Christian apologists. Think, for example, of B. H. Streeter and the impression his book *Reality* (1926) made in the 'twenties. Many Hulsean Lectures by Modernists have been apologetic. However past Hulsean lecturers have also spoken on historical themes, like Marcionism,[73] Alexandrian and Carthaginian Christianity,[74] St Augustine,[75] Erasmus,[76] the Ecclesiastical Expansion of England,[77] and the Platonic Tradition in English Thought.[78]

I hope I have sufficiently justified this course of Lectures on English Modernism. Let me add a personal note. My own interest in English Modernism started in 1954 when I went as a student to Ripon Hall. It was a long time before I had the courage to tell my father I was going there, but the college was at a reasonably respectable stage under Bishop Geoffrey Allen, who though a decided liberal, had come under the influence of Frank Buchman and Karl Barth and was now somewhat critical of Major's Modernism. It was not until I was on the staff of Ripon Hall, from 1962 to 1970, that I began a detailed study of the Modernist movement. At Ripon Hall I was in a fortunate position to do this. The library contained most of Major's books including a unique collection on Modernism. This library got broken up when Ripon Hall was merged with Cuddesdon College. Many of the Modernist books were offered for sale and I bought quite a number of them. No one else was interested in them! Equally important were all the modernist archives, of which the Major papers formed the most considerable part, and which I was allowed to examine through the kindness of Mrs Mollie Hewett, Dr Major's daughter.

Living at Ripon Hall in the 'sixties I was able to witness the end of Anglican Modernism and its supersession by what I have designated Neo-Modernism or Radicalism, and then the period of more positive theological affirmation ushered in by John Macquarrie's *Principles of Christian Theology*. The fact that I am now concerned with St Stephen's House as well as with Ripon College is an indication that I myself have moved in a more orthodox direction; though I note that the only other person who has moved from Ripon Hall to St Stephen's House was the Rev. Frederick William Densham, who became Vicar of Warleggan a remote parish on

Bodmin Moor, who put barbed wire round his vicarage and kept in his garden a pack of savage dogs and instead of having a congregation preached to propped up images in wood and cardboard. You can read about this eccentric in Daphne du Maurier's *Vanishing Cornwall.*

I have entitled the Lectures 'The Rise and Decline of English Modernism'. After having chosen the phrase I noticed that Robert J. Page uses it in his *New Directions in Anglican Theology. A Survey from Temple to Robinson* (1967) but he dates the decline of the movement in 1939, much earlier than I do. One other Liberal Anglican movement has already passed and gone. This is the Anglican Evangelical Group Movement. Some of the leaders of that movement were also leaders in Anglican Modernism, like Bishops Barnes and Hunkin, Charles Raven, Vernon Storr and Guy Rogers. There will not be time to speak about that movement in this series. Those who want to know more about it will find an article on it by L. Hickin in the *Church Quarterly Review* from January to March 1968. The Anglican Evangelical Group Movement ceased to exist in 1967. At the moment the future of English Modernism is precarious. I recently received a document (see Appendix F) from the Council of the Modern Churchmen's Union, stating that the number of its members was steadily declining and the number of attenders at the Conferences was growing smaller; in addition, the quality of the *Modern Churchman* had declined and publishers were no longer sending books for review. Has perhaps the movement done its work and hence will follow the example of the A.E.G.M. and vote for its own demise?

One final word. I was intrigued to discover that I was not the first Stephenson to be chosen to deliver the Hulsean Lectures. There was an H. M. Stephenson who delivered them in 1888.[79] He was then Vicar of Bourn, near Cambridge, and had previously been Headmaster of St Peter's School, York. I was even more intrigued when I discovered that H. stood for Henry and M. for Major. I was sorry, however, to have to admit, that of all the Hulsean Lectures I have read – and I have now read quite a number – they were the dullest.[80]

19

NOTES

1 Evelyn Waugh, *Decline and Fall*, pp.39–41.

2 ibid., pp.169f.

3 ibid., p.198.

4 J. G. Lockhart, *Charles Lindley Viscount Halifax*, Part 1 (1935) and Part 2 (1936).

5 For Anson, see *Looking Forward* (1938).

6 See H. D. A. Major, *English Modernism* (1927), p.39.

7 W. G. Fallows, op. cit., p.6.

8 A. F. Hort, *Life and Letters of Fenton John Anthony Hort*, vol. i, p.215.

9 David Williams, *Genesis and Exodus. A Portrait of the Benson Family* (1979).

10 A. C. Benson, *The Life of Edward White Benson sometime Archbishop of Canterbury*, vol. ii, p.55.

11 See M. Ranchetti, op. cit., p.143. See also H. L. Stewart, *Modernism, Past and Present* (1932), p.4.

12 See S. Angus, *Forgiveness and Life* (1962).

13 On C. J. Cadoux, see Nathaniel Micklem, *The Box and the Puppets*, pp.81ff.

14 And also, presumably, T. R. Glover, author of *The Jesus of History*.

15 For R. J. Campbell, who later settled down as an orthodox Anglican, see his *A Spiritual Pilgrimage* (1916). He died in 1956.

16 See Emmanuel Amand de Mendieta, *Anglican Vision* (1971), p.53.

17 Nineham and Wiles spoke at the Conference of 1967. Wiles also spoke in 1977.

18 Alec R. Vidler, *20th Century Defenders of the Faith* (1965), p.123.

19 Cf. W. R. Inge's words quoted by Adam Fox, *Dean Inge*, pp.263–4, and the words of Rashdall in his *Conscience and Christ*, pp.274–5.

20 The title of a book by two of them, Lily Dougall and Cyril Emmet.

21 One Modernist, Alfred Fawkes, wrote a book with this title.

22 See R. D. Richardson, *The Gospel of Modernism* (1935), p.9.

23 See J. C. Hardwick, *A Professional Christian* (1932) where it is Carpenter Hall and John Michaelhouse (i.e. Joseph McCulloch), *Charming Manners* (1932) where it is York House.

24 Frank Weston, *The Christ and His Critics* (1919), p.138.

25 E. F. Braley, *Letters of Herbert Hensley Henson* (1951), p.205.

26 op. cit., p.205.

27 J. W. C. Wand, *Anglicanism in History and Today* (1961), p.141.

28 C. H. Dodd, *Christian Beginnings*. A Reply to Dr Barnes's 'The Rise of Christianity' (1947).

29 J. N. Sanders, *The Foundations of the Christian Faith* (1950).

30 Alexander Nairne, *The Faith of the New Testament* (1920).

31 J. M. Creed, *The Divinity of Jesus Christ* (1938).

32 For Lilley see Alec R. Vidler, *A Variety of Catholic Modernists*.

33 F. J. Foakes-Jackson, *Christian Difficulties in the Second and Twentieth Centuries* (1903).

34 Charles Earle Raven, *The Creator Spirit* (1927).

35 W. R. Inge, *The Platonic Tradition in English Religious Thought* (1926).

36 See her two volumes, *The Conflict of Duties and other Essays* (1903), and *Within our Limits. Essays on Questions Moral, Religious and Historical* (1913). She also wrote the pamphlet *Our Outlook as changed by the War* (1914).

37 A. C. Bouquet, *The Christian Religion and Its Competitors To-Day* (1925).

38 G. F. Woods, *A Defence of Theological Ethics* (1966).

39 J. S. Boys Smith is still alive, in retirement at Saffron Walden.

40 R. Parkinson, *Rationalism and Revelation*, pp.xix, xx.

41 Christopher Benson, *Evidences of Christianity* (1830), p.23. R. Parkinson, op. cit., p. xxvi.

42 See R. Parkinson, op. cit., pp. xxxi f.: 'His mental faculties were perfect to the last; and he could therefore *watch* the approach of his death, although, as we know he did, with the composure of a Christian, yet doubtless with anxious speculation as to the form which its actual arrival might assume. There being no external symptoms of bodily ailment, animation might be suspended in such a frame as his, who had always lived a dying life, before it was finally extinct; and he therefore directed, it is said, that his grave should be kept open for some days after his interment, and his body watched (which, of course, was a necessary part of his design) day and night. This (if such directions were really given) might be eccentric on his part, but it was nothing more. His simple countrymen, however, assigned a reason of their own for it, which no doubt his retired habits – his reported skill in music, medicine, and divinity – and above all, perhaps, the wonders displayed by his 'diagonal mirror, or optical machine', with the magical revelations of which he had doubtless sometimes astonished the eyes of his rustic neighbours on an occasional holiday – all tended to convince them must be the right one; viz., that the day of his dealings with the Enemy of souls being

over, he wished to be constantly watched lest the Owner should come and carry away the *body*, – the right to which is always understood to form part of the infernal compact! They seem to have forgotten that his temerity in directing the grave to be left *open*, was somewhat inconsistent with their own charitable theory as to the motive; to say nothing of the insufficiency of the *guard* (they, it seems, being certainly no *conjurors*) to whom he had thought proper to entrust the care of his remains. This anecdote, absurd as it was, seems worth recording, as a proof of the disadvantage which always arises to character from seclusion from society, and the slightest symptoms of mystery in conduct.'

43 Christopher Benson, *Evidences of Christianity* (1830), p.26.

44 ibid., pp.26f.

45 For a useful article on past Hulsean lectures see John Hunt, *Religious Thought in England in the Nineteenth Century* (1896), pp.332–8. For a complete up to date list of all Hulsean Lecturers and Lectures see my own Bibliography 1.

46 Henry Alford, *Doctrines of Redemption* (1841).

47 Harvey Goodwin, *Doctrines and Difficulties of the Christian Faith* (1855).

48 James Moorhouse, *Our Lord Jesus Christ* (1866).

49 F. J. A. Hort, *The Way, the Truth, the Life* (1893).

50 Edwin Abbott's Lectures (1876) were not published.

51 William Boyd Carpenter, *The Witness of the Heart to Christ* (1878).

52 Frederick William Farrar, *The Witness of History to Christ* (1880).

53 Thomas George Bonney, *The Influence of Science and Theology* (1885).

54 John Llewellyn Davies, *Order and Growth* (1891).

55 Mandell Creighton, *Persecution and Tolerance* (1893).

56 J. M. Wilson, *The Gospel of the Atonement* (1899).

57 F. R. Tennant, *The Origin and Propagation of Sin* (1902).

58 C. W. Stubbs, *The Christ of English Poetry* (1906).

59 E. A. Edghill, *The Revelation of the Son of God* (1911).

60 W. L. Grane's lectures were not published but his *Church Divisions and Christianity* (1916) was developed out of them.

61 F. E. Hutchinson, *Christian Freedom* (1920).

62 Leonard E. Elliott-Binns, *Erasmus the Reformer*. A Study in Restatement (1923).

63 C. F. Russell, *Religion and Natural Law* (1923).

64 E. C. Dewick, *The Christian Attitude to other Religions* (1953).

65 Miss Wood-Legh's lectures on the subject of Good Works have not yet been published.

66 J. O. F. Murray, *The Goodness and Severity of God* (1924).

67 Robert H. Thouless, *Authority and Freedom* (1954).

68 Peter Baelz, *Prayer and Providence* (1968). Baelz was once on the staff of Ripon Hall.

69 J. A. T. Robinson, *The Human Face of God* (1973).

70 Maurice Wiles, *The Remaking of Christian Doctrine* (1974).

71 H. G. Wood, *Christianity and the Nature of History* (1934).

72 Hendrik Kraemer, *A Theology of the Laity* (1958).

73 F. J. Foakes-Jackson, *Christian Difficulties in the Second and Twentieth Centuries. A Study of Marcion and his Relation to Modern Thought* (1904).

74 John Bickford Heard, *Alexandrian and Carthaginian Theology Contrasted* (1893).

75 William Cunningham, *S. Austin and his Place in the History of Christian Thought* (1886). John Burnaby, *Amor Dei. A Study of the Religion of St Augustine* (1939).

76 L. E. Elliott-Binns, *Erasmus the Reformer* (1923).

77 Alfred Barry, *The Ecclesiastical Expansion of England in the Growth of the Anglican Communion* (1895).

78 W. R. Inge, *The Platonic Tradition in English Religious Thought* (1926).

79 H. M. Stephenson, *Christ the Life of Men* (1890).

80 Mr J. Stevenson, author of *A New Eusebius*, said to me after the Lecture that, though H. M. Stephenson's Hulseans may have been dull, he was an erudite scholar.

2

The Rock whence They were Hewn

The late Dr Routh, President of Magdalen, was a disbeliever in the existence of railways. The unmelodious whistle travelling over Christ Church meadows to the sanctity of his lodgings carried with it no conviction. So far as theory went, no one would have quarrelled with the venerable fossil; but in practice it proved subversive of College discipline. A *demy*, for instance, whose paternal residence was in Norfolk, might turn up any day during the first fortnight of Hilary term. In vain the College officers might carry a complaint to their President. The answer was always the same, 'Bad roads, gentlemen – long distance – snow on the ground.' 'But', would urge the irritated dons, 'the gentleman came by railway.' 'I don't know anything about that', was the centenarian's reply, and authority had to depart unvindicated.[1]

This anecdote, and others equally delightful, appeared in *The Broad Churchman* on 30 January, 1873. It was the first number of a new periodical priced six pence which aimed at acting as a forum for liberal churchmen. It tried to awaken men and women to the existence of a third party in the Church of England. In the Prologue, the Editor, after speaking first of the Evangelicals and, secondly, of the followers of Dr Pusey, went on:

> Last in order of time, but not least in order of influence, has arisen a party more in unison with national sentiment. Its founder, perhaps, was Dr Arnold. Its hagiology comprises the names of Maurice and Robertson.[2]

The editor then referred to the famous article on Church Parties by William John Conybeare in the *Edinburgh Review* for October 1853, in which he gave birth to the expression 'The Broad

Church', unless possibly Arthur Hugh Clough had used it before him.[3] Conybeare had written:

Side by side with these various shades of High and Low Church another party of a different character has always existed in the Church of England. It is called by different names: Moderate, Catholic, or Broad Church, by its friends, Latitudinarian or Indifferent by its enemies. Its distinctive character is the desire for comprehension. Its watchwords are charity and toleration.[4]

The new periodical had an article on a representative Broad Churchman, the Rev. H. R. Haweis, incumbent of St James' Chapel, Westmoreland Street, Marylebone.[5] There was a correspondence column, including one letter, headed 'The Curate's grievance from a Curate's point of view', from Oxoniensis, much political news, including an article on 'Proportional Representation', news from abroad, and a review of Louis (sic) Verne's *Twenty Thousand Leagues under the Seas*, which had just been published in London by Messrs Sampson Low, Marston, Low, and Searle. There were plenty of advertisements, especially for sewing machines, but also ecclesiastical ones, including this:

Episcopal Chapel (Lease of) for Sale, situated in an excellent part of the Metropolis. Present income about £800 per annum, and steadily increasing. Immediate possession. Price low. Apply to Mr. H. W. Bagster, 14, Southampton-street, Strand.[6]

Though full of such good things, the new periodical did not last long – only, in fact, about six months – and hardly any copies of it have survived. This single first issue survives in the Bodleian and I discovered it when I was working on the first Lambeth Conference.[7] There was not a similar attempt at a periodical for the liberal churchmen until the publication of the *Church Gazette* in 1898.

Three years before the publication of *The Broad Churchman*, liberal Anglicans had made their first attempt to organize themselves into a society. This was 'The Church Reform Association', whose programme of reform can be found in the *Life and Letters of Fenton J. A. Hort*. J. Llewelyn Davies wrote to Hort in an attempt to get him to join. The Chairman of its Council was W. Cowper-Temple and its members included Thomas Hughes, the

25

Rev. Edwin Abbott, then Headmaster of the City of London School, John Seeley, who had just become Professor of History at Cambridge, the Rev. W. H. Fremantle, Vicar of St Mary's, Bryanston Square, the Rev. Harry Jones, Vicar of St Luke's, Berwick Street,[8] and Dr Montague Butler, Headmaster of Harrow.

The objects of this Association were threefold:

A.   To obtain legislation giving an organization and certain defined powers in Church matters to the inhabitants of parishes.

Under this heading it was proposed to create a Church Council in each parish which would have a right of veto over alterations in church services and other powers.

B.   To urge the removal of impolitic restrictions.

Here there was the idea of making these alterations.

1.   The abolition of clerical subscription.
2.   The removal of any legal hindrances by which those who have received holy orders are excluded from civil employments.
3.   The discontinuance of the Athanasian Creed in the services of the Church.
4.   Power to be given to an incumbent to invite persons not in Anglican orders to preach, subject to the inhibition of the Ordinary.

C.   To promote improvements in the machinery of the Church system.

Here there was envisaged the subdivision of larger dioceses, the rearrangement of parochial boundaries, more elastic arrangement of church services, and the revision of the Authorised Version of the Bible.[9]

Hort refused to join this Church Reform Association, giving his reasons in a long letter to Llewelyn Davies, reproduced in vol. ii of Hort's Life, pp.125–33, which clearly reveals that he was far more of a High Churchman than a Broad Churchman. 'As far as I can see', he wrote, 'my difference from the Association is fundamental.

Its leading members apparently take as first principles the acknowledgement of the supremacy of "the nation", the subordination of the clergy to the laity, the exclusive "justice" of "popular" government, and the like; which are the negations of my most deeply-rooted convictions.'[10]

As we are indebted to the *Life of Hort* for information about the Church Reform Association, so we are indebted to the life of Henry Sidgwick for information about the 'Free Christian Union', which Sidgwick joined when it began in June 1868. Its object was 'to invite to common action all who deem men responsible, not for the attainment of Divine truth, but only for the serious search for it; and who rely, for the religious improvement of human life, on filial Piety and brotherly Charity, with or without particular agreement in matters of doctrinal theology'.[11] This earlier society of liberal Christians was not confined to Anglicans; indeed it had a distinctly Unitarian flavour. Its President was C. S. Cookson and Henry Sidgwick was its Vice-President; among its leading members were the Rev. J. J. Taylor, Principal of Manchester New College, Dr James Martineau, and the Rev. Charles Kegan Paul. Kegan Paul was then a liberal Anglican and Vicar of Sturminster Marshall, Dorset, from 1862 until 1874 when his doubts became too strong and he went into publishing; years later he became a Roman Catholic. His story is pleasantly told in his *Memories* (1899) recently republished (1971), which speaks about his interest in the Free Christian Union.[12] This Union had met with no more success than the Church Reform Association. To quote the life of Sidgwick:

Notwithstanding an attendance at the religious service held on its first anniversary so large that the meeting had to be adjourned from the room taken for it to a larger hall, it was found impossible to obtain in sufficient amount the active service, personal countenance, and literary and official work needful to its success; and after little more than two years it was dissolved. A contemplated volume of essays was never produced, but the society did arrange for the publication of one or two essays, and one of these was an essay by Sidgwick on the 'Ethics of Conformity and Subscription', originally intended to form part of the volume.[13]

Sidgwick, in an attempt to promote the Free Christian Union, visited Oxford, and his comments about the visit, in a letter to James Martineau, written from Cambridge 22 February, 1869, are worth quoting:

> I write to give you an account of my visit to Oxford, as far as it bears upon the Free Christian Union. The prospect is not very encouraging. It appears that the Liberals at Oxford are chiefly (1) positivists of some shade; (2) Broad Church men of the mildly comprehensive and cautiously vague type, with innovating tendencies, chiefly political; or (3) Metaphysicians, either non-religious or with a religion far too unearthly for them to care about operating directly on the public creeds. Such was my view before I saw [T.H.] Green, and he quite confirms it. The only young man he mentioned as a possible ally is Mr Nettleship, a Fellow of Lincoln . . . I talked to Jowett. He is by no means unsympathetic, and was anxious not to discourage the undertaking. But he seemed to think (1) that Anglican clergymen ought to take the Church of England for their sphere of liberalising work; (2) that the union between enlightened Christians of all denominations, though very real, was too ethereal to be expressed in the concrete form of an association. 'This is an old method,' he said, 'and should be left to the old parties.'
>
> So much I have to say. I will write either to Nettleship or Seeley whenever you like. I think I shall get one or two members for the Union here.[14]

It was not long after writing this that Sidgwick reached a turning point in his life. As he was more and more doubtful about his Christian beliefs, he resigned his Fellowship at Trinity. However, he was immediately appointed Lecturer in Moral Science and so was able to continue teaching at Cambridge. We shall encounter him again, later, engaged in controversy with Hastings Rashdall over possible limits of unbelief in a clergyman. This seems a little ironical when we think of his early activities in the Free Christian Union.

Neither the Church Reform Association nor the Free Christian Union is mentioned in the pamphlet *The Modern Movement in the Church of England* by P. H. Bagenal, which up till now has been all that exists in the way of a history of English Modernism.[15] But he does mention the Curates Clerical Club. These are his words:

> But before the Churchmen's Union came to birth in 1898 there had been in existence for fifty years a private society known as the C.C.C. colloquially, otherwise the Curates' Clerical Club, which still survives.

This Curates Clerical Club is mentioned in the Life of his father by Sir Frederick Maurice, who says that F. D. Maurice and Dean Stanley were the only non-curates admitted to it, but this is corrected by H. R. Haweis in his book *The Dead Pulpit*. Haweis who was a member of it, indicates that J. Llewelyn Davies and Harry Jones were also members; and the life of Dean Fremantle shows that he too belonged to it, when he was a London incumbent, and also mentions J. R. Green the historian. 'Maurice' says Haweis,

> never overawed us; he was rather reluctant to speak, but we laid traps for him, and often drew him. Our plan was to repeat some opinion of his, in almost his own words, and then take some slight exception to it. This almost always brought him to his feet to explain, to our utmost delight and edification. I think it was the Rev. Harry Jones who first named him 'the prophet', a title which he never lost, and which no one ever dreamed of applying to any one else in our company, not even to Dean Stanley.[16]

The slow progress of liberal theology in the eighteen seventies is indicated by a study of the Lambeth Conference of 1878 which was as illiberal as that of 1867, in spite of having Tait as its President. The Conference Committee appointed to report on 'prevailing Infidelity, and on the best practical remedies', drew up a quite innocuous report, which, in spite of re-editing, failed to meet with the approval of the Bishops in plenary session. There was no welcome given in it to any recent biblical criticism; and the chief concern of its drafters seemed to be that Paley's *Evidences, Natural Theology* and *Horae Paulinae* should be re-edited. There is a sentence on the respective functions of Theology and Science. 'Religion', they say, 'appeals to the conscience and to the sense of sin, and aims at restoring the soul to a state of peace, founded on reconciliation with God. This ground Science cannot be said to occupy in any true sense.' The Report is such that it is perhaps as well that it was never published. In fact it was consigned to oblivion until I dug it out.[17] Move on a decade to 1888 and the situation had changed.

A symptom, perhaps, of the change was the publication of the Revised Version of the Bible. We saw how the Church Reform Association was pressing for such a revision. In 1870 the Convocation of Canterbury set up a panel of advisers. On 17 May, 1881, the revision of the New Testament was published by the Universities of Oxford and Cambridge. It was, apparently, the most sensational event, as yet, in publishing history. Public curiosity had been enormous. Demand for early copies was overwhelming. In vain bribes of up to £5,000 had been offered for advance copies. On the first day the Oxford Press sold a million copies. All day long the streets around Paternoster Square were blocked by streams of waggons carrying them to the station. Five days later two Chicago newspapers printed the entire book as a supplement, half the text having been received by telegraph before actual copies were available. The Old Testament followed in 1885 and the Apocrypha in 1895.

Edward Bouverie Pusey, Professor of Hebrew at Oxford since 1827, just lived to see the publication of the Revised Version of the New Testament. His death in 1882 marked the end of an era. What a funeral he had! Canon Scott Holland, who himself later lived in Christ Church as Regius Professor of Divinity, spoke of it in his lovely book *A Bundle of Memories* (1915):

What a passing away it was! In and out of that doorway in the South-west corner of Tom Quad, the wonderful chief had gone ever since 1826. Nobody living could recall the time when he had not been there. And all the amazing days had come and gone: and still the same presence belonged to the same spot. Still, that invincible faithfulness of his persevered, and preserved, and prayed, and toiled, and loved. Still, the grey eyes lifted, now and again, from their lowered bent, and let the prophetic light come through. Still, now and again the burdened face was illuminated by that sudden and incomparable smile which Stanley so vividly remembered. Still he held the fort, and never swerved or shook. Still he spoke, and wrote, and studied, and counselled. It was as if the whole Past was made present to us, as we watched him pass to and fro. And, at last, the end, so long delayed as to have become almost incredible, had come. The old man was dead. And up from every corner of the country came creeping the old men still left to whom his name had been a watchword and an inspiration. It seemed the last act of the historic Movement. Everything that was left from out of the momentous memories must be there. We younger men watched the long procession of men whose names had been familiar but whom we had never before seen in the flesh. Here they were – bowed, grey, tottering, making their final effort, delivering their witness to the end. On and on they filed, round and round the quadrangle, bearing the old hero home to his rest, laying his body by the side of the wife whom he had so absorbingly mourned. As they turned away from the grave, they knew that they would never meet again in such a company, on this earth. They, too, were, now, to pass away with him whose name and presence had meant so much to them. And what would follow?[18]

What was to follow we will see in a moment.

So Edward Bouverie Pusey, the traditionalist, the fundamentalist, the conservative, died. Having turned his back upon his own early liberalism he had fought against the acids of modernity and was now at rest. He had battled with Frederick William Farrar, the grandfather of Field Marshal Montgomery over eternal punishment. When Temple was appointed to Exeter, *Essays and Reviews* brought Pusey into alliance with Lord Shaftesbury in the same way that a century later the Anglican-Methodist Conversations brought together Bishop Graham Leonard and Dr Jim Packer. It was with the more moderate views of the German critics that Pusey did battle, the writings of men like the Baron von Bunsen, for few in England had become advocates and exponents of the heresies of David Friedrich Strauss, whose *Life of Jesus*, a vast tome, George Eliot had painstakingly translated, or of Ferdinand Christian Baur. The only English book favourable to these extremists published in Pusey's lifetime was R. W. Mackay's *The Tübingen School and its Antecedents*, though Mark Pattison, one of the

Septem contra Christum, praised Baur in the volume of essays that Nettleship edited. When he died, Pusey still accepted that the Book of Daniel was written in the sixth century by an exile in Babylon; and he would have subscribed wholeheartedly to the words that J. W. Burgon, a moderate High Churchman, uttered from the University pulpit at Oxford in the year after *Essays and Reviews*:

> The Bible is none other than the voice of Him that sitteth upon the throne. Every book of it, every chapter of it, every word of it, every syllable of it (where are we to stop?), every letter of it, is the direct utterance of the Most High. The Bible is none other than the Word of God, not some part of it more, some part of it less, but all alike the utterance of Him who sitteth upon the throne, faultless, unerring, supreme.[19]

These words, uttered in 1861, were echoed by countless clerical voices, as one can see if one looks at the vast collection of clergy who signed the solemn protest against *Essays and Reviews* and the views therein expressed by Rowland Williams and H. B. Wilson.

But by the Third Lambeth Conference of 1888, as we shall see in a moment, things were changing. Why did they change? I believe that, as far as the Church of England is concerned, the change was due especially to four men, three of them Oxford men and one Cambridge. First, there was Samuel Rolles Driver, who followed Pusey in the Hebrew Chair at Oxford and started to expound as scientifically assured results – here I reflect a phrase of J. Estlin Carpenter – things which his predecessor would have laid down his life to avert. But, as Scott Holland says, 'he saved the day . . . he taught us how to retain and read the Old Testament with sincerity of heart and faith, gaining, and not losing, by all that the new Criticism had to tell us of its origin and its sources, its history, and its growth. To him more than any other man we owe it that we were carried over safely from out of one period of thought into another.'[20] According to Henry Major, who studied under him, his writings were much more palatable than his lectures. The chief of these was his famous *Introduction to the Literature of the Old Testament*, published in 1897, the year of the Fourth Lambeth Conference, the year before the commencement of English Modernism.

The second gentleman I am thinking of is Herbert Edward Ryle, son of J. C. Ryle, first Bishop of Liverpool. The younger Ryle has been largely forgotten today, except perhaps as having been Dean of Westminster when the Unknown Warrior was buried there, about which one can read in Ronald Blythe's *The Age of Illusion* (1963). Before Westminster he was Bishop of Winchester and before that Bishop of Exeter. Before his elevation to the episcopal bench, he was Hulsean Professor at Cambridge and President of Queen's College. Ryle at Cambridge, like Driver at Oxford, did much to get a fair measure of Old Testament criticism accepted and his views reached a wider public in his books *Early Narratives of Genesis* (1892) and *The Canon of the Old Testament* (1892). Professor A. H. McNeile wrote this concerning Ryle:

> But his helpfulness to a wider circle by his writings was very great. Those were the days when Ryle, Kirkpatrick, and Driver represented to many people English Higher criticism of the Old Testament. To countless minds this seemed perilous to the truth of the Bible; and it was thought that the very foundations of the Christian faith were out of course. In the present day [1928] such a state of things is scarcely understandable; but that is due to teachers such as Ryle. By books, lectures, and sermons he advanced the cause. He once assured me that he fully expected a stake in the market place. But the tone of deep reverence and religious devotion which pervaded all that he wrote and said, coupled with a sanity which no opposition could disturb, drew the minds of thinking men to realise that the historical study of the Old Testament, so far from upsetting faith, was its only safe intellectual background.[21]

My third name is that of Charles Gore, another Bishop, happy at Birmingham, unhappy at Oxford, whose *Reconstruction of Belief*, written after his retirement, was widely read in the 'thirties and 'forties. His editing of *Lux Mundi* in 1889 was a great breakthrough. In this book the sons of the Tractarians, the disciples of Pusey, were seen to accept what Pusey never could or would, Evolution and Historical Criticism, for Pusey's mind, to quote Scott Holland once again, 'had been formed before the formulae of Evolution and Development had become the normal determinants of our thinking'.[22] Gore, who to a later age seemed conservative, even reactionary, and who persecuted unfortunate Modernists, like the now forgotten C. E. Beeby,[23] was to Liddon, Father Ignatius and Bishop Stubbs scarcely better than the *Septem contra Christum.* Stubbs in his Second Visitation Charge (1893) asserted against Gore:

> [Christ's] omniscience is of the essence of the personality in which manhood and Godhead united in him. With this belief I feel that I am bound to accept the language of our Lord in reference to the Old Testament Scriptures as beyond appeal . . . Where he speaks of David in spirit calling him Lord, I believe that David in spirit did call him Lord, and I am not affected by doubts thrown on the authorship of the 110th Psalm, except so far as to use his authority to set those doubts aside . . . I cannot bear to anticipate a day when the Church shall cry out to Jesus of Nazareth, 'Thou hast deceived me and I was deceived'; or to the unknown and unknowable, 'Why did'st thou let him deceive himself and us?'[24]

Though he later did battle with Gore, Major was very conscious of what theological liberalism owed to him. When the Bishop died, Major wrote his obituary in the *Modern Churchman* and said this:

> It was Charles Gore and the *Lux Mundi* group whom he led who found the way to fresh advances. With immense courage Gore accepted the results of Biblical Criticism. He dared to acknowledge not only that the Old Testament science and history was inaccurate. He even dared to affirm that modern critics of the Old Testament knew more about the facts of its composition than did the Saviour Himself; in short, that our Lord's human consciousness experienced and exhibited the limits of His terrestrial environment. *Essays and Reviews* was a brave and epoch-making book, but *Lux Mundi* was no less. It gave the Anglo-Catholics a deserved ascendancy over their Evangelical rivals who still clung to Biblical infallibility and shuddered at Gore's doctrine of the *Kenosis* . . .
>
> As an English modernist theologian he deserves to rank with Maurice, Jowett, Westcott, Hort and Rashdall. He would not have felt quite happy in the company of some of them because they were more devoted to truth and less to orthodoxy than he.

Nevertheless he accomplished what they could not have done – he liberalized the Oxford Movement.[25]

Here, of course, Major, in speaking of Gore as a Modernist theologian, uses the word anachronistically.

My fourth name is that of William Sanday, who did in the end throw in his lot with the Modernists, but not until the Great War. He came from Durham to Oxford as Dean Ireland's Professor of Exegesis of Holy Scripture in 1883, the very time when Driver moved into Pusey's old lodgings. From 1895 he was Lady Margaret's Professor of Divinity, his election to that office, which then depended upon clerical votes, having been engineered by A. C. Headlam, in collaboration with whom he wrote the International Critical Commentary on Romans, which has only recently been replaced in the series by the two volumes of Cranfield. Sanday, primarily a New Testament scholar, also popularized the views of Old Testament critics and wrote Bampton Lectures on *Inspiration* in 1893. I believe that it was due to him, perhaps even more than to Driver, that between 1882 and 1920 the clergy accepted the modern approach to the Bible. They constantly looked to him to give them the latest picture of how things stood.[26] The sort of things that Sanday was saying in those years, which formed a preparation for English Modernism, can be seen succinctly summarized in a paper he wrote for the Pan-Anglican Congress of 1908. He made four points:

1.   The theory of Evolution has made sense of the Bible. 'As we look back over the course of Biblical religion, we see at work in it a principle of growth and of what we call providential growth that from first to last has been in the hands of God, accomplishing His purposes, and culminating in the Incarnation of Our Lord Jesus Christ. From the point of view of Evolution, the Incarnation has been the centre and climax of history.'

2.   The study of Comparative Religion has made the study of the Bible more meaningful. Biblical religion has been shown not to be an isolated phenomenon but having many things in common with other religions.

3.   The books of the Bible have been shown up in the light of criticism as living products. Under the old system the Bible had

been treated rather as a collection of proof texts. Then it had a deadness about it. Now the figures of the Bible stand out as living persons.

4. Biblical Criticism has shown how Christian Doctrine arose out of the very life of the Church. Previously it had looked rather like a system of cold abstractions, suspended in mid air.[27]

These four men, Driver, Ryle, Gore and Sanday began their work in the 'eighties. By 1888 even bishops were being influenced by them, as is evident from the Lambeth Conference of that year. I can now add something to what I have written in my *Anglicanism and the Lambeth Conferences* (1978). At the 1888 Conference Frederick Temple, who in spite of his essay in *Essays and Reviews* had been promoted to Exeter and was now Bishop of London, chaired a Committee on 'Definite Teaching of the Faith to various classes and the means thereto'. That sounds a very unexciting title; but in fact, thanks to Temple, it was the most exciting committee to be on. Four years before Frederick Temple had been Bampton Lecturer, and his lectures, *The Relations between Religion and Science*, were a significant contribution to the debate on science and religion. There were two or three copies of this volume in Ripon Hall library when I was there (one of them Dr Major's), but they had never been cut; so I imagined it must be a dull book. Recently I read it in hospital and found it far from dull. Temple was certainly in advance of many of his contemporaries. At the end of Lecture VI, he writes:

> In conclusion, we cannot find that Science, in teaching Evolution, has yet asserted anything that is inconsistent with Revelation, unless we assume that Revelation was intended not to teach spiritual truth only, but physical truth also.[28]

But he is more daring on miracles. In Lecture VII he says:

> For instance, the miraculous healing of the sick may be no miracle in the strictest sense at all. It may be but an instance of the power of mind over body, a power which is undeniably not yet brought within the range of Science, and which nevertheless may be really within its domain. In other ways what seems to be miraculous may be simply unusual. And it must therefore be

always remembered that Revelation is not bound by the scientific definition of a miracle, and that if all the miraculous events recorded in the Bible happened exactly as they are told, and if Science were some day able to show that they could be accounted for by natural causes working at the time in each case, this would not in any way affect their character, as regards the Revelation which they were worked to prove or of which they form a part . . . Thus, for instance, it is quite possible that our Lord's Resurrection may be found hereafter to be no miracle at all in the scientific sense. It foreshadows and begins the general Resurrection; when that general Resurrection comes we may find that it is, after all, the natural issue of physical laws always at work.[29]

When one reads such sentences as these one is, perhaps, surprised that Lord Salisbury appointed Temple Archbishop of Canterbury!

The influence of Temple can be seen in the report on Definite Teaching of the Faith at Lambeth 1888, which was an immense advance on the Conference of 1878. Let me extract a suitable paragraph and you will see how it reflects Temple's Bamptons.

And as we are well assured of the truth of the New Testament, so we accept the Old Testament as the introduction to the New. It is in that character that the Old Testament is part of the Christian Faith. We are not called on to maintain that all the details of the Old Testament History are to be taken as literally true, and that any man who refuses to accept them is an unbeliever. Neither is it essential to the Christian Faith to teach or to believe that the account of the Creation is to be understood as a scientific statement; nor if any man maintains that the opening of the Bible, like the close of it, is a vision or an allegory, and that, in this respect, the first chapters of Genesis are parallel to the Book of Revelation, are we to hold him an unbeliever in Christ. The whole record of God's dealings with man generally, and with the chosen people particularly, is to be accepted in the light of our Lord's teaching, and as He Himself has treated it, as substantially true. But beyond that we are not concerned to go. And if the men who were inspired to make the record were not protected from mistakes of fact which have no bearing on religious truth, nor supplied with scientific knowledge in advance of all their fellow-men, nor able, in all cases where they used past documents, to distinguish between history and poetry, this does not affect the relation of the Old Testament to the New. And when we call on men to accept the Lord Jesus as the One Saviour, we do not require them, as a part of their belief in Him, to say that the account of the Creation is not only a lesson in the great ideas of the omnipotence of God in making all things out of nothing, the order and harmony of all His working, the subordination of the material to the spiritual, but is also an enunciation of scientific truth in the modern sense of these words without any bearing on the Faith.[30]

These words, which have never been quoted since the Conference, anticipated *Lux Mundi*, published a year later. They were too much for some of the Bishops in plenary session and had to be revised. There is no time to quote their revised form. But even that did not meet universal approval and the Report was never published. Temple was bitterly disappointed but held his tongue.[31]

When the Lambeth Bishops as a whole were still showing this timidity – in spite of an advance since 1878 – it is not surprising that the Liberal churchmen were not yet ready to organize themselves. By 1897, however, things were quite different. Frederick Temple was now at Canterbury, having suddenly succeeded Benson when the latter died at Hawarden after being rushed to church for Mattins by his impatient and much younger wife.[32] Temple chaired the 1897 Lambeth Conference instead of Benson. This appointed a committee to consider 'The Critical Study of Holy Scripture' under Bishop Ellicott of Gloucester, a famous Bible commentator. Three sentences are worth noting from their report. 'For many, the process of critical investigation has dissipated certain difficulties, presented by the older historical records . . .' 'Your Committee express their conviction with regard to the New Testament that the results of critical study have confirmed the Christian Faith.' Most remarkable of all is the sentence, 'A faith which is always or often attended by a secret fear that we dare not inquire lest inquiry should lead us to results inconsistent with what we believe, is already infected with a disease which may soon destroy it.' That sentence reminds one of the famous *dictum* of Temple at the time of the *Essays and Reviews* controversy, which is given in the Life of Tait – 'If the conclusions are prescribed, the study is precluded.'[33]

By the time that Temple was at Canterbury, there were other liberal bishops on the bench. His own successor at London was Mandell Creighton. At Ripon, William Boyd Carpenter had been Bishop since 1884 and was starting a theological college at Ripon which was to become the seat of English Modernism. At Hereford, John Perceval, a famous Headmaster of Rugby, full of the Arnoldian spirit, had become Bishop in 1895. He also attempted at Hereford but without much success a small liberal Theological College. At Manchester James Moorhouse, whose Hulsean Lectures of 1865 on 'The Growth of our Lord Jesus Christ in Wisdom' anticipated *Lux Mundi*,[34] had been Bishop since 1886. At Winchester, Randall Davidson, the protégé of Tait, had been Bishop since 1895. With this measure of episcopal support the liberals felt more inclination to organize themselves. So in the very year after the 1897 Lambeth Conference the Churchmen's Union started its career.

Assuming, then, that English Modernism started in 1898, I want to ask the question, who were the spiritual forebears of the Modernists or rather to whom did they look back as their forebears. H. L. Stewart in *Modernism Past and Present*, where he is dealing not with English Modernism but with Modernism in general, takes the story back to Clement of Alexandria and Origen. R. B. Tollinton, a notable English Modernist, learned in Patristics, wrote two volumes on Clement and spoke about him at the 1918 Girton Conference; he also published a volume of selections from Origen. We might go back behind these Alexandrians to the early Apologists, though, perhaps, not include Tertullian.[35] To Tertullian, however, we owe the expression 'anima naturaliter Christiana', and it was he who said, 'Christ called Himself the Truth. He did not call Himself Tradition.'[36] I am sure my old teacher Percival Gardner-Smith would want to include Synesius of Cyrene (370–414) in their pedigree; writing on him in the *Modern Churchman* for March, 1941, he said: 'He represents a type of piety, strong, virile, and non-ascetic, which was rare indeed in the fifth century, but to which the Church, particularly in England, has owed much.' Before Gardner-Smith's article, Alice Gardner, another Modern Churchman, had written

39

a little book on Synesius[37] which she dedicated to her brother Percy.

We might then move on to Peter Abelard (1079-1142), on whom there is an article by A. Henderson in the *Modern Churchman*, January 1928. One of Major's pupils, James Ramsay McCallum, wrote books on *Abelard's Ethics* (1935) and *Abelard's Christian Theology* (1948). He also wrote on him in the *Modern Churchman*, September 1942. From Abelard one would move on to Erasmus, whom Stewart calls 'the typical Modernist'. Most people know that a sentence allegedly from Erasmus used to figure on the cover of the *Modern Churchman*: 'By identifying the new learning with heresy, you make orthodoxy synonymous with ignorance.' Elliott-Binns' Hulsean Lectures for 1921-2 were on Erasmus. G. V. Bennett spoke on him at my request at the Conference of 1969. The name of Erasmus immediately suggests also that of John Colet on whom J. C. Hardwick wrote in the *Modern Churchman*, July 1925.

Then we might trace the line through the Falkland School, in which the chief names were Lucius Cary Lord Falkland, the 'ever-memorable' John Hales of Eton, William Chillingworth and possibly Jeremy Taylor. There is an article on them in the *Modern Churchman* for July 1915, by Gamaliel Milner. From them one would advance to the Cambridge Platonists, of whom Dean Inge was so fond, as one can see from his Bampton and Hulsean Lectures. Arthur W. Adams wrote an article on them in the *Modern Churchman* for April 1939.

Some Modernists might have then brought in Benjamin Hoadley, Bishop of Bangor, Archdeacon Francis Blackburne, and Bishop Richard Watson of Llandaff.

When one comes to the nineteenth century there is a useful guide in the article of H. G. Woods, 'Past Liberalism', in the volume *Anglican Liberalism* (1908), which was published in the series popularly known as 'the Devil's Blue Books'. H. G. Woods would start with the wit Sydney Smith, as also does Miss Isobel Fitzroy in her *Dogma and the Church of England* (1891). Nowell Smith, a notable English Modernist, Headmaster of Sherborne, compiled a two-volume biography of Sydney Smith, from his letters.[38]

It is curious that Woods says nothing of Samuel Taylor Coleridge, who has often been called 'The Father of the Broad Churchmen'. Major in the *Modern Churchman* for December 1956 calls him the 'Father of English Modernism', and H. L. Stewart refers to his *Confessions of an Inquiring Spirit* as a Modernist work. But what has amazed me as I have looked through the files of the *Modern Churchman* is how little there is about him there. I cannot find a single article on him. Not even his great-great-nephew, Gilbert Coleridge, a member of the movement, contributed anything about him.

From Smith and Coleridge one proceeds next to the Noetics, of whom the chief was Thomas Arnold. We saw how the magazine the *Broad Churchman* called him the founder of the Broad Church Party. If there are no articles on Coleridge in the *Modern Churchman* there is a liberal supply of material on Arnold.[39] Modernists like his hatred of ecclesiasticism and his interest in biblical criticism, though they might have been surprised to find him taking Adam seriously and the raising of Lazarus. Some Modernists looked back with admiration to Archbishop Whately. T. F. Royds wrote on his Bampton Lectures, *The Use and Abuse of Party Feeling in Religion*, in the *Modern Churchman* for April 1929, and W. J. Cratchley, then Tutor of Ripon Hall, wrote an article on him in the *Modern Churchman* for January 1937 and H. R. Chillingworth in June 1949. W. A. Cunningham-Craig wrote on Bishop Hampden in the *Modern Churchman* for October 1912, but noted the prelate's condemnation of *Essays and Reviews* and Colenso, remarking, 'We might have expected that one who had himself suffered so much in the cause of religious and theological freedom, would have been the last to set his hand to any documents of that kind, did we not know how easy it is for men to draw a distinction between their own case and that of others, and how often age and high office, if they do not actually distort the judgment, bring with them a caution and perhaps a narrowness of vision which were not there in youth.'[40] It is not surprising that Miss Fitzroy denies that Hampden was a liberal at all.[41]

Robertson of Brighton, whose sermons Charles Smyth praises so highly in his book on preaching, is undoubtedly a Modernist 'hero'. There are four articles on him in the *Modern Churchman*, by Isobel Fitzroy, Felix Asher (one of his successors at Holy Trinity Church, Brighton), N. J. Gould Wickey (an American) and D. L. Scott. The March 1917 number had a hitherto unpublished sermon of Robertson. Bishop Gordon Fallows was working on a book about him when he died in 1979. As well as his sermons, his life by Stopford Brooks carried on his influence.

The writers of *Essays and Reviews* are clearly to be reckoned as Modernist ancestors. We have already said enough about Frederick Temple, who lived to see the birth of English Modernism, unlike Benjamin Jowett, who died in 1893. There are two widely separated articles on Jowett in the *Modern Churchman*, one in May 1915 by Dean Fremantle, who knew him very well; the other, forty years later, by E. D. Mackarness. The sermons of Jowett were still being read, when the writings of Rowland Williams and Henry Bristow Wilson were being forgotten. Rowland Williams was the subject of an article by D. L. Scott in the *Modern Churchman* for June 1955, the centenary year of his *Rational Godliness*. Mark Pattison was the subject of an article by A. M. Coleman in the *Modern Churchman* for January 1936[42] and by Basil Willey for March 1959.

There are two articles on Bishop Colenso of Natal, one by Major and the other by D. L. Scott.[43] Connop Thirlwall of St David's, in spite of his rows with Rowland Williams, is treated favourably as a Broad Churchman by J. C. Hardwick in the *Modern Churchman* for May 1917. Charles Kingsley, whose life in two volumes by Frances Kingsley was more likely to be read by Modernists than were his sermons, is the subject of two articles in the *Modern Churchman*.[44]

So much then for Broad Church heroes. We now move on to men whose works Modernists evidently read, and which had their contribution to make in forging the theology of Modern Churchmen. Pride of place must be given to Frederick Denison Maurice. Articles were written about him in the *Modern Churchman* by W. A. Cunningham-Craig, H. G. Mulliner, Charles E. Raven, W. Moore Ede, D. L. Scott, and H. D. A. Major. Major in the *Modern Churchman* for December 1956 called him 'the father of the Modern Churchman's Movement', but that is wrong; he died too soon and, moreover, he never reckoned himself a Broad Churchman. His writings were not easy.[45] In fact, Major accused him of interpreting Scripture in 'the mystical and allegorical method of the Catechetical School of Alexandria', a statement heavily criticized by Alec Vidler.[46] Whatever the source of his obscurities, the liberal elements were popularized by his admirers, notably J. Llewelyn-Davies, H. R. Haweis, F. W. Farrar and W. Page-Roberts. Of these the most famous was Frederick William Farrar, who lived until 1903 and saw the inception of the Churchmen's Union. His battle over hell with Pusey has been recounted by Geoffrey Rowell in *Hell and the Victorians*. He was a popular figure and his novel *Eric, or Little by Little* was in many Victorian and Edwardian homes, as were also his *Life of Christ* and *St. Paul*. His most lasting contribution to liberal theology was his Bampton Lectures on *The Interpretation of the Bible*. E. J. Martin wrote on Farrar in the *Modern Churchman*, March 1931.

Farrar is still remembered, as also is Dean Stanley. Stanley, the disciple of Thomas Arnold, was the most genuinely liberal Churchman of the nineteenth century, whose *Christian Institutions* and *Essays on Church and State* were regular *pabulum* of Modernists early this century. His life, like those of Arnold, Robertson, Kingsley and Temple, was also widely read by them.

In contrast, one who was widely read when Modernism began, Alfred Williams Momerie, has now been almost completely forgotten. Professor Owen Chadwick does not mention him in *The Victorian Church*, nor is he given a place in F. L. Cross' *Dictionary of the Christian Church*. In 1891 he shared with Maurice the distinction of being expelled from King's College, London, and was reduced to preaching in the Portman Rooms in London. He published a number of short works, with such titles as *Church and Creed* (1890), *Personality* (1895), *Belief in God* (1886), *The Origin of Evil* (1891), *Inspiration* (1890), *The Basis of Religion* (1883), and *A Plea for Truth in Religion*. Miss Isobel Fitzroy dedicated to him her *Dogma and the Church of England* and wrote an article on him in the *Modern Churchman* for March 1914. In 1969 I reminded the Modern Churchman's Conference about this man and someone present was provoked into writing about him in a subsequent number of the *Modern Churchman*.[47] No doubt the praise of Miss Fitzroy in her dedication is excessive, 'I reckon you among the greatest teachers whom the Church of England has ever possessed', but it is remarkable that he has fallen so completely into obscurity. Major read some of his works while still in New Zealand.[48]

Momerie was a Cambridge man who had attended the City of London School, as also had Sir John Seeley and Edwin Abbott. Edwin Abbott I would be prepared to call 'The Father of English

Modernism'. That was the title that Bishop Barnes gave to Fenton Anthony Hort in an article he wrote in *The Challenge* for 8 June, 1923. However, the only person who, as far as I know, accepted that designation for Hort was H. D. A. Major in *English Modernism*, but he went back on it in 1956 and gave the title to Maurice. Barnes in that article tries to contend that Modernism did not come out of the Broad Church Movement. I will quote a short paragraph from that now forgotten article in *The Challenge*:

> It is often assumed that English Modernism is a development of the Broad Church Theology of Arnold, Maurice and Stanley. The assumption is incorrect. The social sympathies of these religious leaders have enriched the outlook of all parties in all English churches. They were champions of intellectual honesty and spiritual freedom; and, in consequence, their memory is revered by Modernists to-day. But they were not fundamentally influenced either by Biblical criticism or by scientific discovery. Maurice's attitude towards the Old Testament seems to a modern scholar curiously naïve. His spiritual earnestness gave a certain splendour to his philosophy; but he did not seize the significance of the discoveries and theories which have since proved singularly important. It was Hort (1828–1892) who first saw their creative power. Just as Newman was the parent of Catholic Modernism, Hort was the man in whose mind English Modernism came to birth.

The work that Barnes uses to prove Hort the 'Father of English Modernism' is his Hulsean Lectures *The Way, the Truth, the Life* delivered in 1871, published posthumously in 1893; or rather, not so much the lectures, but the Notes and Illustrations that are added to them.[49] Admittedly, there are some excellent things in the Notes and Illustrations, but after twice reading Hort's biography, I would conclude it is quite incorrect to call him 'The Father of English Modernism'. Time and time again he criticizes the Broad Churchmen, and, as we have already seen, he will have nothing to do with their attempts at organization. It would be far better to call this great and remarkable man 'The Father of Cambridge Modern Theology'. I note with interest that the Society which in my time at Cambridge was called the Junior Theological Society is now called the Hort Society.

To be justly named the 'Father of English Modernism' one would need to be both a fanatic and a supporter of liberal party programmes. Here the bill was filled by Edwin A. Abbott. Abbott, a St John's College man, was a great Headmaster of the City of London School, who retired early in order to write, though he had already in his teaching days written much. The results of his retirement were thirty volumes of *Diatessarica*, as he called them, learned and original contributions to the study of the Gospels, but so erudite as to repel all but the specialist. Two of these, the *Johannine Vocabulary* and the *Johannine Grammar*, were reprinted not long ago and are still used. His more popular books were his three lives of Jesus – *Philochristus*, the story told by a disciple of the rabbis in beautiful sixteenth-century prose; *Onesimus*, the story told by a Phrygian slave; and *Silanus the Christian*, the story told by a Roman noble, a disciple of Epictetus. His theological thought, which is undoubtedly the embryo of English Modernism, is to be found in his *The Kernel and the Husk* (1886, but published anonymously), *Through Nature to Christ* (1877) and *The Spirit on the Waters* (1897). These all made him suspect in the eyes of the orthodox for he boldly cast aside the whole miraculous element in Christianity. Nevertheless, on his eightieth birthday, he was presented with an address signed by both Archbishops and other bishops and headmasters. He died in 1927 after being bedridden for seven years.[50] We earlier saw his involvement in the Church Reform Association. Though he lived to see the beginning of the Churchmen's Union, he did not join it, nor did he write in *The Modern Churchman*, nor did the magazine give him an obituary notice. Nevertheless, he seems to my mind to foreshadow the Modernist Theology of the 'twenties and 'thirties, with its denial of the miraculous, its emphasis on God working within the evolutionary process, its attachment to the Jesus of history, and its anti-Catholicism. It is significant that Major in the last piece he wrote, 'A Biographical Record of the Modern Churchmen's Union', in the *Modern Churchman*, says quite a lot about Abbott, who certainly influenced him considerably.

A friend of Abbott, also brought up at the City of London School, was Sir John Seeley, whose famous work *Ecce Homo*, a study of the ethical ideals of Jesus, came out in 1865 anonymously, and was at first variously attributed to Newman, Stanley, Gladstone and Temple. Hort said of it 'that the merely ethical aspects of our Lord's Life had never been seized upon with so much power'.[51] Even after all these years it remains a remarkable work. His other book, *Natural Religion*, was less successful and less widely read, but this, like Abbott's works, anticipates the Modernist theology. Attention has been drawn again to Seeley recently in an article 'John Robert Seeley and the Idea of a National Church' by R. T. Shannon in *Ideas and Institutions of Victorian Britain* (1967).[52]

It is worth noting that Major, in that last article of his, to which I have already referred, mistakenly gives Hort the name of Edwin. Clearly there was some confusion here with Edwin Hatch, who is certainly another precursor of English Modernism. Hatch, whose hymn 'Breathe on me, breath of God' is probably sung at most confirmations, was much admired by Harnack. His theory, like that of Harnack's *What is Christianity?*, was that the original Hebraic message of Jesus, summarized in the Sermon on the Mount, had been hopelessly corrupted by Greek metaphysics. One can see this developed in his Hibbert Lectures, *The Influence of Greek Ideas and Usages on the Christian Church* (1900). William Sanday's last public utterance was a lecture on Hatch which appeared in the *Modern Churchman*, September 1920. Hatch died in 1889, at the age of 54, 'when', to quote Sanday, 'he was just coming into his own'.[53]

An important link between the Modernists and Jowett, Stanley, Temple and Tait, was W. H. Fremantle, who unfortunately has been the victim of a poor biography. Major would have written a much better life than that by Draper. Fremantle, a successful Vicar at St Mary's, Bryanston Square, where he had Samuel Augustus Barnett as his curate, was later Dean of Ripon, when Boyd Carpenter was Bishop there. Between them they succeeded in making that cathedral city a Liberal Protestant stronghold. Fremantle, like Tait, was totally Erastian and anti-Ritualist. It was commonly said that the only part of his teaching that was obscure was the doubt whether the Prime Minister ought to be ex-officio Archbishop of Canterbury, or the Archbishop of Canterbury ex-officio Prime Minister.[54] His Bampton Lectures were on *The World as the Subject of Redemption* (1885); and some of his sermons were published under the title *The Gospel of the Secular Life* (1882), which sounds like a title from the nineteen sixties. Fremantle became a Modernist, wrote in the *Modern Churchman*, and was present at the first Conference of Modern Churchmen.

A link between Thomas Arnold and the Modernists was his son Matthew, whose four religious books, *St. Paul and Protestantism* (1870), *Literature and Dogma* (1873), *God and the Bible* (1875) and *Last Essays on Church and Religion* (1877), did an enormous amount to set before the general public the opinions and beliefs of the Higher Critics. Two of his most famous sayings, 'Conduct is three fourths of human life',[55] and his description of God as 'the enduring power not ourselves which makes for righteousness',[56] were beloved of English Modernists, though they hardly liked his criticism of Maurice as having 'passed his life beating the bush with deep emotion and never starting the hare'.[57] There was also the sentence which Major loved to quote: 'Suppose I could change the pen with which I write this into a pen wiper, I would not thus make what I write any the truer or more convincing. That may be so in reality, but the mass of mankind feel differently.'[58] Yet, in spite of Modernists' approval of Matthew Arnold, there are no articles about him in the *Modern Churchman*.

That then is the main Broad Church ancestry from which English Modernism came. These were the men they admired. Here were some of the writings that, with additional material from abroad, were to produce the peculiar beliefs of Modern Churchmen.

Let me, finally, remind you of the ground we have covered. We saw the beginnings of informal coming together of the Broad Churchmen in the Curates Clerical Society. We saw the failure of the Free Christian Union in 1868 and then of the Church Reform Association in 1870. We saw how the publication, *The Broad Churchman*, in 1873 lasted but a few months. A more liberal approach to theology was seen at work among some of the bishops at Lambeth in 1888, but Temple's committee report was not allowed to be published. However in these years Driver, Gore, Sanday and Ryle were all at work and by 1897 Temple, writer in *Essays and Reviews*, was on the archiepiscopal throne of Canterbury and led the bishops into a more liberal theology. Thus the time was ripe for a Broad Church organization that would succeed. This came in 1898, as we shall see in the next chapter, when we examine the fortunes of the Churchmen's Union before the arrival of the

New Zealander, Major, with his great organizing ability. During that period we shall see added to the inherited Broad Church theology the influence of German and French Liberal Protestantism, Roman Catholic Modernism, American Liberal Protestantism and English Liberal Judaism.

NOTES

1   *The Broad Churchman*, 30 Jan., 1878, p.25.

2   ibid., p.1.

3   See C. R. Sanders, *Coleridge and the Broad Church Party*, p.7. The *New English Dictionary* quotes Benjamin Jowett as saying that the term originated with Clough.

4   ibid., p.1.

5   Evidently by Charles M. Davies, who reproduced it in *Orthodox London* (1874 and 1875).

6   *The Broad Churchman*, 30 Jan., 1878, p.26.

7   Cambridge University Library does not possess a single issue. There is a set in the British Library.

8   Harry Jones was a well known Broad Churchman – Vicar of St. Luke's, Berwick Street 1858–72; Rector of St George's in the East, 1879–82; Vicar of Great Barton, Suffolk 1882–5; Vicar of St Philips, Regent Street, London 1886–97; Rector of St Vedast, Foster Lane with St Michael-le-Querne, St Matthew, Friday Street and St Peter, Cheapside 1897–1900.

9   See A. F. Hort, op. cit., vol. ii, pp.58ff.

10   ibid., p.125.

11   A. Sidgwick and E. M. Sidgwick, *Henry Sidgwick. A Memoir*, pp.189f.

12   See op. cit., pp.264f.

13   op. cit., p.190. Sidgwick's essay was published by Williams and Norgate in 1870.

14   See *Henry Sidgwick*, p.191.

15   See also P. H. Bagenal, 'The Modern Movement in the Church of England', in the *Hibbert Journal* (Jan. 1922), pp.220–35, and 'The Origin of the Churchmen's Union' in *Modern Churchman* (December 1920), pp.490–4. The pamphlet to which I have referred was republished in the *Modern Churchman* (April 1937), pp.10–22.

16　See *The Dead Pulpit*, pp.27f. For Fremantle, see W. H. Draper, *Recollections of Dean Fremantle*, p.75, where Wace is also cited as a member.

17　I am indebted to Lambeth Palace Library for letting me see this unpublished Report.

18　op. cit., pp.99f.

19　The passage is quoted in Alan Richardson, *Christian Apologetics*, p.202.

20　H. Scott Holland, *A Bundle of Memories*, p.104.

21　See M. H. Fitzgerald, *A Memoir of Herbert Edward Ryle* (1928), pp.97f.

22　H. Scott Holland, *A Bundle of Memories*, p.101.

23　C. E. Beeby was Vicar of Yardley Wood, Birmingham. He was the author of *Creed and Life* (1897) and *Doctrine and Principles* (1900).

24　Quoted in D. E. Nineham, ed., *The Church's Use of the Bible*, pp.140f.

25　*Modern Churchman* (Feb. 1932), pp.582f.

26　cf. R. A. Knox, *Some Loose Stones* (1914), p.35.

27　See, for further information on Sanday, my article on him in the *Modern Churchman*, vol. ix, No. 4 (N.S.), (July 1966), pp.257–72).

28　F. Temple, *The Relations between Religion and Science* (1884), p.188.

29　ibid, pp.195f.

30　Again I am grateful to the Lambeth Librarian for a sight of this unpublished report.

31　See E. G. Sandford, ed., *Memoirs of Archbishop Temple*, vol. ii, p.628: 'One of the most striking illustrations both of Dr. Temple's self-command and of his lasting sympathy with liberal thought is afforded by the Report on the study of Holy Scripture (*sic*) which he wrote, when Bishop of London, for the Lambeth Conference of 1888. It anticipated conclusions now generally accepted by thoughtful men, which base the defence of Revelation upon sure foundations. The succeeding Conference endorsed many of these conclusions, but the rejection of the Report at the time held back for many years a cause which was dear to him, and he felt it much. He knew (as he told Archbishop Benson on another occasion, p.665) how "to hold his tongue" when he thought silence right; the keenness of his disappointment was, however, well known to his intimate friends. Reference was made to the incident by Archbishop Davidson in the obituary tribute which he paid in Convocation to his predecessor, February 10, 1903.'

32　My understanding of his death seems to be contradicted by David Williams' *Genesis and Exodus*, p.107, who says his wife did not walk.

33　See R. T. Davidson and W. Benham, *Life of Archibald Campbell Tait* (1891), vol. i, p.291.

34 See E. C. Rickards, *Bishop Moorhouse*, p.40, 'It was during his time at St. John's, Fitzroy Square, that James Moorhouse was asked to preach the Hulsean Lectures at Cambridge. He chose for his subject, "The Growth of Our Lord Jesus Christ in Wisdom", a subject to which he had given much thought, and about which he anticipated some of the conclusions arrived at in one of the essays in "Lux Mundi".'

35 H. L. Stewart refers to the Apologists and E. H. Blakeney has an article on them in *Modern Churchman*, July 1941. See also the article 'Liberalism in the Early Church', by W. H. C. Frend, *Modern Churchman*, Conference Number (October 1969).

36 See H. D. A. Major, *Thirty Years After*, p.86.

37 Alice Gardner, *Synesius of Cyrene* (1886).

38 Nowell C. Smith, *Letters of Sydney Smith*, 2 vols. (1953).

39 W. A. Cunningham-Craig, 'Broad Churchmen of the Nineteenth Century II. Thomas Arnold', in *Modern Churchman* (March 1913). R. Meiklejohn, 'The Churchmanship of Thomas Arnold', *Modern Churchman* (April 1919).

40 op. cit., p.338.

41 *Dogma and the Church of England*, p.53.

42 Reprinted in his *Six Liberal Thinkers* (1936).

43 D. L. Scott, *Modern Churchman*, April 1947. H. D. A. Major, *Modern Churchman*, Feb. 1914.

44 E. F. Morison, *Modern Churchman*, April and May 1925. D. L. Scott, *Modern Churchman*, Jan. 1961.

45 cf. Kegan Paul, *Memories*, p.165, 'I saw much of Maurice, but while loving him personally, as did all who came in contact with him, I am free to confess I never could make head or tail of what he taught or what he meant', and H. Anson, *Looking Forward*, p.114, 'Maurice was of all writers on religion the most difficult to understand.'

46 See A. R. Vidler, *F. D. Maurice and Company* (1966), p.139.

47 See *Modern Churchman* (April 1970), Peter Were, 'Forgotten Liberals and "Basic Christianity"'.

48 Yet Major says nothing about him in his 'Biographical Record of the Modern Churchmen's Movement' in *Modern Churchman*, December 1956.

49 Cf. J. A. T. Robinson, *The Human Face of God* (1973), p. viii.

50 See *The Times* obituary.

51 *Life of Hort*, vol. ii, p.65.

52 Edited by Robert Robson.

53   *Modern Churchman* (Sept. 1920), p.379.

54   *Thomas Banks Strong*, by Harold Anson, p.11.

55   *Literature and Dogma*, p.12.

56   op. cit., p.43.

57   op. cit., p.200.

58   cf. *English Modernism*, p.132.

3

English Modernism before Major

My first chapter was introductory, putting English Modernism in the context of the wider Modernism, summarizing the position taken up by the typical English Modernist and indicating the ground we should have to cover. It also said something about the liberal ethos of the Hulsean Lectures. My second chapter dealt with the early failures of Anglican Broad Churchmen to organize themselves; and then examined the theologians and writers whom English Modernists regarded as forerunners, the most important being the nineteenth-century Broad Churchmen. I should like to emphasize that the Broad Churchmen did not present a united front and were not in full agreement with each other – any more than their successors the English Modernists. Thus we find H. R. Haweis complaining that he cannot accept all that Edwin Abbott offers in his *The Kernel and the Husk*,[1] while A. W. Momerie takes Farrar, Haweis and Page-Roberts to task for their failure to sympathize with his position.[2] Yet, on the other hand, Momerie himself is critical of Sir John Seeley's *Natural Religion*, and writes his *The Basis of Religion* against it. Perhaps this very divergence made them slow to organize themselves. This, at any rate, is the view of Philip H. Bagenal in his pamphlet, *The Modern Movement in the Church of England*, where he says:

> Almost to the end of the century men like Llewelyn Davies, Brooke Lambert, and Bradley Alford held that there was no essential unity amongst liberal Churchmen, and that a too pronounced divergence and independence of standpoint would soon split any organisation. Moreover, the evils of partisanship were at the same time so obvious in the disputes between Protestant and Anglo-Catholic organisations that men with wider views and sympathies were not willing to be harnessed to any too pronounced definition in spiritual matters.[3]

During Frederick Temple's episcopate at London and Canterbury the number of liberally inclined parochial clergymen in the metropolis grew. Bagenal mentions Llewelyn Davies, the friend of Hort, Rector of Christ Church, Marylebone 1856–89 (after which he moved to Kirkby Lonsdale), Brooke Lambert,[4] Vicar of Greenwich from 1880, and Bradley Alford, the half-brother of Dean Henry Alford of Canterbury, who was Vicar of St Luke's, Nutford Place, Marylebone, 1877–1903, and for a time Editor of the *Contemporary Review*. Men of similar stamp were Prebendary Harry Jones, Vicar of St Philip's, Regent Street, 1886–97,[5] John E. Kempe, Rector of St James', Piccadilly, and W. Page-Roberts, Perpetual Curate of St Peter's, Vere Street, Marylebone, 1878–1907, when he went to be Dean of Salisbury. Names like these flit across the pages of the life of Samuel Augustus Barnett, who was Fremantle's curate at St Mary's, Bryanston Square, and then Vicar of St Jude's, Whitechapel and Founder of Toynbee Hall.[6] Intermingled with them are references to Jowett, Edwin Abbott, Sir John Seeley, and H. R. Haweis, and there are indications that these were the heroes of the liberal parochial clergymen.

It was amongst these liberal London clergy that English Modernism began, though, of course, it was not then called Modernism, for, as I made clear in my first chapter, English Modernists took over the term from Roman Catholic Modernism. The movement started with a liberal periodical. This was not of course *The Modern Churchman*, which did not begin until 1911, but a weekly publication of which, I imagine, hardly any copies remain, called *The Church Gazette. A Review of Liberal Religious Thought*. The first issue which came out on 23 April, 1898, was of much the same size as the *Broad Churchman*, which had lasted for about six months in 1873, and had a similar coverage – articles, reviews, correspondence column, and advertisements, mostly for books, though there was one for bacon.

> Breakfast bacon – George Young, Teignmouth, Devon, delivers carriage paid, to any railway station in Great Britain, side of his mild-cured, smoked breakfast bacon. 6½d. per lb. Quality perfect.

The first issue contained an article by W. H. Fremantle, on 'The Spiritual Basis of Christian Liberalism', a sermon by Henry Major

Stephenson and an article 'The Church and Modern Thought' by Mandell Creighton. The editorial, headed 'Our Raison d'Etre', read as follows:

> In coming before the public, what is our main object and mission? To this question it is very easy to give a clear reply. Of the various schools of thought and opinion that lie within the limits of the Church of England, all are represented by their special organisations and societies. All, that is, except one, which, if not yet properly forming a party at all, fails to do so merely because it is quite disorganised. The body referred to consists of that very considerable and growing number of thoughtful individuals, known commonly by the name of Liberal, or Broad Churchmen . . .
>
> The fact that no journal creating and representing such a party should have already come into being may be easily accounted for. [Notice, he is oblivious of the *Broad Churchman* of 1873.]
>
> Firstly, Liberalism is essentially divergent, and refuses to be coerced along a united line. From the nature of things, this difficulty must always exist; but though it is a difficulty, it has not hindered the political party known by the name of 'Liberal' from conducting very successful journals. And though we lay stress on the point that Liberalism in Religion is not to be identified with Liberalism in Politics, yet the same divergent tendency is an equal factor to deal with in either case, and need be no more insurmountable in the one than it has proved to be in the other.
>
> And in the second place, the Church Liberals have so recently risen into prominence and recognition, that the time had not yet come for that section to make any attempt to marshal their forces, and pull themselves together, and, from a mass of disintegrated units, to form themselves into a compact whole. That time, we think, has now arrived.
>
> To create such a concerted party an organ is indispensable, and equally so to defend its aims and principles, and to enable them to spread. This demand we propose to supply.

The editorial office of the new magazine was 18–20 Temple House, Temple Avenue, London E.C. The name of the Editor was not revealed but it was the Rev. William Routh, a clergyman who had served in Bishop Boyd Carpenter's diocese of Ripon, having been Headmaster of Bedale Grammar School 1887–92. He was an *alumnus* of St John's College, Cambridge.

Out of the *Church Gazette* there came also, as we shall see, the Churchmen's Union in the same year 1898. There are two other reasons for my dating the rise of English Modernism in the year 1898. One was the foundation in 1898 of Ripon Hall at Ripon in Yorkshire by Bishop Boyd Carpenter. The other was the fact that in 1898 and 1899 four men who were to become leading English Modernists published works of liberal theology. In 1898 Hastings Rashdall, Fellow and Tutor of New College, Oxford, published his *Doctrine and Development*. In 1899 Percy Gardner published his *Exploratio Evangelica. A Survey of the Foundations of Christianity*. In 1899 William Ralph Inge, Fellow of Hertford College, Oxford, published his Bampton Lectures on *Christian Mysticism*. These three men all subsequently became Presidents of the Modern Churchmen's Union, Percy Gardner from 1914 to 1923, Rashdall briefly in 1923–4 (the last year of his life) and Inge from 1924 to 1934. In this same year, 1899, James M. Wilson, Vicar of Rochdale and Archdeacon of Manchester, published his Hulsean Lectures, *The Gospel of the Atonement*. I should like to say something about each of these Modernists as we follow the rise of the Churchmen's Union and see the beginning of each's association with it.

So now we turn to the birth out of the *Church Gazette* of the Churchmen's Union. On 5 April 1898 the Rev. Theodore P. Brocklehurst, Curate of Merstham, Surrey, had a letter in the *Daily Mail* under the heading 'A Churchman's Protest' in which he criticized narrowness of outlook:

Is not the Church of England in these days just in danger of becoming too parochial and too diocesan? Surely it must be healthier for our corporate life that the fittest man should be appointed to a charge, whether he belongs to that or some other diocese?

He belongs to the National Church. Do not let us narrow down our minds to a mere diocesan organization, but let us widen our sympathies and broaden out our methods by contact with any life-giving breeze where the Anglican Communion obtains.

William Routh, who was preparing to launch the *Church Gazette*, saw this letter in the *Daily Mail*, wrote to Brocklehurst and asked him to express himself at greater length for the new Broad Church publication. With this request he readily complied and had a long letter published in the *Church Gazette* on 7 May, 1898, in which his theme was the need of progress and advance in the Church.

> Edmund Burke once neatly said, that 'a state without the means of some change is without the means of its conservation'. Surely this maxim applies to our Church . . . The attempt to hold back the human mind from entering into fuller light is the attempt of the South sea islander, who strives to throw a lasso over the sun, and prevent its rise; as Milton long ago truly said, 'Truth is compared in Scripture to a running fountain: if her waters flow not in a perpetual progression, they sicken into a muddy pool of conformity and tradition.'

Brocklehurst's letter was seen by the Rev. H. G. Rosedale, Vicar of St Peter's, Ladbroke Gardens, Kensington, who thought well of it and wrote to its author. Before long Routh, Brocklehurst and Rosedale met together and mooted the possibility of a centre for Broad Churchmen. On 18 June Rosedale had a letter in the *Church Gazette* suggesting the uniting together of liberal-minded clergy. 'I make an earnest plea' he wrote, 'for a conference of the "liberal-minded clergy". If such could be arranged great would be the result. If such a conference could be held in London, I would for one undertake to try and arrange for hospitality on a large scale, and others, I am sure would do the same.'

> The Church Congress [at Bradford] will do something, but now that we have a weekly paper of our own, the time seems to have arrived for some definite programme. As by far the larger proportion of the learned and highly accomplished clergy and Church laity belong to this school of thought, I am sanguine enough to believe that their deliberations would not be futile.

On 27 July a day conference took place at Kensington with the object of starting a society of Liberal Churchmen. Dean Farrar of Canterbury, Dean Bradley successor to Stanley at Westminster, Dean Fremantle and Archdeacon Waugh of Ripon all regretted their inability to be present. Those who did attend resolved that an organization should be formed 'to unite the body of Churchmen who consider that dogma is susceptible of re-interpretation and re-statement, in accordance with the clearer perception of truth attained by discovery and research'. It was also agreed that the *Church Gazette* should be the official organ of the society.

The next step was a meeting at the time of the Church Congress at the Great Northern Hotel, Bradford, at which Dean Fremantle was present, when it was agreed to meet in October and formally inaugurate the Union. This inaugural meeting took place on 31 October, at the Church House, Westminster (not the present one, of course, but the building which it replaced.)[7] The objects of the Union were now settled. These were:

1. To unite Churchmen who consider that dogma is capable of reinterpretation and restatement in accordance with the clearer perception of truth attained by discovery and research.

2. To take such steps for the advancement of legislation in matters of doctrine, discipline, and dogma as may seem to conduce to the safety, welfare, and progress of the Church. The immediate action of the Union will be directed towards:–
   (a) Enforcing the rights of laymen to adequate share in Church Government.
   (b) Making the use of the Athanasian Creed optional.
   (c) Patronage reform.
   (d) Mutual defence.

3. To promote conciliatory attitudes towards Nonconformists, with a view to making the Church inclusive and truly national.

If we recall what I wrote about the Church Reform Association of 1870, from which Dean Fremantle was a survivor, you will see that the new society's aims had much in common with those of the old.

One of the most significant persons present at this meeting was George Henslow, who had been curate to H. R. Haweis at St

James', Marylebone, and Lecturer in Botany at St Bartholomew's Hospital, and was now Hon. Professor of Botany for the Royal Horticultural Society and President of the Natural History Society. This botanist, who had imbibed the liberal theology of Haweis, was the son of an even more famous botanist, John Stevens Henslow, the friend of Charles Darwin, who was much in evidence in the recent television serial on Darwin.[8] The younger Henslow was a popular preacher on the subject of the reconciliation of science and religion. I have two of his printed sermons, one on *Genesis and Geology. A plea for the Doctrine of Evolution*, and another on *What was the Fall?* He lived until 1926, by which time, as far as I can discover, he had become a spiritualist. Professor George Henslow was elected the first President of the Churchmen's Union, or, to give its full title, The Churchmen's Union for the Advancement of Liberal Religious Thought.

In the first year of its existence the new society got into controversy with the English Church Union, the High Church society founded in 1859, with which the name of Lord Halifax will for ever be associated. That controversy has been completely forgotten. Neither Brocklehurst nor Bagenal, in writing about the early history of the Union, cared to recall it but it can be read about in the pages of the *Church Gazette*, which at this time the Anglican monk, Father Ignatius, was castigating as an 'infidel paper'.[9] It must be remembered that in these last years of the nineteenth century there was another phase of ritualistic controversy, when the Archbishop of Canterbury, Frederick Temple, was called upon to give his opinion on the legality of the reservation of the sacrament and the use of incense. In this atmosphere there were those who wanted the new union to become a society of moderate churchmen who stood for law and order in a period of growing liturgical chaos.

At this time there had been trouble at St Ethelburga's, Bishopsgate, where Mandell Creighton now placed as the new curate-in-charge the Rev. Dr William Frederick Cobb (later Geikie-Cobb), while Messrs. Kensit, Hone and Hill, agitators for the Protestant party, were pleading for the removal of crucifixes and other ornaments. Dr Cobb who was anxious to moderate the churchmanship at St Ethelburga's, was currently Assistant Secretary of the English Church Union, an office he had held since

1892. One of the most amazing episodes in the history of the Churchmen's Union was the transference of the allegiance of Cobb from the English Church Union to the Churchmen's Union. He abandoned the former and had no more to do with it. Cobb, a graduate of Trinity College, Dublin, was already a Doctor of Divinity, and had translated works of St Bernard and Cornelius à Lapide. Not coming from the Broad Church School, he represented a very interesting type of Modernist, as can be seen from his books, notably his *Mysticism and the Creed*. He remained a member of the Union until his death in 1941, and is remembered for the part he played in trying to change the law on divorce and the Church's attitude to divorce.

The first Annual Meeting of the Union, held on 6 October 1899, was notable for the sermon of Hastings Rashdall, who had recently become a member. He was undoubtedly one of the giants of the movement – perhaps the greatest and most erudite exponent of English Modernism. We are fortunate in having a reasonable biography of Rashdall by his friend and colleague P. E. Matheson, though I know that Major (who had immense admiration for Rashdall) had many criticisms to make of it. Someone told me Major always raised his hat when he passed 18 Longwall, Oxford, once the residence of Rashdall, now part of New College. His life can be quickly given. Born in 1858, he went to school at Harrow, where the Broad Church Montague Butler (later Master of Trinity) influenced him, and then to New College. In 1883 he was a lecturer at St David's College, Lampeter, but was hardly settled there before being whisked away to Durham. Then he returned to Oxford as a fellow of Hertford, where he had W. R. Inge as a colleague. It was commonly said at the time, that Rashdall could not believe that Christianity was true, but wished it was, while Inge believed it was true, but wished it was not.[10] In 1895 he became Dean of Divinity and Tutor of New College, where he remained until 1917, combining it, after 1910, with a canonry of Hereford given him by the liberal Bishop Percival, until 1917 when he became Dean of Carlisle. He died of cancer in 1924. Rashdall was learned in history, philosophy and theology and would have graced a chair in any of the three, but none came his way. Nor was he ever a bishop's examining chaplain.

He had been influenced at Oxford by Jowett and had profound

admiration for *Ecce Homo*.[11] He had become well known as a liberal churchman, just before the start of the Churchmen's Union, through controversy with Henry Sidgwick. In April 1896, Sidgwick, now Professor of Moral Philosophy at Cambridge, published a lecture on 'The Ethics of Religious Controversy', delivered on 24 November 1895 at the West London Ethical Society, in which he affirmed that any clergyman who 'concludes against the miraculous element in the Gospel history, and, in particular, rejects the story of the miraculous birth of Jesus should not continue in the Church'.[12] In January 1897 Rashdall took up arms against Sidgwick and defended liberal clergymen. In speaking of miracles, he says, 'Whatever his theory of miracles may be, the clergyman who can tell the sick man that Christ went about curing diseases and who can point to the disciples' vision as an illustration or manifestation of the immortality of Christ, and, therefore, of all men, has enough in common with the beliefs of simple people to make it quite possible for him to perform the duties of a clergyman without any painful sense of unreality to himself, and with advantage to his flock.'[13]

However he made it clear that there were limits to liberalism. 'In speaking of theological liberalism', he says, 'let me, however, say at once that there are some kinds of theological liberalism which do unfit a man for the ministry of the Church of England.'[14] Later he indicates what these are: 'anyone who regarded (say) the Resurrection as a mere case of ordinary subjective delusion would, at present at least, find his position in the Church of England a somewhat difficult one.'[15] On the divinity of Christ he says, 'But the man who cannot accept the Divine Sonship of Christ in some real, distinctive, exceptional sense is (I should personally be disposed to think) too far out of sympathy with ordinary religious feeling to make his ministrations useful to the ordinary Church of England congregation, or to enable him to throw the expression of his own devotional feeling with any naturalness into the forms provided by the Church of England.'[16]

In 1898 Rashdall published his book, *Doctrine and Development*. In this fascinating book of sermons, in which one can see the influence upon him of Maurice, Robertson, Seeley and many others, one gets a glimpse of his uncompromising theism and his degree Christology which was to create such a disturbance in the aftermath of Girton 1921. One can see also in his sermon on 'The Abelardian Doctrine of the Atonement' the embryo of his later Bampton Lectures. The earliest of these sermons was preached before the University of Cambridge on 23 December 1889, and was on the 'Limitations of Knowledge in Christ', where he said much in common with Gore. *Doctrine and Development* really contains a great deal of the theology of English Modernism.

We must now get back to the Churchmen's Union in 1899. Rashdall preached the annual sermon that year at St Peter's, Bayswater on 6 October. This sermon, which was published in the *Church Gazette*, 14 October 1899, can be read today in that other volume of Rashdall's sermons, *Christus in Ecclesia*, which is on the Church and the sacraments. In the *Church Gazette* the sermon is headed 'Unity in Diversity'; in *Christus in Ecclesia* it is headed 'The Broad Church Party'. Rashdall here stands firmly in defence of Christian liberalism, but again he insists that there are limits. Let me quote the relevant passage:

> In modern language, I think we might say that we adhere to the three great essentials of the Christian religion – belief in a personal God, in a personal immortality, and (while not limiting the idea of revelation to the Old and New Testaments) in a unique and paramount revelation of God in the historic Christ. But we recognise that to this one foundation there has, in the course of ages, been added much building-upon. Of the vast superstructure of doctrinal and ritual and ethical tradition which has been built upon and around the essential Christianity which we find in the moral and religious consciousness of Jesus the Son of God, not all is of equal value. There is a great deal of hay and stubble that has simply got to be cleared away.[17]

This attitude of Rashdall on the limits of theological liberalism can also be seen in his essay on 'Clerical Liberalism' in the book *Anglican Liberalism* (1908), where Rashdall says:

> I would say that I do not myself wish to see the ministry of the Church of England made accessible to persons who do not believe in Theism and human immortality, and who do not recognise the unique and paramount character of the Christian revelation in a sense which makes it possible for them, without a

61

feeling of unreality, to use the ordinary language of the Church about the Divinity of our Lord. (p.106)

Here we must leave Rashdall and get back to the Churchmen's Union, which under the influence of the ex-High Churchman Cobb now set about rewriting the objects for which it stood. Before long these were set out as follows. You will see how more moderate they now are:

1. To defend and maintain the teaching of the Church of England as the Historic Church of the country, as being Apostolic and Reformed.

2. To uphold the Historic Comprehensiveness and Corporate Life of the Church of England and her Christian tolerance in all things non-essential.

3. To give all the support in their power to those who are honestly and loyally endeavouring to vindicate the truths of Christianity by the light of scholarship and research, while paying due regard to continuity, to work for such changes in the formularies and practices of the Church of England as from time to time are made necessary by the needs and knowledge of the day.

4. To work for the restoration to the laity of an effective voice in all Church matters.

5. To encourage friendly relations between the Church of England and all other Christian bodies.[18]

A little later the first of these aims was changed to this: 'To maintain the right and duty of the Church to restate her belief from time to time as required by the progressive revelation of the Holy Spirit'. There were very minor alterations in the others. Otherwise these aims of the Union held good until they were redrafted in 1918.

Cobb now did all he could to promote the extension of the Union as a society of moderate churchmen. But one finds in the *Church Gazette* plenty of dissatisfaction with his policy. People complained that the Union was supposed to be a society of Broad

Churchmen and asked what had happened to it. A rift developed between Cobb and William Routh, the Editor of the *Church Gazette*, who gave notice that his magazine did not accept the policy of the Churchmen's Union as it was now being presented. In due course, instead of working through the *Church Gazette*, Cobb found a forum in the *Church of England Pulpit and Ecclesiastical Review*. At the end of 1900 the *Church Gazette* went out of existence. The last issue, which noted the death of Dr Momerie, was dated 29 December 1900. William Routh remained in the Churchmen's Union until his death in 1912, by which time H. D. A. Major had become its leading figure.

The Second Annual Meeting of the Churchmen's Union, held in May 1900, was controversial because of people's doubts about Cobb and his moderate policy. It began with a communion service at St Edmund's, Lombard Street, taken by the incumbent, William Benham, who had been a friend of Archbishops Longley and Tait and who, with Randall Davidson, wrote the life of Tait. At the meeting which followed Cobb was highly criticized by some but Rosedale defended him, saying that though at first he had looked upon Cobb as a 'snake in the grass', he had now changed his mind. In the end the annual report was passed by 21 votes to 14. Then the meeting settled down to hear a paper on 'The Claims and Duties of the Church of England' from the Rev. Arthur Galton, who had once been a Roman Catholic priest. Three other notable Anglican Modernists had been Roman Catholic priests, viz. Alfred Fawkes (about whom Alec Vidler has written in his *A Variety of Catholic Modernists*, calling him a Liberal Protestant even in the days when he was supposed to be a Roman Catholic Modernist), W. E. Addis, who for a time was a Unitarian, and A. W. Hutton, about whom I will say more in a moment. It was to the memory of this trio that Major dedicated his book, *The Roman Church and the Modern Man* (1934).

In spite of the controversy over the position of Cobb and what he wanted the Union's programme to be, several well known persons were now members – like Sir John Lubbock (later Lord Avebury), to whom the nation owed August Bank Holiday, often originally called 'St Lubbock's Day', Dr R. H. Charles, the authority on apocalyptic, Sir Edward Russell, Dr E. A. Wallis Budge the Egyptologist and Archdeacon J. M. Wilson.

James M. Wilson I have already mentioned for his Hulsean Lectures of 1898. We are fortunate in having quite a good biography of him by his son Sir Arnold Wilson. He went from St John's College, Cambridge, to be for twenty years mathematics master at Rugby, where he greatly admired Frederick Temple. Ordained in 1879, he later became Headmaster at Clifton, then Vicar of Rochdale and Archdeacon of Manchester, and finally a Canon of Worcester. His Hulsean Lectures were a shock to some at the time. He contended that it was not God who has to be reconciled to man. 'How can we think', he asked, 'of the eternal, omnipresent God, of whom all forces, all life, all personality, are the incipient expression, as altered in his disposition towards creation by an incident in time?'[19] Wilson strove to revive the Greek idea of atonement, seeing the incarnation as the at-one-ment, as showing an identity of nature between God and man in the person of Christ. The Lectures were put out in a more popular form under the title, *How God saves us*. They were a leading Modernist contribution to the doctrine of the atonement.

On 19 June 1900 Dr Cobb suddenly resigned the post of Organizing Secretary of the Churchmen's Union, possibly because of a breakdown. A little later Bishop Mandell Creighton of London appointed him the Vicar of St Ethelburga's. He remained in the Union, becoming more and more liberal as the years went on. His last work, published in 1934, was entitled *The Humanist's Hornbook*. His place as Secretary was filled by William Manning, then Vicar of St Andrew's, Leytonstone, a living he had held since 1885. Manning remained Secretary up to the Great War, but he is rather a shadowy figure today, and Major wrote nothing about him. He seems to have been a popular Broad Church preacher and a volume of his sermons, *Some Elements of Religion*, was published in 1908. He was later Vicar of Chipping Barnet.

A much more interesting figure, who came into the movement at this time, was Arthur Wolloston Hutton, the ex-Roman Catholic priest. He had started life as an Anglican and studied at Exeter College, Oxford, gaining the intimate friendship of Liddon, Bright, and Bishop King. He became curate of St Barnabas', Oxford, and then Rector of Spridlington, Lincolnshire. In 1876, finding High Anglicanism no longer tenable, he was received into the Church of Rome, and became a member of

Cardinal Newman's Community at the Oratory, Edgbaston. After seven or eight years, finding the Roman system did not satisfy him intellectually, he left the Church completely. For fifteen years he was an agnostic. During this period he acted for a while as Librarian of the Gladstone Library at the National Liberal Club. He did not recover his religious beliefs until towards the end of the century. Then in 1898 he became curate of St Margaret's, Westminster. After other parochial positions, he was appointed Rector of St Mary-le-Bow in 1903. In the first decade of the century his vestry hall became the London meeting place of the Churchmen's Union. Hutton remained a staunch member of the Union till his death in 1912. Among his writings was a book on Cardinal Manning. His theological position can be seen in his book *Ecclesia Discens* (1904), which contains a paper he read to the Churchmen's Union in 1902 where he describes how he recovered his faith, thanks to the writings of Albrecht Ritschl, Seeley's *Ecce Homo* and Percy Gardner.

We must continue the early fortunes of the Churchmen's Union. In May 1901 the connection with the magazine *The Church of England Pulpit* came to an end, and the Union was left without any forum in a periodical. At the Annual Meeting that year it was announced that the Union had a membership of 281. Arthur Galton preached the sermon, but instead of an address there was a discussion of Harnack's *What is Christianity?* which had just come out.

The long connection of Percy Gardner with the Union began in 1902. Gardner, a layman, was a classicist, whose life story can be read in his rather unexciting *Autobiographica*. He went to the City of London School, when John Seeley was in charge of the Sixth. At Cambridge he came under the influence of Maurice. 'I only went occasionally', he says, 'to the discourses of Professor Maurice which were ethically very stimulating but not of great value from the philosophic point of view.'[20] He later held the Disney Professorship of Archaeology at Cambridge and then in 1885 succeeded Sir William Ramsay as Professor of Classical Archaeology at Oxford and remained there the rest of his life. He read most of the works of Auguste Comte. William James and the French Roman Catholic Modernists influenced him and he became, philosophically, very much a pragmatist. His great work of Modernist Theology was his *Exploratio Evangelica* published in 1899. The aim of this book which I imagine hardly anyone has read today is neatly expressed in the summary at the end:

> I have tried to clear away the accumulation of the dust of ages, which lies about the Foundation of the Christian Creed, and to see wherein the foundation really consists, and what kind of superstructure it is capable of supporting. To build any such superstructure is not in my plan. I conceive that many structures of Christian faith, differing by race, by historic tendency, by personal prepossession, might all justify themselves to a criticism such as I have endeavoured to develop. It is not a particular set of beliefs that I have advocated, but a particular way of founding and regarding belief. I have tried to show that religious beliefs, like all the active principles of our lives, can only be justified when they are based on realities and experience, and can only lead to success and happiness when they are suited to their environment, psychological, intellectual and spiritual.

His *Exploratio* seemed to many at that time a totally reductionist Christianity. Major says, it 'led those who did not really know him to think of him as an unbeliever, though of a very unusual type. I remember a younger member of the University saying to me: "There is no one in Oxford who prays more and believes less than Percy Gardner".' Major adds that Gardner was a friend of von Hügel whose religious mysticism he shared. My reading of the *Exploratio* and his other works has given indications of the effect of the Broad Churchmen upon him, like *Ecce Homo*, Edwin Abbott, Robertson of Brighton and Charles Kingsley.

On 23 April Gardner addressed the Churchmen's Union on 'The Translation of Christian Doctrine' in St Martin's Vestry, Charing Cross Road, at that time a frequent place of meeting for them. Here he indicated the limited value of doctrinal definition.

> True doctrine seems to be definable as that which accords with the essential facts of man's spiritual surroundings in relation to nature. Thus it seems that no statement of doctrine can be true save generally, or in spirit, for no formula, no words can

permanently embody it. If such doctrine is expressed reasonably and in full accordance with the intellectual conditions of a particular age, it is true for that age, even in its words; but the truth is after all not to be taken too literally. If even a truly formulated true doctrine be taken as if it were an axiom in Euclid or a formula in logic it cannot endure the test. At best man can but adumbrate in words any divine idea; he cannot enclose it in words.[21]

At the Annual Meeting of 1902 another newcomer appeared in William Douglas Morrison, a Scot educated at Glenalmond, who was ordained to a curacy at Wakefield by Bishop Bickersteth and then entered the prison chaplaincy service at Wakefield. Later he was chaplain at Wandsworth until 1898. Major says of his prison work: 'In this sphere he did much valuable work which led to reforms in our prison service, especially in the treatment of young criminals and earned for him public recognition by Lord Haldane. Morrison's researches and recommendations were published in two books, *Crime and its Causes* (1890) and *Juvenile Offenders* (1896). The findings of these books were not based solely on Morrison's personal experience. He was a profound student of the literature of criminology.'[22] When he came out of the prison service he lived at New Romney, Kent, and engaged in literary work, writing in 1889 *The Jews under the Romans*, in the series 'The Story of the Nations'. He also acted as editor of the volumes of the Theological Translation Library, his fellow editors being James Moffatt, Allan Menzies and T. K. Cheyne (another supporter of the Churchmen's Union). He was thus fairly well known in London as one interested in modern, especially German, theology, as well as crime. Morrison remained connected with the Union until his death in 1943, at the age of 91, when he was still Rector of St Marylebone, the Crown living to which he was appointed in 1908, though hardly with any pleasure to the Bishop of London, Winnington-Ingram, who opposed Modernists, allegedly refusing to ordain any student of Ripon Hall. Morrison was preacher to the Union at their annual meeting in 1902 and he also succeeded Henslow as President of the Union. Henslow now became one of the Vice-Presidents. At that annual meeting Hensley Henson was also present and spoke on 'Home Reunion'. Though he never actually joined the Union, and later opposed it, he had some contact with it and flirted with it in these first years.

Dean Fremantle, who as yet had had little personal contact with the Union, now brought it into notoriety in October 1902 and convinced the world it was not a society of Moderates! In that month he delivered, in St Martin's Vestry Hall, a lecture on 'Natural Christianity'. This was never published but still exists in manuscript. An expanded version of it came out in a book of the same title in 1911. Fremantle contended that God is at work in all nature and in all men. He presented Christ as the morally supreme man, sharing the sort of degree Christology that Rashdall offered in *Doctrine and Development*. What caused the scandal was his statement on the virgin birth. Speaking of the unimportance of this dogma, he contended that it was a natural and not a miraculous event, explainable by parthenogenesis. 'But supposing', he said,

> the accounts to be genuine, that is integral parts of the Gospels, is there not enough to suggest that the account might have arisen from a misunderstanding in the fact that the word of Isaiah which is said to have been fulfilled refers to a natural birth?
>
> Supposing however, we think ourselves bound to believe that the birth took place without the intervention of the male element, this is a process well known to biologists, under the name of Parthenogenesis, so well known and occurring so high in the scale of biology that Darwin said he could not account for the need of the male except as giving strength and energy to the ovum or germ in the female, which is already complete in itself. Suppose that the accounts are literally true, the meaning could be that a Hebrew woman of exceptional purity of character having the hopes which women of her race widely and naturally entertained, longing with a pure and divinely inspired hope that she might be the mother of the Messiah, was stirred amd quickened by that hope: in other words that this spiritual longing and Divine influence gave the vivifying energy which would otherwise have been given by a husband. I think this would give a satisfactory explanation of the words 'Conceived by the Holy Ghost' nor do I know of any other which is possible.[23]

I may interject here that this years later was the viewpoint of Bishop Barnes. Fremantle then dealt with miracles in general, contending that they need not necessarily be thought of as *contra naturam*. He went on to say that he had never been able to think of the resurrection of Christ as a violation of natural law.

This lecture by Fremantle started a first-class row. Though many in his audience were prepared to go all the way with him, there was some opposition even within the ranks of the Churchmen's Union. The *Daily Express* said it was impossible for the Dean of Ripon to speak in these terms and call himself a Christian. On the whole there was far more opposition than support in the country in general. The Dean's Minor Canons called upon him to undo the mischief he was doing. His Evangelical neighbour at Holy Trinity, Ripon, labelled him another Paul of Samosata. He was also involved in correspondence with Bishop Boyd Carpenter over what he had said. However, a number of members of the Churchmen's Union defended him, like Lord Avebury, Theodore Brocklehurst, by then Vicar of Giggleswick, and William Manning, the Organizing Secretary. Canon T. L. Papillon, however, was unhappy at the Dean's views and the Principal of King's College London, Archibald Robertson, the authority on Athanasius, who surprisingly up till now had been a member of the Union, handed in his resignation from it. When the Churchmen's Union met on 29 November to hear Dr John Hunter (father of Leslie Hunter, a recent Bishop of Sheffield) of the King's Weigh House Congregational Church, there was a move to pass a motion of sympathy with Fremantle but, when Rosedale doubted whether this would be agreeable to the Dean, it was dropped. In 1903 there was a move in the York Convocation to pass a motion that the Church still believed in the Lord's virgin birth and his resurrection. The proposer of this motion did not refer to Fremantle but to the article on the nativity (by H. Usener) in the notorious *Encyclopedia Biblica* edited by T. K. Cheyne, C. E. Beeby's *Creed and Life* and Dr Cobb's book *Theology Old and New* in the Church's Outlook Series. However, Fremantle was, not unnaturally, very interested in the discussion and rose to defend the view that the incarnation did not necessarily involve a virgin birth. In doing so he quoted from a recent work by Dean Armitage Robinson of Westminster (the successor of Bradley), *Some Thoughts on the*

Incarnation, at the beginning of which he addressed an open letter to Archbishop Davidson, in which he said, 'If the Bishops were asked to declare that the Incarnation is a cardinal doctrine of the faith, such a statement would be superfluous, indeed, but it would be true. But to say that the historical fact of the Virgin-birth is a cardinal doctrine is to use language which no Synod of Bishops, so far as I am aware, has ever ventured to use. It is to confuse the Incarnation with the special mode of the Incarnation in a way for which Christian theology offers no precedent.' This was a valuable sentence from an unquestionably orthodox theologian and Modernists underlined it in their copies. While Dean Fremantle defended the liberals, one of the Ripon Canons, Malcolm MacColl, a moderate High Churchman, spoke against the Dean and attacked Rashdall's article in the *International Journal of Ethics*. He was also scathing about the volume *Contentio Veritatis* which had just been published. This was a volume of essays by Six Oxford Tutors, of which the most significant ones were Rashdall's on 'The Ultimate Basis of Theism', and W. R. Inge's two on 'The Person of Christ' and 'The Sacraments'.

Eventually the Fremantle episode went out of the news, and the member of the Churchmen's Union who now came under attack was Charles Evans Beeby, Vicar of Yardley Wood, Birmingham, who then had Charles Gore as his diocesan Bishop. In October 1903 an article was written by Beeby in the *Hibbert Journal* on the 'Doctrinal Significance of a Miraculous Birth', because of which he was subjected to such an attack by Gore that he was compelled to resign. The Council of the Churchmen's Union supported Beeby, signing a document which demanded that accused clergymen should be granted the protection of a formal judicial inquiry.[24] At the Annual Meeting of 1904 further sympathy was expressed with Beeby. But after this we hear little more about him. He is on a 1908 list of members of the Union, when his address is given as Yardley Wood. Was he still living in his old parish in retirement?

In 1903 Mrs Humphrey Ward, granddaughter of Thomas Arnold, joined the Union. On 9 December she was booked to speak to its members on 'Church Membership', but was unable in the event to do so. Two new members were the Rev. John Richard Wilkinson, Rector of Winford, Somerset, from 1903 until his death in 1940, and remembered for his translations of Harnack in the Crown Theological Library, and Mr (later Sir) Richard Stapley.[25] At the 1903 Annual Meeting Lord Avebury gave the address and the Secretary reported a further growth in membership.[26] Hastings Rashdall had the privilege once again of preaching the annual sermon (on this occasion at St Stephen's, Walbrook) which was published in one of the Union's Occasional Papers. The subject was, 'In what sense was Christ the Son of God?' It is a succinct summary of the Rashdall Christology from which I will extract a characteristic paragraph:

> Now what is the natural inference that we should draw from the facts that our Lord talked of Himself as the Son of God in some distinctive sense, and yet that he called other men sons of God too? Does not the question almost carry its own answer with it? Does it not show that He felt Himself to be preeminently all that he meant by the phrase 'Son of God', when He told His disciples that they should think of themselves as sons of God? To all men some measure of the Divine Nature was communicated; He felt that to Him it was communicated in an exceptional degree. Human nature in general is a revelation of God. He felt that to Him in an exceptional way was committed the task of revealing God to his fellow men, of revealing to others their true sonship. He felt in Himself, a sense of intimate communion with God, felt that God was His Father, felt that He knew His nature and understood His love for Himself and for all mankind, felt that other men were sons of God, and He longed to make them worthy of their sonship. He felt, He *saw*, if we may so say, the ideal of Sonship, of filial love to God and fraternal love to other men, as the true ideal of human nature. All that He felt Himself with such depth and anxiety and intensity He believed that He was called upon to make others feel. God, he felt, was revealing himself not merely to Him but through Him and in Him to other men.[27]

At the Annual Meeting of 1904 Hensley Henson spoke on 'Sincerity and Subscription', a lecture which was subsequently published as a hard-backed booklet. That year found R. B. Tollinton, son-in-law of Bishop Boyd Carpenter, an authority on Clement of Alexandria, a Balliol man and disciple of Jowett,

71

joining the Union. Professor T. K. Cheyne lectured to the members on 14 June 1904, and this lecture was later expanded into his book *Bible Problems*. Years later Cheyne became more and more unorthodox and ended up a member of the Bahai faith.

Perhaps the most notable newcomer in 1904 was Hubert Handley, who remained an adherent of the Modernist Movement until his death in 1943. Handley was at Lincoln College, Oxford, under Mark Pattison, and was ordained as curate to Prebendary Harry Jones of St Philip's, Regent Street. In 1894 Gladstone appointed him to the living of St Thomas, Camden Town, where he stayed for the rest of his life. He was a member of the Quiet XII, a company of twelve men bound together in prayer for the Modern Movement in the Church of England. This brotherhood is mentioned in the life of Rashdall who was also a member.[28] In 1901 Handley wrote a book with the intriguing title, *The Fatal Opulence of Bishops*. That subject came up again in his work *Theological Room* (1914) which, however, is mainly a collection of his papers on liberal theology. He also edited the volume *Anglican Liberalism* (1908) from which we have already quoted. Handley was also very much involved in the *Declaration on Biblical Criticism* (1906) which was signed by 1725 clergymen scattered over the world. Many members of the Churchmen's Union signed this declaration; but there are some surprising absences, e.g. Dean Fremantle and Dr W. D. Morrison. I notice too the absence of W. R. Inge's signature.

Inge first made his appearance on the platform of the Churchmen's Union at the Annual Meeting of 1905 when he preached the sermon. He was then Vicar of All Saints', Ennismore Gardens, where he stayed two years before becoming Lady Margaret's Professor of Divinity at Cambridge. From 1911 to his retirement in 1934 he was Dean of St Paul's and popularly labelled 'the Gloomy Dean'. He did not die till February 1954 and I remember his memorial service in King's College Chapel. As Dean of St Paul's he did a great deal of popular journalism, but in the realm of theology he will be especially remembered for his Bampton Lectures for 1899 on *Christian Mysticism*, which remain a remarkably thorough introduction to the subject, and his Gifford Lectures on *The Philosophy of Plotinus* (1918). His Bampton Lectures were also a contribution to English Modernism, inasmuch as they were an attempt to go to another seat of authority, in contrast to those who believed in an infallible Bible or an infallible Church. Let me quote from his last lecture:

> It is not claimed that Mysticism, even in its widest sense, is, or can ever be, the whole of Christianity. Every religion must have an institutional as well as a mystical element. Just as, if the feeling of immediate communion with God has faded, we shall have a dead Church worshipping 'a dead Christ', as Fox the Quaker said of the Anglican Church in his day; so, if the seer and prophet expel the priest, there will be no discipline and no cohesion. Still, at the present time, the greatest need seems to be that we should return to the fundamentals of spiritual religion. We cannot shut our eyes to the fact that both the old seats of authority, the infallible Church and the infallible book, are fiercely assailed, and that our faith needs reinforcements. These can only come from the depths of the religious consciousness itself, and if summoned from thence, they will not be found wanting. The 'impregnable rock' is neither an institution nor a book, but a life or experience.[29]

The modernists have often been accused of a lack of a devotional spirit. There is the famous *dictum* of Tait at the time of the *Essays and Reviews* controversy, 'The great evil is that the liberals are deficient in religion . . .'[30] Gordon Milburn in his book *A Study of Anglicanism* remarked, 'There is a lack, or apparent lack, of reverence and devotion among Liberals which seems to be the cause of that flippant irreligious tone so common among them.'[31] That charge, however, is hardly one that could be levelled against Inge. Prayer for him was absolutely essential. In his *Truth and Falsehood in Religion* he wrote, 'Let no one think that he is religious, or knows what religion means, if he does not pray habitually and spontaneously.'[32]

Inge could be decidedly bitter against the Roman Catholic Modernists, and especially Loisy, whom he violently attacked in a sermon preached in St Mary's, Oxford, and published in his *Faith and Knowledge*. He condemned Loisy's historical negativism. Yet in his last years he got quite close to Loisy and Tyrrell. Thus on 18 March 1951 he wrote in his diary:

George Tyrrell once said that some day nothing might be left of Christianity except the Pauline-mysticism and the law of love – I have been moving in that direction, willing to blot from the page 'unborn to-morrow and dead yesterday.' What happened 2,000 years ago cannot matter to us now, and there has been no relevation of the future.[33]

Adam Fox in his *Dean Inge* does not say when Inge joined the Churchmen's Union. He was not yet a member when in 1916 he contributed to Foakes-Jackson's symposium *The Faith and the War*, nor is he on a 1918 list of members, but he seems to have come into the Union in 1920. He was President from 1924 to 1934.

Returning to the Annual Meeting of 1904, when Inge, though not a member, made his appearance on the Churchmen's Union platform, one is surprised to find, on that occasion, no reference at all to the new Broad Church periodical, the *Liberal Churchman*. This had come out for the first time in November 1904. Its Editor was Dr Morrison, the President of the Churchmen's Union, and it was published quarterly by Williams and Norgate, who were bringing out so much liberal theology at this time, and especially translations of Continental theologians. In his introductory article on 'The Task of Liberal Theology', Morrison wrote:

Modern Theology must emancipate the facts of the Christian faith from the mists of theory which have gathered around it in the course of centuries; it must proclaim that men are perfectly free to form what theories they please. It must teach the Church to renounce the inculcation of theories and to announce the great fundamental truth that the Christian religion is not a theory but a profound, transforming, ethical and spiritual experience, drawing its vitality from a conviction which transcends experience – a conviction that the spirit of Christ is the incarnate spirit of goodness, that Goodness is the supreme Reality and union with it the supreme life.[34]

The *Liberal Churchman* continued until January 1908. During its short lifetime – short, but longer than any of the two previous liberal periodicals – each issue had a tripartite division into (a) Notes (b) Articles and (c) Reviews. Among those who wrote in it were Rashdall, Henson, William Routh, Dean Fremantle, George

Henslow, and John Gamble, Vicar of Leigh Woods, Clifton, another new adherent to the movement.

The Annual Meetings of the Union in 1906 and 1907 need not detain us. In 1908 there was a change of President. Dr Morrison retired from the office and was succeeded by Sir Thomas Dyke Acland, a Devonian landowner and liberal churchman, whose family seat, Killerton, is now owned by the National Trust, and whose descendant, Sir Richard Acland, has remained in the liberal theological tradition, as one can see from his book *We Teach them Wrong*.[35] The annual meeting of 1908 was the first Annual Meeting that Major went to. It was the year of the Pan-Anglican Congress and the Fifth Lambeth Conference when many overseas bishops were in England and the preacher to the Union was the Rt Rev. Charles D. Williams, Bishop of Michigan. By 1908 the Union could boast 494 members. As I look through the list I note the names of the two Oxford professors (Percy Gardner and T. K. Cheyne) but none from Cambridge, Professor Ashley of Birmingham, and Professor Allan Menzies of St Andrews (the Presbyterian New Testament scholar). Two notable canons were Samuel Augustus Barnett of Westminster and M. G. Glazebrook of Ely.

As I have already indicated, 1908 was the year of the Fifth Lambeth Conference. That conference had a committee working on 'The Faith and Modern Thought', chaired by Bishop E. S. Talbot, who wrote in *Lux Mundi*. One notes the effect of English Modernism upon the episcopal utterances, for, in a footnote to their report, they say:

> In using the word miracles in a report dealing with scientific thought we must guard ourselves against the often repeated misapprehension that the Church by that word means breaches or suspensions of the law of Nature. To this end, instead of using any modern words, we prefer to quote the noble words of St. Augustine, so often quoted by theologians (e.g. Trench, on 'The Miracles' p.15, ed. 1966): 'Contra naturam non incongrue dicimus aliquid Deum facere, quod facit contra id quod novimus in natura . . .

One can see from this and other passages in the report that liberal theology was having its effect on the Church in general.

NOTES

1   See H. R. Haweis, *The Broad Church*, p.13: 'Let us confess plainly that the Broad Churchism of such books as *The Kernel and the Husk* seems to us completely sterile and impossible.'

2   See *Dr. Momerie. His Life and Work.* Written and edited by his Wife (1905), p.193

3   op. cit., p.3.

4   For Brooke Lambert, see *Sermons and Lectures*, ed. R. Bayne. With a Memoir by J. E. de Montmorency (1902).

5   For Harry Jones, see his *Fifty Years or Dead Leaves and Living Seeds*.

6   See *Canon Barnett, his Life, Work and Friends* by his wife. 2 vols. (1918).

7   See *Church Gazette* (5 Nov., 1898), pp.59f.

8   His correspondence with Darwin has been published.

9   See *Church Gazette*, 10 September 1898.

10   See Adam Fox, *Dean Inge*, p.58.

11   P. E. Matheson, *The Life of Hastings Rashdall*, pp.79 and 216.

12   *International Journal of Ethics* (April 1896), p.289.

13   *International Journal of Ethics* (January 1897), p.156.

14   op. cit., p.138.

15   op. cit., p.154.

16   op. cit., p.155.

17   *Church Gazette* (14 Oct. 1899), p.715. *Christus in Ecclesia*, p.335.

18   P. H. Bagenal, *The Modern Movement in the Church of England*, pp.5f.

19   *The Gospel of the Atonement*, p.75

20   *Autobiographica*, p.15.

21   P. Gardner, *The Translation of Christian Doctrine*. A Paper read before members of the Churchmen's Union at St. Martin's Vestry Hall, Charing Cross on Wednesday, April 23rd 1902, p.26.

22   *Modern Churchman* (Dec. 1956), pp.196f. Only recently I received a letter from a prison chaplain asking about his work in prisons.

23   I take this from the original Manuscript.

24   See *Hibbert Journal*, vol. ii, pp.591ff.

25   It is curious that there is no obituary of Richard Stapley in the *Modern*

Churchman. He died in 1920. For J. R. Wilkinson see *Modern Churchman,* vol. xxx, pp.75–8 (S. E. Seamer).

26   For his address see *Occasional Paper* No. VI, pp.7–13.

27   The Churchmen's Union. *Occasional Paper* No. VI, p.3.

28   P. E. Matheson, *The Life of Hastings Rashdall* p.105.

29   op. cit., pp.329f.

30   See R. T. Davidson and W. Benham, *Life of A. C. Tait,* vol. i, p.325.

31   See H. Handley, *Theological Room,* p.69.

32   op. cit., p.11.

33   op. cit., p.264.

34   This passage was heavily lined in Major's copy.

35   For Sir Thomas Dyke Acland, see *Modern Churchman,* vol. ix, pp.1f. (Major).

4

English Modernism after Major

Our subject in this chapter is Henry D. A. Major but I should like first to say something about the history of Ripon Hall before he became associated with it, for Ripon Hall, Major and Modernism are inextricably linked together.

Ripon Hall dates its beginnings in 1898. You will remember that this was an added reason for my dating the rise of Modernism then. To be quite accurate, it can be taken back to 1897, when the third Bishop of Ripon, William Boyd Carpenter, founded a small hostel in Ripon and put it under the guidance of William Frederick Wright, a St John's College Cambridge man, until then curate of Holy Trinity church, Ripon, who had been sent to him from Cambridge by Herbert Ryle, the President of Queen's, who was his Examining Chaplain. Boyd Carpenter, most eloquent of Victorian bishops, had earlier been associated with the Evangelicalism of Islington rather than with the Broad Church party. But after being made Bishop of Ripon in 1885 he became more liberal in outlook. Once W. H. Fremantle had succeeded his uncle W. R. Fremantle as Dean of Ripon, the town became very much a Broad Church centre, because there were also two liberal-minded canons, Arthur Thornhill Waugh and William Danks.[1] The Ripon Hostel was one of many such small colleges arising at that time all over the country. Leeds, with its already established Leeds Clergy School, was not a little annoyed at their Bishop's planting of another training establishment in the diocese. But Boyd Carpenter was anxious to pursue different methods from that institution which he regarded as over-ecclesiastical, as also did Donald Hankey, the famous 'Student in arms'.[2] His objectives can be seen neatly summarized in his article, 'The Education of a Minister of God', which he contributed to the *Hibbert Journal* in 1905, where he makes in effect eight points.

1.   The approach to theology must be scientific. The correct reason for believing in certain doctrines must be ascertained and there must be no resting content with any false or no longer valid position.

2.   All dogmas of theology must be judged by the highest ethical ideals. The only avenue to spiritual conviction is an ethical one. One might reach intellectual assent, theological harmony, neat and compact systems of belief, through other channels, but, without the sanction of the moral nature, there is no faith.

3.   There must be a prophetic conception of the ministry. 'Whatever official dignity, whatever splendour of historic association, whatever rights of ruling, may belong to the minister of any Church, he is a merely negative quantity unless he stands in the prophetic relation to his people.'

4.   There must be a willingness to recognize that all new knowledge, of whatever kind, has relevance for theology.

5.   There must be some study of comparative religion.

6.   There must be some study of the psychology of religion. Here Boyd Carpenter himself had led the way in the sphere of the psychology of religion in his Hulsean Lectures for 1878, *The Witness of the Heart to God.*

7.   Historical study must hold a conspicuous place and be widely interpreted.

8.   There must be a recognition that the supreme and most important doctrine is that of the love of God.[3]

The initial success of this precarious venture was due wholly to the Bishop and Fred Wright, who were in entire agreement over principles and methods. As numbers grew an increased staff was necessary, and in 1900 Dr Henry Gee, who had been a pupil of Percival at Clifton and was a noted Reformation scholar, was imported from the London College of Divinity to become first Principal. What had previously been known as Bishop's Hostel, Ripon, became Bishop's College, Ripon, and Wright, a popular figure in Ripon, remembered for his reluctant motor-cycle – he was the first person in Ripon to possess one – and his climbing of the walls of the college house in preparation for the Alps, modestly accepted the post of Vice-Principal.

In the meantime a not dissimilar institution had been started at Birmingham, then in the diocese of Worcester, whose Bishop was J. J. S. Perowne, a past Hulsean Professor and Hulsean Lecturer, editor of the works of Connop Thirlwall. This likewise began in a diocese which already had a theological college, for Queen's College, Birmingham, had been in existence for many years. The new college arose in a time of ritualist controversy which occasioned much correspondence in the press. Hastings Rashdall, one of those who wrote on the subject in *The Times*, said, 'The real evil is the prevalence of a certain theological temper among the clergy, which is getting more and more out of harmony with that of the laity and particularly of the more thoughtful and educated laity.'[4] A plea was now made for another theological college like Ridley Hall and Wycliffe Hall, which would be anti-sacerdotal. The leaders in this movement were T. B. Jex-Blake, Dean of Wells, an Arnoldian Evangelical, who had been at Rugby under Tait and was later himself Headmaster there, and whose daughter was one of the Mistresses of Girton, F. J. Chavasse, Principal of Wycliffe, and three notable Broad Churchmen, W. W. Jackson, Rector of Exeter College, Oxford, Hastings Rashdall and Michael George Glazebrook. Glazebrook, whom I briefly mentioned in the last chapter, became a distinguished Anglican Modernist. He was a disciple of Jowett at Balliol, who then served under Montague Butler at Harrow, before in 1888 becoming Head of Manchester Grammar School. In 1891, the year after his ordination, he followed in the steps of Percival and James M. Wilson as Headmaster of Clifton, where he remained until his resignation in 1905. In that year he was appointed a Canon of Ely. He will come into our story later in the time of the Great War as the author of *The Faith of a Modern Churchman* (1918). This group, with others, formed themselves into the Midland Clergy Corporation. In October 1899 the Midland Clergy College was opened by Bishop Perowne in a large house in Edgbaston, the first Principal being John H. B. Masterman, a St John's College, Cambridge man, brother of the future author of *The Condition of England* (1909) and *The Life of F. D.*

Maurice, who came from a living in Devonport. The college was pledged to objects decidedly Protestant, rather than Liberal:

1. A special devotion to the study of Holy Scripture.
2. A loyal adherence to the Book of Common Prayer, without authorized variations, doctrinal or ceremonial.
3. A large measure of instruction in practical work.

Obviously no ritualist would have been at home there! Yet Masterman was soon suspected of ritualist leanings. J. Armitage Robinson was invited to the college to take a retreat for the Birmingham clergy when the eastward position was taken and coloured stoles worn and a mixed chalice used at the communion. There was a commotion. We soon find Masterman had resigned as Principal of the Midland Clergy College, and become Principal of the already existing establishment, Queen's College, Birmingham! He combined this with the Professorship of History in the University of Birmingham. He was Hulsean Lecturer at Cambridge in 1907–8, on the subject 'Rights and Responsibilities of National Churches'. Later he became Bishop of Plymouth.

Masterman was replaced at the Midland Clergy College by the Rev. John Battersby Harford, then Vice-Principal of Ridley Hall, who had just changed his name round from Harford-Battersby. He was the son of T. D. Harford-Battersby, founder of the Keswick Convention. He had assimilated quite a lot of modern biblical criticism and was an Old Testament scholar. Like Fred Wright he was an Alpine climber who had conquered the Matterhorn. He moved to Birmingham in January 1901 and shortly afterwards changed the name of the Midland Clergy College to Lightfoot Hall, being devoted to the Cambridge Triumvirate. However, numbers remained small – about half a dozen. In January 1902 a large meeting was held at Lambeth Palace under the chairmanship of Frederick Temple, Archbishop of Canterbury, to try and arouse interest in the college. The occasion was chiefly noteworthy for the forward-looking conception which the new Principal held out for the college.

He said that 'Lightfoot Hall had been established to provide Oxford and Cambridge graduates with such a training as had been indicated by the previous speakers. The name was a token of the tone and temper of the instruction given within its walls. The qualities of the three great scholars – Lightfoot, Westcott and Hort – under whom it had been his privilege to study at Cambridge as an undergraduate, were the qualities which they aimed at developing at Lightfoot Hall. There was (1) *Love of Truth*, not of a certain set of views, received by tradition and labelled 'The Truth', but of reality, the truth of things as it appeared in the sight of God, as far as that truth can be ascertained by truthful methods. And that involved (2) *Patient Scholarship*, that thinks no pains too great to ascertain the exact meaning of every word and phrase in the Bible and in the early Christian writings. And, further, (3) *The Use of Historical Methods*, seeking to read the Bible and early Christian writers, not in the light of succeeding centuries – whether the fourth or the sixteenth – but in the light of their own day; asking, What did St. Paul say to the men of his own day, and what would they have understood him to mean? not 'What can he be made to say in support of my own views?' And (4) *The Fearless Welcoming of Light from every Quarter*. The man who knows God will not fear Light. Seeing God in all, he welcomes every addition to our knowledge of the world around and the world within, assured that it can only throw welcome light upon God and His truth. Dr. Hort has taught us in his lectures *The Way, the Truth and the Life* [sic] to see that science, psychology, sociology, have each their testimony to bear to the truth of God. One more quality was (5) *The Patient Zeal to apply the Truths thus ascertained to the Pressing Problems of Individual and Social Life*. In this they sought the guidance of the late Bishop Westcott, whose books were upon their library shelves.

The germ of all these things could be implanted and fostered at the college. The maturing of them must come in after-life. The aim now was rather to implant principles and methods than to cram with ready-made results – to teach men to observe facts and so put them in a position to test theories and views on either side by the extent to which they face and explain the facts.'

No less important than the intellectual training was the cultivation of the spiritual life.[5] This was a remarkable speech by a liberal

Evangelical who never became a Modernist. Battersby-Harford's ideal, which, as you can see, had much in common with Boyd Carpenter's, eventually became the ideal of Ripon Hall, though it was forgotten that the ideal was his and later it was attributed to Boyd Carpenter or Rashdall or Major.

Lightfoot Hall was uneconomic, being too small. It did not flourish. Hence a move to unite the Birmingham venture and the Ripon one. This became possible when Dr Gee was promoted to the Mastership of University College, Durham. It was agreed by the two governing bodies that the few Birmingham students should move to Ripon and that their Principal should become the Principal of the combined college, henceforth known as Ripon Clergy College. It meant that the interest of Rashdall, Ryle, Glazebrook and Jackson was transferred to the Ripon foundation, which up to then had been governed mostly by local Ripon clergy. Professor Gwatkin also became a Governor at this time. Fred Wright was unfortunately killed in a climbing accident in the Alps in 1904. Among the tutors of the college early in the century were the distinguished New Testament scholar S. C. E. Legg and the Old Testament scholar S. Lawrence Brown. Brown's replacement stayed but a few months and so, at the end of 1905, Battersby Harford was looking for another member of staff. This was where Major came in. To the 'Apostle of English Modernism' we now turn.

Henry Dewsbury Alves Major was born on 28 July 1871. His paternal grandmother, Jane Dewsbury, had also been born on 28 July; hence his second name. Alves was the name of his mother. He was born not in New Zealand (as most people think), nor in Australia (as Bishop Wand thought) but at Plymouth in Devon. But in 1878 his father, Henry Daniel Major, and his mother Mary Ursula, left the British Isles (Belfast to be exact) to emigrate to New Zealand. They never saw the homeland again. They sailed in the *Lady Jocelyn* to the settlement at Kati Kati, pioneered by Vesey Stewart, in the Bay of Plenty in the North Island.

In New Zealand his education was somewhat uneven. His father was his first teacher. Then he came under two important influences. The first was that of William Katterns, the local Vicar, famous for his ostrich farm, a traditional and orthodox High Churchman, trained at Queen's College, Birmingham. Through his encouragement Major managed to get to St John's College, Auckland, the theological college founded by Bishop Selwyn, where he came under a second influence, that of William Beatty the Principal, a disciple of the works of Coleridge and Maurice. Encouraged by Beatty, Major read both theologians. I have Major's copy of *Aids to Reflection* and *Confessions of an Inquiring Spirit* in the Bohn Library which he read at Auckland. Major read Maurice but confessed he found his style difficult and obscure. So from being a High Churchman Major developed Broad Church leanings. His father, however, was bitterly opposed to his ordination. Hence the young man had to earn money in the vacations working on farms. Bishop W. G. Cowie of Auckland, the successor of Selwyn, wanted to see Major ordained. Cowie was a great admirer of Archbishop Tait and once showed Major an engraving of him, with the words 'The greatest primate since St Augustine', a very extravagant praise which Major swallowed whole. Besides being a member of St John's, Major was also a student of University College, Auckland and took a pass degree. At ordination he became curate of St Mark's, Remuera, where Beatty, who had just left St John's, was now Vicar. While serving his curacy Major took another degree, a first class honours in geology. He was immensely popular at St Mark's, especially amongst the younger section of the community who admired his athletic prowess. There he met his wife, Mary Macmillan, the daughter of a wealthy leading citizen of Auckland, a remarkable lady to whom he later owed much.

In 1889 Major left the diocese of Auckland for that of Wellington, presided over by an ex-don from Cambridge, Frederic Wallis, who placed him in charge of the parish of Waitotara. There he contracted rheumatism of the ears (as he describes it) which brought about increasing deafness as the years went on, so that people who now remember Major recall a very clerical looking gentleman, in a good shepherd hat and with an ear-trumpet or else his battery hearing aid. His highly clerical appearance dated from the time when Rashdall said to him, 'It is as well at least to look orthodox even if you are not.' After a short while he came back to Auckland diocese, marrying and settling down as Vicar of Hamilton. The Majors lived in a terrible rat-infested vicarage by the river Waikato. The unsuitability of the vicarage and the failure of the parishioners, in spite of his popularity, to do anything about it was one of the factors which brought about his return to England in 1903. The other factor was a feeling of inadequacy in theological scholarship – in spite of the excellent results he had obtained in the examinations set by the New Zealand church. He wanted to go to England to become more expert in theology.

So instead of staying in New Zealand, where (providing he had advanced no further as a Broad Churchman) he would doubtless have become a bishop, he returned to England with his wife and baby daughter to study theology at Oxford. At that time Samuel R. Driver and William Sanday were the leaders of a very distinguished Theological Faculty. Being a Devonian by birth, Major chose to become a student of Exeter College, the college also of F. D. Maurice and now presided over by W. W. Jackson, the Rector. There, three years later, he obtained one of the two Firsts in the Theological Schools; the other went to D. C. Simpson, later the author of a once well-read book *Pentateuchal Criticism*, and Oriel Professor of the Interpretation of the Holy Scripture. Major's tutor was Willoughby Charles Allen, Sub-Rector of Exeter, a keen teacher of Hebrew but best known in the field of New Testament for his I.C.C. *Commentary on Matthew* (1907). He had also written in *Contentio Veritatis* (1902). Major also came under the influence of the Vicar of the University Church, C. A. Whittuck, a disciple of Ritschl and Lotze, whom he served for a while as curate. All these liberal influences left their mark. It was W. C. Allen who recommended Major to Battersby Harford as a member of staff for Ripon College. On 19 January 1906 Major went north to start at Ripon College. He remained connected with the college for the rest of his life.

Ripon brought him under three further influences. First, there was that of the eloquent Bishop Boyd Carpenter, who later appointed him Librarian of the Holden Library, a theological library then housed at Ripon Palace, now at the University of Leeds. Secondly, there was that of Dean Fremantle, who doubtless encouraged him to read Jowett. The third influence was that of Hastings Rashdall, who was a Governor of the College and with whom he had not had contact at Oxford.

I should like now to stop for a moment and see the other

ingredients besides the Broad Churchmen I outlined in my second chapter which were producing the theology of English Modernism in the period 1898 to 1908, for we can see their influence upon Major, the typical Modernist.

a.   First there was German and French Liberal Protestantism. Here the most important influence were the disciples of Albrecht Ritschl, Wilhelm Herrmann, particularly his *Communion of the Christian with God*, and Adolf von Harnack, especially his *What is Christianity?*, which we saw the Churchmen's Union discussing at one of their Annual Meetings. The most notable French Liberal Protestant who contributed to the theology of English Modernism was Auguste Sabatier, particularly his *The Religions of Authority and the Religion of the Spirit* and his *Outlines of a Philosophy of Religion*. Sabatier strove to keep people in the Christian fold by his 'symbolism'. Religion, he contended, as conceived by the minds of men was forced to express itself in images, in symbols, which varied with the mentality and outlook of a country or an age. They represented the variable factor of dogma.

A friend of Sabatier, who is not alluded to by Bernard Reardon in his *Liberal Protestantism*, must also be mentioned. This was Eugène Ménégoz, who developed the Lutheran conception of salvation by faith, but faith with him was essentially a state of heart, of feeling, of trust. Faith was the consecration of the whole individual to God, and such faith was independent of any special beliefs held by the individual or the age. Ménégoz has been largely forgotten but Major was influenced by all that he wrote and later published some of his essays in the *Modern Churchman*. Finally there was Jean Réville, whose *Liberal Christianity* was published here in 1903.

b.   Then there was the impact of Roman Catholic Modernism. Here the influence of Alfred Loisy was much less than that of George Tyrrell and the Baron von Hügel. Tyrrell influenced Major the most and he wrote an article on him in the series *Great Christians*, edited by R. S. Forman (1933). Norman Pittenger refers to von Hügel in most laudatory terms in his *The Christian Understanding of Human Nature*, where he says, 'Many of us feel that Baron von Hügel was the wisest, the most balanced and in general the most profound writer on religious subjects in this century.'[6]

There are numerous articles on all three of them in the files of the *Modern Churchman*. The two Modernists who especially became their exponents were Alfred Fawkes and A. L. Lilley.

c.   There was also the influence of American Liberalism. Here of special significance were the two Anglicans, Phillips Brooks, the American equivalent of Robertson of Brighton, and his disciple A. V. G. Allen, whose books *Freedom in the Church* (1907), *The Continuity of Christian Thought* (1884) and *Christian Institutions* (1898) were widely read by Liberals in this country. Two non-Anglicans whose works were influential here were Newman Smyth and William Adams Brown whose *The Essence of Christianity* (1902) impressed Major.

d.   A fourth background is that of Liberal Judaism, by which I mean really the writings of the Liberal Jew, Claude Montefiore, who was himself a disciple of Jowett. His Hibbert Lectures, *The Origin and Development of the Religion of the Ancient Hebrews*, which came out in 1892, made quite an impression; and even more so later his Commentary on the Synoptic Gospels.

In 1907, the year after he moved to Ripon, Major went with his wife and her parents on a voyage to Egypt and the Holy Land. He often makes allusions to that tour in his biblical writings. On the return journey he became ill and back at Ripon was so unwell that he nearly died. During the recovery from that illness he decided to throw in his lot with the Churchmen's Union. He had already associated himself with liberal theology by contributing to a book *Lux Hominum*, edited by F. W. Orde Ward, a book remarkable because of its contributions from three women, one of them Miss Lily Dougall, the Modernist. His first Annual Meeting was that of 29 June 1908 when the preacher was an American Bishop, the Rt Rev. Charles D. Williams, Bishop of Michigan, over here for the Lambeth Conference and the Pan-Anglican Congress.[7] Major himself addressed the Union for the first time in St Martin's Vestry Hall in May 1909 on the subject of 'Theological Colleges'.[8] He then set about spreading the message of Modernism in Yorkshire, with varying success. Major's entrance in the Union was providential, for it needed new life. There were some in 1908 who wanted him to take over the editorship of *The Liberal Churchman*, which Dr W. D. Morrison gave up when he was appointed Rector of Marylebone by the Crown. Major refused, probably because he was not at that time flushed with funds. So the *Liberal Churchman* came to an end. But by this time there were plenty of Modernistic clergymen and laymen ready to write for a journal, as one can see from the twelve contributions to the book *Anglican Liberalism* (1908).[9]

By 1911, however, the year he became a member of the Council of the Churchmen's Union, he felt able to take on the editorship of a liberal magazine. He consulted the President of the Churchmen's Union, Sir Thomas Dyke Acland, who thought that liberal theology was being sufficiently catered for by the *Hibbert Journal* founded in 1902. Percy Gardner, however, did not agree. He wrote to Major, 'Dyke Acland is wrong. What we need for our purpose is a Liberal Church of England Magazine. The Hibbert Journal is not that.' Rashdall evidently agreed with Gardner. So Major proceeded to start a new magazine. He called it *The Modern Churchman*. As yet the group were not yet using the name Modernist, because of its association with Roman Catholic Modernism, with which they were not totally in sympathy. In particular Loisy was too radical for most of them. The first number of the *Modern Churchman* came out in April 1911. It was printed at Parrs, the Printers and Stationers at Knaresborough, a firm which still existed when I was a curate there in the late 1950s. At first it had a red cover, but after a year this changed to yellow and remained yellow until the change to white in 1972. While yellow coated it was popularly known as the 'Yellow Peril'. On the front cover was a motto from Carlyle, 'The old never dies until this happens, Till all the soul of good that was in it have itself transformed into the practical New.' When the magazine changed to yellow that motto was removed and there were two new ones: the sentence allegedly from Erasmus, 'By identifying the new learning with heresy you make orthodoxy synonymous with ignorance', and one from Edmund Burke, 'A State without the means of some change is without the means of its conservation.' It was described as 'A Mid-Monthly Magazine to maintain the cause of truth, freedom, and progress in the National Church', and sold at 5/- per annum. The most fascinating feature of the new magazine was 'The Signs of the Times', pithy comments by Major on current ecclesiastical events and theological writings. These became famous and in the 'twenties people would rush to read what the Apostle of English Modernism had said. Major remained Editor until 1956 when the *Modern Churchman* was taken over by Arthur Adams and William Frend; the latter remains Editor today. *The Modern Churchman* was a success and it immediately gave liberal churchmen a literary organ once again. The new magazine has lasted a very long time. One of the first people to take out a subscription for it was Lord Halifax, the life-long opponent of English Modernism.

In its very first year the *Modern Churchman* gained some notoriety because of its editor's defence of J. M. Thompson, whose book *Miracles in the New Testament* came out in that year. Thompson, a nephew of Francis Paget, Bishop of Oxford, was Fellow and Dean of Magdalen College, Oxford. The tenor of his notorious book can be seen from this typical quotation:

> Though no miracles accompanied His entry into, or presence in, or departure from the world; though He did not think or speak otherwise than as a man; yet in Jesus Christ God is incarnate – discovered and worshipped, as God alone can be, by the insight of faith.[10]

Thompson's book brought its author a great deal of abuse and criticism. Major rushed in to defend it and upbraided the Bishop of Winchester (Talbot) for withdrawing Thompson's licence. The book also confirmed his own negative beliefs about the miraculous, which he had developed independently of Thompson. Thompson later ceased to function as a clergyman, though he never gave up his orders. He penned no more theology but turned to French history, particularly the French Revolution.[11] He also wrote a long poem on his ecclesiastical vicissitudes.[12]

The year 1912 saw another volume of Liberal Theology, which Major defended. This was the book *Foundations. A Statement of Christian Belief in terms of Modern Thought*. Its editor B. H. Streeter, soon to join the Modernist camp, wrote the particularly offending article on 'The Historic Christ'. The other contributors were mostly Liberal Catholics – William Temple, Neville Talbot, A. E. J. Rawlinson, R. G. Parsons, R. Brooke and Walter Moberly, though Parsons dabbled with Modernism. The essayists were

89

attacked by Ronald Knox, still an Anglican, in his poem 'Absolute and Abitofhell', and then, more substantially, in his book *Some Loose Stones*. Streeter gave offence for advocating a non-physical resurrection of Christ and for his seeming commendation of the subjective vision theory of the resurrection. Major defended the book and demanded that the church authorities should allow a latitude of belief on the resurrection and other questions.

The same year saw the publication by Fisher Unwin of Major's first book *The Gospel of Freedom*, a collection of articles, most of which had previously been published in the magazine *The Interpreter*, whose editor was Hewlett Johnson, later the famous 'Red Dean' at Canterbury.[13] The book shows how his theological liberalism had now developed. When in the 'twenties he brought out *English Modernism*, there was not really much advance on *The Gospel of Freedom*. *The Gospel of Freedom* had on its cover two quotations. One from Richard Baxter, 'The plague of the Church for above a thousand years has been the enlarging our Creed and making more fundamentals than God ever made.' The second was from Bishop Diggle of Carlisle, 'The more complex the Creed, the more it obscures the Christ.'

Perhaps, at this point, it would be appropriate to say something about Major's theology. First, he was completely sure of his belief in a loving God. As a Christian apologist he never spent much time trying to defend the existence of God. He was as sure of God as the author of Genesis and, in this respect, he was at one with his Oxford contemporary, William Temple. Major also never doubted the existence of Jesus Christ. Moreover, he followed William Sanday in believing that Mark's Gospel was the eye-witness testimony of St Peter and therefore represented a true account of Jesus' ministry. But, as Major believed in a non-miraculous incarnation, all the miracles had to be rationalized. That is precisely what he did in his book *Jesus by an Eyewitness*, his study of St Mark which was the basis of his Oxford doctorate of divinity in the 'twenties.

Major also had no hesitation in accepting the divinity of Christ. His theology of the incarnation is contained in his pamphlet 'A Modern View of the Incarnation', privately printed for the Anglican Fellowship in 1915 by Parrs of Knaresborough and which was really an expansion of an article of the same title published in the *Modern Churchman* for 1913. Behind that article lay what he had earlier written on the Logos doctrine for the Ellerton Prize Essay at Oxford. In this pamphlet he started by stating he wished to present the incarnation from a non-miraculous standpoint. That seemed to the traditionalist an absurdity, but biblical criticism had made us revise our estimate of the miraculous in the Bible; moreover, the overthrow of the miraculous did not mean the overthrow of the supernatural. A non-miraculous view of the universe did not mean expelling God from the universe. There was a growing number of philosophers, scientists, and historians, who, while not admitting the miraculous, believed in the incarnation. Here he referred to Edwin Abbott. He then turned to the *fact* of the incarnation and asked where in Jesus Christ are we to find the indwelling by God, who is the Ideal of all rational, moral and spiritual perfection? He saw the divine indwelling in four aspects:

1. The teaching of Jesus, remarkable for piercing spiritual insight, intense moral force, and unfailing grasp of principles.

2. The conduct of Jesus, who utterly obeyed the will of God.

3. The influence of Jesus, which was of the most magnetic kind.

4. The self-consciousness of Jesus. Major saw our Lord's two great themes as the Fatherhood of God and the Kingdom. The correlative of divine Fatherhood was divine Sonship. Jesus' conception of divine Sonship was twofold.
   a. He taught that all men were sons of God. Jesus shared in that divine Sonship.
   b. He was also conscious of possessing messianic Sonship.

Jesus regarded Himself [Major says] as the Anointed Son of God and Vice-gerent of the Kingdom of God, thus possessing a relationship to God shared by no one else. It ought to be observed perhaps that to the ideal of Messianic Kingship, He united that of the Suffering Servant of the second Isaiah. Now it is this Messianic consciousness, a fact not sufficiently taken into account by some liberal theologians, which is the dominant aspect of our Lord's personality. It was this which severs Him from all men and gives Him an unique relationship to God and to humanity.[14]

Major then goes on to say that Jesus never claimed to be God absolutely; and he suggests that he was not conscious of pre-existence. He then passes from the *fact* of the incarnation to the *mode*. Here he took up, as he had done in his Ellerton Prize Essay, the Logos Christology. He contends that Jesus can be regarded as divine because the Logos, the moral and rational principle of the universe, dwelt in him. Moreover, the title Logos when applied to Jesus implied a fundamental relationship between Jesus and every human being, since it was only by sharing in the divine Logos that a human being became really human.

Major then goes on to say something about creation which he sees as a process still not complete. The modern view sees creation as an immanent rather than transcendent process. 'In proportion as the creative process becomes more rational, moral and spiritual, so it becomes more and more "in God". In this sense Jesus is most "in God", while the hardened sinner is least in God.'[15] He also contended that this method of creation involved suffering for God. 'God the Creator suffers with and in His creatures. His creatures may suffer in and with God.'[16] This, incidentally, was a theological conception which G. A. Studdert-Kennedy, who was a Ripon College student, derived from Major's lectures.[17] Major then asks what bearing this modern understanding of the creation has on the incarnation. The creative process is clearly, in its rational, moral and spiritual stages, a process of incarnation, and the process of incarnation reached the completion of one great stage in the personality of Jesus. 'What seems to be clear', says Major, 'is that the Incarnation process is not the mechanical addition of a Divine Personality to a human personality, but the *development of human consciousness until within the sphere of human limitations it may be said to coincide with the Divine consciousness.*'[18] That sentence admirably sums up the Modernist evolutionary liberalism. As the process did not begin with Jesus, so it did not end with him. His personality is extended to the sacred society, consisting of those who recognize incarnate deity in Jesus, and, as the result of that, receive themselves the privilege of becoming sons of God.

In his final section, Major deals with possible objections. He might be criticized for making Jesus' difference from us one of degree rather than kind. But once the evolutionary process is accepted then a difference in kind may be seen as a difference in degree. To the argument that he seemed to be ignoring the atonement, he argues that the only theory of the atonement that is excluded is a propitiatory one.

This pamphlet Major sent to Boyd Carpenter, Sanday, Rashdall, Edwin Abbott and Charles Raven. All except Raven largely agreed with him, though Boyd Carpenter and Rashdall suggested he did not publish the pamphlet to the world. Raven felt too much of an Augustinian to agree completely with Major and thought that his view of the incarnation did not cater for man's need of redemption.

We must move on in our brief summary of Major's position and leave the pamphlet on the incarnation. On the resurrection he held that one could subscribe to Jesus' resurrection without believing in the empty tomb. On the issue of man's resurrection he could not contemplate Christianity without belief in the afterlife. But, to quote from *English Modernism*, 'Yet while the Modernist believes in a future life, he is opposed, in the interests of the higher morality, to stressing its rewards and penalties as the motive for right conduct in this life.'[19] Major was undoubtedly anti-dogmatic, but he believed that there were some dogmas which were an essential part of Christianity. Like Edwin Abbott he wanted to separate the kernel from the husk. Thus on the question of church order he was prepared to accept episcopacy as of the *bene esse* of the Church but not of its *esse*. He loved the Book of Common Prayer but was a strong advocate of its revision and engaged in some amateur liturgical revision himself, which was hardly noticed by the experts.[20] He loved the Bible, was a competent Hebraist, but his great delight was in the Greek text of the New Testament. Those who studied under him at Oxford will recall his New Testament Greek seminars. Some, like the late Ian Ramsey, were given to taking down notes of all that he said in exposition of the Greek New Testament.

The idea of a Modern Churchman's Creed was first suggested by Major in a short piece, 'The Creed as an ethical stimulus' in the *Modern Churchman* of September 1911. This included sentences from the Johannine writings and a sentence from Galatians. In July 1917 Major put out his suggested creed in a revised form in his article 'The Problem of the Creeds'. Here then is his Modern Churchmen's Creed, which at the time of the 1927–8 Prayer Book controversy was adopted in the Grey Book. It was set to music by Charles Lesley Bradley and appears in *Hymns of Praise*. It reads:

We believe that God is Spirit, and they that worship Him must worship Him in Spirit and in truth.

God is Light, and if we walk in the light, as He is in the light, we have fellowship one with another.

God is Love, and everyone that loveth is born of God and knoweth God.

Jesus is the Son of God, and God hath given to us Eternal Life, and this life is in His Son.

We are the children of God, and He hath given us of His Spirit.

If we confess our sins, He is faithful and just to forgive us our sins.

The world passeth away and the lust thereof, but he that doeth the will of God abideth for ever.

This creed is entirely in Johannine language and gets rid of any historical statements, in spite of Major's belief in the historicity of Mark's Gospel.

As he was working for the propagation of English Modernism, Major was at the same time Vice-Principal of Ripon Clergy College. It was, not unnaturally, his ambition to try and turn the college into a fully liberal and modernistic institution. Major worked quite well with Battersby Harford but regarded him as too timid a liberal. When the *Modern Churchman* started, there was an element of hostility towards him from some of the more conservative Governors and from the Evangelical Vicar of Holy Trinity, Ripon. This opposition at one point almost made Major accept an offer of the desirable living of Timaru in New Zealand. He suggested to Battersby Harford the addition of some liberal Governors, and gave him the names of Percy Gardner, Inge, Kirsopp Lake and Glazebrook, but Glazebrook was the only name taken up. In 1911 Boyd Carpenter resigned the see of Ripon and was appointed to a canonry of Westminster. There is an amusing story of Lloyd George going to the Abbey and hearing him preach and wanting to make him a bishop until he was told he had been a bishop in the northern province for close on 30 years. One of Carpenter's last acts was to appoint Battersby Harford to a Ripon canonry. What now would happen to the college? Would Major be elected in his place and turn the college into a fully Modernist institution? This hardly seemed likely when T. W. Drury, the

94

Evangelical Bishop of the Isle of Man, was translated to Ripon, though Major had strong support in Dean Fremantle, Rashdall and Archdeacon Waugh. When the new Bishop was in the saddle and the question of a new Principal for the college was discussed there were no less than sixteen names suggested. Among them were B. K. Cunningham, W. K. Lowther Clarke, G. Foster-Clark, the Rector of St Aldate's, A. W. F. Blunt (later Bishop of Bradford),[21] R. B. Tollinton, J. R. Wilkinson, C. H. K. Boughton, the Vice-Principal of Wycliffe Hall and Major himself. Eventually C. H. K. Boughton was elected, Major being defeated by the local Governors. On 30 May Dean Fremantle wrote thus to Major.

The Deanery,
Ripon,
May 30th 1912

My dear Mr. Major,

I am sorry we did not elect you yesterday. But I doubt whether more could have been done than was done. Canon Waugh made an excellent speech, good humoured but telling. It was good of Canon Rashdall to come from such a distance; and he too spoke excellently. The Bishop would, I think, have come round if you had met with the support of the Governors. But men like W. Austin and W. Sheepshanks were evidently determined to use all resources of timidity and ignorance (though professing, and I think truly, that they had no ill feeling) and men like the Bishop of Knaresborough[22] did not vote.

I hope you will hang on. Opinion is rapidly changing in the points on which you have incurred mistrust. I wish I could have pointed this out, as Rashdall did in part. The precedent of Maurice in 1853, turned out of King's College, ought to be a warning. Also, since there are 3 Schools in Anglican Theology & the High are more than abundantly supplied with training places & the Evangelicals have colleges at Oxford and Cambridge & Highbury, it would be just to let liberals have a place of their own. If Boughton after a time is moved on, I think everyone will welcome you. I remember when I was Chaplain to Archbishop Tait (then Bishop of London) when Archbishop Sumner died, that the Government fell back on Longley as the safe man; but 6 years after, when Longley died, everyone accepted Tait, if not with enthusiasm, at least as inevitable . . .

Major, who was now 40, endeavoured to try and work with Boughton, who was 29. Boughton got married and moved into the college. Major by this time was Rector of Copgrove, a very small hamlet outside Ripon, where he was a model country parson, but spent most of the week in college. Boughton seems to have been unpopular from the start. Friction developed between the two men. At a meeting of the Governors in 1914 Boughton asked for Major to be dismissed. This was passed by the local Governors present. Later Rashdall, Boyd Carpenter (still a Governor), Ryle and Waugh objected. Major was indignant. The students rushed to his support. There were some who suggested a Westminster living for Major. Pershore and Steventon were vacant; but he was not ready so to be disposed of. Dean Foakes-Jackson of Jesus College told him not to resign. Rashdall pressed for the rescinding of the motion getting rid of Major. The students made it clear that Major who was immensely popular was not exactly pushing his Modernist views upon his students. At this juncture the Great War broke out, which put a different complexion upon things. Major seemed to think that the solution was for Boughton to go off to a living. That suggestion was taken up. Boughton was persuaded to accept the living of Calverley, Bradford, and Canon Battersby Harford was brought back to take on again the Principalship of the college as 'war work', in addition to his Ripon canonry. Major remained on as Vice-Principal. Bishop Drury gave up being Chairman of the Governors and Boyd Carpenter took on the job once again. The college went on until 1915. By then the army had invaded Ripon and officers were quartered in the vacant college rooms. Major retired to Copgrove and took on other clerical duties. He also trained to make munitions, but once trained could not get a job. Alan Wilkinson's recent excellent book, *The Church of England in the First World War* (1978), shows how strong a patriot Major was.

NOTES

1   For Danks, see *The Gospel of Consolation. University and Cathedral Sermons* by William Danks M.A., late Canon Residentiary of Canterbury and sometime Canon Residentiary of Ripon and Archdeacon of Richmond. Preface by the Very Rev. the Dean of Canterbury [H. Wace] and an Appreciation by the Right Rev. Bishop Boyd Carpenter (1917).

2   See K. G. Budd, *The Story of Donald Hankey. A Student in Arms* (1931) and especially pp.47–58.

3   See *Hibbert Journal*, vol. iii, pp.433–51.

4   *The Times*, 31 March 1899.

5   See *Report of a Meeting held at Lambeth Palace in support of the claims of Lightfoot Hall*, His Grace the Archbishop of Canterbury in the Chair, on Saturday, 18 January 1902.

6   op. cit., p.388.

7   See the pamphlet, *The Churchmen's Union for the Advancement of Liberal Religious Thought. Annual Sermon 1908* preached in St Martin's-in-the-Fields, Charing Cross, by The Right Reverend Chas. D. Williams D.D. Bishop of Michigan.

8   See *Modern Churchman*, vol. i, pp.441–7 and 505–13.

9   Hubert Handley, 'Religious Liberalism'.
    F. C Burkitt, 'Theological Liberalism'.
    J. R. Wilkinson, 'Biblical Liberalism'.
    C. R. Shaw Stewart, 'Devotional Liberalism'.
    Hastings Rashdall, 'Clerical Liberalism'.
    Percy Gardner, 'Lay Liberalism'.
    Sir C. Thomas Dyke Acland, 'Political Liberalism'.
    A. J. Carlyle, 'Social Liberalism'.
    H. G. Woods, 'Past Liberalism'.
    Alfred Caldecott, 'Nonconformist Liberalism'.
    William D. Morrison, 'German Evangelic Liberalism'.
    A. L. Lilley, 'Roman Catholic Liberalism'.

10   *Miracles in the New Testament*, p.217. Thompson prints these words in italics.

11   See 'A Martyr of the Miraculous', by H. D. A. Major in *Modern Churchman* (Dec. 1948), pp.336–8.

12   James Matthew Thompson, *My Apologia* (1940). There is a copy in the Bodleian Library.

13   For Hewlett Johnson and *The Interpreter* see his autobiography *Searching for Light* (1968).

14   op. cit., p.7.

15   op. cit., p.19.

16 op. cit., p.21.

17 See William Purcell, *Woodbine Willie*.

18 op. cit., p.22.

19 op. cit., p.116.

20 For his views on the revision of the Prayer Book see G. L. H. Harvey, ed., *The Church and the Twentieth Century* (1936), pp.51–106.

21 This fact was unknown to John S. Peart-Binns when he wrote *Blunt*.

22 Lucius Bottomley Smith. Actually he voted against Major.

5

Men of Girton

In my fourth chapter I dealt with Henry Dewsbury Alves Major, the 'Apostle of English Modernism', and we arrived at the year 1915, with Major as Rector of Copgrove near Ripon and running other neighbouring parishes. He had trained to make munitions but, for one reason or another, no factory would take him on. The Great War was in full swing. Ripon College was temporarily closed and officers were quartered in the students' rooms. Bishop Boyd Carpenter, its founder, was now a Canon of Westminster; so that there seemed no reason for keeping the liberal theological college at Ripon. Major felt determined that after the war the college should start again somewhere with himself as Principal and preferably in a University.

We must now go back briefly to the year 1914 to witness the beginning of the series of Conferences of Modern Churchmen. This was another of Major's gifts to the Modernist Movement which still continues. By 1913 Major was dissatisfied with the inactivity of William Manning, the Secretary of the Churchmen's Union. He was also critical of its President, the west country landowner, Sir Thomas Dyke Acland. Above all, he felt convinced that Modernists should meet in Conference. This suggestion met with support and encouragement from two men whose names are well known in the history of New Testament scholarship, F. J. Foakes-Jackson, then Dean of Jesus College, and his friend Kirsopp Lake, Professor of Theology at Leyden and the author of a then rather radical book on Christ's resurrection and *The Earlier Epistles of St. Paul* which made Paul into a great sacramentalist. Both these scholars had moved away from the Liberal Protestant position and had rather more affinity with the Catholic Modernist school. That had repercussions in the first Conference and in that of Girton 1921. Major, Foakes-Jackson and Lake then recruited two

Yorkshire ladies who had attended Major's Oxford University Extension lectures on the Old Testament, Miss Dora Nussey and Mrs Lucy Reith of Ilkley, to help with the domestic arrangements. Ripon seemed to them the place for the Conference, so the group approached Dean Fremantle over the possibility of using the cathedral. After some initial hesitation he agreed. One is not surprised to discover that William Manning, the Secretary of the Churchmen's Union, was not a little annoyed at all this being done behind his back. Major told him, with complete candour, that he ought to resign his secretaryship and make way for a younger man.

Durham was not so very far away from Ripon and some had hoped that Hensley Henson who was now Dean there would give his blessing to the proposed Conference. This was not to be. Henson, who never spoke at a single Conference of Modern Churchmen, was very critical of many of them. When Foakes-Jackson approached Henson, he replied:

> It seems to me very important at the present time to effect a *modus vivendi* between Liberal Anglicans and Evangelicals. It is to that end I am directing my efforts. The point of danger is precisely at this moment liberal handling of the creeds. If some reckless or unwise declaration were now to be flung before the public, it would go far to undo such progress as has been made.

One must recall the controversial theological background to this letter from Dean Henson. There was the Kikuyu controversy and the attack by Bishop Frank Weston of Zanzibar upon the liberal theology of *Foundations* (1911) and Henson's own book *The Creed in the Pulpit* (1912). J. M. Thomson's *Miracles in the New Testament* was still being discussed. The year 1914 saw an immense number of pamplets issued on the question of miracles. Sanday, B. H. Streeter, Gwatkin and Bethune-Baker rushed to the defence of Modernist beliefs, while Charles Gore and N. P. Williams vehemently attacked them.[1] It may be recalled that a year or two later, N. P. Williams was to write this remarkable sentence in a controversy with the Modernist William Sanday:

> I trust that I am not insensible to the effect of genuine *a posteriori* evidence: and *if* at any future time an ostrakon or a papyrus is unearthed at Nazareth which proves beyond the shadow of

doubt that Jesus was the son of Joseph, I shall be prepared to take the consequences. I shall frankly admit that Catholic Christianity has tumbled down with a crash, and I shall proceed to look round for some other theory of the universe.[2]

The whole subject of theological liberalism has been discussed in Canterbury Convocation in 1914 and resolutions not totally condemnatory were passed.

Foakes-Jackson wanted boldness and felt strongly that they should refuse to give way to Henson. 'I am sure', he said, 'we should rouse England if we go to work, not as statesmen, but as Knights errant with an almost exaggerated sense of honour. I want to see our meeting light a candle in England.' By April 1914 all was pretty well settled. Percy Gardner, Philip Bagenal, Cyril Emmet and John Gamble had joined the other organizers. The Conference was planned from 3 July until Tuesday 7 July and was open to anyone in sympathy with the aims of the Churchmen's Union. The meeting place was to be the Spa Hotel, which ought now to have a commemorative tablet somewhere. A full ticket would cost 35/-. The Cathedral was to be the place of worship. The Dean who felt that he had not been given enough to do – only an address of welcome was assigned to him – was later placated by being allowed to talk on 'What is the Church of England?' The two preachers were to be Canon Waugh of Ripon and E. W. Barnes, Fellow of Trinity College, Cambridge. Waugh as a 'local' wanted to hand his preachment over to Dean Inge of St Paul's, but Fremantle evidently did not like him – he thought he was too sarcastic – and Inge never came to the first Conference.

When 3 July came Ripon had the most remarkable gathering of Anglican Liberals that the century had yet seen. Dean Fremantle acted as the link between them and Temple, Tait and Jowett. Percy Gardner, soon to succeed Dyke Acland as President of the Churchmen's Union, linked them with Maurice and Seeley. Hastings Rashdall was there and Michael George Glazebrook, Canon of Ely, soon to achieve unwanted notoriety for his little volume *The Faith of a Modern Churchman*. The Chairman of the Union, Canon T. L. Papillon, and the Secretary, William Manning, were both there; and Hubert Handley, A. L. Lilley, J. E. Symes, author of *Broad Church* (soon to become assistant organizing secretary), Cyril Emmet and his brother P. B. Emmet, a missionary from India, Edwyn Bevan, John Gamble, F. E. Hutchinson, J. M. Thompson, the most notorious of Anglican Modernists, still Dean of Magdalen, J. R. Wilkinson, the translator of Harnack, and G. G. Coulton, who was to achieve fame as a Cambridge medievalist. An unexpected supporter was Edwyn Clement Hoskyns, the son of the Bishop of Southwell. Both Bishop and son gave their support to the Churchmen's Union that year, but those who have written about Hoskyns are either ignorant of, or have totally ignored, the brief flirtation of this famous New Testament theologian with Anglican Modernism. There was also an American Bishop present – the Bishop of Arizona, Dr Attwood. The ladies included Miss Alice Gardner of Newnham College, Mrs Rashdall, Mrs Coulton, Mrs Glazebrook and Mrs Major.

Obviously there is not space to deal with all the papers delivered, most of which were published in the July *Modern Churchman* at 6d. The speed with which they were published is remarkable, since they came out before the month of July was over. Really the Conference was the preview of Girton 1921, for Foakes Jackson and Lake delivered an attack upon Liberal Protestantism, which was the standpoint of most of the participants, and Rashdall expressed the views which were to be so heavily criticized in the popular press in 1921. Rashdall affirmed that Jesus never claimed to be divine; the Church concluded that he was divine because of the moral and spiritual appeal he made to men, but his participation in Godhead did not make him infallible. He attacked both Schweitzer and Tyrrell, though their views were congenial to Kirsopp Lake, whose paper was entitled 'The Society of the Logos'. For Lake the important thing was Catholic Christianity. 'It was not the Christianity which stood still and remained where it was, even with the teaching of Jesus Himself, which won the world, but it was the Christianity which went out into the world and took from that world a great part of the truths which it went to preach, which won the world.' It was the old problem of the acorn or the oak. Lake put his money on the oak, like Loisy, while most of the others were for going back to the acorn. Lake, however, had some support from Hoskyns, who asked his auditors not to depreciate the Logos teaching of St John and St Paul, though it was an addition to the original message of Jesus.

Michael Glazebrook spoke on 'The Second Reformation', and praised Erasmus, Colet and More and felt that the Churchmen's Union were the successors of this trio, as well as of Origen and Jerome. Jerome got a mention, perhaps, because of Fremantle, who had written a monograph on that church Father. The Bishop of Arizona contended that American Anglicans were ahead of English Anglicans since they were opening their pulpits to other religious bodies. Kirsopp Lake suggested that continental theology was several years ahead of English theology.

Before the Conference broke up, its members passed a resolution of tribute to Major for his editing of the *Modern Churchman*. Though the Conference had profited through its tactful chairman, Foakes Jackson, yet the bulk of the work in preparation had been done by Major. In 1915, in spite of the Great War, there was a similar conference at Rugby, where A. A. David, a supporter of the movement, was Headmaster of the famous school, though the meeting took place not in his school but in a girls' academy. In 1916 they met at Lady Margaret Hall, Oxford and in 1917 at Girton College. On that occasion Major was given a document in which it was stated: 'The undersigned . . . feel that the growing reputation and increasing usefulness of the Churchmen's Union is largely due to your energy and ability.' Certainly Major was very much the organizing brains of the Union. He managed to get Michael Glazebrook as Chairman in place of Canon Papillon, and had Dyke Acland supplanted by Percy Gardner as President. When Manning did give up the secretaryship, Major put in one of his own old Ripon pupils, Cavendish Moxon, Rector of Marske, in his place. Indeed, there were some who thought that the centre of gravity of the movement was passing from London to Yorkshire. This was not quite true. There were groups of Modern Churchmen appearing in various parts of the country, including Bristol, Manchester, West London and Oxford. In 1915 a Churchmen's Union Lending Library was inaugurated. There was also talk of cheap manuals on Modernism. These again came about largely through Major.

Though such manuals were suggested in 1914, the wheels were not set in motion until 1917. That was the year of the 'Hereford

Scandal', when there was so much acrimonious debate over the appointment of Dean Hensley Henson of Durham as Bishop of Hereford and another spate of pamphlets appeared. Henson had never really been a Modernist and, as we have seen, had not been happy about the First Conference of Modern Churchmen, but now he was treated as if he were one of the leaders of the school! However, the episode ended with Henson very much in disfavour with Modernists when he rather climbed down in correspondence with Archbishop Davidson and said that he affirmed all the articles of the Creed *ex animo*. Kirsopp Lake remarked that he thought Henson's meaning was more correctly expressed in another Latin phrase, *cum grano salis*.

The first of the new manuals, which were known as the Modern Churchmen's Library, came out in 1918 and was by the Chairman of the Council of the Modern Churchmen's Union, Michael George Glazebrook, entitled, *The Faith of a Modern Churchman*. The controversy over liberal beliefs in connection with Henson perhaps brought special attention to this book, which was given a full page review in the *Church Times* for 15 March 1918. Glazebrook accepted the sort of degree Christology that we associate with Rashdall.[3] He was careful what he said about the miracles. He did not make an outright denial of the virgin birth and the physical resurrection of Jesus, but he pleaded that men who declined to affirm them should not be branded as heretics.[4] J. K. Mozley in his review in the *Church Times* criticized the book for the absence of any belief in the breaking in of God *ab extra* into human history. The great objection to the book came from Glazebrook's Bishop, F. H. Chase, who wrote to *The Times* on 26 April and criticized Glazebrook for what he had written on the virgin birth and resurrection. He said it was distasteful to him to challenge Glazebrook's conclusions without a lengthy reply, but pressure of work at that moment prevented this. Foakes-Jackson, hearing in America of the contents of the letter, was indignant. He wrote to Glazebrook:

But what is really astonishing is that the Bishop says he disagrees with you but has not time to publicly challenge your arguments. I believe Dr. Chase is the only professional theologian on the bench. He is the only bishop whose life has been entirely academic, who resided in Cambridge for at least 30 years as a student and ended up a Divinity Professor. He has one of the easiest of dioceses and ought to have leisure. . . . Even however if he had not, his equipment, for he lectured for years on dogmatics, ought to be enough to demolish a man, who has for the greater part of his life been a particularly hard worked schoolmaster. He has no right to address you in such a way, to reprove you for error & then to plead the excuse of pressure of work. It is a mean evasion. I do hope and trust you will not do the Henson trick and climb down.

In the end Chase did sit down and write a reply to Glazebrook's book, with the title *Belief and Creed*, which dealt mainly with the virgin birth and physical resurrection of Jesus. Chase objected to the Erasmian motto on Glazebrook's book, 'By identifying the new learning with heresy you make orthodoxy synonymous with ignorance', disliking the menacing implications of the words. This greatly annoyed Major, for the motto appeared regularly on the *Modern Churchman*, and he suggested that the best commentary on the motto was Cyril Emmet's book *Conscience, Creeds and Critics* which came out in 1918 and showed how in the nineteenth century ecclesiastical authority was wrong when it condemned in turn Colenso, Maurice, Jowett, Temple and Kingsley as unorthodox. Chase's book was not, however, the end of the matter. Glazebrook wrote a reply, *The Letter and the Spirit. A Reply to the Bishop of Ely's Criticism* (1920), which was well argued and made good use of another recent Modernist publication, Professor J. F. Bethune-Baker's *The Faith of the Apostles Creed. An Essay in adjustment of Belief and Faith* (1919), a book which years later was republished in America in an abridged and edited version by Dr Norman Pittenger. Bethune-Baker's book put forward in a striking way what many Modernists were saying but it went beyond them at one point in almost suggesting that Jesus had a sense of sin.[5] The sinlessness of Jesus was a dogma which most Modernists did not argue about.

The other Manuals of Modern Churchmanship need not delay us. The second was by Alfred Fawkes, ex-Roman Catholic priest and very liberal Protestant Vicar of Ashby St Ledger, on *The Genius of the Church of England*. The third was J. R Cohu, Rector of

Aston Clinton and a former Fellow of Jesus College, Oxford on *The Evolution of the Christian Ministry*, the most erudite of the Manuals – though Major as Editor rewrote quite a lot of it – and very dependent on J. B. Lightfoot's famous essay in *Philippians* and Gwatkin's Church History. The fourth was by John Gamble, Vicar of St Mary's, Leigh Woods, Clifton on *Baptism Confirmation and the Eucharist* which had nothing very outrageous in it, though on the matter of the virgin birth he wrote, 'The devout believer, whatever opinion he may himself form on this question, or whether he decline to form any opinion, will deeply resent the suggestion that faith in Christ as God Incarnate must involve a belief upon which our Lord Himself, as far as we know, based no claim, of which the first generation of Christians were in ignorance, and which appears to have had no influence upon the mind of St Paul.'[6] Percy Gardner wrote a volume but Murrays refused to publish anything by Gardner. His book, *The Evolution of Christian Doctrine*, was published by Williams and Norgate.

By the time these Manuals were published, Ripon College, soon to become the centre of the Modernist movement, was being transferred to Oxford. As we have seen, Major was intent upon the reopening of the college after the war. In July 1916 he wrote to Rashdall that Oxford would be a good place for it, and, if not Oxford, then London or Birmingham. 'My own view', he wrote,

is quite clear that I can hold only one post in the college and that is Principal. The course is full of difficulty and will require careful steering and I do not feel inclined to work under another man who in days of disaster will himself or his friends declare that I am the Jonah. Moreover I have strong views as to methods after 10 years at Ripon and have never had any opportunity of carrying them out. One of my ideals is that we should have a number of lectures and addresses from our Liberal teachers who should be invited to share our life and get to know our students.

There is no personal ambition in my saying this. The post is in some ways a very precarious one and is uncongenial to my wife. As you know I was willing to stand aside four years ago and take a subordinate place. The compromise was a failure and a cause of misunderstanding. If anyone can make the college succeed I can. If not I feel it is not likely to succeed as a Liberal College.

Rashdall in his reply was doubtful about Oxford as it was the see of Charles Gore and thought it would be better to go to Southwark where there was a liberal Bishop, Hubert Burge. There was a suggestion of Major going as Vicar of St Olave's, Hart Street, London, then vacant, and Charles Raven joining him as curate and becoming the nucleus of a new college. In the next few months all sorts of possibilities were mooted. There seemed much in favour of the idea of bringing the college to London because Bishop Boyd Carpenter at Westminster was taking an active interest in the revival of the college, but Major felt he was insufficiently committed to the liberal cause and advocated the increase of the Governing Body by a dozen genuine liberals. One of these was Sir Richard Stapley and another Professor Bethune-Baker. In October 1918, Bishop Boyd Carpenter died. His death brought an end to the idea of bringing the college near Westminster. Canon Glazebrook, who favoured Oxford, wrote to Major, 'Your proposal to collect information about the Universities is most acceptable. Oxford, Cambridge, London, Birmingham, Leeds seem to me the only possibilities. Bristol is hopeless at present. Personally I favour Oxford, and incline to something like Mansfield and Westcott House i.e. an institution with a chapel and lecture room but only a few residents as a centre of men in the ordinary colleges.' Then he went on to the question of electing a new Warden or Visitor in place of Boyd Carpenter. Ryle would be 'safe and respectable but not enterprising.' Henson would be dangerous, but a live wire. Needless to say, Major would never have countenanced Henson. John H. Skrine, Vicar of St Peter's-in-the-East, wanted the college to come to Oxford, and thought that Professors Headlam and Watson and Dean Strong would welcome it. A. W. Fletcher, an old Riponian, now studying theology at Oxford, thought Manchester would be better. At this point Henrietta Barnett, the widow of Canon Barnett, suggested Hampstead Garden Suburb. Major thought even that worth investigating. 'Tea and tennis and suburbia generally I loathe, but we might rise to higher things.' However, by December 1918 things seemed to be decidedly in favour of Oxford.

On 23 January 1919 at a meeting in Church House Bishop Burge was appointed Warden in place of Boyd Carpenter and Major was unanimously elected Principal. There was no other candidate.

Major, who had been in an adjoining room, was ushered in by Cyril Norwood to meet the assembled Governors. Rashdall asked him about moving the college to Oxford, and said some Governors were doubtful of the wisdom of placing it there. Major replied that the permanent location of the college should not be determined by the temporary accident that Charles Gore was Bishop of Oxford. A policy based on apprehensiveness about the future was not sound. Bethune-Baker, in congratulating Major, said he was sorry he was not bringing the college to Cambridge. The *Church Times*, in reporting what had happened, noted with some glee that Bishop Percival's attempt at a liberal theological college at Hereford had ended in failure. But, though Oxford was decided upon, they still had to find buildings there. Houses in Banbury Road, Woodstock Road and St Giles were looked at. The Rector of Exeter, Dr Farnell, said, 'Secure a site in St Giles', whereas Nowell Smith, the Headmaster of Sherborne, said, 'Keep out of that cockpit of religions'. At this point it was heard that St Stephen's House were moving from the site opposite Wadham to Norham Gardens. Major wrote, 'I then heard confidentially from my bank manager that St Stephen's House must inevitably come on to the market and I purchased it in the name of Sir Richard Stapley, Mecklenburg Square, our Treasurer and Governor. I had no desire to admit the *odium theologicum* into a commercial transaction to the prejudice of sound business. My prescience was judicious for I heard later from Canon N. P. Williams, the most influential personage at St Stephen's House, with what pained surprise at the last stage of the transaction they learned they had sold their property to Ripon Hall.'

Major now looked for a Vice-Principal. The name of Charles Raven was suggested and Major tried to get him appointed to a church at Oxford but without success. Raven suggested Oliver Quick for the post but suspected he would be too orthodox. I note, however, that Quick once spoke at a Modern Churchmen's Conference. In the end Major appointed Cyril Emmet, who also held the post of Chaplain of University College, having recently left the living of West Hendred. He died a few years later of pneumonia when lecturing in New York.[7]

In September 1919 Major said goodbye to Yorkshire and Copgrove Rectory and after a stay in the King's Arms at Oxford moved his wife and family into a house he renamed Copgrove Cottage in Bagley Wood. The opening of the new college was planned for 7 October but the railway strike delayed it until 9 October. So Major had achieved his ambition. He had opened his liberal theological college in Oxford, and had added to its Governing Body liberal Churchmen like B. H. Streeter, J. M. Creed, J. F. Bethune-Baker, R. H. Charles and Bishop Barnes. What Ripon Hall was like in the 'twenties can be seen from Hubert Handley's pamphlet *A Visit to Ripon Hall* and that delightful novel of John Michaelhouse (i.e. Joseph McCulloch), *Charming Manners*. The 'twenties saw many students who later became famous as liberal Churchmen, like Norman Sykes, once Dixie Professor of Ecclesiastical History at Cambridge, J. S. Bezzant, a former Dean of St John's, Cambridge, James Parkes, R. D. Richardson, Geoffrey Allen, A. Tindal Hart, Alan Richardson and many others. The historian A. L. Rowse was once invited by James Parkes to dine at the new Ripon Hall and he quoted his diary entry recording the experience in *A Cornishman at Oxford*:

> A fellow named Parkes . . . invited me to dine at Ripon Hall. A nice little place; altogether life there seems rather like that of an old-world family. We dined in a long room at an oak table, candles burning in silver candlesticks. About a dozen and a half were there, two being guests. I sat at the right hand of the Principal, who turned out no less than the celebrated Major, against whom the attack was launched for heresy. Major appeared to be a kindly old man, very deaf, but not wanting in wit and repartee, of a rather noble countenance, fair hair, shaggy brows.[8]

The reason why Major was so celebrated when Rowse went to dinner was because of the famous Girton Conference of 1921. To this we must now turn.

The subject of this most famous of all Modern Churchmen's Conferences was 'Christ and the Creeds' and the reason for the choice of subject was the publication by Foakes Jackson and Kirsopp Lake of Part I of their *The Beginnings of Christianity* which had a section on 'Primitive Christianity' in four chapters:

    1.   The Public Teaching of Jesus and the Choice of the Twelve.

2. The Disciples in Jerusalem and the Rise of Gentile Christianity.

3. The Development of thought on the Spirit, the Church and Baptism.

4. Christology.

This section of the book has been widely criticized as excessively negative. J. M. Creed wrote a review of the book in the December number of the *Modern Churchman*, 1920. He was critical. Reviewing the section on Christology he said, 'The editors then discuss the significance and origin of other titles which were applied to Jesus – Son of Man, Son of David, the suffering Servant, the prophet of Deuteronomy XVIII, and, lastly, the Lord. But the writers do not go on to show us how this miscellaneous assortment of concepts came, in the minds of actual people, to describe an actual person, who had lived an historic life on earth.' Years later Charles Raven in a footnote in his Hulsean Lectures said that it was the only treatment known to him which made Jesus merely dull.[9] As well as this joint work there were also two recent works of Kirsopp Lake. In 1915 he had written *The Stewardship of Faith* and in 1920 *Landmarks in the History of Early Christianity*. In the former book he had been critical of Liberal Protestantism and written:

> If we go back a little we find that man believed in an infallible bible, and that belief has been forced from us by the undeniable proof of fallibility. The same may be said of the belief in an infallible Church. But Liberal Protestantism thought that historical criticism would remove all the misrepresentations of later tradition and reveal the figure of the historic Jesus as infallible. Is that hope also to go? Yes, I fear so. It is impossible to find its fulfilment in Jesus if he conditioned his teaching by Jewish apocalypticism, and believed in what was, after all, an illusory expectation of the coming of the Kingdom of God. But is this a tragedy?[10]

Clearly Lake was far more tolerant of the views of Schweitzer, Loisy and Tyrrell than Major and the other English Modernists except Lilley could ever be.

Another part of the background to the Conference was Frank

Weston's book *The Christ and His Critics* (1919), in which he had attacked Hensley Henson's *The Creed in the Pulpit* (1912) and a review by Bethune-Baker of H. M. Relton's *A Study in Christology* (1917), in which the Cambridge professor had written, 'There is no kind of "evidence" that He [Jesus] ever thought of Himself as God in any sense.' The book had also contained an attack on Ripon Hall which I quoted in my first chapter. Weston did not go unanswered. William Sanday's last work was a reply to Weston entitled *The Position of Liberal Theology*. There, as in his *Divine Overruling*, he stated his unwillingness any longer to accept the concept of miracle. Another attack on liberal Theology came in W. J. Sparrow-Simpson's *Broad Church Theology* (1919). Other liberal books, which formed a background to the Conference, were Rashdall's Bampton Lectures *The Idea of the Atonement in Christian Theology* (1919), A. Seth Pringle Pattison's *The Idea of God in the Light of Recent Thought* (1920), W. R. Sorley's *Moral Values and the Idea of God* and W. R. Inge's first series of very readable *Outspoken Essays* (1919).

Though undoubtedly he had suggested the subject of the Conference, Major did not himself organize it but Canon Glazebrook. Glazebrook had opposed the choice of subject, as also had the President of the Churchmen's Union, Percy Gardner, and William Manning, a member of the Council, and Philip Bagenal, now the Secretary of the Union. It is remarkable that with this opposition, Major managed to get the subject accepted. The first announcement of the forthcoming Conference came in February 1921, when Major wrote in the *Modern Churchman*, 'The eighth conference of Modern Churchmen will be held this year at Girton College, Cambridge, from August 8–15, by the kind permission of the authorities. The morning subject, to which a number of papers are assigned, will be our Lord Jesus Christ. Such a subject is full of difficulties today, and for responsible and practical Modernists to select it and speak about it frankly and fearlessly demands courage. Final conclusions may not be reached on many points, but the selection of the subject is neither needless nor premature in view of the interest in it which has been aroused by Professor Lake's two recent books . . . The evening subject at the Conference, which will be treated in a series of brief papers, will be the Faith of a Re-United Church.'

Major's words were read by Henson now Bishop of Durham, who feared that Major might be capitulating to Lake's views. He wrote off to his Examining Chaplain, Alfred Fawkes:

I am really troubled about Lake, for his tone and teaching with respect to our Saviour do not seem to me suggestive of anything which could reasonably be described as a personal discipleship. He is less respectful to the Founder of Christianity than a pious Jew like Claude Montefiore, and far less reverent than Unitarians like Martineau and Drummond. He does not seem to realize the awful issues of his reasoning. No doubt truth must at all hazards be pursued and held fast; but a Christian might be expected to perceive that the whole validity of his religion is at stake when Jesus Christ's character, teaching, and credit are in debate. I notice with some apprehension that the Churchmen's Union proposes to discuss Lake's theories in August. It would be well if the organizers considered what would be the probable consequence of any extravagances on the part of the speakers.

Fawkes asked Henson if he could make use of his letter among the organizers of the Conference. Henson agreed, and wrote:

I agree that Christological questions in the 20th century are taking in the religious world something of the central importance which they held in that of the 4th. But there is this difference, that while in the earlier age the intellectual debate proceeded against a background of belief, that of the latter proceeds against a background of aggressive and all-penetrating scepticism. I do not think that critics of Lake's type, who live in the atmosphere of questioning, and do not possess in many cases the habit of devotion, realize how very far they have moved from the standpoints of the Church, which believes and worships. I am persuaded that it will be grossly uncharitable and highly impolitic to thrust on the public notice exasperating and unproved theories about our Saviour, which cannot possibly be reconciled with the traditional belief of the Church, and which may be altogether incompatible with any living faith in Christ as uniquely Son of God and Revealer of the Father. At this juncture a religious panic would be particularly unfortunate, and might easily create a situation in which the Liberal elements of the National Church might be actually thrust out of membership on the wave of offended feeling.

Glazebrook was alarmed at this and wondered if Major had not given some suggestion, albeit mistakenly, to Henson that the Union would support Lake. He himself was anxious to remove Lake from his position as a Vice-President of the Union. Major stood fast and said that if Henson's views influenced the policy of the Union, he would resign from it.

In April the speakers were announced. The lecturers on Christology were to be Cyril Emmet, R. H. Lightfoot, R. B. Tollinton, J. W. Hunkin, E. W. Barnes, Nowell Smith, Hastings Rashdall, Major, Bethune-Baker and R. G. Parsons. The speakers on the Creeds were to be W. R. Sorley, T. H. Bindley, Cyril Norwood, Leslie S. Hunter, J. C. Hardwick, Dr Douglas White, Percy Gardner and Harold Anson. Some notable absentees from this list were Alfred Fawkes, W. R. Inge, B. H. Streeter, J. M. Creed and Charles Raven. We should note, however, the presence of R. H Lightfoot, as earlier we noted the presence of Sir Edwyn Hoskyns at the first Conference at Ripon. Like Hoskyns, Lightfoot later fell out of sympathy with the Modernist movement, though he remained a great admirer of Dean Inge and collected his every utterance. The July issue of the *Modern Churchman* gave a list of 'Books for the Girton Conference', which included T. R. Glover's *The Jesus of History*, which had come out with an introduction from Randall Davidson in 1917, Harnack's *What is Christianity?*, Schweitzer's *The Quest of the Historical Jesus* and Shirley Case's *The Historicity of Jesus*.

So we come to the Conference itself, which a number of the students of Ripon Hall attended. Some of them have written to me their impressions of it. One recalls that they were intrigued by the number of clergymen wearing lay collars or the white bow tie, proper to orthodox Victorian clergymen, and the absence of dog collars. Bishop Townley and Charles Jenkinson cycled from Oxford to attend it. We will leave on one side the papers on the Creeds, as being the less controversial and deal with the christological lectures. Glazebrook as chairman led off with an opening address which sounded a decidedly cautious note. Then came Cyril Emmet, who in 1922 (the year before his death) was to combine with Lily Dougall in the anti-eschatological portrait of Jesus, *The Lord of Thought.* He dismissed traditional orthodoxy and the Christ myth school and then characterized the eschatological view as making Jesus a 'one-sided fanatic and implying that the sane and permanent element in the Gospels comes from some other source'.[11] Turning to Foakes-Jackson and Lake, he said they 'appear to give us the picture of a very commonplace and uninspiring prophet, differing from the prophet of the Liberal-Protestant, in that he only taught much what other people had already taught, except for a few original remarks which were either untrue or quite unpractical . . . The fundamental criticism on these books is that they fail historically because they make Jesus unimportant and uninteresting. Such a view explains neither the figure of Jesus as given us in the Gospels, nor the impact of Jesus on His age.'[12] Rather artfully Emmet went back to an earlier essay of Foakes-Jackson in *Cambridge Theological Essays* (1905) on 'Christ in the Church; the testimony of History' where he had written, 'The personal fascination which He exercised (i.e. on his contemporaries) has renewed itself from age to age and is perhaps stronger than ever; whereas the influence of others has decreased as time went on. This may be considered as part of the historic testimony to the divine nature of Christ.'[13]

R. H. Lightfoot, who followed Emmet, quoted frequently from the Gospels but only one modern authority, Heinrich Weinel, whose words from the volume *Jesus or Christ?* 'We know Jesus full well' he completely endorsed. 'I do not think', he said, 'that we need have any doubt at all as to His personality or the general nature of His teaching.'[14]

Foakes-Jackson who was present – Lake was not there – was given a chance to reply. He had not been included among the original speakers. Ramsey is wrong there. He said that *The Beginnings* had been well received on the Continent and by Nonconformists and the non-sectarian press. He maintained that Harnack's *What is Christianity?* would not do in 1921. He and Lake believed that the Jesus whom the early Church preached was not 'a character of singular charm and beauty during his life on earth, but a Risen Saviour who was expected to come speedily to judge the quick and the dead'. He felt that Liberal Protestants like Harry Emerson Fosdick in America were preaching a Christ who had no historical foundation. 'They have lost the historical Christ, and have not regained Him by converting Him into a social reformer, a moral legislator, a revealer of a new conception of God. They are really preaching an entirely new religion, and concealing the fact even from themselves by disguising it in the phraseology of the old, which as employed by them is sometimes without meaning.'[15] Foakes-Jackson maintained – as Lake had maintained in 1914 – that the religion of the early Church was a 'sacramental Catholicism'. When it passed from Palestine into the Graeco-Roman world it became a mystery religion.

On the next day (Wednesday) R. B. Tollinton, Boyd Carpenter's son-in-law, an authority on Clement of Alexandria, showed himself on the side of Emmet against Foakes-Jackson and Lake, though he exhibited more sympathy for Schweitzer and Tyrrell than most of the other speakers. There followed J. W. Hunkin, Dean of Caius College, who sympathized with Tollinton. A paragraph expresses his position. 'Few details of His life have survived; but we can picture Him clearly enough, going about doing good, speaking as never man spoke, not ministered unto, but ministering and giving His life a ransom for many, and finally rising again from the dead. The exact form in which He rose may be a matter of dispute, but that He did rise there can be no doubt whatever.'

> There is no question but that He is unique in history. If we had a thousand times as many details of His life as we have, we should still have no logical proof of his sinlessness. But it was only natural that His disciples, after their experience of Him, of His life and death and resurrection, should think of Him as such. The human mind works that way. After a certain point affection becomes an all-or-none reaction. Love reaches a stage when it throws away its last reserve.[16]

One wonders whether he was not here getting near to Bethune-Baker's position.

On Thursday, E. W. Barnes, who later delivered the sermon in Girton chapel when he said he was an Evangelical and not a Modernist, spoke on 'The Centrality of the Person and Work of Jesus' and joined in the chorus of opposition to Foakes-Jackson and Lake. 'The authors of such a work as *The Beginnings of Christianity*', he said, 'appear to reach what we may not unfairly term rejective conclusions by an ingenuity of atomic disintegration which a physicist might envy.'[17] Barnes was thoroughly Liberal Protestant in his contention that the essence of the gospel was in 'the Fatherhood of God, the brotherhood of man, the Kingdom of God, Eternal Life'.[18] He was followed by Nowell Smith, Headmaster of Sherborne, who referred to *The Beginnings* as a 'disturbing book' but seemed more favourable to it than anyone else.

On Friday Major spoke of 'Jesus, the Son of God', a paper showing his usual gift of clear analysis. He praised Lake for at least dissociating Jesus from political messianism. All Modernists except Brandon have here followed Lake. After attacking apocalypticism, he maintained, against Lake, that Jesus was conscious of messianic Sonship. 'It was His consciousness of Messiahship which gave Jesus that note of supreme spiritual and moral authority which marks His teaching and His character. He promulgates a new Divine Law: He pronounces forgiveness of sins: He recognizes the importance of His message and its inestimable worth: He feels Himself to stand in an unique relation to God and mankind. Moreover, it must not be forgotten that He died for making this tremendous claim; but not before He had warned His judges that they should see Him coming as their Judge with divine authority and power.'[19]

Another paragraph of Major's, often quoted in the debate that followed the Conference, needs to be noticed:

> First, let it be clearly realized that Jesus Himself did not claim to be the Son of God in a *physical* sense, such as the narratives of the Virgin Birth affirm, nor did He claim to be the Son of God in a *metaphysical* sense such as is required by the Nicene theology. He claimed to be God's Son in a *moral* sense, in the sense in which all human beings are sons of God, *viz.* as standing in a filial and moral relationship to God and as capable of acting on those moral principles on which God acts.[20]

Clearly then, the Conference were pretty well united in their opposition to Foakes-Jackson and Lake. Their own conservatism in this respect has been noted even by Roger Lloyd who remarks, 'The Christology of the conference was often strikingly positive.' When Major published the papers in the *Modern Churchman* he remarked, 'The Liberalism which Prof. Lake jettisons may be alleged to have stript our Lord of His miraculous characteristics, but it left Him His moral and spiritual supremacy. But Prof. Lake's conclusions seem to deprive Him of the latter as well as of the former.'[21]

However, it was the two of the next day's papers, those of Rashdall and Bethune-Baker – that by R. G. Parsons in spite of the fact that he was the only speaker who became a bishop can be neglected – which really brought about the notoriety of the Conference in the eyes of the popular press and traditional theologians. Rashdall, whose subject was 'Christ as Logos and Son of God', said nothing that he had not said many times before. He started with five points:

1. Jesus did not claim Divinity for Himself.

2. Jesus was in the fullest sense man.

3. It is unorthodox to suppose that the human soul of Jesus pre-existed.

4. The Divinity of Christ does not necessarily imply the Virgin Birth or any other miracle.

5. The Divinity of Christ does not imply omniscience.

No one would disagree with these points today. Going on to elaborate on his conception of how Jesus was divine, he maintained that we must believe that every human soul incarnates God to a certain extent, but that in Christ we see the fullest disclosure of God in man.

> If we believe that every human soul reveals, reproduces, incarnates God *to some extent*; if we believe that in the great ethical teachers of mankind, the great religious personalities, the founders, the reformers of religions, the heroes, the prophets, the saints, God is more fully revealed than in other men: if we believe that up to the coming of Christ there had been a gradual, continuous, and on the whole progressive revelation of God (especially, though by no means exclusively, in the development of Jewish Monotheism), then it becomes possible to believe that in one Man the self-revelation of God

117

has been signal, supreme, unique. That we are justified in thinking of God as like Christ, that the character and teaching of Christ contains the fullest disclosure both of the character of God Himself and of His will for man – that is (so far as so momentous a truth can be summed up in a few words) the true meaning for us of the doctrine of Christ's Divinity.[22]

Rashdall concluded with a consideration of the Logos doctrine, contending that we must follow Augustine and Aquinas and not those Fathers who made the Logos into a separate consciousness of Deity. In this connection he criticized the High Churchmen, A. J. Mason and Peter Green.

The morning after Rashdall's speech the *Daily Telegraph* in a leader on the Conference said, 'The Conference of "Modern Churchmen", now in session at Cambridge, is more interesting, and in reality more important, than a good many of the other conferences, whose "proceedings" congest the newspaper columns.' Then they commended Dean Inge (who was not at the Conference), Canon Glazebrook, from whose opening address they quoted, and Canon Barnes. This sympathetic note was soon to be overshadowed by a great deal of abuse and criticism.

On Saturday the other paper that achieved notoriety was delivered by Professor Bethune-Baker, whose book *The Faith of the Apostles' Creed* marked him out as a Modernist, though he never joined the Churchmen's Union. He agreed with much of what Rashdall had said but was more radical, and I doubt whether Rashdall approved of everything in the lecture, though he would have agreed with him when he said, 'I do not for a moment suppose that Jesus ever thought of himself as God.' His final paragraph sums up his outlook very well.

It is not from anything that I know beforehand about God that I infer that Jesus is God incarnate. I know almost nothing about God's character apart from Jesus. But I attribute to God the character of Jesus. I say my conception of God is formed by my conception of Jesus. The God I recognize is a supreme 'person' like Jesus in all that makes 'personality'. In thinking of God personally as Jesus did and as we do, I believe that I am, at all events, thinking along the lines of truth, in the right direction. So Jesus is the creator of my God. I know, of course, that I may be the victim of illusion; it is my faith that, through this estimate of Him, of His significance I am in touch with reality.[23]

This was more or less what he had said in *The Faith of the Apostles' Creed*. Rashdall would have expressed himself differently. Nor, do I imagine, would he have approved of this following passage: 'The Creator is not separated from His creatures; they do not exist apart from Him. They have their origin in the will and love of God; they are the counterparts of that will and love, as necessary to the existence of God as He is to theirs. Neither is complete without the other. Language almost fails us, but God is always being actualized, fulfilled, expressed in man, and only comes to full consciousness – the fulness of potentiality – in God.'[24]

This seems the most vulnerable utterance of the whole Conference. I am glad to find that Norman Pittenger, a disciple of Bethune-Baker, agrees that his language here is dangerous. In his *The Word Incarnate* (1959), he says:

> Is man really as necessary to God as God is to man? Such an implied evolutionary monism has terrible dangers; the loss of the sense of the transcendence of God, no matter how active He may be in the world, and the failure to recognise the dependence upon Him of all derived reality can only lead to pantheism if followed to their logical conclusion. This, of course, is not done by Bethune-Baker; and a more careful statement of what he intended would have led him to a panentheistic conception, in which God is seen as above and beyond the world yet ceaselessly active in it and intimately related to it.[25]

Bethune-Baker was thus reckless and I suspect many members of the Conference found him so.

Most people derive their notions about Girton 1921 from Roger Lloyd's account in *The Church of England 1900–1965*, where he is very condemnatory – though I have discovered that he himself spoke at the Conference of Modern Churchmen in 1937, and indeed a large number of non-Modernists, including Bishop Mervyn Stockwood, have spoken at their Conferences. Lloyd accused the men of Girton of believing in the perfectibility of man and showing themselves unwilling to be impressed by the depressing picture of man that had been apparent in the Great War. He accused them of agreeing with Swinburne, 'Glory to Man in the highest! For Man is the master of things.' What truth is there in this verdict? In 1969 I wrote as follows in the volume *Liberal Christianity in History*:

> When Roger Lloyd looked back at the Modernist Movement in *The Church of England in the Twentieth Century* it struck him as excessively negative. He made the great mistake of seeing it as a this-worldly version of Christianity, concerned simply with building the Kingdom of God upon Earth. This was a very grave error. They were (and Dean Inge especially) preachers of otherworldliness. Lloyd seems to have confused them with the preachers of the social Gospel. It is a regrettable mistake. They were not believers in a this-worldly Utopia. In fact, today, it might be said that they laid too much emphasis on the spiritual rather than the material.[26]

Do I agree in 1980 with what I wrote in 1969? I have read yet again the Girton papers and looked out especially for anything that might suggest a Spencerian or Wellsian belief in the perfectibility of man. I found nothing, though I rather felt that Bethune-Baker might be approaching it. I went back to his *The Faith of the Apostles' Creed* (1918) and there I did find, I am afraid, what Lloyd denounces, though I think he is, perhaps, alone among the Modernists in being guilty of it. Here are the relevant sentences.

> Yet belief in the ultimate establishment of the Kingdom of God in the world is paramount in belief in Him as Christ (p.53).
>
> Human society has in it the immortal germs of progress towards its perfection and the conditions of its perfectibility were described in such sayings as are collected in the Sermon on the Mount (p.54).

So there is a little to be said for Roger Lloyd, but only a little.

A statement made by Bishop Stephen Neill, who seems to have swallowed Roger Lloyd whole, in *The Truth of God Incarnate* is the suggestion that Girton 1921 anticipated *The Myth of God Incarnate*. That is quite wrong. None of the men of Girton 1921 refused to believe that Jesus Christ was God incarnate.

In the next chapter we shall see why, in spite of their

conservative approach to the Jesus of History – conservative in relation to Foakes-Jackson and Kirsopp Lake and the Continental Roman Catholic Modernists – the members of the Conference suffered an immense amount of abuse in the press. Major was even accused of heresy. We shall see how one of the outcomes of the Conference was the setting up of the Commission on Doctrine in the Church of England. The Conference obviously was important because of what resulted from it. So Girton College ought to have a tablet to commemorate the Girton Conference of Modern Churchmen 1921.

NOTES

1   See William Sanday, *Bishop Gore's Challenge to Criticism*. A Reply to the Bishop of Oxford's Open Letter on the basis of Anglican Fellowship (1914). B. H. Streeter, *Restatement and Reunion*. A Study in First Principles (1914). H. M. Gwatkin, *The Bishop of Oxford's Open Letter*. An Open Letter in reply (1914). J. F. Bethune-Baker, *The Miracle of Christianity*. A Plea for 'The Critical School' in regard to the use of the Creed. A Letter to the Rt Rev Charles Gore (1914). N. P. Williams, *Miracles* (1914). Charles Gore, *The Basis of Anglican Fellowship*. An Open Letter to the Diocese of Oxford (1914). For Major's review of Gore see *Modern Churchman* III, pp.66–73.

2   See *Form and Content in the Christian Religion. A Friendly Discussion between W. Sanday and N. P. Williams* (1916), p.90.

3   See p.7 in second edn (1925).

4   See p.87.

5   op. cit., p.117.

6   op. cit., p.55.

7   For Emmet see *Modern Churchman* (Dec. 1956), pp.247f.

8   op. cit., p.64.

9   *The Creator Spirit* (Hulsean Lectures 1927), p.235.

10   op. cit., p.43f.

11   *Modern Churchman* (Sept. 1921), p.215.

12   ibid., pp.215f.

13   op. cit., p.478.

14   *Modern Churchman* (Sept. 1921), p.224.

15   *Modern Churchman* (Sept. 1921), p.231.

16 *Modern Churchman* (Sept. 1921), p.251.

17 ibid., p.258.

18 ibid., p.254.

19 *Modern Churchman* (Sept. 1921), p.275.

20 *Modern Churchman* (Sept. 1921), p.276.

21 ibid., p.194.

22 *Modern Churchman* (Sept. 1921), p.283.

23 *Modern Churchman* (Sept. 1921), p.301.

24 *Modern Churchman* (Sept. 1921), p.292.

25 op. cit., pp.199f.

26 *Liberal Christianity in History*, p.151.

6

Heresy Accusation and Doctrine Commission

We turn now to the aftermath of Girton 1921 which culminated in 1922 in the appointment of the Commission on Doctrine in the Church of England which finally reported in 1938.

As Bishop Townley cycled back to Ripon Hall from Cambridge on Monday, 15 August 1921, having enjoyed the experience of the Conference, he scarcely thought, he says, that they would hear so much about it in the months ahead. The Conference papers were not published until half way through September, but reporters had been present at Girton and they made a great deal out of what Rashdall and Bethune-Baker had said. Max Pemberton writing in the *Sunday Pictorial* for 21 August said: 'There are some of us still left who believe in the divinity of Christ, and who totally fail to understand how men who believe the contrary can honestly occupy the pulpits of our State churches and take money for teaching people to deride the ancient faith.' The *Star* contained an attack on the Conference from Bishop Gore who said:

> I feel sure that the denial of miracles and the abandonment of belief in Christ's Godhead will be found to carry with them an abandonment of Divine Revelation altogether, and those who abandon the specific Christian Creed will find themselves not in the Unitarianism of Dr. Martineau, but much lower down.

Rashdall replied quite rightly, 'My paper distinctly asserted the Divinity of Christ. All my philosophical writings are a protest against Modern Pantheism and strongly defend the Personality of God. I have no sympathy with the views of Dr. Foakes-Jackson.' According to J. F. W. Boden-Worsley, writing in *Theology*, September 1940, Rashdall obtained damages out of court on the ground of a quite unwarrantable misrepresentation of his conference paper. Gore attacked again in the *Church Times* on

23 September but now he was milder. He described Rashdall as an adoptionist, but said that Modernists 'have a real devotion to Christ, that He has for them "the Value of God"'. The Roman Catholic journal *The Tablet* was bitter in its attack. 'Our very separated brethren, the Anglicans, have been holding a feast of infidelity at Cambridge. One would have thought that Anglican unbelief had reached its high-water mark in Professor [*sic*] Thompson, the Bishop of Durham, and Dean Inge, but. . .'[1] The Roman Catholic Bishop of Southwark, Louis Charles, in view of the Girton infidelity, ordered a Day of Reparation on Sunday, 2 October.[2] Even a Riponian joined in a procession of reparation for the damage done to the historic Creeds organized by an East London Anglican parish. The Rev. William Manning, who was one of the Vice-Presidents of the Churchmen's Union and had been Secretary for several years resigned from it. On the other hand, E. S. Woods, Vicar of Holy Trinity, Cambridge, joined the Union because of the Girton Conference.

The *Western Morning News and Mercury* had a whole column of letters on 22 August. One defended Rashdall, but most were like that written by 'Mordecai at the King's Gate' who said, 'If it were possible for Arius, Pelagius, Socinus and Arminius to re-visit earth, these arch-heretics and anti-Christian preachers of erroneous and poisonous doctrines evidently would be welcomed by our learned theologians and spiritual guides.' The *Daily Express* for 16 August had a defence of Rashdall from the Congregationalist R. F. Horton. In the same issue even Edgar Wallace, whose detective stories Bishop Barnes was fond of reading, defended him and asked, 'What does divinity mean? It means no more than inspiration, and nobody denies or questions the inspiration of Christ.' The prize piece – to my mind – in the way of newspaper correspondence was in the *Manchester Guardian* of 6 September – a letter from W. A. Loyd from Constantinople. He had happened to be in Gumleik, the ancient Kios, the residence of the Archbishop of Nicaea, to whom he had shown the *Manchester Guardian* report on the Conference. One would have thought an Orthodox prelate would have been horrified, but apparently not so.

'My son' he said, 'read your Bible intelligently, but don't read into it meanings that are not there, however sanctified by tradition. Then study your Plato, and you will see that most of these so-called modern problems are in reality as old as human thought. The trouble is that good and terribly earnest people worry about matters of secondary importance. Many Modernists as they delight to call themselves are not modern at all, but I am afraid some of them are not very modest either. I notice the Cambridge Congress discussed the difficulties of a literal acceptance of the Nicene Creed. But I do not regard the Symbol as a really vital matter, or its literal acceptance as being a matter of life and death to Christians. I always encourage my clergy to present the human Christ, the Christos Anthropos, in their sermons, as well as the Divine Christ . . . We must bring the people to Christ, but we must also bring Christ to the people. The living, loving, sympathetic, understanding Christ.'

When the Conference number of the *Modern Churchman* came out, a flood of letters descended upon Major, whose introduction to the papers was criticized by Glazebrook. Harold Anson reported that he had had a talk with William Temple, Bishop of Manchester, about the papers. Temple, who had been friendly, but regretted that Major had given a negative expression, defended the paper of R. G. Parsons, one of his Manchester incumbents.

Let us look at the two controversies which now went on. There was first the continuation of the controversy between Foakes Jackson and Lake and the Churchmen's Union. Major wrote to Foakes Jackson to assure him that his paper would be published with the others in the September *Modern Churchman*. Foakes Jackson was glad to hear this as he had felt there had been some reluctance on the part of the Modernists to put it in print. At the same time he complained that he had been treated discourteously by Glazebrook, though he felt that *hoi polloi* at the Conference were on his side. He said he had nearly left the Union but he had heard from a Ripon Hall student how Major had resisted Henson. He told Major that the last remarks in his speech at the Conference were prompted by Glazebrook saying it was a pity that Lake was still a Vice-President of the Union, since he was practically not a Churchman. But Foakes-Jackson was not content to have his apologia published in the *Modern Churchman*, he also wrote an article for the January number of the *Hibbert Journal,* where he accused the Modernists of wanting to substitute Jesuanity for Christianity. Perhaps if he were alive today he might make a similar criticism of Don Cupitt.[3] He went on:

> Modernist Churchmanship in England fails in two aspects. It is too rational and also too unscientific. In its desire to save Protestantism it has protested against the catholicism of the Anglican community, while its anxiety for the future of the Church has made its leaders repudiate those who are determined to follow criticism to the full. It will have to choose one side or the other, for the fence on which it is now sitting is giving way.[4]

Foakes-Jackson felt that Protestantism was losing ground, while the Anglo-Catholic party were gaining ground. They had had a great Congress in 1920. The Catholic party looked with more favour upon himself and Lake than on the Modern Churchmen's Union. Both Catholics and advanced New Testament critics were opposed to Liberal Protestantism. The former said, 'This is not the Christ I worship.' The latter said, 'This is not the Jesus of History.'

Dean Inge condemned both Foakes-Jackson and Lake and wrote in a letter to Major, 'I do not think Lake and his friends have any right to call themselves Christians', and added that there were some regrettable lapses in the Girton papers. Headlam wrote on 'The Modernist Christology' in the January number of the *Church Quarterly Review.* He said quite a lot in praise of the Girton Conference but made a devastating attack on Lake and Foakes-Jackson and called them (quite unjustly) second-rate scholars. H. L. Goudge, the Principal of Ely Theological College, wrote in the same number of the *Church Quarterly Review* and made a very interesting observation.

> Nothing at the Conference was more interesting . . . than the appearance of Dr. Foakes-Jackson. If he once belonged to the group, he does so no longer; and he appeared at the Conference as a sort of accusing historical conscience. He came as a visitor rather than a member, and his view rightly found no favour. But none the less he and his fellow-worker see what the others do not see – that the message of the Church as it appears in the New Testament is essentially Catholic, and that the fact

must be explained. If the view taken of our Lord by the Cambridge Conference is correct, the early Church and its Gospel ought to have been quite different from what we actually find it to have been. What for example ought St. Peter to have said at the Day of Pentecost? The centre of his teaching ought to have been the Fatherhood of God as the Lord had revealed it, and the need to love Him and our human brothers for His Sake . . . Yet St. Peter says not a word of all this . . . Their love for God and for our Lord is most ardent and puts ours utterly to shame; but it rests little upon God's Fatherhood, or upon the goodness displayed in the Lord's human life, but upon a mysterious salvation worked by the determinate counsel and foreknowledge of God, and by a Resurrection which had followed it. In a word they are Catholics and no religion other than Catholicism is discoverable in the New Testament.[5]

Here of course Goudge assumes – what most then believed – that Acts has the *ipsissima verba* of Peter.

What about Kirsopp Lake? He also wrote in the *Hibbert Journal.* In October 1924, in an article on Jesus, he defended himself and Foakes-Jackson from an attack by Inge in the second volume of *Outspoken Essays.*[6] In February 1927 Major tried to get Lake to speak at another Conference, but he was unable to come. After that the cleavage between him and English Modernism grew. In 1932 he wrote to have his name removed from the list of Vice-Presidents. His later position can be seen in his book, *Paul. His Heritage and Legacy* (1934). What Henson thought of this can be read in his diary:

> June 24th 1934.
>
> I finished reading Kirsopp Lake's latest book, *Paul; his heritage and legacy.* It is rather painful, and gives the impression of a man who is casting himself away in a kind of desperation. He has parted company with every recognizable version of Christianity.
>
> 'I do not believe [he writes] in the existence of any creator, and when I use the word "God", I mean the totality of values, not a person or a "personal being", who created values, which are eternal and neither created nor derived.'[7]

It is not surprising that Lake's chair at Harvard changed its title.

He began as 'Professor of Early Christian Literature'. This changed to 'Professor of Ecclesiastical History'. He ended as 'Professor of History'. He retired in 1938 and died in 1946. If Lake moved further away from traditional Christianity, I think I am not wrong in suggesting that Foakes-Jackson moved nearer it. Thus he dropped out of the editorship of *The Beginnings of Christianity*, his place being taken by H. J. Cadbury, author of *The Peril of Modernizing Jesus*. Moreover in 1938 we find him adding an approving preface to Percival Gardner Smith's *The Christ of the Gospels*, a book written from a Liberal Protestant angle. He died at the age of eighty-six in 1941 still a Fellow of Jesus College, Cambridge, though living most of the year in New York. In his obituary of him Major wrote, 'Research . . . was not really his sphere. His gifts were primarily those of an educationalist . . . It was said that there were at one time no less than ten Deans of Cambridge Colleges who had been tutored by Foakes-Jackson.'[8]

What about Rashdall? When the newspapers attacked him he began preaching sermons of defence. These sermons together with his original Conference paper were printed in his little book, *Jesus Human and Divine* (1922). He also replied to Gore's attack upon him in the *Church Times* of 23 September in articles in the *Modern Churchman* in December 1921 entitled 'Some Plain Words to Bishop Gore'. Some further plain words to Bishop Gore appeared in the *Modern Churchman* for April 1922, where he dealt mostly with Athanasius. A third article appeared in July 1922, where he interpreted St Thomas Aquinas. The articles on Athanasius and Aquinas were republished by Major and Cross in the volume of Rashdall's essays entitled *God and Man* (1930). It is interesting to discover that Vincent McNabb, the head of the Oxford Dominicans, supported Rashdall's interpretation of Aquinas, in an article in *Blackfriars*, reproduced in his collected essays, *From a Friar's Cell* (1923). Gore never replied to Rashdall who died in 1924 without anyone having attempted to arraign him for heresy.[9] Emmet died in 1923, Glazebrook in 1926, and Alfred Fawkes in 1930. Percy Gardner lived on until 1937, but remained silent about Girton 1921. No letters of his to Major about it survive, and he says nothing about it in his *Autobiographica*. In 1923 he resigned as President of the Churchmen's Union and Rashdall took over from him for the last year of his life. He was then succeeded by Dean Inge who was President from 1924 to 1934.

The one Conference speaker who was accused of heresy was Major, and then it was not on the basis of a sentence in his paper but because of a subsequent letter in the *Church Times*. Canon Peter Green attacked Major in the *Church Times* for 19 August 1921, when as yet the Conference papers were unpublished.

Perhaps we may take the opinion of the Rev. H. C. A. Major [*sic*] Principal of Ripon Hall, as expressing the views of the Conference. He said that Christ claimed to be the Son of God only 'in a moral sense, in the sense in which all human beings were sons of God, as standing in a filial and moral relationship to God, and capable of acting on those moral principles on which God acts.' Let us take that and see what modification it logically implies 'in what was once meant by Christianity', however little the members of the Conference may desire, or even realize such implication.

The Virgin Birth has, in this view, gone already. But surely the Resurrection must go too. Not merely gross views of a material resurrection (which in view of I Cor. xv.36–54, could never have been truly part of the Church's teaching), but all ideas of a resurrection at all. Christ surely must be held, if Mr Major is right, to have risen only 'in the sense in which all human beings' may be said to live again in their influence after death. Christ, that is to say, must be thought of as living in the minds of His followers as Shakespeare lives in the minds of deep students of poetry; He must be thought of as living in the Church as Napoleon lives in the 'Code Napoléon'.

With the Resurrection goes the Atonement. It is no more possible to think of Him 'dying for our sins' than to believe that He 'rose again for our justification'. Some efficacy may be allowed to his example, but even that is seriously affected . . .[10]

A great deal of correspondence then followed in the *Church Times*. Cyril Emmet defended the Conference, but it was not until 9 September that Major's reply was published. As the subsequent charge of heresy was based upon it I must quote it in full.

Ripon Hall,
Oxford,
September 5.

Sir,

I regret that pressure of work has prohibited until to-day my reading Canon Peter Green's article, 'Modernists at Cambridge', in your issue of August 19.

Canon Green credits me with various views on the strength of a brief quotation from a paper of 2,000 words in length and has, I regret to say, not only gone astray himself but may become the means of leading others astray.

He writes—

'But surely the Resurrection must go too. Not merely gross views of a material resurrection . . . but all idea of a resurrection at all. Christ surely must be held, if Mr Major is right, to have risen only in the sense in which all human beings may be said to live again in their influence after death. Christ, that is to say, must be thought of as living in the minds of His followers as Shakespeare lives in the minds of deep students of poetry; He must be thought of as living in the Church as Napoleon lives in the "Code Napoléon".'

These words are calculated to give your readers the impression that not only do I not believe in our Lord's Resurrection, but that I do not believe in the resurrection of Christians either. This I wish unreservedly to contradict. Canon Green's ingenious supposition that as I do not believe in the resurrection of the material body from the grave the only form in which I can believe in the resurrection is in the form in which Napoleon survives in the 'code Napoléon' suggests that he has never heard of a *tertium quid* – viz., the survival of death by a personality which has shed its physical integument for ever. This happens to be the form which the doctrine of the Resurrection assumes in my mind.

Perhaps, I ought to add, as Canon Green does not explicitly state it, that there was no reference to the Resurrection in my Conference paper, nor in any speech which I made at the Conference.

Henry D. A. Major

Peter Green wrote a reply in which he said that Major's conception of the resurrection represented 'a fairly adequate statement of the doctrine of immortality . . . But it is not what I believe of my Saviour, and I could not call it a statement, in any way adequate, of the Christian doctrine of the Resurrection'. He obviously conceded that Major believed in some form of life beyond the grave. Green then asked whether there was a sense in which Major could say that 'Christ is risen' in which he could not as truly say that 'St Paul is risen'. 'Certainly there is such a sense,' Major replied, 'Christ is risen to the right hand of God.' That could not be affirmed of Paul. Green replied, 'To suggest that our Lord may be said more truly to have risen than other men in that he occupies a more exalted place in Heaven is to empty the Easter message of all special significance and to make the Christian doctrine of Christ's Resurrection mean no more than the Doctrine (held by Jews, Mohammedans, and many other non-Christians) of Human Immortality.' He concluded that if this was the teaching being given to the students of Ripon Hall then he was dismayed.

It was not long before Bishop Burge of Oxford was reporting to Major that a priest from the diocese of Southwark, whom he had known when Bishop of that diocese, wished to arraign Major for heresy. This was the Rev C. E. Douglas, Curate of St Luke's, Camberwell, founder of the Faith Press. His brother J. A. Douglas was Vicar of St Luke's.[11] C. E. Douglas was for a long time Prolocutor in Convocation. His letter to Bishop Burge read as follows:

> I, Charles Edward Douglas, priest of the diocese of Southwark, in the Province of Canterbury, hereby accuse Henry Dewsbury Alves Major, priest of your Lordship's diocese in the same province, of openly teaching Doctrine concerning the Resurrection which is contrary to the Christian Religion as set forth:
>
> a. in the ancient Creeds of the said Province in the Book of Common Prayer,
> b. in Holy Scripture where the Resurrection of the Body is taught explicitly and is a vital element in the general theological and philosophical system.
>
> Further, I accuse Mr Major of importing the teaching of a

131

heathen mystic (Gautama) into the Christian religion without warrant or reason or of observed fact.

These accusations I am prepared to substantiate and, in accordance with canonical precedent, I require that your Lordship hold inquisition into the matter forthwith.

C. E. Douglas

When Burge sent the letter to Major he referred to Douglas as an 'earnest unbalanced fellow'. The Bishop now consulted Headlam, the Regius Professor of Divinity, who suggested that Douglas should be asked to withdraw the accusation, since it was ridiculous. 'Really Douglas seems to me to have gone out of his way to select one of the more orthodox of Major's utterances. If they care to delate the new number of the *Modern Churchman*, it might cause much more trouble, although I think the meeting on the whole constructive and some of the papers excellent. Emmet and Lightfoot have some admirable things in them.' In view of Headlam's letter, Burge asked Douglas to withdraw the charge, but he refused. Burge therefore was obliged to take further action. He suggested that Major should answer the charge and then he (Burge) would consult with a panel of theologians. One of the names suggested to him was Darwell Stone, the Principal of Pusey House, but Major objected that Stone was billed to speak at an English Church Union demonstration against Girton. Major suggested that Burge should consult the Oxford Professors, Headlam, Lock, Ottley, Watson and C. H. Turner. He added, 'An excellent precedent would be set for judgement in such cases; sound learning would be honoured; the Theological Faculty of the University would be gratified; and the question delivered from the fatal partizan ecclesiastical atmosphere.' In the end, Burge consulted all these Professors except Ottley.

Major now set to in order to refute the charge. He prepared a lengthy document of fifty-three typed pages. In this he was assisted by his student Charles Jenkinson, famous later for the Quarry Hill flats in Leeds, who after Girton had spent a great deal of time pasting on black sheets of paper all the newspaper cuttings about the Conference.[12] The defence was ready by 10 December – pretty quick work. Later it was printed by Blackwells under the heading *A Resurrection of Relics*. Major examined the teaching of notable Christians on resurrection from the first days until the twentieth century. I believe that he made use of the library of the Dominicans at Blackfriars. He showed how with certain brilliant exceptions, such as Origen, the general teaching of the Church on the resurrection up to the nineteenth century was thoroughly materialistic in character. When he got to the nineteenth century he quoted as what he considered authorities for his own enlightened view, F. D. Maurice, who had used the phrase 'resurrection of relics', Bishop Harvey Goodwin, Brooke Foss Westcott, Charles Gore, and in the twentieth century, Charles H. Robinson, Dean Beeching of Norwich, Hensley Henson, W. C. Allen (his old teacher), Bishop F. H. Chase (the opponent of Glazebrook), and Professor Bethune-Baker. He ended by saying, 'It is obvious that the traditional theory of the resurrection of the flesh is essentially a product of the thought, exegesis, and polemic of an age which has long passed away.' When he received the statement Burge said he would consult the Oxford Professors, but that he was being pestered with a flow of letters from Douglas asking him to get a move on. The matter did not get into the press until December 1921 when London and Yorkshire papers reported it.

Early in January Burge received the replies of the Oxford Professors. Turner had refused to judge the matter since he was a layman, and had already committed himself in a paper at the Anglo-Catholic Congress. Professors Headlam, Watson and Lock had examined the charge both separately and in consultation. In the light of what they said, Burge could not proceed with any charge, 'I am satisfied', he said in his official statement, 'that Mr Major's teaching is not in conflict with what Holy Scripture reveals to us of the Resurrection of the Body. I do not find that Mr Major denies the doctrine of the Resurrection of the Body: in fact he positively asserts his belief in "the full survival of all that constitutes whatever is essential to human personality, in short all that is meant by personal identity".' In due course Burge published his statement and the statements of the Oxford Professors and Major's statement.[13]

If Major was pleased with Burge, Douglas was full of wrath. The *Church Times* published the Bishop of Oxford's decision on 13 January. It pointed out that the judgement did not give any approval to the Girton papers or Major's introduction to them, and added that, though Major's language on the resurrection was not heretical it was 'temerarious'. Douglas now appealed against the decision to the Archbishop of Canterbury, Randall Davidson. Later in January the Archbishop spoke, 'The issue before me is a simple one. The Bishop of Oxford has with great care and after taking competent advice exercised a discretion which belongs to him as diocesan. I have neither the right nor the wish to interfere with the Bishop's action in the matter.' Douglas was flattened. On 27 January he wrote to the *Daily Telegraph*, 'It should be noted that this judgment deals only with the particular case and does not affect the subject of general ecclesiastical jurisdiction. With this reservation, I unhesitatingly accept his Grace's decision. Indeed, under present conditions it has been (to me) inevitable all along.' The *Church Times* also was flattened. On 3 February it said, 'We are of opinion that in some points Mr Douglas has acted with less than wisdom, and that in others he has been treated with less than fairness. Mr Major and several minors have secured from the incident a magnificent advertisement, and are pursuing their advantage with the zest of the Modern Publicist.'

Major certainly gained great notoriety at Oxford. Speaking years later at the Jubilee of Ripon Hall in 1948, Major remarked:

When we moved to Oxford I admit our Anglo-Catholic brethren did not welcome our arrival there. We bought the buildings of a former theological college, and a cross was removed from the entrance as it belonged to the former foundation. This immediately raised a storm of protest. We substituted in the place of the cross the horn of the Ripon municipality, and we put under the horn the motto, Nisi Dominus. I remember two clergymen remarking, 'You know how they translate that, "Everything except the Lord".' I can remember dining with a kind friend, Dr. A. J. Carlyle, and coming into the drawing room before dinner, he said, 'Pickard-Cambridge, you know Major.' Pickard-Cambridge said, 'Oh, yes, we all know the devil of Oxford.' Our rooms at the Hall looked into Wadham College, and on one occasion one of our number saw a great demonstration going on. Suddenly a white sheet fell over the window, and he saw the words, 'Major, anti-Christ'.

C. E. Douglas drowned his disappointment by publishing a little book, *The Redemption of the Body*, which consisted of four lectures on the resurrection, preceded by a preface by the Anglo-Catholic layman Hakluyt Egerton examining Bishop Burge's pamphlet.

Bishop Burge defended Major at a private meeting of the bishops in February 1922 when the Bishop of Gloucester, E. C. S. Gibson, author of a then well-known book on the Thirty Nine Articles, broached the matter. Burge pointed to Major's article in the *Hibbert Journal*, 'Modern Churchmen or Unitarians?'.[14] Later in the month he seemed to move back a bit when he suggested that Major might withdraw his introduction to the Girton papers since it was generally regarded as misleading. Major naturally refused.

In February the Girton Conference was attacked in Canterbury Convocation. On 15 February, the Bishop of Gloucester presented a petition from the English Church Union which made five accusations against the Conference number of the *Modern Churchman*. This contained these points: (1) The denial of the unique and distinctive character of the being of God; (2) The repudiation of the doctrine of the incarnation as taught in Creeds and Bible; (3) The substitution of the idea that a divine character was infused into a human person instead of the scriptural doctrine of the word being made flesh; (4) The repudiation of the authority of the Nicene Creed; (5) The desire expressed to abolish creeds or formulate new ones. On the same day in the Lower House Darwell Stone presented a gravamen signed by sixty members, which asked that the Upper House should declare the teachings of Girton to be contrary to the teaching of Bible and Church. Nothing was done until 2 May when the Bishop of Oxford, in the absence of the Bishop of Edmundsbury (A. A. David) brought forward a petition signed by forty-one very well known ecclesiastical persons. This asked that any attempt to condemn the Girton papers should be made in the proper ecclesiastical courts with chapter and verse clearly identified. This petition was, in fact, the work of the Council of the Churchmen's Union, though not everyone who signed it was a member of that body. A long debate followed. The result was the agreement upon a resolution which said that adhesion to the Nicene Creed – and in particular concerning the eternal pre-existence of the Son of God, his true

135

Godhead and his incarnation – was essential to the life of the Church; it recognized the value of fearless and reverent inquiry, but saw the danger of the publication of debatable suggestions as if they were ascertained truths. At the same time debates went on in York Convocation.

Randall Davidson now summoned Major to see him. In an autobiographical fragment, Major says that before he left home, his wife urged him to listen attentively to the Primate and not to argue with him. He continues,

> As I climbed the flight of stairs to the Primate's quarters at the end of the long gallery, I recalled a story Bishop Gore told of himself when making a similar ascent, 'Now Charles,' he said to himself, 'you are to be interviewed by Randall Davidson. You must be careful, you must be very careful what you say'; and then going down the stairs after the interview, 'Well, Charles you were not half careful enough.'

He went on to describe the interview, 'The Primate relaxed on a sofa. There was nothing aloof about him, certainly nothing archiepiscopal. He was dressed in an ordinary suit. His manner was not clerical, but simple and natural. Although Scotch by descent his accent was pure English. He was entirely delightful and made a very different impression from the Archbishop of York (Lang).' Major then recalled how he had been told by Foakes Jackson after the latter had stayed with Archbishop Lang at Bishopthorpe, 'Lang drives himself like an Archbishop. You should have seen him say "Goodnight" to his mother. Two feelings were struggling for supremacy. He could not forget she was his mother and he could not forget that he was an Archbishop.' 'Davidson was never anything but a kind, intelligent and modest man.' Major gave no detailed report of the discussion anywhere, but he recalled, 'On parting, the next day, his Grace said, "I know that I am no scholar and I know that I am no theologian, but I hold an ecclesiastical post of considerable responsibility and should wish to be consulted."'

While Davidson had been concerned with the Girton Conference, he had also been involved in consideration of the possibility of a Doctrinal Commission. It was undoubtedly Girton 1921 that clinched the matter. The initiative towards this began with Mr

Will Spens (as he was then), Fellow of Corpus Christi College, who approached Bishop Burge about the matter after the 1920 Anglo-Catholic Congress. Bishop Burge met with others and proposed a Doctrinal Commission of representatives of the Anglo-Catholic, Evangelical and Liberal schools of thought. The proposal was brought to Davidson in August 1921. He did not welcome it and much correspondence went on between him and Burge. An official letter asking for the Commission came to him in January 1922, signed by nine diocesan bishops, seventeen clergymen and one layman (Mr Will Spens). Amongst the liberals were Burge, Temple (though he ceased to be a liberal before long), Glazebrook, Raven, Guy Rogers and C. J. Shebbeare. Further correspondence followed and later in 1922 Davidson gave way. In a letter of 28 December 1922 he agreed to set up, with the Archbishop of York, a Doctrinal Commission and appended a number of names. The men named – there were no women – in due course joined the commission. Burge of Oxford, Temple of Manchester, Dean Burroughs of Bristol (later Bishop of Ripon), F. R. Barry, E. J. Bicknell, J. M. Creed, C. W. Emmet, H. B. Gooding, L. W. Grensted, W. L. Knox, W. R. Matthews, Walter Moberly, J. K. Mozley, O. C. Quick, A. E. J. Rawlinson, E. G. Selwyn, C. J. Shebbeare, Will Spens, Vernon F. Storr, B. H. Streeter, A. E. Taylor, L. S. Thornton, C. C. J. Webb, H. A. Wilson (later Bishop of Chelmsford). Rashdall had evidently been asked to serve on it but declined; he said he did not believe it was a good idea.[15] He died in the following year. The definite Modernists on it were Creed, Emmet, Matthews, Shebbeare and B. H. Streeter. Barry and Grensted were liberals and Storr a Liberal Evangelical but also a member of the Churchmen's Union. Raven was not placed on it – perhaps he had excluded himself through his strong advocacy of the ordination of women. Nor was Major on it. It was probably felt that he would be too aggressive and that his Vice-Principal, Emmet, would be more cautious. Emmet, however, soon died and was replaced by another Modernist, C. F. Russell. The last survivors from this body were Barry, Matthews, and Moberly, though they are all dead now. The late Dean Matthews wrote of the Commission in his *Memories and Meanings*:

It is clear that one of the dominant purposes of the archbishops in setting up the Commission was a practical one. The conflicting currents in the Church of England had become violent. The extremes at either end aimed at purging their opposites from the Church and both agreed that the majority who were attached to the middle way and hoped that they were both Catholic and Reformed were feeble compromisers. The expressed aim of the Commission was to formulate the limits within which disagreements were tolerable. The members included theologians of all hues except the orange of Fundamentalist Protestantism. Most welcome to me was the inclusion of professors of philosophy – all laymen: A. E Taylor, Professor in Edinburgh; Clement C. J. Webb, Nolloth Professor, Oxford; Professor W. H. Moberly of Birmingham; and Will Spens, a chemist who was Master of Corpus Christi College, Cambridge. One wonders whether a comparable number of Anglican lay philosophers could be gathered today to serve on a doctrinal commission.[16]

On the recent Doctrinal Commission there was but one layman – the philosopher J. R. Lucas – and, as on the previous Commission, no laywoman.

What I find rather puzzling is the lack of reference to the Doctrinal Commission in the *Modern Churchman* in 1923. After all, Major was in favour of the idea and indeed had advocated it long ago in 1911 at the time of the Thompson scandal.[17] Is it possible he was annoyed at not being included? He does, however, mention the Commission in an appendix to his *English Modernism*. The Commission did not report until 1938. Let us look at some of the main Modernist events between the setting up of the Commission and its report. There followed after Girton a large amount of anti-Modernist literature, of which the most substantial contribution was A. E. Harris' *Creeds or no Creeds* (1922) when he accused Major of having the Christology of Paul of Samosata.

In 1924 Major became a Doctor of Divinity at Oxford. His thesis was, from the point of view of New Testament criticism, the now rather conservative one that Mark's Gospel was the eyewitness testimony of Peter. It would seem today a rather slim piece for a D.D. but Professor Goudge accepted it. Major then published it as a Modern Churchman's Manual, *Jesus by an Eyewitness* (1925).

In 1925 Major was elected to the William Noble Belden Lectureship at Harvard. Both Dean Fremantle and Bishop Boyd Carpenter had been previous lecturers on the foundation. Major and his wife sailed to America in November 1925, leaving James Bezzant in charge of Ripon Hall. Bezzant was now Vice-Principal. Emmet had died in 1923 and Major had received several suggestions for a successor, among them E. C. Ratcliff, R. H. Lightfoot, Mervyn Haigh, L. W. Grensted, and V. J. K. Brook; but none of these would take it on, and his choice fell upon an old Riponian, A. T. W. Dowding; but his stay was brief, and in the end Major brought back James Bezzant from a curacy at Hartlebury. Bishop E. H. Pearce of Worcester was at first opposed to Bezzant's returning to Oxford after only a few months as deacon, saying he should have more parochial experience. Major then wrote and gave a list of first-class bishops who had not had any parochial experience. The Bishop of Worcester in his reply from Hartlebury Castle admitted the truth of Major's contention and added, 'If you had made a list of bishops of the second or third class it might have included myself.'

The Majors sailed for New York on the Minnesota on 7 November 1925. There is not time to speak at length of that visit. But Mrs Major's description of their first night in a New York Hotel ought to be heard.

> Our first night was a veritable nightmare. The ten dollar room was some 20 stories [*sic*] up. There are no bells but each room has a telephone but just at first we did not understand how to use it. Nor could we discover how to turn out the electric light. Something had gone wrong with the heating, for though we told the man who brought up our baggage to turn it off, it became each hour more intolerable. We opened wide the windows so as to be able to breathe & then could not hear ourselves speak for the roar of the traffic Then all night long fires seemed to be raging in the city. For above the noise of the traffic every now & then there were piercing shrieks & ringing of bells & screeching of sirens. It was so noisy and near that we thought the hotel was on fire & the inmates were all being

warned. Anyhow we felt nothing could be done. We were 20 stories up; we knew of no fire escape nor of any stairs so it was no use making investigations.

The Apostle of English Modernism survived that experience to visit the Union Seminary, with which he fell in love, and saw again his old friend Foakes Jackson. The Majors went on to Boston and there and on the way met many American Modernists including people who had been connected with Phillips Brooks and A. V. G. Allen. One of the men he met, Dr Karl Reiland, later was elected a Vice-President of the Modern Churchmen's Union as the Churchmen's Union was known after 1928. Though he travelled only in New England, Major was much impressed with American civilization, with its hospitality and its sanitation. When he returned his lectures were published as *English Modernism*. They remain the standard exposition of his position.

In 1926 came the publication of *Essays Catholic and Critical*. This was a volume by Anglo-Catholics, but important as showing how far they were prepared to go in the modernist direction. Major gave the book to James Bezzant to review for the *Modern Churchman* and he wrote at length and very favourably about it in the March 1927 issue. 'Their work', he said, 'testifies to the acceptance of Modernist principles, if not of what are regarded as Modernist views, in circles wherein even Modernists are apt to deny their existence.' The work contains the celebrated essay of Sir Edwyn Hoskyns on 'The Christ of the Synoptic Gospels' which has largely been accepted as proving that the Jesus of Liberal Protestantism cannot be found in any of the strands of the Synoptic sources. It also contained Kirk's criticism of Rashdall's book on the atonement.

In 1928 Major was asked to speak at the Church Congress at Cheltenham, as also were Bishop Barnes and B. H. Streeter. The Anglo-Catholics, led by Lord Halifax, made a protest. There was an enormous amount of controversy in the newspapers over Modernism. It was felt by Halifax that Modernist views should not be represented at the Congress as being inadmissible in the Church of England. Headlam, now Bishop of Gloucester (in succession to Gibson), the President, waved aside this protest. His letter to Lord Halifax appeared in *The Times* for 2 October. 'I often do not agree with Dr. Major,' he said, 'I dislike the tendency he shows to build up what may be called an Unorthodox Orthodoxy: I think sometimes he is nearly as dogmatic as his opponents: some of his language is precarious but I have found no evidence that he does not believe in the truth of the Incarnation.'[18] It is curious how the Cheltenham Congress row has been forgotten. The life of Headlam and the recent life of Barnes are the only books I know that refer to it. But at the time it filled the headlines – I have a whole large volume of newspaper cuttings about it.

The years 1927 – 8 saw all the Prayer Book controversies and the reaction of Modernists and Major in particular to them can be seen in the *Modern Churchman*. In an article 'The Composite Book from the Modernist Point of View' in March 1927 Major wrote, 'Taken all in all, the Composite Book provides much for which the Modernist may feel truly thankful. There are certainly some things retained, and even some things added, which he wishes the authorities had eliminated, i.e. the terrible word *satisfaction* retained in the Prayer of Consecration.' He was also a bit worried about the precautions taken against the abuse of reservation, but not perhaps as worried as Bishop Barnes whose attacks on the Deposited Book helped to defeat it.

At the end of 1928 the Majors went to New Zealand for a visit of several months. They had not been back since they had left in 1902. Major's fame as a Modernist went before him, since he had just been involved in the Cheltenham Congress controversy, but his Modernism would hardly make much appeal in Australia (which he visited on the way) or New Zealand. However he was welcomed as one who had grown up there and was the most distinguished ex-resident of Kati-Kati. Major tried to strike the note of simplicity, and this can be seen in the sermons he delivered there which were published under the title *Thirty Years After. A New Zealander's Religion*. The expedition at least enabled Major to visit all his old haunts, none of which was he to see again.[19]

Major had moved his private residence from Bagley Wood to Eastleach Turville in the Cotswolds where he purchased a most beautiful cottage in country associated with John Keble and right by Keble's Bridge. Major always had great respect for John Keble, and took pride in the fact that his mother had spoken as a child to the Oxford Tractarian. However he was anxious to strengthen his position by becoming a country incumbent again. Major's Oxford College, Exeter, was seeking an incumbent for the little living of Merton near Bicester, which had been held by an advanced High Churchman, and was hardly as attractive a place to reside in as the Cotswolds. High Churchmen now protested against the introduction of a Modernist there. One of the vocal opponents was Dr Scott, the Rector of nearby Oddington, an authority on the Eastern Orthodox Church and its relations with Rome. *The Referee* protested in these words:

> This presentation creates a graver issue than Dr. Major's appearance at the Church Congress. The objection then was that the Church Congress chose him and other Modernists as representative exponents of the Church of England teaching. Now, by being instituted by a Bishop to a cure of souls, it will be claimed that he has the sanction of the Church for his teaching.

The Bishop of Oxford was now Tommy Strong, who had succeeded Burge in 1925. He also succeeded Burge as Warden of Ripon Hall. Protests against Major's appointment came to the Bishop. He wrote to Major, who refused to make any special declaration in response to the agitation and simply submitted to Strong some of his published statements. A great deal of correspondence in the *Church Times* followed, but Strong had no hesitation in inducting Major to the living on 31 January 1930.

The Conferences of Modern Churchmen continued each summer through these years between the setting up of the Doctrine Commission and its report of 1938. In 1925 at Oxford the subject was 'The Faith of a Modern Churchman'; while at Girton, in 1926, they devoted their time to the Sacraments. In 1927, at Selly Oak, Birmingham, they had a Conference on 'The Modern Movement in the English Church', which had a paper on 'Intellectual Causes of the Modern Movement' by a newcomer to Modernism John Sandwith Boys Smith, who years later became Master of St John's College, Cambridge and now lives in retirement at Saffron Walden.[20] The Conference which received most press coverage was that of 1930 when the subject was 'Problems of Personal Life'. Perhaps the choice of subject was due to the fact that Dr Douglas White was now Chairman of the Council of the Modern Churchmen's Union in succession to

Glazebrook. Dr W. F. Geikie-Cobb spoke on Marriage and Divorce in the Modern State. There were two papers on Birth Control, one by Mrs J. L. Stocks on its social aspects and one by C. J. Bond on medical aspects. It will be recalled that this was the year of the Lambeth Conference which gave some very grudging acceptance of birth control and roused a great deal of controversy. The 1932 Conference was devoted to the Reformation and the 1934 Conference to 'The Bible and the Modern Man'. The subject in 1935 was 'The Church of England; its constitution, character and call'.

The year 1932 saw the publication of a new series of Modernist Manuals, produced by Skeffington and Son. Six of these were published. The first was by Major himself *The Church's Creeds and the Modern Man*. The second was by J. C. Hardwick, who had been Chaplain of Ripon Hall, and was now Vicar of Partington in Cheshire, on *Freedom and Authority in Religion*. The third was by T. F. Royds, Rector of Haughton in Staffordshire, on *Sorrow, Sin and Suffering*.[21] The fourth was by Dr Douglas White on *Modern Light on Sex and Marriage*, which doubtless today seems very old fashioned, but did not then. The fifth was by R. Gladstone Griffith on *The Necessity of Modernism*. The sixth was the most notable of these books, R. D. Richardson's *The Gospel of Modernism*. Richardson's book went into a very much expanded second edition in 1935 and can, like Major's *English Modernism*, be regarded as one of the textbooks on the English Modernist Movement. Bishop Barnes endorsed it with a Foreword and this had repercussions in his diocese.[22]

Modernists in 1932 were very much involved in what became known as the Liverpool scandal. Liverpool had a Liberal Evangelical Bishop in A. A. David, who had been translated from St Edmundsbury, and a Liberal Dean in Dean Dwelly. Charles Raven, a Modernist, was also a member of the Chapter until in this year 1932 he returned to Cambridge as Regius Professor of Divinity. The scandal arose through the invitation of two Unitarian clergymen, Laurence Redfern and the well known L. P. Jacks, Principal of Manchester College, to occupy the Liverpool Cathedral pulpit, though not at statutory services. Lord Hugh Cecil led the objectors and Hensley Henson at Durham added fuel to the fire. Major in the *Modern Churchman* was full of praise for

Liverpool and its friendliness towards Nonconformists. Dean Inge, the President of the Modern Churchmen's Union, likewise supported Liverpool, and recorded in his diary for 5 February 1934, 'I found that Herbert Henson was annoyed with me for approving of the invitation to a Unitarian to preach in Liverpool Cathedral. I have never read better sermons than those of J. H. Thom, a Unitarian divine, and Martineau's books are of great apologetic value. I have never found much to differ from in my talks with Jacks, though he goes too far, in my opinion, with Loisy about the historical Christ.[23] Surely there are many subjects on which an Anglican congregation might profit by sitting under a devout and thoughtful Unitarian, or a Quaker. I am all in favour of trying to close schisms, if it can be done without sacrifice of principle. I think an earlier Henson would have agreed with me.'[24]

But if the Modern Churchmen were ready to listen to Unitarians they were not much interested in the commemoration of the Oxford Movement in 1933. On 12 October 1932 Inge wrote in his diary, 'A committee meeting of the Modern Churchmen's Union to decide whether we should take any part in the commemoration of the Oxford Movement. Opinion was divided; I think I turned the scale in deciding that as a Society we should not associate ourselves with it. When we consider the attitude of the Tractarians towards any kind of Liberalism in theology, it seems absurd that we should profess sympathy with them.'[25] What Bishop Barnes thought of Newman and the Oxford Movement can be seen in the recent life.[26]

Ripon Hall was flourishing under Major, in spite of his increasing deafness, but it became apparent, late in 1932, that the University wanted to purchase its buildings to extend the Bodleian Library. Hence a search started for new premises. Major tried unsuccessfully to buy Frewin Hall and there was also talk of taking on Sir William Osler's house near St Stephen's House in Norham Gardens. In the end they were persuaded by Dr R. W. Macan, who had been Master of University College, Oxford, and was a leading Modernist, and lived in retirement on Boar's Hill, to purchase Foxcombe, the residence of Lord Berkeley, which had been empty for many years.[27] Lord Berkeley had built his mansion on to a smaller house which had been put up by H. G. Woods, President of Trinity, at the end of the nineteenth century as a retreat where his wife could write rather indifferent novels. H. G. Woods had been a notable liberal churchman, Barnes' predecessor as Master of the Temple, and according to Sir John Barnes had a reputation as a dull preacher.[28] Obviously the move brought controversy amongst Modernists. Foxcombe was a lovely and spacious site but it took the college several miles out of Oxford. In some sense they were biting off more than they could chew. Boar's Hill at any rate was the final resting place of Boyd Carpenter's foundation until it united with Cuddesdon in the 'seventies. A fire which occurred soon after the move enabled useful reconstruction to be done.

It is fascinating to the historian of New Testament scholarship to discover that the New Testament scholar who spoke at the Modern Churchmen's Conference of 1914, viz. Sir Edwyn Hoskyns who then parted with Modernism, and the New Testament Scholar who spoke in 1921 and then would have nothing further to do with it, R. H. Lightfoot, occupied the forefront of biblical scholarship in the 'thirties. The views of both men proved unacceptable to the majority of Modernists. In 1935 Lightfoot's famous Bampton Lectures – a book which ought to be reprinted – were published under the title *History and Interpretation in the Gospels*. They were a decided acceptance of the standpoint of the German scholar Wilhelm Wrede and the Form Critics, Bultmann and Dibelius. Major read them, received a shock, and was totally bewildered for he had accepted Sanday's dismissal of Wrede. In his review of them 'The Latest Phase of Gospel Criticism', he wrote as follows in the *Modern Churchman* for June 1935, the number which also reported the death of Professor Burkitt:

Plain men and women, if ever they read this volume, may be much disconcerted by it. They really ought not to be so. It is by no means assured that the Form-critics in what is really original in their contributions, can be relied on. In the estimation of many eminent New Testament scholars the historical element in the Gospels is very much larger than the Form-critics are disposed to admit. Criticism has been carried by them to what some will regard as absurd lengths. They perhaps need to be criticized in their turn after the manner in which Archbishop Whatley criticized contemporary historical scepticism in his famous pamphlet, Historic Doubts as to the existence of Napoleon Buonaparte. The writer of this article sat at the feet of a distinguished New Testament scholar who used to insist that 'the critical faculty, when it is once aroused in this kind of work, cannot be repressed. When there is no more wheat to gather, then it collects chaff.'

But suppose the reverent agnosticism of our Form-critics is justified at the bar of history, it will not follow that we have necessarily lost the Christian religion in its most essential form. It may be that these critics have completed the work of the liberation of that religion from the limitations and swathing bands of the past. God the Creator may be unknown and unknowable. God the Incarnate Son may be a myth and an illusion; but God the indwelling Spirit remains to us. He is ours and we are His. This suffices.

Major now prepared to restate his own beliefs about the Gospels and prepared the massive work, which he and Riponians called the 'Pedestrian', *The Mission and Message of Jesus* (1937). He assigned the sayings of Jesus to the notable New Testament scholar T. W. Manson, and allocated the Fourth Gospel to C. J. Wright, a Methodist, who had written a doctoral thesis on the miracles which Major had examined and which was later published as *Miracle in History and in Modern Thought* (1930). Later Wright became an Anglican and fell foul of Archbishop Fisher while on the staff of St Augustine's College, Canterbury. In this work Major dealt with the Gospel of Mark and the narrative parts of Luke and Matthew. The Form Critics had not caused Major to alter his opinions, because he calls Mark's Gospel, 'My year with the Lord Jesus. The Reminiscences of Peter, His chief apostle, reported and translated by his Dragoman, John Mark for Christians in Rome.'

There were, however, younger Modernists, who were prepared to be more sympathetic to this latest phase of Gospel criticism. One of these was Professor J. M. Creed, whose commentary on St Luke's Gospel had been a notable theological publication of 1930. There was also H. K. Luce's Cambridge commentary on St Luke of 1933. Luce, like Major, was an Examining Chaplain to Bishop Barnes of Birmingham. On Good Friday, 30 March 1934, Bishop Hensley Henson read this book and was horrified.

From the standpoint of the Humanitarians what special and perpetual significance can the Crucifixion of Jesus be said to possess? The critics have passed their rough desecrating hands over the Evangelical narratives, and left little in them of all that has most touched the hearts of men. I read through the Cambridge Commentary on the Passion Chapters in St. Luke's Gospel and realized how spiritually desolating is the method of Bible study which it represents. At every point the Editor quotes with approval some destructive comment from a modern scholar, generally the Liberal Jew, Montefiore, or the ex-Roman Catholic Modernist, Loisy. 'A sublime touch but probably not historic', is the note on the words, 'the Lord turned and looked on Peter'. The dramatic episode in which Barabbas is preferred to Jesus is 'somewhat unlikely'.

The whole account of Pilate's contact with the people is contained in a narrative which 'it is impossible to accept as history'. The wailing of the women 'is probably unhistorical', being made up of a number of O.T. reminiscences. The words, 'Father, forgive them, for they know not what they do', are marked as doubtful. But whether the words are part of Luke or not, they are entirely characteristic of the spirit of Christianity, and of Jesus Himself. Even if not historical, they are a supreme tribute to his memory. The mockery by the soldiers is unlikely. The touching record of the two robbers 'seems to be rather in the realm of legend than of history.' It is difficult to make devotional use of a Sacred Scripture which is thus to be regarded.[29]

Henson also took Luce to task for the appendix in which he gave his Christology, which was exactly the Christology of Girton, but which Henson seemed unable to accept. In the *Modern Churchman* Luce's volume was reviewed by the young Hedley Sparks, a protégé of Major. He was certainly not appalled like Henson. He wrote, 'This is undoubtedly the best commentary for its size on any part of Holy Scripture that it has been my pleasure to read – full of information, always concise, absolutely up to date, above all fundamentally healthy . . . Mr. Luce's book is an excellent piece of work.'[30] If Henson was horrified over Luce, he was not very pleased with the Report on Doctrine which Modernists regarded as a triumph, to which we shall return in the next chapter, and was even more displeased at *The Rise of Christianity*, by Bishop Barnes, to whom Luce had dedicated his commentary, and which many Modernists regarded as an embarrassment.

NOTES

1 Quoted in *Modern Churchman* (Oct. 1920), p.359.

2 ibid., pp.360f.

3 See Don Cupitt, *The Debate about Christ*, p.139, 'The historical Jesus is the real Christ for today.'

4 *Hibbert Journal* (Jan. 1922), p.205.

5 *Church Quarterly Review*, vol. xciii (Jan. 1922), pp.205f.

6 This article of Lake's was republished in the Jubilee Number of the *Hibbert Journal* (July 1952), pp.348–58. In the same volume Major's article 'Modern Churchmen or Unitarians?' was republished.

7 See *The Retrospect of an Unimportant Life*, vol. ii, p.324. For the words of Lake see his *Paul*, pp.85f.

8 See *Modern Churchman* (Dec. 1956), pp.329f.

9 A. M. Ramsey suggests that the answer to Rashdall is in E. J. Bicknell's note, 'The Trinitarian Doctrine of Augustine and Aquinas', in *Essays Catholic and Critical*, pp.148–50.

10 *Church Times*, 19 August 1921.

11 For C. E. Douglas, see *Parson and Parish* (October 1965), p.28.

12 For Jenkinson, see the life by H. J. Hammerton, *This Turbulent Priest* (1952).

13 H. M. Burge, *The Doctrine of the Resurrection of the Body* (1922).

14 *Hibbert Journal*, Jan. 1922.

15 P. E. Matheson, *The Life of Hastings Rashdall*, p.228.

16 op. cit., pp.144f.

17 See *Modern Churchman*, vol. i, pp.242f.

18 See R. Jasper, *Arthur Cayley Headlam*, p.335.

19 It is interesting to discover that he was not asked to preach at his old college – St John's College, Auckland. Was he thought too unorthodox?

20 In 1930 J. S. Boys Smith wrote *Christian Doctrine and the Idea of Evolution* (a pamphlet).

21 For Thomas Fletcher Royds, see his *Haughton Rectory or Four Country Parsons* (1953).

22 See John Barnes, *Ahead of His Age*, p.294.

23 Jacks was responsible for translations into English of Loisy's works.

24 *Diary of a Dean*, p.177.

25 *Diary of a Dean*, p.167.

26 John Barnes, *Ahead of His Age*, p.292.

27 For Reginald Walter Macan, see *Modern Churchman* (Dec. 1956), pp.309–14. Macan's book, *The Resurrection of Jesus Christ* (1877), lost him the favour of Pusey. He lived till 1941.

28 John Barnes, *Ahead of His Age*, p.78.

29 *Retrospect of an Unimportant Life*, vol. ii, pp.317f.

30 *Modern Churchman*, vol. xxv, pp.51f.

7

Modernism in the 'Thirties and 'Forties. Doctrine Report and Bishop Barnes' 'The Rise of Christianity'

In our excursion into the history of English Modernism we deal in this chapter with the Report of the Commission on Doctrine of 1938 and then turn to Bishop E. W. Barnes of Birmingham and his notorious book, *The Rise of Christianity* (1947).

We saw how the Commission on Doctrine was appointed in 1922, following upon the Girton Conference, and how Modernists were represented upon it, as well as Evangelicals and Anglo-Catholics, but not extreme Fundamentalists. When the report came out in the year 1938, it was greeted by Modernists as a victory for their party. In the previous year there had been a crisis in English Modernism. Again it was a battle, as at Girton in 1921, and as at Ripon in 1914, between Liberal Protestants and Catholic Modernists. It involved the President of the Modern Churchmen's Union, Walter R. Matthews, who had succeeded W. R. Inge both as Dean of St Paul's and as President of the Modern Churchmen's Union. The trouble arose over the Report on negotiations between the Church of England and the Rumanian Church which came out in 1936.[1] A Committee of the Modern Churchmen's Union examined the report and a memorandum on it drawn up by Max Dunlop, who had been Tutor of Ripon Hall and was then Vicar of West Hendred (Emmet's old parish). This memorandum, which expressed some unhappiness over the eucharistic doctrine countenanced by the negotiators at Bucharest and felt it was out of step with Anglican doctrine, was examined at the meeting of the Council of the Modern Churchmen's Union on 19 January 1937. Controversy followed, the details of which I was given by the late Rev. T. J Wood, Secretary of the Modern Churchmen's Union from 1927, when he succeeded the Rev. John R. Bentley, till 1940. I also heard about it from Dean Matthews himself, though he is silent about it in his autobiography.[2] Most of the members of the council supported the memorandum, but Matthews objected to it as insufficiently positive and seeming to militate against the Anglo-Catholics. So strong were his feelings that he withdrew from the meeting and on the next day resigned as President of the Union. Others supported him and resigned their positions on the Council. These were the Chairman of the Council, Edward St George Schomberg, Master of the Charterhouse, the Rev. H. R. L. Sheppard (Dick Sheppard), Canon Harold Anson, the Master of the Temple, the Ven. M. W. Browne, Archdeacon of Rochester and Dr Norman Sykes, then Professor of History in the University of London. The Dean put his view of the situation in *The Times* for 3 February. It became clear that the rift went deeper than the question of the Rumanian church.

> We are anxious for a wider and more tolerant form of Modernism, which shall include Anglo-Catholic Modernists as well as Liberal Evangelicals.
>
> We feel ourselves often out of sympathy with the line taken by the *Modern Churchman*, which, although not under the control of the Union, is generally thought by the public to be its official organ.
>
> We realize how much the *Modern Churchman* has done for the Union, but we feel that a wider Modernism, which interests itself perhaps less with academic theology and more with those issues which fill the thoughts of the younger generation, is the need of our age, and the cause to which we want to give whatever energies we have.

Clearly it was felt that Major was being too much of a Pope in Modernism. He now had a rebellion on his hands. He and other leading Modernists replied in *The Times* on 13 February.

> No member of the Council desires that the union should be exclusively Protestant in colour. It never has been nor is it likely to become so. Anglo-Catholics have always been welcome, and they will be no less welcome in the future. But it ought to be clear that no one will be likely to feel at home in the union unless he is liberal in his conception of the character of the Christian Church as well as in doctrine. That is the immediate cause of the divergence between the minority and the majority

of the council. The majority were as eager as the minority for intercommunion with the Rumanian church. They objected, however, to intercommunion being based on an alleged doctrinal agreement.

At a meeting of the Council on 9 March a committee was appointed to meet with the Dean and the other malcontents to see if the breach could be mended. At that meeting Major was criticized for his tight control on the *Modern Churchman* and the Conferences of Modern Churchmen. Major's letter to the *Guardian* of 19 March did not help matters, when he said:

> Anglo-Catholicism is the dominant power in the Church to-day, and Socialism is the coming power in the State. It is therefore natural enough that the circumspective and forward glancing eye of Dean Matthews should desire to see the M.C.U. more Anglo-Catholic and more Socialist than it is. But whilst there is a place and a welcome for all Anglo-Catholics and for all Socialists who wish to join the M.C.U., they must find their spiritual home there not because they are Anglo-Catholics or because they are Socialists, but because they are Liberal or Modernist Churchmen.

On 19 March Matthews replied with an article in the *Spectator* on 'The Dilemma of Modernism', which summed up the real cause of the whole controversy.

> The Modernist movement in England today is to a large extent, though not entirely, derived from two different and partly incompatible sources. There are those who derive inspiration from Protestantism of the end of the nineteenth century, which found its most persuasive expression in Harnack's famous lectures, *Das Wesen des Christentums.* There are others who have an intellectual and spiritual affinity with those thinkers to whom the name 'Modernists' was first applied – the Roman Catholic scholars who, in opposition to Harnack and Liberal Protestantism, believed that it was possible to interpret the Christian dogmatic system, constitution and worship, in the light of modern conceptions. These men were not indifferent to Biblical criticism, indeed they were often more radical in their treatment of Christian origins than their Protestant adversaries.

They held, however, that the Church was an essential element in the complex which is called Christianity and that its continuous life and experience was the datum for all efforts towards reinterpretation and reconstruction. It is well known that these ideas could find no permanent home in the Roman Church, and were, condemned as the 'synthesis of all heresies', but they have not been killed; they have found a more congenial environment in the Anglican Church . . . The Liberal Protestant tends to become impatient with the Catholic Modernist when the latter finds meaning in the traditional forms of worship and values mythological statements as vehicles of religious truth. The Catholic Modernist, on the other hand, is tempted to wonder whether his Protestant brother has sufficiently pondered the relation between religion and poetry.

Eventually a compromise was patched up between the disputing parties. Matthews, however, did not withdraw his resignation of the post of President and in the end Sir Cyril Norwood, then President of St John's College, Oxford, was elected to replace him. Other names that had been suggested were Charles Raven, Major, Bishop Barnes and the Bishop of St Edmundsbury (W. G. Whittingham). Really the trouble had been brewing earlier since before the Rumanian crisis it had been agreed that there should be another Modern Churchmen's Union publication alongside the *Modern Churchman*. This was a quarterly journal called *The Way*, edited at first by Kenneth Budd and later by an Oxford don, Henry Paul Kingdon, which went on until 1942. It was aimed at being a forum for the sort of articles that Major might refuse for the *Modern Churchman*. What Dean Inge thought of it in his retirement at Brightwell Manor can be seen in a letter he penned to Major on 29 April 1937.

To what extent is the MCU implicated in a Bolshevist rag called 'The Way'. Its object is plainly to entangle the Society in revolutionary propaganda. Nothing could be more alien to the objects of the Society, and to the principle which has always guided it – to keep clear of politics.

Let us now look a bit more at the general theological background when the Doctrine Report was published. As we saw last time, there was the appearance of advocates of Form Criticism in the Church, of whom the chief was the ex-Modernist, R. H. Lightfoot. We saw last time the horror with which Major greeted it.

Another background was the Oxford Group Movement, started by the controversial American Frank Buchman, and later known as Moral Rearmament or MRA. One notable Modernist, B. H. Streeter, was won over by the movement, but he and his wife met their deaths in a plane accident in Switzerland in September 1937.[3] Geoffrey Allen found inspiration in the movement, as one can see in his book, *He that Cometh* (1930), written when he was Chaplain of Lincoln College, Oxford. Major defended the Group from the attacks of the Bishop of Durham, but there was no wholesale espousing of the Group movement by Modernists.

Then there was the Barthian movement which brought to many men and women a renewed realization of the transcendence of God. The emergence of Bathianism in this country is generally linked with the publication in 1933 of Sir Edwyn Hoskyns' translation of Barth's *Epistle to the Romans*. It is well known that Barth's condemnation of natural religion and his emphasis on revelation produced opposition from the Modernist Charles Raven. Dillistone in his life of Raven speaks of Cambridge in the 'thirties as divided in its allegiance between Raven at Christ's and Hoskyns at Corpus.[4] This is denied by Vidler in his review of Dillistone's book,[5] and Gordon S. Wakefield in *Theology* for November 1975 rather supports Vidler and suggests the cleavage was between Hoskyns and Bethune-Baker.[6] At any rate Major called the Barthian movement 'the revolt from reason' and 'the great blight'. But some Modernists like Geoffrey Allen were influenced by it.

Akin to the Barthian movement was the biblical theology movement. Here again the father-figure was Hoskyns, the ex-Modernist. His leading disciple was A. M. Ramsey whose book *The Gospel and the Catholic Church* was an important contribution in 1936. He took things a stage further in his inaugural lecture at Durham in 1940 on *Jesus Christ in Faith and History*. One might have thought that Bishop Henson would have been pleased with this move from history to theology, but not so. He wrote to Dean Alington:

Does he [i.e. Ramsey] really understand historical method? Does he imagine that History can be seriously handled under the domination of theological assumptions? To my mind Theology cannot *begin* its work until History has provided so much of its material as is properly called '*historical*'.[7]

Yet another background was the liturgical movement, and especially the Parish and People movement, which has recently been chronicled by Peter Jagger.[8] In this the Kelham Father, Gabriel Hebert, played a leading part and his *Liturgy and Society* (1935) remains a great and important book, which the late Ernest Southcott said every clergyman should read every year. Hebert was of course hostile to Modernists and says on p.179 of his book, 'The utterances of Modernism as represented by the *Modern Churchman* are not those of men beset by intellectual difficulties and hazardly impudent hypotheses; they reflect a dogmatism which is satisfied that it has comprehended all that orthodoxy has to say and propounds an alternative teaching.' Hebert like Ramsey was to play an important part in the biblical theology movement, though today he has largely been forgotten, and I doubt whether his books on the Bible are much read.

There was also the influence of the theology of Reinhold Niebuhr and his emphasis on the sinfulness of man. We can see the impact made upon one liberal (though not an Anglican Modernist), D. R. Davies, who describes his return to orthodoxy and transfer to the Church of England in his *In Search of Myself* (1961).

Finally there was the movement in philosophy known as logical positivism which ruled out the possibility of theological statement and was sparked off by A. J. Ayer's *Language, Truth and Logic* in 1936. Not long after its publication Ian Ramsey enrolled as a student of Ripon Hall. He was to spend the greater part of his life showing the necessity of 'odd' language to create a 'disclosure' situation in which God could be revealed.[9]

Such was the atmosphere when the Doctrine Report came out in 1938. At that time the Anglican theologians most widely read were Oliver Chase Quick, whose *The Doctrines of the Creed* (1938) and *Christian Sacraments* (1927) are still probably read today,[10] and W. R. Matthews the ex-President of the Modern Churchmen's Union. Matthews' books *God in Christian Thought and Experience, Studies in Christian Philosophy* and *The Purpose of God* were all widely read in the 'thirties and 'forties. Clearly Matthews was what Winnington Ingram called 'an orthodox Modernist'. Both Quick and Matthews were on the Doctrine Commission.

When the Commission's first chairman, Bishop Burge, died in 1925, William Temple became his successor. He had a great deal to do with the actual writing of the Report and contributed an Introduction. The Report, a document of 242 pages, was in four sections: (1) The Sources and Authority of Christian Doctrine. (2) The Doctrine of God and Redemption. (3) The Church and the Sacraments. (4) Eschatology. Modernists came to regard this document as giving them a justification for their existence in the Church of England. This is, presumably, why Roger Lloyd, who was hostile to Modernism when he wrote his book *The Church of England in the Twentieth Century*, completely ignored the Report in that book. Let us look at the passages which Modernists delighted to quote. First miracles. Temple in his Introduction, wrote:

> On the question whether or not events occur which are strictly miraculous, the Commission is divided; but the reluctance of some to admit miraculous events, or the strictly miraculous character of events admitted, is based on the supposition, not that God *could* not do such works, but that he *would* not.[11]

Then in the Report itself was the statement on the Virgin Birth on page 82.

> There are, however, some among us who hold that a full belief in the historical Incarnation is more consistent with the supposition that our Lord's birth took place under the normal conditions of human generation. In their minds the notion of a Virgin Birth tends to mar the completeness of the belief that in the Incarnation God revealed Himself at every point in and through human nature.

The Resurrection was dealt with on p.84.

> To speak more positively, we are of opinion that it ought to be affirmed that Jesus was veritably alive and victorious; that He showed Himself alive from the dead, to the disciples; and that the fact of His rising, however explained (and it involves

probably an element beyond our explaining), is to be understood to have been an event as real and concrete as the crucifixion itself (which it reversed) and an act of God, wholly unique in human history. The symbol of this fact in the Gospels is the story of the empty tomb. More than one explanation of this has been suggested; but the majority of the Commission are agreed in holding the traditional explanation – viz., that the tomb was empty because the Lord had risen.

On p.209 they spoke about the resurrection of Christians. 'While, in the judgment of the Commission, we ought to reject quite frankly the literalist belief in a future resurrection of the actual physical frame which is laid in the tomb, it is to be affirmed, none the less, that in the life of the world to come the soul or spirit will still have its appropriate organ of expression and activity, which is one with the body of earthly life in the sense that it bears the same relation to the same spiritual entity.' That vindicated Major.

What was the reaction to the Report? The *Church Times* on 16 January called it a 'momentous document'. 'Not since the 16th century has a body of doctrine been set forth on behalf of the Church of England of such intrinsic importance or of such profound weight . . . Charles Gore would have found a number of points in the Report with which he would certainly have disagreed, and at which he would have been profoundly grieved. But we are certain that the Report, as a whole, would have been hailed by him with exultant satisfaction.' Canon Peter Green writing several articles on it in the *Church Times* welcomed it and said we could thank God for it. The *Observer* said, 'Few pronouncements backed by any kind of ecclesiastical authority have faced more candidly the points of collision between Christian tradition and the modern mind.' Dean Inge in the *Church of England Newspaper* said the Report had 'a somewhat more liberal appearance than the majority of members probably desired'. On the other hand the Evangelical Church Association heavily criticized the document and its setting aside of the Thirty-Nine Articles. In the *Church Times* for 28 January there were pieces on it by the Anglo-Catholic N. P. Williams and Major. Williams was pleased that the Commission had accepted prayers for the dead, the invocation of saints, and confession, but he did not relish the idea of the Commission admitting that some members did not believe in the virgin birth or empty tomb. Major naturally was full of praise for the report. Its treatment, he said, was essentially modern. (1) It was critical. (2) It was evolutionary. (3) It was psychological. (4) It was essentially English in that (a) it was comprehensive and (b) marked by a real spirit of English liberalism. (c) It was English in its timidity, in its spirit of compromise and robust optimism, its belief that somehow, somewhere, somewhen, our present antitheses would be sublimated into a higher synthesis.'

Henson criticized the Report for falling too much into the hands of Anglo-Catholics, but Matthews repudiated this charge in a letter in the *Sunday Times*. Roman Catholics were horrified by the document. The *Universe* said, 'We beg them [Anglicans] to read it and ponder it and ask themselves if the picture it presents corresponds to anything history has ever known as Catholic truth and doctrine.'

A younger Modernist, James Bezzant, Raven's successor as a Canon of Liverpool, wrote of it in the *Guardian*: 'When first I read the report I had an impression that it was rather little for which to have waited so long . . . A more careful reading of the report in the light of that limitation has convinced me that the commission has succeeded beyond what I should have predicted and thought possible . . . In my judgement those who call themselves or are called Modernists will receive the report as the most important landmark in the progress of true liberalism since the Reformation.'

E. G. Selwyn, the Anglo-Catholic Dean of Winchester, one of the Commissioners, answered criticisms in the *Guardian* and said of the virgin birth that 'the commission consider that the symbolic truth of the Virgin Birth was felt to be more important than the historical, and that if some people regarded the infancy narrative as poetry rather than as history, that need not discourage us too much provided that they affirmed wholeheartedly the truth represented in these miracles, namely that He Who was born at Bethlehem was Very God of Very God.' Perhaps it is not surprising to find Dean Inge writing in his book *Our Present Discontents*, 'The MCU has very little to fight about. Our occupation is gone.'[12]

However in spite of the satisfaction of N. P. Williams and Peter Green and E. G. Selwyn, there was opposition to the Report from many Anglo-Catholics, particularly in the religious communities. Evangelicals joined up with Anglo-Catholics in a petition to Canterbury Convocation. The leading opponents of the Report were C. M. Chavasse, Master of St Peter's Hall, Oxford, and H. M. Hinde, an Evangelical, and the Anglo-Catholics, E. D. Merrit, of the Federation of Catholic Priests and W. B. O'Brien, one of the Cowley Fathers. They drew up a petition which dealt with virgin birth, resurrection and ascension, which seems to have been signed by between 6,000 and 8,000 signatories. Percival Gardner-Smith in a letter to *The Times* asked how many of the people who signed the petition had actually read the Report. There was an attempt to draw up a Modernist counterblast, but Major discouraged it. On 10 May 1938 he wrote to J. T. Wood, the Secretary of the Modern Churchmen's Union, from Merton Vicarage.

> I am sure to consult Raven, Creed and Bezzant is a good thing & if the three of them agree you can act safely. May I say you ought on no account to ask any of our bishops to take part in such a committee or any similar project. It would probably only lead to their prompt resignation of the MCU. Personally I take the view that we shall not help matters by attempting a forward move at this juncture. We may very easily by such an effort increase the difficulties of the liberally minded bishops & a definite document put forward by us would be cited by their opponents as stamping the episcopal policy of defence as definitely Modernist. Of course their policy would be modernist; it has got to be so. I do not see how they can go back on the report. We should help them by giving them good arguments for the report but I think we ought not to take definite action.

In the end Wood let the matter drop.

The petition against the Report was presented in Canterbury Convocation in June. Fortunately the bishops, as Major predicted, stood by the report. At this time Bishop Kirk of Oxford selecting the subject of the virgin birth to speak on at his first Diocesan Conference, expressed his view that it was a cardinal doctrine of the faith. Major, who was one of his incumbents, put the contrary view in direct opposition to Kirk in the *Modern Churchman* for June 1938 and published his article as a separate pamphlet.

The controversy continued into 1939. On 22 May of that year a deputation which included Chavasse and Father Talbot of Mirfield waited upon both Archbishops at Lambeth Palace. Later Archbishop Lang expressed in a letter what they had said to the group. 'We said that we had every sympathy with sincere scholars or thinkers within the Church, who, while accepting the Incarnation and Resurrection as truths essential to the Christian Faith, and as events which occurred in human history, were doubtful as to the exact circumstances in which these events occurred. We had no wish to attempt authoritatively to close their minds or the continuance of their thought or study. We believed that this is not the way in which the cause of truth has been or can be best achieved.'[13] In this same year 1939 Gabriel Hebert produced a Memorandum of thirty-six pages on the Report for the Council of the Church Union. He said that in some sense the report marked a decisive stage in the retreat from Modernism, citing the fact that the Commission had not endorsed Rashdall's view of the atonement. He then went on: 'It gives for example, what is in many ways an admirable statement of the doctrine of the Church; it acknowledges the Eucharistic sacrifice, though its explanation of it is hardly satisfying; it gives sympathetic treatment to certain aspects of Penance and Absolution; it accepts prayers for the dead and even the Invocation of Saints.'[14] However, there were concessions to Modernism he did not like: 'But, on the other hand, it concedes points that are far more vital than any of these, points that belong to the very basis of faith. Implicitly and even explicitly it allows the Virginal Conception of our Lord and his bodily Resurrection to be denied; it allows any clause in the Creed to be interpreted 'symbolically'; and it allows a conception of Revelation radically different from that assumed in the Bible and the tradition of the Church.'[15]

I have already quoted Bishop Wand's praise for the Report in my first chapter. May I add what Bishop Barry says in his *Period of My Life*? 'The findings were dated before they were published. Yet the report is still worth reading, and if anyone reads it today he might be surprised to discover how "liberal" it was, and what a width of interpretation it allowed as legitimate in the Church of England. Thus it still has contemporary relevance.'[16]

With the outbreak of the Second World War the Doctrine

Report and its liberalism were forgotten. Even Major himself seemed for a moment less fanatical and somewhat chastened, as one can see in his article in the *Modern Churchman*, June 1939, not long before the outbreak of war.

To-day Liberal Christianity is spoken of with contempt; as something which is discredited as it has proved itself to be futile. The Liberal Gospel, the Liberal Jesus and the Liberal God are derided, and the theologies of Neo-Thomism, Neo-Calvinism, Neo-Lutheranism are claimed as infinitely more deserving of faith and obedience. Liberal Theology undoubtedly had its limitations. Loisy on the one hand, and Schweitzer on the other, criticized these limitations effectively. When the Great War came, the Anglo-Catholic and Evangelical Press in England seized the opportunity to assail Liberal Christian theology as 'Theology made in Germany', apparently forgetting the existence in France of Auguste Sabatier and the Fidei-Symbolist school, and in English-speaking lands the existence of such Liberal scholars as William Robertson Smith, Estlin Carpenter, Edwin Hatch, J. F. Hort, Sanday, Burkitt, Streeter, and a galaxy of American critics and theologians who, while in large agreement with German Liberal scholarship, were in some respects both independent and critical of it.

Like all great movements, the Liberal Christian movement had its defects and weaknesses and its injudicious followers. It was too optimistic and too ready to believe that the Kingdom of God would immediately appear; it had too strong a belief in the essential goodness and reasonableness of human nature; it lacked confidence in ecclesiastical organizations and institutions as divine instruments for bringing in the Kingdom of God, and as a consequence neglected both to support and reform them. Its axioms – 'We needs must love the highest when we see it'; 'God's in His heaven; all's right with the world'; '*Vox populi, vox Dei*', and so on – are seen to-day to have been more sentimental than sensible. They failed to recognize a number of very important countervailing considerations. For instance, that human beings although children of God, are also inheritors of a brute ancestry.[17]

Major, however, remained a determined Modernist. Through the war years he went on editing the *Modern Churchman*, though it became less frequent than monthly. The Conferences suffered some curtailment. One planned for 1940 did not take place and the next was in 1943 on 'National Church and National Life'. The next after that was in 1945 on 'The Religion the World needs', followed in 1946 when they turned once again to the subject of the Historic Jesus and the Gospel. R. D. Richardson, L. B. Cross, the Chaplain of Jesus College, Oxford, and Vice-Principal of Ripon Hall, T. J. Wood and Percival Gardner-Smith were now frequent speakers. Then younger Modernists like David Scott, Denys Whiteley, A. W. Adams and Ian Ramsey began to make their appearance in the late 'forties.

Major was determined to see his theological college, Ripon Hall, survive the war. He achieved this by handing over the main building to a hospital, and then moving first into the building known as the Hostel (Lord Berkeley's laboratory, now a laboratory once again for the Open University), and then from there into Tutor's Lodge which was enlarged.[18] There with a little band of students the Apostle of English Modernism carried on the movement which owed so much to him. With the development of Basic English and the translation by the Modernist S. H. Hooke of the Bible into Basic English he took up the word 'Basic' and now called Modernism 'Basic Christianity' and his sermons on that title, delivered in Ripon Hall chapel to people living on Boar's Hill, were published in 1944. They contained nothing he had not said before. Two other notable books on liberal Christianity were James Parkes' *Good God* which Penguin published in 1941 under the pseudonym John Hadham. Parkes tells the story of the genesis of the book in his delightful autobiography, *Voyage of Discoveries*. It evidently aroused much interest at the time. Parkes asserts that Temple claimed it was the most important contribution to theology for fifty years. I read it again recently and felt it still remarkably good.[19] The other book was also a Penguin, Bishop Hunkin of Truro's *The Gospel for Tomorrow*. All these books, however, received nothing like the publicity given to *The Rise of Christianity*, which Bishop Barnes wrote during the war and which Cambridge University Press refused to publish and which did not see the light until 1947. To Barnes we must now turn.

When I began writing these chapters, I did not know that a life of Ernest William Barnes would be published. This was long awaited, since Barnes died in 1953. Before the life we had to be content with an article on him in the *Dictionary of National Biography* by Bishop A. E. J. Rawlinson, who was hardly a close friend, and articles in the *Modern Churchman* from Sir Henry Self, successor to Sir Cyril Norwood as President of the Modern Churchmen's Union, and from Charles Raven and Alec Vidler.[20] Now we are glad to have a biography even though we would like even more information at some points and even though the list of Barnes' articles in it is incomplete.

Ernest William Barnes, who in 1924 became Bishop of Birmingham, was born at Altrincham on April Fool's day, 1874, the son of an elementary school master. But the family soon moved to Birmingham where he went to St Edward's school – the school of Westcott, Lightfoot and E. W. Benson. His father was a Baptist and his mother a Wesleyan, but they allowed their son to become an Anglican and he began to worship on his own at St John's, Sparkhill. He went from school to Trinity College and won fame as a mathematician; he was also President of the Union. The list in Sir John Barnes' life of his mathematical articles dating from 1897 to 1910 looks most impressive. They earned him his Doctorate of Science in 1906 and his Fellowship of the Royal Society in 1909. It is curious that Rawlinson does not mention his doctorate of science. He was elected a Fellow of Trinity in 1898 and became what Raven calls 'an austere and rather frightening fellow'. Rawlinson suggests that Barnes came to Cambridge as an atheist and underwent some sort of conversion experience as an undergraduate. That is not corroborated by the *Life*, which makes no allusion to the *Dictionary of National Biography* article, but Sir John Barnes seems to suggest some mystical experience round about ordination time. His affiliation with Evangelicalism does seem to indicate a conversion experience at some point. He was ordained not by the Bishop of Ely but by the rigidly orthodox Winnington-Ingram of London. He was always very much the Liberal Protestant, but his anti-sacramentalism did not make him unfriendly to Roman Catholics. It was Anglo-Catholicism which made him angry, since he thought it foreign to English religion. Relations with his fellow dons at Trinity were not always happy, especially when, after the outbreak of the Great War, he remained a firm pacifist. Both he and they were glad when he succeeded H. G. Woods as Master of the Temple, even though his salary was considerably reduced. Later he moved to Westminster as a Canon, and there started delivering what were popularly called 'gorilla' sermons advocating an evolutionary outlook. Many people maintained that evolution had been long accepted so that they were not necessary. He also fulminated against the doctrine of the real presence.

In 1924 he succeeded Russell Wakefield at Birmingham, being appointed by Ramsey MacDonald. It is likely that Lord Parmoor suggested him. At any rate it became the stock appointment to criticize by those who wished to see the appointment of bishops taken away from the State. In Birmingham he disliked Anglo-Catholic disobedience to the Book of Common Prayer and wished to see reservation forbidden. That whole subject is described in an illuminating article in *Theology* for January 1965 by James Bezzant, who says that Barnes 'was widely accused of having said that if any change in the Eucharistic bread was effected by consecration it could have been detected by physical experiment. Neither Dr. Vidler nor I have been able to trace any such statement, and the bishop assured me that he had never made it; but he did use language liable to be misinterpreted.' In fact, the Bishop did make some offensive remark of this character, which can be read in his *Can Such a Faith Offend?*, a book of sermons and addresses which Bezzant edited. On p.321 of that book these words occur in a sermon preached on 6 October 1927, in Birmingham Parish Church:

There are among ourselves today men and women whose sacramental beliefs are not far from those of the cultured Hindu idolator. They pretend that a priest, using the right words and acts, can change a piece of bread so that within it there is the real presence of Christ. The idea is absurd and can be disproved by experiment. If there were a *physical* change in the bread, chemical analysis would enable us to detect it. All are agreed that this type of change does not take place. Yet if there be a *spiritual* change, it must surely be possible for a man to recognise it by his spiritual perception. Now I assert – and who will gainsay me? – that there is no man living who, if a piece of bread were presented to him, could say whether or not it had been consecrated. Personally, I find it hard to attach any meaning to a spiritual change in dead matter; but if it exists there must surely be some living person who can perceive its existence. If there be no such position, belief in such a change is an idle superstition.

What the Bishop seems to be saying is that no one postulates a physical change in the elements. High Churchmen suggest there is a spiritual change. But if there were a spiritual change surely a spiritual person could discern it. As he later wrote to Archbishop Davidson, 'We have no right to assume the existence of spiritual properties in an inanimate object unless they can be spiritually discerned. Yet there is no man living who possesses the spiritual discernment by which to discriminate between consecrated and unconsecrated.'[21] All this sort of talk was obviously highly offensive to many and Barnes was lacking in good taste and tact to speak in that way. But why was he led into it? Bezzant suggests that it was because he was convinced that Catholic sacramentalism owed much to paganism and the mystery religions. For him the Catholicizing of Christianity was its paganization. This became a psychological obsession with him.

However in spite of all this anti-Anglo-Catholicism one gets the impression that Barnes was not entirely unpopular at Birmingham and some of the clergy and laity greatly admired him. But it is perhaps unfortunate that the life was written by his son.

While Master of the Temple he contributed to two volumes of essays by Liberal Evangelicals, *Liberal Evangelicalism* (1923) in which he wrote on 'The Future of the Evangelical Movement', and *The Inner Life* in which he wrote on 'The Rise and Growth of Man's Spiritual Consciousness'. Barnes' association with the Liberal Evangelicals has been largely omitted in Sir John Barnes' life and there is but one reference to the Anglican Evangelical Group Movement and no mention of his pamphlets for the movement.

Barnes wrote but three books. The first is the one from which we have already quoted, *Can Such a Faith Offend?* In that volume we see his devotion to Jesus Christ, whose sinlessness he sharply defended. There we see his total hostility to the Anglo-Catholic movement. Take such a passage as this:

In Latin Catholicism the ancestral sacramental paganism of the

Mediterranean is veneered by Christian sentiment. To attempt to graft it on to the English Church is hopeless. The Englishman will not lean on the priest and the sacraments even though he be given that permission to sin boldly which Tyrrell, himself a Jesuit, accused the Jesuits of allowing. Therein our Englishman, though he may be a bad Catholic, is a good Christian, for it is certain that Christ gave neither the command nor the permission.[22]

(This was from a sermon preached at the 1924 Modern Churchmen's Conference.)

On p.162 there is a remarkably good summary of his position, which is the English Modernist position:

Now Modernists can equally be divided into two main groups. On the one side there are the typically English Modernists of the right. They preserve the Jewish – in fact, Christ's – idea of God. He is transcendent, with an independent existence, apart from the Universe which He created. His kingdom is the spiritual realm, non-spatial and probably extra-temporal. He works through men and in men; yet they are not divine, though through obedience to His will they can enter into communion with Him. And the reward of such communion is Eternal Life, which after death implies personal immortality. To the English Modernist the Incarnation is the fundamental fact of human history. However Jesus was born, God was manifested in Him as in no other human being. He lived the divine Life on earth, so far as was possible under the restrictions of human existence. Limited, necessarily, though his human knowledge was, His moral and spiritual insight was perfect. He is the Teacher of humanity for all time. His Spirit, still active on earth, leads men to the one goal of perfect truth and righteousness, to which the Spirit of God also guides men in their evolution. The work of the Holy Spirit must be discerned, not merely within the Church, but in the whole intellectual, moral, and spiritual progress of humanity. The authority which discriminates true progress from false change is not external, a Pope, a Council, a Synod; but is the agreement of individual minds. Such agreement is reached through the working of conscience and reason; and it *gradually* becomes an authority to which separate

166

individuals yield. The English Modernist is not an agnostic, for he affirms that conscience is a gift of God, and that through reason we can discover truth.

Then comes a criticism of Catholic Modernism which he sees as tending to pantheism. 'They think', he says, 'of God realising Himself in and through humanity, and especially in Jesus of Nazareth.' In this volume he shows his enormous respect for Hort whom he regards (wrongly, as I have earlier argued), as the Father of English Modernism.

In his Trinity and London days, and perhaps still in 1927, he was a believer in miracles. Sir John Barnes quotes some words of his father in 1914:

> That parthenogenesis should be a commonplace of biology and yet impossible in the Birth of Christ I cannot accept. The other supernatural miracles associated with the life of Jesus I do not find incredible . . . I am compelled to accept the Resurrection as a literal fact and the empty tomb causes me no difficulty . . . My own imagination, my own sense of the infinite power of God and the unique personality of God lead me to find no difficulty in the supernatural miracles of the Gospels.[23]

However when he got to Birmingham he began to call himself a Modernist and he became more inclined to deny the miraculous. In the end he denied it completely. His largest and most important book is his Gifford Lectures. These lectures were delivered at Aberdeen in 1927 and 1928 and Sir John Barnes remarks 'the large but mostly uncomprehending audience had gone into ripples of laughter as Barnes inscribed ever longer mathematical formulae across two or three widths of blackboards'.[24] There is certainly much maths in the book which was entitled *Scientific Theory and Religion. The World described by science and its spiritual interpretation.* This was a remarkable achievement for a twentieth-century bishop, especially when one realizes that it was written as the Bishop was having all the trouble over St Aidan's, Small Heath. Barnes, in this book, which perhaps has never received the recognition due to it, travels through chapters on Matter, Space, Riemann's General Theory of Space, Space-Time; the Special Theory of Relativity, General Relativity, the Electrical Theory of Matter, Heat and

167

Light, Quantum Theory and Röntgen rays, the Solar System, the Galactic Universe and Great Nebulae, the Origin of Life and the Geological Record, the Evolution of Plants and Sex, the Evolution of Animals and Mendelism, the Machinery of Evolution, Man's Origin and Past, Scientific Theory and the Real World, God and our Belief in His Existence, Religious Experience, Immortality. His heroes on the scientific side are Newton, Darwin and Einstein; and on the theological side, Hort and Rashdall. There is not much on miracles but he is strong in his belief in a transcendent and immanent God and on human immortality. With Rashdall he maintained that belief in God and belief in immortality must stand or fall together. This volume of 685 pages was scarcely a best seller but one might have expected Cambridge would have given him an honorary D.D. for it. However his honorary doctorates were all from Scotland.

He would have done best to have written nothing further. However during the grim days of the Second World War he studied and wrote on Jesus and the first days of the Christian Church. This was the famous or infamous book, *The Rise of Christianity*, which the Cambridge University Press, which had published his Giffords, were (understandably) unwilling to publish. The book was issued by Longmans, Green and Co. in 1947. There are eighteen chapters in it and the work is subdivided into 334 numbered paragraphs. He holds firmly to the belief in God and immortality and the centrality of Christ which he had outlined in his Giffords. But now he embarks on a consideration of the history of Christ's religion. He starts with man's remote beginnings, and takes a look at the Sumerians, Egypt and Babylon, Syria, Assyria, Persia, the Hebrews, the Greeks, the Etruscans and the Romans. There is much on the mystery religions which, he thinks, considerably influenced Christianity, and the influence was bad. Then comes a chapter on the miracles, which he totally discards, including the virgin birth and the physical resurrection. Many Modernists would have had no quarrel with him there, though what he says about the resurrection was rather too negative even for them, and smacks of what Rudolf Bultmann was saying in Germany – not that the Bishop knew anything about Bultmann. However, why some Modernists took exception to the book and found it an embarrassment was because of the extreme positions which the Bishop took up in dealing with the New Testament documents, an aspect which Sir John Barnes skates over lightly. He feels we can know next to nothing of the facts of the death of Christ. Luke-Acts he dates late; but, today, probably many people would agree with him. He simply cannot understand St Paul's theology which obviously is repellent to him. The Epistle to the Romans, one of the most important documents for Christian history, is totally written off. 'Parts of it could hardly have come from a Jew carefully brought up in the traditions of his people. It must be due . . . to some man of a primitive mentality, whose speculations with regard to social conduct were as confused as those of an untaught adolescent grappling with a fundamental philosophical problem.'[25] Sections of 1 Cor. including chapter 13 are non-Pauline. St John's Gospel is 'sustained allegory rather than fact'.[26] On the other hand Barnes simply loves the *Didache* which appeals to the Modern Christian humanist. Revelation is a 'fantastic work' and Hebrews is 'hardly less extravagant'. Early Christians are depicted as both pacifists and socialists.

Barnes' book is certainly clearly written but his allusions to his authorities are very vague. He never quotes specifically any modern authorities. He claims to be impartial but it is an extremely prejudiced work. It never became the sort of book that one could recommend a person to read on the subject of Christian origins. The reviews of the book were led off by Charles Raven in the *Spectator*. 'This', he said, 'is the chief value of the book; it is convincing proof that a man of outstanding intellectual integrity can give full effect to the work of critical scholarship and without shirking or minimizing its results can find it consistent to remain not only as a confessing Christian but as an Anglican bishop. To those who know Dr Barnes this is a fact of great apologetic importance: no man would more readily have resigned his position had his conscience allowed him to do so . . .' He goes on, one is glad to say, 'But if (as is the case) the present reviewer would take a very different view on many particular points and especially as to the character and writings of St. Paul, this is not due to any difference of principle. Such matters must be decided in accordance with the evidence.'

The most effusive review of the book which Sir John Barnes does not quote came from the Modernist Canon R. D. Richardson, the Vicar of Harborne, Birmingham, where Barnes had his residence, who wrote in the *Birmingham Diocesan Bulletin*:

This book should be received thankfully: by anxious Christians as a bulwark against modern scepticism: by serious critics as an account of it which then enables them to become believers . . .
   The Bishop's views on the original forms of the text of our documents, on their dates and authorship, and on the background of circumstance, knowledge, experience and purpose of the authors, are not likely to be seriously modified . . . Whatever the immediate reception of this book, it will long stand as a classic . . . I draw attention to one heresy in this book i.e. the author's insistent declaration that he worships Jesus Christ. Orthodoxy requires the worship of God in Christ. Yet in a Church which lays more and more stress on orthodoxy but – may I say it? – knows less and less what it is, the Bishop's over-belief at a fundamental point should cover a multitude of critical conclusions.

Major, still editor of the *Modern Churchman*, handed over the book to Pervical Gardner-Smith, the Dean of Jesus, for review. Gardner-Smith, whom Sir John Barnes does not mention by name, was a well known Modernist who had not long before reviewed A. M. Ramsey's book on *The Resurrection of Christ*, an exposition of biblical theology criticizing Modernism for not believing in the breaking in of God into history from outside history. In the review Gardner-Smith dismissed the story of the empty tomb as not an essential part of Christianity. Ramsey replied that the resurrection was the mighty act of God entering into human history – empty tomb or not – and not simply the illustration of human immortality. What would Gardner-Smith say about *The Rise of Christianity*? On 25 April 1947 he wrote to Dr Major.

I have been very much troubled by Barnes' book, and I was on the point of sending it back with a request that you should choose another reviewer.
   I know the Bishop slightly, I admire his courage and his devotion to what he conceives to be the truth. He is a distinguished member of the M.C.U., and I do not wish to offend him. But honesty compels me to say that I think *The Rise*

of Christianity is a very bad book indeed, amateurish, arrogant and dogmatic. I think it will do harm to the author; to the cause of Modernism, and to the Church. The Bishop is completely off his beat, and he exhibits not only a very superficial knowledge of the very wide field which he attempts to cover, but an extraordinary lack of sympathy towards those whose minds have not been trained on the same lines as his own. Because St. Paul and St. John were not modern scientific rationalists he can see nothing good in their work, and he has none of the historian's ability to cast his mind into another age.

I have written a review, which I think you may very likely prefer not to print. If so, I shall not take offence, for I see that your position is difficult. But I think that if you print it you may reassure some of your readers.

Well, Major did print it after consulting Barnes. The review came out in the July 1947 *Modern Churchman*. Major made some preliminary remarks about the book in his 'Signs of the Times' and called Barnes a 'Second Colenso'. 'No more fearless book than *The Rise of Christianity* has been written by an English bishop since Bishop Colenso (who like Bishop Barnes was a Second Wrangler and Smith's Prizeman) published his critical commentary on the *Pentateuch* nearly three generations ago.'

Gardner-Smith's review (which runs through several pages of small type) is very thorough. I will quote a few of the prize sentences. 'The tone of the book is predominantly sceptical, and very little of traditional Christian theology remains . . . Modern churchmen are rightly suspicious of miraculous stories, but that is a different thing from ruling them out *a priori*, and we may well hesitate to declare dogmatically what may or may not have happened in the presence of the incarnate Son of God . . . This does not make credible every tale of miracles in which the vulgar of all ages have delighted, but it does suggest that to begin an enquiry into the rise of Christianity with the assumption that no 'miracles' can ever have occurred is an unscientific method . . . The Church's net enclosed some fish of every class, but there is no evidence that Christianity was specially a movement of the lowest classes who found in it the hope of social emancipation. No doubt the intelligentsia held aloof, as they always do, and Celsus and

Lucian scoffed; but to describe the Church which included Flavius Clemens, Clement of Rome, and a host of educated men from the *Auctor ad Hebraeos* to Clement and Origen, as 'proletarian' is a misrepresentation . . . Scarcely less open to question is Dr. Barnes' characterization of the Church as socialist and pacifist . . .' Turning to St Paul he is quite rightly horrified over Barnes' rejection of 1 Corinthians 13 as Pauline, and adds 'If Marcion "criticized with a penknife", Dr. Barnes criticizes with a hatchet.' Turning to the general tendency of the author, he continues:

> Dr. Barnes approves of socialism, pacifism, and internationalism, and therefore he thinks that they were the dominating characteristics of early Christianity. He has small sympathy with mysticism and sacramentalism which offend his austere rationalism, and therefore he represents them as incursions into Christianity from the heathen world. He dislikes speculative theology, and to him the Logos doctrine, by which, it has been said, the Greek world was led to accept Christianity, seems fanciful and useless theorizing (p.331). Throughout the book the subjective element predominates, and many will feel that the facts are made to fit the theory rather than the theory based upon the facts . . . *The Rise of Christianity* cannot be accepted as a serious contribution to critical study. It is too arbitrary, too dogmatic, and too much indebted to a few extreme critics . . . All modern churchmen will pay tribute to the honesty and courage which have gone to make this book, and no less the industry which has enabled a diocesan bishop to produce so considerable a work. Yet many will regret its publication. A bishop necessarily speaks *ex cathedra*, and the eminence of Dr. Barnes in one field may easily give to his pronouncements in another field an authority which they do not possess . . . Many will feel that Dr. Barnes has not provided a possible explanation of the rise of Christianity. Mountains may produce mice, but mice do not give birth to mountains.

Most people seemed to have felt that Barnes had swallowed whole one book in particular in his bibliography, Guignebert's book on Jesus. A review as equally scathing as Gardner-Smith's came from the pen of Wilfrid Knox, who had been on the Doctrine Commission, in the *Cambridge Review*. Unfortunately he began with the sentence, 'Dr. Barnes is well-known as an exponent of the view of the Modern Churchmen's Union in a somewhat extreme form.' This annoyed Gardner-Smith who quickly wrote in and said, 'The Modern Churchmen's Union has no views. Its object is to defend freedom of thought, and it includes among its members people of widely different opinions. If Dr. Knox cares to turn up the current number of *The Modern Churchman* he will find a review of the Bishop of Birmingham's book scarcely less critical than his own.'

There were others who heavily criticized the Bishop's book, like C. H. Dodd, who wrote *Christian Beginnings. A Reply to Dr. Barnes' 'The Rise of Christianity'*, and the elderly Sir Frederic Kenyon who dealt with it in his *The Bible and Modern Scholarship* (1948). When I started Theology at Cambridge in 1951 one of the books I was recommended to read was the late J. N. Sanders' *The Foundations of the Christian Faith. A Study of the Teaching of the New Testament in the Light of Historical Criticism* (1950), which had the subsidiary purpose of pointing out the errors of Bishop Barnes.

Major continued to defend Barnes' right to hold his opinions. In the *Hibbert Journal* for April 1948, the Rev. Dr A. H. Birch, late Headmaster of Chepstow Grammar School, had an article attacking Barnes, entitled 'Creed and Conscience', and said that he ought to give up his office as an Anglican bishop, because of his non-belief in miracles. In the same issue Major rushed to the defence in an article 'Criticism and Conscience', in which he went back over attempts to exclude Colenso, the writers of *Essays and Reviews* and *Lux Mundi*, and the participants at Girton from the Church of England. He then spoke of a recent attack upon a clergyman, the Rev. Frank Moyle, Vicar of Allesley, Coventry, a Modernist who had made some remarks at the Conference of Modern Churchmen in 1946, and was widely reported as having said that the virgin birth was a myth. Seventeen clerics of Coventry had publicly charged him with making a statement which was not compatible with his clerical faith and honour. The Bishop of Coventry, Neville Gorton, had intervened, and while dissenting from Moyle's statement, defended his right to make it and cited the Report on Doctrine.[27] Major then concluded his defence of Barnes with the words, 'To-day nothing further in the way of *doctrinal* freedom is desired or demanded by Liberal or Modernist Churchmen, but in the sphere of *liturgical* freedom it is otherwise.' In this connection he suggested the authorization of alternative Creeds.

The story of the condemnation of Barnes' book by Archbishop Fisher has been told in Purcell's life of the Archbishop, and the late Dean Matthews in his *Memories and Meanings* describes the scene.

> The Archbishop pronounced his judgement on Barnes's book *The Rise of Christianity* in Convocation on October 15th, 1947. I came in about half way through and found all the bishops grouped together on one side of the hall and the Bishop of Birmingham isolated, sitting all by himself as though he had been sent to Coventry. On the spur of the moment I went and sat by his side, hoping that my rank as prolocutor would excuse me for sitting in the bishops' row of chairs. Barnes was quite silent and I wondered if he was feeling an outcast. I think not, for when he saw me he said, 'Well, you see I'm not deposed yet.'[28]

Extracts from the book were published in the *Sunday Pictorial*. I cut them out at the time – they were my first theological newspaper cuttings. Bishop Blunt of Bradford was allowed to reply, though apparently he complained that he had been treated unfairly. Sir John Barnes suggests that Blunt's replies were trivial and dogmatic, a charge which I am sure is unjust.

What did Dean Inge think of it all? He was worried in case the Modern Churchmen's Union as a group defended the book and on 25 October 1947 he wrote to Major saying how distressed he was to receive a suggested defence. 'I thought', he said,

> from what Gardner-Smith told me, that our Society was *not* going to take any action about the book. In my opinion the Abp. did exactly the right thing in expressing his personal disapproval. It was the *least* that he could do, and I was grateful to him for taking this course. If we provoke the Bishops into issuing a statement of the things that a clergyman must not say, great harm will be done. [The old dog-fight between dogmatic materialism and materialistic dogmatism is out of date because intelligent people on both sides realise that the question is the

174

metaphysical problem as to the status in ultimate reality of the world of space and time. Man the *amphibean* [*sic*] has intercalated the untransparent middle terms of myth and symbol, to bring together the two world of things and values, of visible and invisible, of time and eternity, put it how we will.] The traditional symbols do not suit us all; there is no standardised pair of spectacles to suit the learned professor and his kitchen-maid. But it is not right for a Bishop to discredit the symbols which for simple folk are the only way of escaping from materialism. The bishop is no philosopher; for him there is no alternative between accepting miracles as facts in the physical order and denying them as falsehoods. Moreover, his view of the historical Christ leaves us next to nothing of the Christian belief in Christ as the Logos made flesh. I do hope you agree with me. I doubt whether our Society could survive a false step on this occasion.

Hensley Henson condemned as much as Inge. On 5 April 1947 he wrote to Dean Selwyn of Winchester. He said he had been reading both Kirk's *The Apostolic Ministry* and Barnes' *The Rise of Christianity*. 'The first is in my judgment definitely, in tone, in type, temper and tendency not Anglican but *Roman*, and the last is not even in any tolerable sense, Christian.' 'Under the pretence of complete detachment and impartiality the Bishop has produced a book which might more fitly have been published by the *Rationalist Press*.'[29]

Soon after the discussion of *The Rise of Christianity* Major at long last left Ripon Hall. His successor was Barnes' disciple, R. D. Richardson. It meant, inevitably, that Ripon Hall became associated with the theology of Bishop Barnes, whose book was soon finding its way into the second-hand shelves and treated as a joke. In contrast, the discussion of *The Apostolic Ministry* went on for years. Henson died in 1947, Barnes in 1953 and Inge in 1954. One wonders what they would have thought of the next theological ferment, that of the 'sixties, when the doctrines of both God and life after death seemed to be questioned. At any rate Gardner-Smith lived on to write another devastating review. Major lived long enough to see the beginnings of the new Radicalism which can be dated back to a Modern Churchmen's

Union pamphlet of 1955 some years before *Soundings* and *Honest to God*. More of this in the next chapter when we conclude with 'The Old Modernism and the New Radicalism'.

NOTES

1   See *Lambeth Occasional Reports 1937–8* (1948), pp.189–205.

2   W. R. Matthews, *Memories and Meanings* (1969).

3   See Alan Thornhill, *One Fight More* (1943).

4   F. W. Dillistone, *Charles Raven*, pp.205ff.

5   For Vidler's review see *Guardian*, 12 Feb. 1975.

6   Gordon S. Wakefield, 'Hoskyns and Raven. The Theological Issue', in *Theology* (Nov. 1975), pp.568–76. See also Michael Ramsey's review of Dillistone's book in *Theology* (Nov. 1975), pp.603–5.

7   E. F. Braley, ed., *Letters of Herbert Hensley Henson*, p.169.

8   Peter J. Jagger, *A History of the Parish and People Movement* (1978).

9   See David L. Edwards, *Ian Ramsey Bishop of Durham – a Memoir* (1973).

10 Dr Robinson in *Honest to God* refers to Quick's *Doctrines of the Creed* as 'one of the outstanding books on Christian doctrine of our generation'.

11 op. cit., p.10.

12 *Modern Churchman* (Dec. 1938), p.464.

13 *Church Times*, 30 June 1939.

14 op. cit., p.8.

15 op. cit., p.8.

16 op. cit., p.87f.

17 *Modern Churchman* (June 1939), pp.119f.

18 When I became Vice-Principal of Ripon Hall in 1962, Tutor's Lodge became Vice-Principal's Lodge. I lived in it for nine years.

19 It was republished by SCM in the 'sixties.

20 See Sir Henry Self, 'Bishop Barnes' in *Modern Churchman*, March 1954, pp.14–24. C. E. Raven, 'E.W.B. – The Man for the Moment' in *Modern Churchman*, March 1955, pp.11–24. Alex Vidler, 'Bishop Barnes. A Centenary Retrospect' in *Modern Churchman*, Spring 1975, pp.87–98. (See also his *Scenes from a Clerical Life*).

21 Sir John Barnes, *Ahead of His Age*, p.198.

22 op. cit., p.182.

23 op. cit., p.54.

24 op. cit., pp.308f.

25 op. cit., p.234.

26 op. cit., p.145.

27 For Neville Gorton, see *Neville Gorton Bishop of Coventry 1943–55*, edited by Frank W. Moyle.

28 op. cit., pp.309f.

29 See *Letters of Herbert Hensley Henson*, Letter No. 187, pp.203ff.

8

The Old Modernism and the New Radicalism

Our subject in this last chapter is the old Modernism and the new radicalism, an almost impossible assignment in so short a space. It is our aim to ask what relation, if any, there is between Modernism and the new radicalism. After all, as we have looked back through Anglican Liberalism we have witnessed a sort of liberal succession from Thomas Arnold down to Henry Major and his disciples. Then there is the question, What attitude did the Modernists adopt towards the new radicalism? There is also the question of when the new radicalism began. Most people would date it in the period 1962–3. Some might take it back to Gabriel Vahanian's *The Death of God* which was published in America in 1960. I would suggest, however, that it can be taken back to 1955, in which year the Modern Churchmen's Union published a pamphlet entitled *Return to the Roots*. I am sure that many will be surprised to hear this; but I hope to show that it is so.

We left the story of English Modernism with the general hostility bestowed upon Bishop Barnes' *The Rise of Christianity* in 1947–8 and the embarrassment which it gave to many Modernists. We saw Percival Gardner-Smith prophesying (correctly) that it would do harm to the Modernist cause. Soon after the publication of the book, Major at last retired to Merton Vicarage and handed over Ripon Hall to a successor after thirty years as Principal and a connection with it going back to 1906. The man he would have liked to succeed him was L. B. Cross, the Vice-Principal of Ripon Hall and Chaplain of Jesus College, Oxford; and to attract him to Boar's Hill he had managed to buy a delightful Principal's House with an equally delightful garden. But L. B. Cross did not rise to the bait. Instead the man appointed to enjoy the new acquisition was Canon R. D. Richardson, who had the reputation of being an uncritical admirer of Barnes and whose review of *The Rise of*

Christianity, as we saw, had been so effusive. Soon after the appointment, Bishop Henson wrote to Dean Selwyn of Winchester, 'You will have seen that Canon Richardson, the Vicar of Harborne, is to succeed Major at Ripon Hall. He is of course, a friend, a disciple and a champion of his present Bishop, though I think he is a man of a more spiritual type and will express himself less crudely. In some respect he would be well suited for guiding young men *in spiritualibus*, but whether he has any power of discipline remains to be seen.' Richardson, whose interests were in early liturgy, took over in 1948, by which time the college was recovering its full complement of buildings. The task of following the Apostle of English Modernism was difficult. Major hardly found it easy to hand things over, made Richardson do a term's apprenticeship under him, and then, as Treasurer, constantly interfered in the college's running. Richardson, in any case, had not been the choice of all the Governors and had critics from the start. Student numbers went down and there was talk of the college moving back into smaller quarters in Oxford. In the midst of these troubles there was a great Modernist occasion when Major was presented with a bronze bust at Ripon Hall, unveiled by the new Warden (or Episcopal Visitor) of the college, Bishop Hunkin of Truro. There was also an inspection of the college by Canons Michael Ramsey and C. E. Hudson. It is a little amusing to think of the college where what the *Church Times* then called 'the Gospel of negativity' had been preached, inspected by the leading exponent of biblical theology, who was highly critical of Modernism. But the report said nothing particularly detrimental and characterized Richardson and his assistant, Thorold, as 'men of devotedness, kindness and patience who were always accessible to ordinands'. However, the college did not flourish for several reasons. In the end, Richardson was persuaded to leave and he accepted the living of Boynton in the Salisbury diocese, where he was again as conscientious and devoted a parish priest as he had been before at Harborne.

To fill the gap and build up the college once again came Bishop Geoffrey Allen, a pupil of Major's, who had been Archdeacon of Birmingham under Barnes and then gone out to be Bishop in Egypt. He was a different man from Richardson and especially so in theology. At Oxford he had come under the influence of Frank

Buchman and then Karl Barth and so had moved far on from Major's Modernism. Moreover he had experience as a missionary in China. Though he remained associated with the Modern Churchmen's Union, he was ever critical of the old Modernism. Certainly when at Ripon Hall we were given no encouragement to read Major's works. Nevertheless he remained a liberal in theology, and was the advocate of what he termed 'a Penitent Liberalism'. That was the subject of his Annual Sermon for the Modern Churchmen's Union, delivered in St Martin's-in-the-Fields on 21 May 1953, the year after he had taken over Ripon Hall with but two students. In that sermon he described what liberalism was. 'First liberalism stands for a spirit of initiative or spontaneity. In the realm of thought it means a freedom to explore new fields of learning with honest inquiry; it means also a creative vigour of mind, to bring a Christ-formed judgement to bear on the issues of the present hour . . . Liberalism stands also for a spirit that is liberal in the other sense of the word, generous. . . There is a third characteristic . . . Liberty does not exist in a vacuum; it thrives and flourishes in a setting of law and order.' (Here he was echoing what he had written in his book *Law with Liberty* (1942).) He said, 'The earlier liberalism of the nineteenth century and the beginning of the twentieth century was a little too facile, a little too Utopian, both in its religious and political forms. We thought we had merely to liberate people from the chains of old authorities, to give them the vote, and to speed up a little the processes of education, and an ideal world would be waiting round the corner. In theology we questioned at that time the historicity of the stories of Adam and the Fall. We said, as of course I should still say, that these stories were myth and not exact history. We did not always discern that as myth they contained deeply significant abiding truths, concerning the forces of evil which dwell in the human soul and which all too often frustrate our strivings for human perfection.' Geoffrey Allen pleaded for a penitent liberalism but he was equally emphatic in his demand that there should be a revival of liberalism, as one can see in his article 'The Coming Revival of Liberalism' in the *Modern Churchman*, December 1953 (republished from an article in the *Church of England Newspaper* in July).

So Ripon Hall, which a year or two before had had such a

questionable reputation, now with a changed atmosphere recovered. I was one of those attracted from Cambridge by Geoffrey Allen's message and as I have always been interested in the history of the places with which I have been associated I started delving into the history of Ripon Hall and hence into Modernism. Certainly in the 'fifties Modernism was at a discount. *Crockford's Clerical Directory* in 1956 remarked in its preface:

> Although the annual conference of the Modern Churchmen's Union continues to be favoured above all others by *The Times*, it cannot be said that this group counts for much in the life of the Church of England today. That they do not is largely their own fault, for allowing themselves to convey the impression that they are a body of bitter ancients whose modernism is that of the day before yesterday.

In the 'fifties people were reading Karl Barth, C. S. Lewis and the writings of the exponents of biblical theology. I mentioned in the last chapter the contribution of Gabriel Hebert and Michael Ramsey. Now we can add the name of Alan Richardson, who had been Chaplain of Ripon Hall in the 'thirties, but had rebelled against Modernism perhaps even more strongly than Geoffrey Allen. He expressed his thoughts in his book *The Redemption of Modernism* in 1935, when a Northumberland incumbent. In 1941 came his famous book *The Miracle Stories of the Gospels*, in 1947 his *Christian Apologetics*, and in 1958 his *An Introduction to the Theology of the New Testament*. Undoubtedly in the 'fifties this ex-Chaplain of Ripon Hall was one of the most popular of English theological writers, whose works went into many impressions. At Nottingham he was joined by Robert Leaney, who had served for a time as Vice-Principal of Ripon Hall under Geoffrey Allen. In fact, the Theological Faculty at Nottingham at this time, which included R. P. C. Hanson, were very much exponents of biblical theology. The old over-concentration on historical criticism and questions of dates and sources everywhere receded into the background. The emphasis was on 'the God Who acts' and 'the God Who speaks in His Acts'. The Bible was 'the Book of the Acts of God in history'. But there seemed little questioning of whether this God existed. There was a proclamation of the unity of the Bible, which was the title of a well-known book by H. H. Rowley, one of the Old

181

Testament scholars who were protagonists of biblical theology. A further contribution to the movement came in Michael Ramsey's *The Glory of God and the Transfiguration of Christ* (1949) and in J. A. T. Robinson's *The Body. A Study in Pauline Theology* (1952). The great climax of this movement was in 1958 by which time Ramsey was Archbishop of York and the Lambeth Conference took 'The Bible' as its main subject of debate. Ramsey was Chairman of the Committee dealing with the subject. A London journalist painted the scene at the Conference.

> Dr. Ramsey, Archbishop of York, is giving many hours to the Lambeth Conference report on the Bible. Proofs are now coming from the printer. He is a swift worker, able to read a passage at a glance. In the Bishops' discussions on the Bible Dr. Ramsey presides. Sometimes the Bishops think that he is asleep in the chair. For he sits with his hands grasped over his purple robe. But he is not asleep. He is on his feet in a second if he disagrees.

The Report on the Bible, largely the work of Ramsey, was symptomatic of biblical theology triumphalism, and seemed to speak with great certainty. It began with a section on 'The Bible and the Church'. 'The New Testament', it said, 'is not to be seen in isolation: the Church preceded it in time, and it was within the Church, with its sacraments, Creeds and Apostolic Ministry, that the New Testament was canonised. The Church is the witness and keeper of Holy Writ, charged to interpret and expound it by the aid of the Spirit of Truth which is in the Church.' There followed a commendation of biblical criticism:

> Biblical criticism has brought about a number of widely accepted results: that certain narratives which had been taken to be literal history cannot be so taken; that certain books were not written by the writers traditionally ascribed to them; that some of the books were written in several stages at different periods; that some of the features of the religion described in the Bible were less unique than had been supposed and were more interwoven with the religion and culture of other peoples.[2]

Then came an attack on evolutionary liberalism which simply saw the Bible as a record of moral and religious progress and did not believe in 'particular divine interventions'. Many Modernists would have fallen into that category. 'But', the report continues, 'more recently amongst Biblical scholars in every part of the world there has been a strong reaction from this outlook. Scholars, thorough and rigorous in criticism and historical method, have studied the Bible without prejudice against belief in the living God who is active in history, and have shown how the varied library of books in the Bible has its origin in the unique action of God in Israel and in Jesus Christ. This point of view, powerfully represented at the present day, is often called by the name of "Biblical theology".'[3] Later there is an attack on the 'radical reinterpretations of the biblical message which try to discard the elements belonging to primitive culture and to retain an essential core relevant to the modern world'. Clearly the reference here is to Rudolf Bultmann and *Kerygma and Myth* which had been translated into English in 1953.

Biblical theology appeared to have triumphed. Demythologization was the great subject of debate. Modernism and liberalism in general seemed dead. Charles Raven's Gifford Lectures on *Natural Religion and Christian Theology*, published in the early 'fifties, were read and then forgotten. Yet there were four theologians in the Modernist Movement trying to present anew some of the things that Modernism had stood for. One of these was Norman Pittenger, whose *The Word Incarnate* came out in 1959; he was in no way ashamed to refer to some of the old Modernist authorities and assumptions and unite them with process theology. Then there was F. W. Dillistone, who came from the Evangelical camp, and wrote on Christian symbolism; later (in the 'sixties) he was to write on the atonement. Then there was Ian Ramsey, disciple of Major, alumnus of Ripon Hall, whose fine book *Religious Language; an Empirical Placing of Theological Phrases* came out in 1957. Finally there were Frank Cleobury, the idealist philosopher, disciple of Berkeley and Bradley, whose story can be read in *From Clerk to Cleric* (1976) and who wrote *The Armour of Saul* (1957) (on the resurrection) and *Rationalism and Philosophical Analysis* in 1959.

None of these four had any inkling of the period of liberal Christianity which was to be ushered in throughout the whole Church by the papacy of John XXIII which began in 1958 and which became a swift current in the Church of England when

Michael Ramsey moved south to Canterbury in 1961. At that moment it was the magazine *Prism* which was the *avant garde* magazine of the Church of England, not the *Modern Churchman*.

Major lived to see the beginnings of the new radicalism when it was the size of a cloud no bigger than a man's hand. It began within the Modern Churchmen's Union, though that fact has been quite forgotten. From 1947 the President of the Modern Churchmen's Union, in succession to Sir Cyril Norwood, who had held the post ten years, was Sir Henry Self, the Chairman of the Electricity Board. Self was a remarkable layman who was a Master of Science, a Doctor of Philosophy and a Bachelor of Divinity; an intellectual with considerable executive capacity. Self brought Clifford Rhodes, a journalist priest, into the Movement as its Director. The new President felt that the Union should be turning itself from theology to social and industrial problems. But Rhodes, in spite of the fact that he was very much a man of the world and not an academic theologian, began to feel that this was a mistake. Deciding that the Union had not been founded with this intention, Rhodes used his efforts for the Union on three fronts.

1. First there was the ecumenical task. That was not the major occupation that it became in later years for so many in the Church. Out of Modernism at this period came a manifesto on South India, published in 1955, and largely written by E. C. Dewick, a former Hulsean lecturer, which recommended the acceptance of non-episcopally ordained presbyters.[4] In 1961 many Modernists were among the twenty-one who signed the Open Letter to the Archbishop of Canterbury on Intercommunion.

2. Then there was the revision of canon law which was the main task being attempted during Archbishop Fisher's primacy. Modernists were anxious to resist too rigid a system of canon law and the transference of too much power into the hands of the bishops. In this endeavour they engaged in considerable consultation, along with other organizations, at Lambeth Palace with Archbishop Fisher.

3. There was the question of the marriage of the divorced in church. This had always been part of the programme of English Modernism. Indeed, they had in 1952 produced a document on

Marriage and Divorce in the Church of England, with substantial essays by P. Gardner-Smith, Denys Whiteley and others. Rhodes maintains that the Modern Churchmen's Union did in this sphere make an impact up and down the country.

In addition to promoting the cause of Modernism, Rhodes was also editing the *Church of England Newspaper*. Among the panel of advisers for that paper, which included Sir Kenneth Grubb, were John Drewett, Rector of St Margaret's, Lothbury, and Rural Dean of London, and John Wren Lewis, a scientist. Both these men became involved in the Modern Churchmen's Union. Indeed, St Margaret's, Lothbury, not far from the Bank of England, became the London centre of the movement until John Drewett's death in 1973. It was here that John Wren Lewis gave some lunch-time lectures on the meaning of God. He then sent the manuscripts to Rhodes who, sensing their brilliance, published them in the *Church of England Newspaper*. Later Rhodes had them published as a pamphlet under the auspices of the Modern Churchmen's Union. They were entitled *Return to the Roots. A Study in the Meaning of the Word 'God'* (1956). I did not read it until years later and I never remember anyone alluding to it when I was a student at Ripon Hall. But to my mind it was the beginning of the new radicalism. When people reviewed *Honest to God* they saw the influence upon Dr Robinson of three Teutonic theologians, Bultmann, Tillich and Bonhoeffer. But few made much of his debt to the Englishman, John Wren Lewis, the mathematician and physicist, who had rebelled against Christianity as a boy and then adopted it again through the influence of an enlightened Anglican clergyman. John Wren Lewis has told the story in *They Became Anglicans*, edited by Dewi Morgan, a book which Dr Robinson quotes several times in *Honest to God*. It is very remarkable how this forgotten pamphlet, *Return to the Roots*, anticipated much of what Dr Robinson says in *Honest to God*. He starts by asking why the Church is so weak and says it is because our hearers cannot see what the word 'God' means. 'When we say that God means "the infinite power who is creator and sustainer of the universe" it conjures up in most people's minds the notion of a Being of immense proportions somewhere "above" or "outside" the Universe of stars and galaxies, who created it all at some distant date in the past and now

185

supervises it like a foreman.'[5] He goes on to deride the idea of God as an 'Old Man above the Sky' and criticizes an Anglican clergyman who explained the incarnation by saying that 'in Jesus, God visited His world personally'. John Wren Lewis now demands a return to the roots, a radically new approach. Picking up Martin Buber's conception of the 'I-Thou' relationship, he stresses the ultimate importance of our personal relationships. 'Our very being as persons in fact, comes from our encounters with each other – and since this is true for each of us then there must really be something between us which is there before us and is bigger than all of us. Here, in fact, at the heart of personal life, we have an actual *experience* of creation – not just an idea of the Universe being made by somebody, but direct knowledge of ourselves being created by a Power "between man and man".'[6] Is God being reduced in speaking thus? No. 'To say that "God" means the creative power between people, the power of what we usually call love, is not to reduce God to anything, but rather *to increase our ordinary estimate of love*, and that is just what we need to do if we are to see life the right way up.'[7] He contends that this is not denying the personality of God – unless 'by personality of God' is meant a sort of individual person or super-person, in which case it ought to be denied.[8]

> To say that the Controlling Intelligence behind the scenes of the Universe ought to be imagined as like a father is superstitious nonsense, but that is not what the doctrine of the Fatherhood of God means. The genuine doctrine, like all doctrines about God, *is a descriptive statement about the character of the Creative Power which we experience directly in our relations with one another*. Those who have made the great discovery 'that love can love and be loved' know that love is a personally active Reality which (or Who) works continually towards our growth into personal maturity-in-relationship: love, in fact, exercises towards us a Fatherhood of which ordinary biological fatherhood is a pale and distorted reflection.[9]

Then come the paragraphs on what later was called 'Situation Ethics'.

> Real sensitiveness is sensitiveness *to what Love which is between us*

requires at any given moment. That is what real religion means by 'Doing God's will', not doing things which the Old Man above the Sky is supposed to have commanded but being sufficiently aware of the Presence and Demand of Love in any situation that the right thing is done in the right way *spontaneously*.[10]

After talking about prayer, on which there is no space to quote, he moved on to Jesus Christ. The incarnation is not the Old Man in the Sky visiting the earth personally. 'Jesus was fully human *because* he partook fully of, was wholly open to, was indeed a complete embodiment of, the Creative Power of Love. The whole uniqueness of the personality of Jesus, on the Christian view, was that he never attempted to achieve it by being an individual on his own account, but lived wholly *in Love*, even when – perhaps especially when – he was alone . . . This shows us, incidentally, just why it was that the Incarnation was also a revelation, for to say that Jesus lived wholly in Love means, among other things, that he lived wholly in Love with his friends, so that *they* saw God too in knowing him. That in fact was their message, that in this man's life with them God had been made manifest to them.'[11]

There is no space to quote more from this remarkable pamphlet, which, according to the *Modern Churchmen's Newsletter* for December 1955, was commended by that Grand Old Man of the ecumenical movement, J. H. Oldham. Major was still alive when this first document of the new radicalism came out. What did he think about it? Fortunately we know, for he reviewed it in the *Modern Churchman* for December 1955, when he wrote:

> We are not sure that we are in agreement with some of the statements made by Mr Lewis in these lectures but we do agree with him that the Church's theologians have sought in their Christian apologies to maintain that God is a *personal* being and that we can hold *personal* intercourse with Him and He with us if we go the right way about it. We also agree with Mr Lewis that God is a moral being and that His morality must be interpreted supremely in terms of love. We recall Dean Rashdall saying that he regarded St. Augustine's treatise on the Trinity as the best of his theological expositions because St. Augustine interpreted the Trinity in terms of love.[12]

Undoubtedly Major was somewhat bewildered by the pamphlet which to him in some aspects represented an entirely new approach

Major's days of editing the *Modern Churchman* were almost over. The December 1956 number with its biographical record of English Modernists was the last he produced. It was both praised and criticized by Archbishop Ramsey in the *York Quarterly*. Major had founded and successfully edited the *Modern Churchman* for forty-six years. Has anyone edited a magazine longer? Major, on his retirement from the editorship, in a letter to Rhodes, said he felt convinced that Modernists should stand for the following:

1. That the Revised Canons be not legalised nor be claimed to possess legal authority.

2. That the Revised Canons be not imposed on the clergy or included in any form of subscription required from them.

3. That our policy of church reunion should authorise intercommunion when desired by communicants of any Christian denomination at the Lord's table in our national church.[13]

Since then the Canons have come into being and been promulgated in 1964 and 1969, but the clergy do not have to take any rigid subscription to them. As regards intercommunion the situation that Major asked for has largely come about. He handed over the *Modern Churchman* to an editorial committee and to his disciple Arthur Adams, Dean of Magdalen, as Editor in chief. Adams later shared this office with William Frend and then handed the magazine over to Frend completely.

The first issue of the new series of the *Modern Churchman* contained an article by Archbishop Fisher on Dr Major; he must have been the first Archbishop of Canterbury to write in it. He said:

Though I have never had the opportunity of close acquaintance with Dr. Major, I have from time to time had correspondence with him. I was often inclined to think that he was too firmly tied to certain unvarying modes of thought or expression in the realm of Christian doctrine to be in my sense of the word liberal. But he was always very learned, very lucid and very persistent and with a passion for truth as he saw it.[14]

In the same issue was an article by John Wren Lewis on 'The Real Significance of Demythologization'.

Major lived on in Merton Vicarage until his death at the end of January 1961; he ceased to be Vicar only a few months before his death.[15] He had lived to see yet another change in the Presidency of the Modern Churchmen's Union. Bishop Leonard Wilson, Barnes' successor at Birmingham, took over from Sir Henry Self in 1957.[16] In 1961 Rhodes handed over the Secretaryship of the Union to the Rev. F. E. Compton, a Birmingham vicar who soon moved to a country parish near Ludlow and remains the Secretary today. Major's funeral was a notable gathering of Modern Churchmen, with four Bishops present – Leonard Wilson of Birmingham, Geoffrey Allen, who had left Ripon Hall to be Bishop of Derby, the Bishop of Oxford (Harry Carpenter) and the Bishop of Dorchester (David Loveday). The Roman Catholic theologian Bernard Leeming also was present with Major's two Jesuit grandsons. Gordon Fallows, successor to Bishop Allen at Ripon Hall, preached the sermon. Later that year Norman Sykes, another notable Modernist, who owed to Major his introduction to Edmund Gibson, died at Winchester where he had ended his days as Dean.

In the very year of Major's death came the book which brought to an end the triumphalism of biblical theology. This was James Barr's *The Semantics of Biblical Language* which showed how the exponents of biblical theology had often been barking up the wrong tree. It particularly criticized T. Boman's *Hebrew Thought compared with Greek*, which the Nottingham school of Alan Richardson with their over-emphasis on Semitic thought forms had seized upon with open arms. How J. Langmead Casserley rejoiced over the publication of Barr's book, since he had contended that English theology had degenerated into work with Concordances and Biblical Word Books – so he had argued in *The Retreat from Christianity in the Modern World*, his Maurice Lectures for 1951. In 1962 the new radicalism started moving more strongly with the publication of *Soundings*, edited by Dr Alec Vidler. This had contributions from two disciples of Major, G. F. Woods and

Howard Root; and from Geoffrey Lampe, who though he had had nothing to do with Ripon Hall, was a member of the Modernist camp. *Soundings*, which had been in preparation for a few years (Howard Root had reported its projection to Dr Major in 1957), had been intended for 1960 to commemorate *Essays and Reviews* but it was too late for that. In view of *Honest to God* one is surprised to find no contribution from Dr Robinson in it. Vidler gives the answer in his *Scenes from a Clerical Life*, 'Although he had been a don at Cambridge when we formed the *Soundings* group, we had deliberately not invited him to join us, because he seemed then to be still an apostle of biblical theology and of the liturgical movement.'[17] But one is still surprised, since in his book *In the end, God* (1950) Robinson had showed himself a universalist, like the Modernists, and in *Jesus and His Coming* (1957) he had, like the Modernists, with the help of T. F. Glasson, tried to get rid of the notion that the historical Jesus believed in a second coming on the clouds of heaven, at the end of the world.

So we come to *Honest to God*, written by one who had had nothing to do with Modernism or Liberalism and yet which seemed to some to be the most negative book of theology that the century had yet seen. Dr Robinson had already been in the public eye over *Lady Chatterley's Lover* by D. H. Lawrence.[18] What did Modernists make of this book? On the whole they were somewhat critical, in spite of the fact that the Modern Churchmen's Union had published John Wren Lewis' pamphlet. As Percival Gardner-Smith had reviewed Barnes' *The Rise of Christianity*, so now he was given to review *Honest To God*. He wrote as much about the one as the other and equally trenchantly. But he clearly recognized that *Honest to God* was a very different book from *The Rise of Christianity*. He found the book very disturbing, as in the same year he found Samuel Angus' *Forgiveness and Life* far too radical, though this had had the commendation of Henry Major.[19]

It is not easy to assess the permanent value of this book [wrote Gardner-Smith of *Honest to God*]. Of the author's honest intention there can be no doubt, and his courage in trying to meet the difficulties of those who find the anthropomorphism of popular religion a stumbling-block will win the admiration of Modern Churchmen. Nevertheless it is to be regretted that he has fallen so completely under the influence of such extremists as Tillich, Bonhoeffer, and Bultmann. In some passages he hardly seems to realise the implications of his position. A vague ethical pantheism may provide consolation for a few philosophers, but it would be quite useless as a working faith for the vast majority of men, and it could not provide a foundation for the active life of a Christian Church. Many of the parochial clergy have read the book with dismay. How can they deliver a message to the uninstructed masses of their congregations? How long will any form of institutional religion remain possible.[20]

I note that this was not one of the reviews republished in *The Honest to God Debate*. In his last sentence Gardner-Smith commended Michael Ramsey's answer to *Honest to God*, entitled *Image Old and New*. His reaction was not untypical of the reaction of many traditional Modernists, though some of them like C. J. Wright were far more willing to welcome Tillich. They felt, on the one hand, there was much to be thankful for in *Honest to God*. After all Robinson seemed to be rejecting, like them, the miraculous and the God who intervenes in history from his throne on high. They also agreed with him in his assessment of the importance of love over Law. It was an old Riponian, Douglas Rhymes, who wrote on the same lines as Robinson in *No New Morality*. On the other hand they were irked that Robinson did not accept the Modernist degree Christology – for he rejects it on p.68. What, perhaps, annoyed them most of all was that he had arrived at some Modernist views, with no help from Rashdall and Major, and, in spite of that fact, had nothing complimentary to say about Modernists! But the main region where they were critical was over his doctrine of God. We saw how Major had been hesitant there in respect to John Wren Lewis. That Robinson was unclear in *Honest to God* and open to criticism is obvious from the fact that the philosopher Alasdair McIntyre maintained that he was an episcopal atheist. The nervousness of some Modernists regarding his doctrine of God, as far as it was developed in *Honest to God*, can be seen in the *Modern Churchman* for April 1963.

Modern Churchmen may be pardoned if they noted somewhat wryly the impact upon the public, of hydrogen bomb magnitude, made by the Bishop of Woolwich's book *Honest to God*. This book, and *Soundings* published a few months ago, are propounding theological questions, assertions and attitudes which the Modern Churchmen's Union has been discussing or advocating for fifty years. It might appear that the whole world has awakened to find itself Modernist.[21]

Yet the Editor went on to voice criticisms of *Honest to God's* doctrine of God – the sort of criticism that Rashdall might well have made.

The Christian must resist any tendency to identify God with reality, even though it be termed Ultimate Reality, if that be taken to comprehend the world we see. It is indeed difficult to know what connotation to give to the word 'Creator' as an ascription of God in what may prove to be a steady-state universe. But the importance of the doctrine of creation, as the opening of Genesis makes plain, lies precisely in its assertion of the transcendence of God and so in his separatedness from His creatures. Upon this doctrine rests man's identity and freedom. And the Christian must resist any tendency to identify God with one of His attributes, even that of love. Love presupposes somebody who loves. On both grounds an impersonal view of God must be rejected. Perhaps we can go no further than did C. C. J. Webb when he concluded that God cannot be less than personal.[22]

Thus William Frend (I take it to be by him) rebukes the Bishop, but forgets that the Modern Churchmen's Union had published similar views in John Wren Lewis' pamphlet.

Criticism of *Honest to God* and *Soundings* was also voiced by *alumni* of Ripon Hall in the pamphlet *Four Anchors from the Stern* containing essays by Alan Richardson, Robert Leaney, Stuart Hall and James Richmond.[23] That Nottingham pamphlet also criticized *Objections to Christian Belief*, edited by Vidler, which was a further contribution to the new radicalism, though one of its authors was the Modernist James Bezzant who wrote on 'Intellectual Objections'. Criticisms of *Honest to God* and *Soundings* were heard at the Girton Conference of Modern Churchmen in August 1963. Charles Raven in his sermon at that gathering – it was the year before his death –

remarked with respect to both books that 'if certain of their constituents are accepted, it will change the whole relationship between religion and science, change it I am afraid for the worse. The grounds for this conviction are matters of basic importance and of general as opposed to particular importance.' In fact I understand that the only two Modernists who evinced sympathy with the new radicalism at that Conference were Norman Pittenger and A. O. Dyson, who in 1965 edited for the Union a new but short-lived periodical called *Impetus*. The biggest blast against *Honest to God* came from an old Riponian of the 'twenties, Fielding Clarke, who penned the volume *For Christ's Sake*. Though this, apparently, sold quite well – so Clarke maintains in his autobiography – I do not think anyone (except Eric Mascall) thought it was particularly successful.[24]

Quickly after *Honest to God* came Paul van Buren's *The Secular Meaning of the Gospel*. Here the Christian Doctrine of God did seem to be categorically rejected by an American ex-disciple of Karl Barth. Though Dr Robinson welcomed it, he was critical, as one can see in *The Honest to God Debate*, and in *The New Reformation?* Robinson had said nothing about the Creeds in *Honest to God* but now in *The New Reformation?* Modernists rejoiced to find him agreeing with them in their desire to keep credal formulae to a minimum. He also welcomed *God is no More* by Werner and Lotte Pelz, though this is as doubtful as van Buren about the possibility of making statements about God, and reduces Christianity to situation ethics and no more.

In 1966 the Modernists held a Conference at Southlands Training College, London, under the chairmanship of Canon John Pearce-Higgins, on Honest Religion (the title of a book published in 1941 by John Oman, but in fact the subject was suggested by *Honest to God*). Here Frank Cleobury delivered a considered attack on *Honest to God*, of which you will get the flavour if I quote the opening paragraph.

The subject of this Conference – *Honest Religion* – was suggested by the discussion that followed the publication of the book *Honest to God*. The Conference must start where the book started – with the discussion of the concept of 'God'. The Bishop began by criticising the notion of a God 'out there', as he

193

put it, and he seemed not merely to be saying that we must not take this spatial reference literally. Indeed, there would have been no need for him to say that, for not even the simplest Christian believes that God lives, shall we say, halfway along the Milky Way. The Bishop seemed to be going further, and lining up with those theologians who decry all attempts to demonstrate rationally that there must be a Cosmic Creative Mind. I shall show in this paper that the Bishop was barking up the wrong tree. If the words 'out there' are used as a metaphor for objectivity, there are far stronger rational grounds for believing in God 'out there' than in a material world 'out there', completely independent of Mind. Belief in God is far more rational than belief in matter.[25]

Whether Cleobury was successful I leave readers to decide for themselves.

Modernists took heart when Dr Robinson wrote his next book *Exploration into God*, which I personally found very satisfying. Here he started using the term 'panentheism' which had been used early in the century by Dr Major and later by Norman Pittenger in *The Word Incarnate*. This is the belief 'that the Being of God includes the whole universe, so that every part of it exists in Him but (as against pantheism) that His Being is more than, and is not exhausted by, the Universe.' However, if Robinson seemed to be reaching a position acceptable to Modernists there were others who were going further and further away from them. Such were the 'Death of God' School in America, i.e. Thomas J. J. Altizer and William Hamilton, and in this country Alistair Kee, whose *The Way of Transcendence* (1971) had the bold subtitle 'Christian Faith without Belief in God' Norman Pittenger, the Modernist who was most sympathetic to the new radicalism, and who was becoming well known for his radical attitude to the problem of homosexuality,[26] reviewed the book in *The Modern Churchman*[27] and made it clear that he categorically disagreed with it, though he encouraged people to read it. One can say no more about the debate about God. Broadly speaking, Modernists did not agree with the slogan 'Our image of God must go', but rather, as James Parke suggested, 'Our image of God must grow'.

What about Christology? There was much that they agreed

with in *Honest to God* about Jesus as 'the man for others'. They remained adamant in their belief in the divinity of Christ – that Christ was the window through which men could see God. In the same year as *Honest to God* came Dennis Nineham's Pelican commentary on Mark which accepted completely the insights of Form Criticism. How did Modernists react to that? There were many older Modernists who could not turn their back on the view that Mark represented the direct eye-witness testimony of St Peter. I myself tried to put across the new approach to them at the 'Honest Religion' conference in 1966, but expressed the view that, when modern criticism had done its worst, one could still find in the New Testament a portrait of Jesus. 'We shall still find enough of uniqueness [in Jesus] and shall be compelled to say that here were sown the seeds of the most complete revelation given by God to man. We shall, I am sure, find enough of the historical Jesus in the Gospels to feel persuaded that the reaction of the rest of the New Testament to him was deserved and appropriate.'[28] That was roughly the position that Norman Pittenger took up in his *Christology Reconsidered* (1970), and which John Baker took up in *The Foolishness of God* (1970).

Christology was the subject of the most famous of the more recent Modern Churchmen's Conferences which Norman Pittenger organized at Somerville in 1967, which was the Jubilee Conference. By now the Modernists, led by Edward Carpenter, Archdeacon of Westminster, who had succeeded Bishop Leonard Wilson as President of the Modern Churchmen's Union in 1966, were so respectable that even the Archbishop of Canterbury, Dr Michael Ramsey, was present to preach the opening sermon. The *Church Times*' anonymous correspondent (who happened to be myself – though I have not revealed that fact to anyone until now) wrote of that Conference.

It seems to have been the intention of Dr. Pittenger, to wake up the ideas of the Modern Churchmen's Union, and especially of that large number of its adherents who are still protagonists of Arnoldism, Erastianism, British Colonialism, Municipal Anglicanism and Public School Religion, who seem to the outsider to represent the Conservative party at prayer. If this was his intention it was certainly successful, since the Conference presented the Union with questions even more momentous than those engaged on at Girton in 1921.[29]

In contrast to Girton there was a paper on the Religions of the World from Professor Parrinder. Eric Heaton followed on the Old Testament Preparation. Then came the most disturbing paper of all, that of Dennis Nineham on the Jesus of the Gospels. Dr George Caird spoke on the Doctrine of Christ in the New Testament. He mistook his audience and imagined he had strayed into one of F. L. Cross' Oxford Biblical Congresses, and his erudite exposition seemed out of place in the series, and in spite of his pleas for the revival of Liberal Protestantism, he did not seem to fit the bill as a Modern Churchman. Professor Wiles gave evidence of his great ability to analyse and simplify the intricacies of patristic Christology, and the members of the Conference were pleased at his enthusiasm for Origen. Canon Dillistone won the affection of the audience for his demand that truths of religion should be expounded through the poetic. Canon Hugh Montefiore, whose recent book *Truth to Tell*, like Dr Robinson's *But that I can't Believe*, had echoed a lot of early Modernism, made the mistake of devoting too much time in his talk to discussing whether Jesus was a homosexual (a suggestion which would have horrified the Girton Fathers of 1921 and equally horrified some old Modernists in 1967), though he was careful not to cast any aspersions on the purity of Jesus. He spoke of Christ as the lens through which one could see straight to God. Geoffrey Lampe then dealt with the atonement and said much that Modernists had always said, though he was critical of mere exemplarism. Professor Reid spoke of the philosopher's point of view and the series ended with Peter Hamilton, a pupil of Pittenger and disciple of Whitehead; he devoted some time to the resurrection and seemed to be advocating a corporate non-personal survival, for which he was roundly taken to task by Frank Cleobury. Why did it seem to me that the Conference was so important? I gave the reason in the *Church Times*. It seemed to me that Nineham's New Testament radicalism was shared by only one other speaker, Professor Reid. As I said at the time, if Nineham was right, then the positions of Montefiore, Lampe and Hamilton could hardly be sustained. The trouble was that none of the speakers attempted to build up a

Christology on the basis of what was left when Nineham had done his devastating criticism. Hence the Conference was quite divided. The older members, and hence the majority, sided with the more conservative speakers, the younger ones with Nineham and Reid. One was reminded of the cleavage at Girton. My *Church Times* review of the Conference concluded with these words, 'Where do we go from here? If Nineham is right, then Christology will have to receive a far more radical treatment than this Conference gave it. Indeed, we shall have to talk about "the event of Christ" rather than "the person of Christ". But is Nineham right?' When the papers were published by the SCM (not in the *Modern Churchman*),[30] Leonard Hodgson greeted them favourably in *The New Christian*.

That Jubilee Conference of Modern Churchmen, which was addressed by mostly non-Modernists, ushered in over a decade of Christological debate. The far more radical treatment which Nineham had begun was continued by him and Maurice Wiles and Don Cupitt. Their contributions can be seen, with arguments against, in the Cambridge symposium *Christ Faith and History*, where Stephen Sykes and Peter Baelz (the one a former student the other a former member of staff at Ripon Hall) defended a more traditional approach. Wiles also wrote on the question in *The Remaking of Christian Doctrine* (1974). In 1977 came *The Myth of God Incarnate*. Representing a more conservative position than these was Dr Robinson's *The Human Face of God* (1973). How have Modern Churchmen reacted to the position of Nineham, Wiles and Cupitt who broadly speaking, have tended to question whether the Church was right in declaring Jesus to be God incarnate? On the whole Modernists have not been rushing to accept this position. Thus the Editor of the *Modern Churchman* for Winter 1977 wrote of *The Myth of God Incarnate*, 'We do not believe that *The Myth of God Incarnate* will compare with *Essays and Reviews* or *Foundations* as a milestone in Anglican thought. It is the sort of compilation to be expected from able writers who, however, lack historical sense . . . To declare him (Jesus) "possibly the most wonderful human being who has ever lived" (academics are careful folk) is pathetic.'[31] Dr Frend had been equally critical of the new Doctrine Report which had come out under the chairmanship of Maurice Wiles in 1976.[32] Yet one would have thought that there was much in the report which traditional Modern Churchmen would have commended – that the Creeds are not infallible, that we need pluriformity in theology, that there is not one single unified theology in the New Testament. Moreover there is the clear acceptance of dogma as necessary and a recognition that there are limits beyond which a Christian cannot go. Thus on p.71 of that report J. R. Lucas wrote:

> If I believed that Jesus of Nazareth never existed, or that he was just an ordinary man of no great interest to us, or that he was not crucified or never rose from the dead, or if I were to turn my back on him, and decided that the Analects or the Quran or the New Statesman were equally good statements about the nature of man and his place in the universe, then, although I might be an excellent man in other respects, I should have no business to pass myself off as a Christian believer or full professing member of the Church.

Professor Wiles certainly felt grieved over the *Modern Churchman*'s criticism of the report and wrote a letter in the next issue.

Moving away from Christology, two contributions of Modern Churchmen in the period of the 'sixties were to my mind of great value, though I can merely allude to them. One was the bringing together of scientists and theologians at Jesus College, Oxford, in 1962. The group, led by Ian Ramsey, included Cleobury, Raven, Arthur Peacocke and Alister Hardy and resulted in the publication of the volume *Biology and Personality* (1965). Later there was a similar gathering of theologians and sociologists under the leadership of Denys Whiteley, which resulted in the volume *Sociology, Theology and Conflict* (1969).

When I told someone that the subject of my Hulsean Lectures was 'The Rise and Decline of English Modernism', he could not understand the word 'decline' and felt it ought perhaps to be 'triumph'. I used the word 'decline' for the simple reason that the Modernists were pushed out of the scene by the new radicals and left in a conservative position. Yet in this period of the new radicalism some of the old Modernist endeavours have triumphed. Thus the relaxation of subscription to the Thirty-Nine Articles came about in the 'sixties. This began with Dean Matthews' little book *Thirty-Nine Articles* in 1961. Then came Canon Pearce-

Higgins' histrionic denunciation of them at his installation as Vice-Provost of Southwark Cathedral in 1963. Then came David Edwards' sermon about them entitled 'One last Heave' in 1967[33] and finally in 1968, the Lambeth Conference year, the report on them chaired by Ian Ramsey which subsequently resulted in the alteration in subscription. Again the Modernist ambition to ordain women, on which Charles Raven and Bishop Barnes were so keen, has spread to other sections of the Church, so that the literature on the subject in the 'sixties and 'seventies has been immense. Yet again the Modernist desire for the remarriage of the divorced in church has been advocated in two official Church reports. The first, *Marriage, Divorce and the Church*, was chaired by an ex-Riponian, Howard Root. The second, *Marriage and the Church's Task*, was chaired by Kenneth Skelton, Bishop of Lichfield. Again this period has seen the fulfilment of the Modernist hope that non-Anglicans would be readily admitted to Holy Communion, by the passing of Canon B15a.

Looking at Modernism in the last two decades one notices that the battles between high churchmen and low churchmen within the movement came to an end, and the antisacramentalist position of Barnes died out. Even vestments were introduced at Ripon Hall by Geoffrey Allen. But the battles between activists and their opponents have continued. One of the leading activists has been the Rev. Malcolm Goldsmith, who delivered the Annual Sermon to Modern Churchmen in 1970, and called upon his hearers to give up their concern with theological *minutiae* and move into the real world with its many problems. He quoted Colin Morris, 'A lot of contemporary theology . . . has Christians searching their heads instead of clutching their bellies. There are plenty of stimulants on the market to agitate their already fevered brains; there's room for an emetic to clear out their clogged-up systems.'[34] He commended Morris' books *Include me out* and *Unyoung Uncoloured Unpoor*. This brought down upon him the heavy wrath of Frank Cleobury, who felt that Goldsmith and Morris were representing Christianity as a this-worldly business only. Cleobury abandoned the Modern Churchmen's Union in disgust.[35]

The *Modern Churchman* is still alive, but only just, and its future is uncertain. Looking over its issues of the last two decades, one finds how wide it has cast its net in the way of contributors. Certainly any suggestion of a Modernist orthodoxy in that period is wide of the mark. Again, the Conferences of the Modern Churchmen's Union have continued though they have developed a different pattern and the daily newspapers now take little notice of them. The last one on the traditional pattern was that on Liberal Christianity in History which I chaired in 1969. But since then the variety of speakers that have been netted is truly remarkable. The new radicals have probably well outnumbered the old Modernists. What about Ripon Hall? When Gordon Fallows who was very much a traditional Modernist and disciple of Dr Major left to be Bishop of Pontefract in 1968, after adding to the college a large new building, there were among the Governors strong sympathizers with the new radicalism, though there were several traditional Modernists to whom it was abhorrent. Hence a certain amount of conflict. In the end, the new radicals carried the day and an old Riponian was appointed, A. O. Dyson, whose sympathies were entirely with the new radicalism. By then, however, most theological colleges were feeling a lack of numbers. Ripon Hall had done so under Fallows though one might have expected the prevailing liberalism to have benefited Ripon Hall. He had attempted to fill in the gaps by taking in women, an experiment that was not very successful. So in the 'seventies amalgamation with Cuddesdon was talked about. That would have seemed odd and indeed impossible earlier in the century. But in the 'seventies it was found that the men of Ripon Hall under A. O. Dyson and the men of Cuddesdon under Leslie Houlden were thinking on very similar lines. So the merger took place and one had the ironical situation of the relics of English Modernism finding a home in Samuel Wilberforce's foundation. After initial teething troubles, the college now seems to be on a steady course, though old Riponians are outnumbered by old Cuddesdonians at the annual reunions. 1975 saw the publication of Crockford again, and the Editor remarked in astonishment on this amalgamation of Ripon Hall, the college of Dr Major, with Cuddesdon, 'the Eton of theological colleges and firmly Tractarian'.

The Editor of Crockford also remarked, 'As a movement the "Modernists" or "Broad Church" is negligible.' The Editor of the *Modern Churchman* picked this up and rushed to the defence.

The M.C.U. may not be the force it was in the 'twenties or 'thirties when nearly every churchman of academic standing was associated with it, but this is to some extent because so many of its original aims have been fulfilled. No one is likely to be turned out of the Church for failing to subscribe to the Definition of the Council of Chalcedon on the Person of Christ. Moreover, the Union has concentrated on doing its job. It has sought to enlighten, criticise and construct. It has not come out with headline-catching phrases. It has attempted to think through some of the fundamental issues that face Christianity in the western world. It has aimed at bringing together people of all Christian traditions and none, to understand each other's viewpoint in an era of increasing frustration and intolerance. Where else in the Anglican or any other Communion would it be possible to hold a conference of more than a hundred participants addressed by Christian, Buddhist, Jewish and Moslem scholars? It has shown informed concern for the problems of the pluralistic society that is emerging in parts of the Midlands and northern England. Its role as a watch-dog over freedom of doctrinal expression may have changed, but it has much to do, and many years before it.[36]

Dr Frend there draws attention to one sphere of recent activity of the Union which owed much to Edward Carpenter, that of the dialogue with other faiths. The Modernists who included in their number both Alan Bouquet and S. G. F. Brandon have often demanded that theological students should know something about other great religions. But it is still not a necessary part of their training; and in this sphere Ripon Hall was never very strong, in spite of the wish of its founder Bishop Boyd Carpenter.

What then does the Church owe to traditional Modernists? It owes to them the demand that doctrinal thinking should be controlled by ethical thinking. Any characterization of God which would be criticized if it were posited of a human being had to be ruled out. It owes to them in the first half of the century the inculcation of the necessity of biblical criticism. It owes to them the pressing for the final acceptance of an evolutionary outlook on life. They certainly rejoiced at the publication of Teilhard de Chardin's *The Phenomenon of Man*. It owes to them the promotion of

201

high standards of scholarship in ordination training. It owes to them the realization that credal formulae are but mere approximations to reality. It owes to them the acceptance of the legitimacy of a position of agnosticism on the miraculous. Note how their position was taken up in the work *Miracles* which came from Cambridge in 1965, and in the work *Catholic Anglicans Today* (1968) where a young Anglo-Catholic wrote, 'A Christian is free to believe that Jesus was born by a particular process, parthenogenesis, but this belief is not something which the Church has the power, right, or need to make necessary for salvation.'[37]

Admittedly they can be criticized for their at times naive optimism, their failure to see the value of *some* modern methods in biblical criticism, their at times anti-sacramentalism. Perhaps on occasion they were too Pelagian and failed to emphasize man's need of redemption besides illumination. Perhaps at times they felt they could build the Kingdom of God on earth – though they certainly were not, I think, guilty of a belief in inevitable progress. Perhaps they were too individualistic, and perhaps at times – curiously enough – they emphasized the spiritual to the detriment of the material. Certainly Henry Major was too prone to work out a Modernist orthodoxy.[38]

Bishop Mandell Creighton in his Hulsean Lectures *Persecution and Tolerance* said,

> The Church is a witness to the truth, and her primary duty is to see that her witness is true. The means by which she is to accomplish that duty is to see that no teaching is given under her authority which contradicts or impairs the essential elements of that truth committed to her charge.

He then went on to use of those claiming an irresponsible liberty the words of Amiel, 'They confuse the right of the individual to be free with the duty of the institution to be something.'[39] I would claim that classical Modernism always maintained that there was a duty of the Christian Church to be something. From its start it always maintained three aspects of the Christian faith as essential.

1.   The belief in a supra-personal God – the reality 'undergirding and penetrating through the whole derived creation', to quote some words of Norman Pittenger. They would still cling to that,

though today they would see creation as more necessary to the very being of God than was apparent in earlier thinking. One can add that Modernists have always been ready to depict God as suffering with and in his creation.

2.   Then there is the belief that Jesus Christ is the window or lens through which we can see God. Traditional Modernism has always believed that we know sufficient of the historical Jesus to contend that it is right to bow down before Christ and say with St Thomas, 'My Lord and my God'. Modernists have never been persuaded that the historical Jesus was unimportant or insignificant or unknowable.

3.   Then there is the belief in eternal life, beginning here and now and continuing beyond the grave. One of the most remarkable experiences that some of us had in the 'sixties was that of teaching ordinands who had given up belief in any after-life. Indeed on 10 December 1965 a letter appeared in the *Church Times* from the Rev. P. G. Hardman bidding the Church to give up this last ditch stand and accept that what it had said about resurrection or after-life was nothing more than imagery. In contrast classical Modernism always maintained with St Paul, 'If in this life only we have hoped in Christ, we are of all men most pitiable.'

I began this book with Evelyn Waugh's *Decline and Fall*. May I end then with the favourite text of both Charles Raven and Ian Ramsey, which is also really the text behind *Honest to God* – the last section of Romans 8 which speaks of God and of Christ and of eternal life?

With all this in mind, what are we to say? If God is on our side, who is against us? He did not spare his own Son, but gave him up for us all; and with this gift how can he fail to lavish upon us all he has to give? Who will be the accuser of God's chosen ones? It is God who pronounces acquittal; then who can condemn? It is Christ – Christ who died, and, more than that, was raised from the dead – who is at God's right hand, and indeed pleads our cause. Then what can separate us from the love of Christ? Can affliction or hardship? Can persecution, hunger, nakedness, peril or the sword? 'We are being done to death for thy sake all day long,' as Scripture says; 'we have been treated like sheep for slaughter' – and yet, in spite of all, overwhelming victory is ours through him who loved us. For I am convinced that there is nothing in death or life, in the realm of spirits or superhuman powers, in the world as it is or the world as it shall be, in the forces of the universe, in heights or depths – nothing in all creation that can separate us from the love of God in Christ Jesus our Lord. (NEB)

NOTES

1   E. F. Braley, ed., *Letters of Herbert Hensley Henson*, p.204f.

2   *Lambeth Conference 1958.* Report, p.5.

3   *Lambeth Conference 1958.* Report, pp.6f.

4   *The Churches of England and South India.* A Joint Statement by the Anglican Evangelical Group Movement, the Church Society, and the Modern Churchmen's Union.

5   op. cit., p.4.

6   op. cit., p.1

7   op. cit., p.10.

8   op. cit., p.11.

9   op. cit., p.16.

10   op. cit., p.18.

11   op. cit., p.23.

12   *Modern Churchman* (Dec. 1958), p.354.

13   *Modern Churchman* (Dec. 1956), pp.193f.

14   *Modern Churchman* (July 1957), p.11.

15   Gordon Fallows preached a sermon at Merton on Major's retirement, which was printed.

16   For Wilson, see Roy McKay, *John Leonard Wilson Confessor of the Faith* (1973), which is not very full on Wilson's Modernist activities.

17   op. cit., p.179.

18   D. H. Lawrence was being commemorated the week this Lecture was delivered.

19 *Forgiveness and Life. Chapters from an uncompleted book The Historical Approach to Jesus* by the late Samuel Angus. Edited by Ernest H. Vines (1962). I reviewed the book in *Theology*.

20 *Modern Churchman* (July 1963), p.296.

21 *Modern Churchman* (April 1963), p.193.

22 ibid., p.194.

23 *Four Anchors from the Stern*. Nottingham Reactions to Recent Cambridge Essays edited by Alan Richardson (1963).

24 For the sake of completeness it is worth noting two trenchant criticisms by Eric Mascall, the Anglo-Catholic, *Up and Down in Adria. Some Considerations of Soundings* (1963) and *The Secularisation of Christianity* (1965).

25 *Modern Churchman* (Oct. 1966), p.7.

26 See his *Time for Consent. A Christian's Approach to Homosexuality* (1970).

27 *Modern Churchman* (Jan. 1972), pp.111–15.

28 *Modern Churchman* (Oct. 1966), p.51.

29 *Church Times* (4 Aug. 1967), p.15.

30 See *Christ for Us Today*. Papers from the Fiftieth Annual Conference of Modern Churchmen, held at Somerville College, Oxford, 24–28 July, 1967 (1968).

31 *Modern Churchman* (Winter 1977), p.3.

32 See *Modern Churchman* (Spring 1976), pp.25f. For Wiles' letter see *Modern Churchman* (Summer 1976), pp.181f.

33 See *Modern Churchman* (Jan. 1967), pp.135–41.

34 *Modern Churchman* (Oct. 1970), p.6.

35 See Cleobury's letter in *The Modern Churchmen's Union Newsletter*, No. 27, April 1971.

36 *Modern Churchman* (Summer 1975), pp.141f.

37 op. cit., p.105.

38 For similar criticisms of Modernism in America see Harry Emerson Fosdick's *The Living of These Days* (1957), chapter 9, which I have read since delivering these Lectures.

39 Major always mistakenly quoted these words as Creighton's. Creighton quoted them in his Hulsean Lectures. See also Francis J. Hall, *Christianity and Modernism* (1924), p.91, where probably Major got the quotation.

Appendices

9. T. F. Royds, 'The Church and Nonconformity'
10. J. M. Jeakes, 'Towards Unity'
11. Arthur Thomas Bannister, 'Joint Communion'
12. W. B. Gordon, 'Lay Representation'
13. Miss K. M. Emery, 'Lay Representation'
14. H. D. A. Major, 'The Training of the Clergy' (not published)
15. R. G. Parsons, 'Training of Ordinands' (not published)
16. James Granville Adderley (Sermon, not published)
17. Thomas Leslie Papillon (Sermon, not published)
18. Hubert Handley (Sermon) 'Our Needs of Power'

The papers, with the exceptions noted, were published in *The Modern Churchman*, vol. v, Nos. 7 and 8.

3. Oxford (Lady Margaret Hall). 21–5 August 1916

Chairman. Hastings Rashdall

1. Percy Gardner, 'Law in the World of Ethics'
2. F. B. Jevons, 'What is Conscience?'
3. Miss Lily Dougall, 'Conscience and Authority'
4. G. H. Rendall, 'The Ethics of Jesus'
5. R. B. Tollinton, 'The Ethical Teaching of Christ in relation to Human Society'
6. Alfred Fawkes, 'Ethical Development'
7. H. D. A. Major, 'Christian Ethical Development; Helps and Hindrances'
8. Alfred Caldecott, 'Some Objections to Christian Ethics'
9. J. M. Thompson, 'Christian Ethics and International Relations'
10. C. H. S. Matthews, 'Christian Ethics and Social Reform'
11. Hastings Rashdall (Sermon) 'Theism or Pantheism'

The papers were published in *The Modern Churchman* (October 1916), vol. vi, Nos. 7–8.

4. Cambridge (Girton College). 8–13 August 1917

The Church and Modern Churchman

1. Percy Gardner, 'Christian Art' (not published)
2. Michael George Glazebrook, 'The Church and the World'
3. W. R. Inge, 'Did Christ found the Church?'

4. Sir William Ashley, 'A Layman's View of the Church's Ministry'
5. Alfred Fawkes, 'The Origin of the Christian Ministry'
6. Henry Herbert Symonds, 'What is Church Authority?'
7. Bishop J. E. Mercer, 'Church Authority and Liberty of Thought'
8. Hastings Rashdall, 'The Spiritual Independence of the Church'
9. Cyril Norwood, 'The Church and the Churches'
10. C. F. Russell, 'Psychology and the Sacraments'
11. John Gamble, 'The Symbolisms of the Eucharist'
12. Bishop Mercer, 'The Church and Social Hope' (Sermon)
13. Arnold Page, 'The Church of England and its Nonconformist Members'
14. G. H. Rendall, 'The Church of the Spirit'

The papers were published in *The Modern Churchman*, vol. vii, Nos. 6 and 7. As indicated, Percy Gardner's paper was not published and also, it seems (see *The Modern Churchman*, vol. vii, pp.45f.) papers by A. E. J. Rawlinson, C. R. Shaw Stewart and C. C. J. Webb.

5. Cambridge (Girton College). 5–12 August 1918

Psychology of Religious Experience

1. Percy Gardner (Presidential Address), 'The Psychology of Religious Experience'
2. F. R. Tennant, 'The Psychology of Sin'
3. Neville Talbot, 'The Sense of Sin'
4. Hastings Rashdall, 'The Validity of the Argument from Religious Experience'
5. Professor Granger, 'The Validity of the Argument from Religious Experience'
6. Alice Gardner, 'The Psychology of Repentance and Forgiveness'
7. E. C. Dewick, 'The Psychology of Forgiveness'
8. F. B. Jevons, 'Inspiration and Comparative Religion'
9. C. W. Emmet, 'The Psychology of Inspiration'
10. Kenneth Saunders, 'The Psychology of Conversion and Saintliness'
11. Alfred Caldecott, 'Saintliness'
12. Cavendish Moxon, 'The Psychology of Christian Fellowship'
13. Eric Milner White (not published)
14. Mrs Constantine Graham (Aelfrida Tillyard) (not published)
15. A. A. Cock, 'The Religious Experience of Childhood and Adolescence'
16. Lily Dougall (not published)

17. Hubert Handley, 'Thomas à Kempis'
18. Michael Glazebrook (not published)
19. Professor Widgery (not published)
20. Alfred Fawkes, 'Blaise Pascal'
21. Nowell Smith, 'Thomas Carlyle'
22. R. B. Tollinton, 'Clement of Alexandria'
23. A. H. Peppin, 'Bach' (not published)

The papers were published in *The Modern Churchman* (August to October 1918), vol. viii, Nos. 5-7.

6. London (Kensington Town Hall and Queen Mary's Hostel, Campden Hill). 7-12 July 1919

The Ideals of Modern Churchmen

1. Percy Gardner, 'The Ideals of Modern Churchmen'
2. W. R. Matthews, 'The Church of England – Catholic and National'
3. Alfred Caldecott, 'Modern Churchmanship and Missions'
4. H. D. A. Major, 'Self-Government of the Church'
5. C. J. Sharp, 'Marriage and Divorce'
6. A. H. Sewell, 'Problems of Public Worship'
7. Cyril Norwood, 'Modern Preaching'
8. Harold Anson, 'The Teaching of Modern Theology in Parochial Life'
9. Sydney H. Nicholson, 'Music and Worship'
10. W. R. Inge, 'The Inscrutable Future'
11. S. K. Knight, 'Our Work for the National Church'
12. R. J. Campbell, 'The New Outlook'
13. C. F. Russell, 'Providence and Law'
14. Douglas White, 'Suffering and Forgiveness'

There were unpublished addresses by H. A. Wilson, C. T. Shebbeare, F. Lenwood, Jane Walker, C. E. Raven, A. S. Duncan Jones, Gilbert Coleridge, H. L. C. Vully de Candole, W. Bainbridge Bell and G. G. Coulton.
The papers were published in *The Modern Churchman*, vol. ix, Nos. 4 and 5 (August 1919) and No. 6 (September 1919).

7. Oxford (Somerville College). 23–31 August 1920

The Relation between Modern Knowledge and Traditional Christianity

1. Percy Gardner (Presidential Address)
2. J. C. Hardwick, 'Modern Conceptions of the Universe and Traditional Christianity'
3. G. G. Coulton, 'History and Christianity'
4. B. W. Bacon, 'Miracle and Scripture'
5. F. B. Jevons, 'Modern Conceptions of Morality'
6. Michael Glazebrook, 'The Evolution of Christian Ethics'
7. Alfred Fawkes, 'Inspiration and Infallibility'
8. Sir William Ashley, 'Modern Political Ideas'
9. Maurice Pryke, 'The Danger of Biblical Infallibility'
10. J. M. Creed, 'History and the Old Testament'
11. C. F. Russell, 'The Right of Private Judgment'
12. Alfred Caldecott, 'The Recent Extension of Psychology'
13. C. W. Emmet, 'Psychology and Traditional Christianity'
14. William Sanday, 'Edwin Hatch, 1835–1889'
15. H. J. D. Astley, 'Galileo, 1564–1642'
16. F. G. Given-Wilson, 'Joseph Mazzini, 1805–1872'
17. H. D. A. Major, 'Raymond Lull, 1236–1315'

The papers were published in *The Modern Churchman* (September 1920), vol. x, Nos. 6 and 7.

8. Cambridge (Girton College). 8–15 August 1921

Christ and the Creeds

1. Michael G. Glazebrook (Opening Address)
2. C. W. Emmet, 'What do we know of Jesus?'
3. R. H. Lightfoot, 'What do we know about Jesus?'
4. F. J. Foakes Jackson, 'Christ and the Creeds' (not part of published programme)
5. R. B. Tollinton, 'Jesus as the Revealer of God'
6. E. W. Barnes, 'The Centrality of the Person and Work of Jesus'
7. H. D. A. Major, 'Jesus, the Son of God'
8. Hastings Rashdall, 'Christ as Logos and Son of God'
9. J. F. Bethune-Baker, 'Jesus as both Human and Divine'
10. R. G. Parsons, 'Jesus: Human and Divine'
11. T. H. Bindley, 'The Faith of a Re-United Church'
12. W. R. Sorley, 'The Faith of a Re-United Church'

13. J. C. Hardwick, 'The Nature of an Ideal Creed'
14. Percy Gardner, 'The Uses of a Creed'
15. Harold Anson, 'The Proper Uses of a Creed'
16. Douglas White, 'What Creed should be used?'

The papers of this most famous of all Conferences of Modern Churchmen can be found in *The Modern Churchman* (September 1921), vol. xi, Nos. 5 and 6. (One brief paper by L. S. Hunter was not published.)

9. Oxford (Somerville College). 22–8 August 1922

Christianity as the World Religion

1. Percy Gardner (Introductory Address)
2. F. B. Jevons, 'The Evolution of Religion'
3. J. M. Creed, 'Early Christian Universalism'
4. C. W. Emmet, 'Primitive Christianity and its Competitors'
5. Lily Dougall, 'Christianity and the Western World'
6. H. J. D. Astley, 'Christianity and the Non-Christian World; The Primitive Races'
7. A. G. Widgery, 'Christianity and the East'
8. W. R. Matthews, 'The Finality of Christianity'
9. W. B. Selbie, 'Christianity and the Future'
10. R. F. McNeile, 'Mohammedanism'
11. W. E. Soothill, 'Buddhism'
12. Edwin Greaves, 'Hinduism'
13. R. H. Charles, 'To Love God with the Mind' (Sermon)
14. J. C. Hardwick, 'The Outlook' (Sermon)

There were also unpublished addresses of A. Clutton-Brock, Maude Royden, G. R. S. Mead, Vernon Bartlett, Hastings Rashdall and Sir William Ashley.

The published papers can be read in *The Modern Churchman* (October 1922), vol. xii, Nos. 6 and 7.

10. Cambridge (Girton College). 24 September–1 October 1923

Christ and Human Society

1. M. Glazebrook (Opening Address)
2. Douglas White, 'The Sexual Basis of Marriage'
3. T. F. Royds, 'The Christian Ideal of Marriage'
4. F. B. Jevons, 'Is the Family the Fundamental Social Unit?'

5. J. R. Wilkinson, 'Women and Priesthood'
6. Edmond G. A. Holmes, 'The Child: the Aim of Education'
7. Ernest Barker, 'The Results of Education at present'
8. Claud Mullins, 'Marriage and Divorce in the modern State'
9. R. B. Tollinton, 'The contribution of Races and Nations to the Kingdom of God'
10. W. W. Longford, 'Is the ultimate aim to be Uniformity or Variety of national life?'
11. A. J. Carlyle, 'Competition, Acquisition, and Service, as Motives for effort'
12. Percy Gardner, 'The sons of the Kingdom, their relation to (a) God' C. S. Woodward (b) the State'
13. J. W. Hunkin, 'The Church and the Kingdom'
14. Oliver C. Quick, 'God the King and the Father'
15. W. M. Pryke, 'The City of God'
16. J. H. Bentley, 'Is the group-mind personal?' This address was either not delivered, or at any rate not published.

The papers were published in *The Modern Churchman* (November 1923), vol. xiii, Nos. 7 and 8.

11. Oxford (Somerville College and St Hugh's College). 25 August–1 September 1924

The Scientific Approach to Religion

1. W. R. Inge (Opening Address)
2. E. W. Macbride, 'Evolution, a vital phenomenon'
3. S. A. McDowall (in place of Prof. J. G. Adami), 'The Possibility of Purpose'
4. Hector Macpherson, 'The Universe as revealed by Modern Astronomy'
5. J. S. Haldane, 'Biology and Religion'
6. C. Lloyd Morgan, 'Autonomy of Life and Mind'
7. W. G. de Burgh, 'The Time-Process, Eternity and God'
8. F. R. Tennant, 'The Reign of Law'
9. C. C. J. Webb, 'The Religious Consciousness in the Light of the History of Religion'
10. J. A. Hadfield, 'Psychology and Religion'
11. B. H. Streeter, 'Creative prayer'
12. W. J. R. Calvert, 'The development of modern ideas of the structure of matter'

13. C. F. Russell, 'The Natural and the Supernatural'
14. J. C. Hardwick, 'The Miraculous'
15. J. E. Turner, 'Immortality – Absolute or Conditional?'
16. Richard Hanson, 'The Sacramental View of Nature'
17. E. W. Barnes, 'The Faith and the Future'
18. M. G. Glazebrook, 'The Christian Interpretation of the Universe'

The papers were published in *The Modern Churchman* (September 1924), vol. xiv, Nos. 5, 6 and 7.

12. Oxford (Somerville College and St Hugh's College). 24–30 August 1925

The Faith of a Modern Churchman

1. W. R. Inge, 'Faith and Reason'
2. Alfred Caldecott, 'Why we believe in God'
3. J. S. Bezzant, 'What we believe about God'
4. J. C. Hardwick, 'Man – His nature'
5. Hubert Handley, 'Man's Needs'
6. W. M. Pryke, 'Modernism and Life after Death'
7. J. F. Bethune-Baker, 'Why we believe in Jesus Christ'
8. Maude Royden, 'Why do we believe in Jesus Christ?'
9. W. R. Sorley, 'The Ethic of the Kingdom'
10. R. G. Parsons, 'Why we are members of the Church of Christ?'
11. T. F. Royds, 'Why we are members of the Church of England?'
12. M. G. Glazebrook, 'The Bible and Modern Churchmen'
13. H. D. A. Major, 'Why we value Baptism and Confirmation'
14. E. W. Barnes, 'The Eucharist'
15. Alfred Fawkes, 'Superstition'
16. P. Gardner, 'Are Modern Churchmen dishonest?'
17. Arthur Hort, 'The Confessio Fidei of a Broad Church Layman'
18. W. W. Longford, 'The Loss of Vital Religion'
19. E. L. Elliott-Binns, 'The Vindication of the Faith of a Modern Churchman'

The papers were published in *The Modern Churchman* (September 1925), vol. xv, Nos. 6, 7 and 8.

13. Cambridge (Girton College). 6–13 September 1926

Sacraments. Their Psychology and History

1. C. F. Russell (Opening Address)

2. H. J. D. Astley, 'Primitive Sacramentalism'
3. Alexander Nairne, 'Semitic Sacramental Rites'
4. P. Gardner, 'The Pagan Mysteries'
5. Douglas White, 'Sacraments and the Synoptic Gospels'
6. J. S. Bezzant, 'Sacraments in Acts and Pauline Epistles'
7. J. M. Creed, 'Sacraments in the Fourth Gospel'
8. F. L. Cross, 'The Patristic Doctrines of the Sacraments'
9. A. L. Lilley, 'The Sacramentalism of Aquinas'
10. Norman Sykes, 'The Reformers and the Sacraments'
11. R. B. Tollinton, 'Sacraments since the Reformation'
12. R. D. Richardson, 'The Mystics and the Sacraments'
13. T. Guy Rogers, 'The Value of the Sacraments today'
14. H. A. Wilson, 'The Misuse of the Sacraments'
15. L. S. Hunter, 'The Arts in relation to the Sacraments'
16. J. C. Hardwick, 'Sacramental Tolerance'
17. W. F. Geikie-Cobb, 'The Task of the Modernist'

The papers were published in *The Modern Churchman* (October 1926), vol. xvi, Nos. 6, 7 and 8.

14. Selly Oak, Birmingham. 22–9 August 1927

The Modern Movement in the English Church

1. W. R. Inge (Opening Address), 'The Spiritual Nature of the Christian Religion'
2. J. S. Boys Smith, 'The Intellectual Causes of the Modern Movement'
3. Alfred Fawkes, 'History of the Modern Movement'
4. A. L. Lilley, 'Roman Catholic Modernism'
5. W. R. Matthews, 'Christianity and the Modern Outlook. Is a Synthesis possible?'
6. B. H. Streeter, 'Christian Faith and Knowledge'
7. J. F. Bethune-Baker, 'The Reinterpretation of Traditional Formularies'
8. W. W. Longford, 'Affinities of the Modern Movement with Catholicism'
9. J. P. Hodges, 'Affinities of the Modern Movement with Evangelical Protestantism'
10. J. C. Hardwick, 'Modernism and Agnosticism'
11. H. D. A. Major, 'Modernism and the Reunion of Christendom'
12. J. R. Wilkinson, 'The Actual and Potential Contributions of Modern Thought to the Teaching of Theology'

13. Francis Younghusband, 'The Modern Movement and Foreign Missions'
14. R. B. Henderson, 'A Christian Basis of National Education'
15. E. J. Martin, 'A National Basis for Religious Education. Some Practical Considerations'
16. E. W. Barnes, 'The Birmingham Conference. A Survey'
17. T. J. Wood, 'The Extension and Development of the Modern Movement'
18. Leonard Patterson, 'The Scholar-Saints of Antioch'
19. H. G. Mulliner, 'John Frederick Denison Maurice'
20. P. J. Kirkby, 'Hastings Rashdall'
21. Arthur Hort, 'Fenton John Anthony Hort'

The papers were published in *The Modern Churchman* (October 1927), vol. xvii, Nos. 6, 7 and 8.

15. Cambridge (Girton College). 17–24 September 1928

Christianity and History

1. G. G. Coulton, 'Is a Science of History possible?'
2. A. S. Pringle Pattison, 'Is a Philosophy of History possible?'
3. C. C. J. Webb, 'The Significance of the Historical Element for Religion'
4. F. C. Burkitt, 'The Importance of the Historical Element in Christianity'
5. M. J. Oakeshott, 'The Importance of the Historical Element in Christianity'
6. J. S. Boys Smith, 'The Significance of the Historical Element in the Christian Idea of Incarnation'
7. Geoffrey Allen, 'The Jewish Contribution to Christianity'
8. R. B. Tollinton, 'The Hellenic Contribution to Christianity'
9. Alfred Fawkes, 'The Roman Contribution to Christianity'
10. A. C. Bouquet, 'Christianity as World-renouncing'
11. Norman Sykes, 'Christianity as World-accepting'
12. J. F. Bethune-Baker, 'Christianity as World-redeeming'
13. J. S. Bezzant, 'The Authority of Jesus Christ'
14. J. C. Hardwick, 'The Finality of Christianity'

The papers were published in *The Modern Churchman* (October 1928), vol. xviii, Nos. 6, 7 and 8.

16. Cambridge (Girton College). 23–30 September 1929

The Problem of Authority

1. W. R. Inge, 'Authority and the Life of the Spirit'
2. Ernest Barker, 'Corporate Authority and its Sanctions'
3. M. J. Oakeshott, 'The State'
4. A. L. Lilley, 'The Idea of a Transcendent Order of Society'
5. J. C. Hardwick, 'The Meaning of "Spiritual" and "Religious"'
6. W. R. Sorley, 'The Scope of Authority in the Sphere of Science, Ethics and Art'
7. A. C. Bouquet, 'The Scope of Authority in the Sphere of Religion'
8. Alfred Fawkes, 'The Church as a Divine Institution'
9. F. C. Burkitt, 'A Corpus of Sacred Writings'
10. George Galloway, 'A System of Doctrine as revealed Truth'
11. J. M. Creed, 'The Idea of a National Church'
12. Norman Sykes, 'The Actual Position in England to-day'
13. J. S. Bezzant, 'Establishment and Alternatives'
14. Geoffrey Allen, 'The "Sacred" and the "Secular"'
15. J. S. Boys Smith, 'The Spirit of Christ and the Spirit of Man'
16. T. F. Royds, 'Righteousness and Truth'
17. J. W. Hunkin, 'Vision and Authority'

The papers were published in *The Modern Churchman* (September, October and November 1929), vol. xix, Nos. 6, 7 and 8.

17. Oxford (Somerville College and St Hugh's College). 18–23 August 1930

Problems of Personal Life

1. W. R. Inge, 'The Modern Outlook in Ethics'
2. J. C. Hardwick, 'The Disintegration of Morality'
3. J. S. Bezzant, 'The Nature of Man. The Old Background and the New'
4. Frederick Augustus Morland Spencer, 'The Christian Moral Ideal; its Nature and Validity'
5. Douglas White, 'Principles of Sexual Conduct'
6. H. D. A. Major, 'Christian Marriage in Idea and History'
7. W. F. Geikie-Cobb, 'Marriage and Divorce in the Modern State'
8. Mrs J. L. Stocks, 'The Social Aspects of Birth Control'
9. C. J. Bond, 'The Influence of Birth Control on Individual and Racial Health'

10. Eldon Moore, 'Eugenetics and Population'
11. Rene Sellon, 'The Acquisition and Expenditure of Money'
12. Harold Mulliner, 'The Ethics of Gambling'
13. L. P. Jacks (Unitarian), 'The Science and Art of Leisure'
14. Hewlett Johnson, 'The Claims of Beauty in Modern Life'

All the papers, except that of L. P. Jacks, were published in *The Modern Churchman* (September 1930), vol. xx, Nos. 5, 6 and 7.

18. Oxford (Somerville College). 7–12 September 1931

Man

1. W. R. Inge, 'Humanism, Pagan and Christian'
2. J. Arthur Thompson, 'The Nature of Man'
3. M. C. Burkitt, 'Man's Conflict with, Control of, and Adaptation to, External Nature'
4. William Brown, 'Man's Progress in the Understanding, Expression and Control of his own Nature'
5. Francis Younghusband, 'The Root of Religion'
6. C. F. Russell, 'The Root of Morals'
7. A. L. Lilley, 'The Nature of Grace'
8. Arnold Wilson, 'The Epic and the Tragedies of Civilization'
9. H. D. A. Major, 'The Role of Religion in Civilization'
10. Charles Raven, 'The Crisis of Modern Civilization'
11. J. A. Fraser Roberts, 'The Terrestrial Prospects of Man'
12. Oliver Lodge, 'The Evidence for Human Survival of Physical Death'
13. J. S. Bezzant, 'Human Immortality and Eternal Life'
14. J. C. Hardwick, 'The Challenge of Life'

The papers were published in *The Modern Churchman* (August, September and October 1931), vol. xxi, Nos. 5, 6 and 7.

19. Bristol (The Victoria Rooms, University). 5–10 September 1932

The Reformation Old and New

1. W. R. Inge, 'The Future of Protestantism'
2. G. G. Coulton, 'The Reformation and Historical Study'
3. E. W. Watson, 'Precursors of the Reformation'
4. V. J. K. Brook, 'The Renaissance in relation to the Reformation'

5. J. W. Hunkin, 'The Reformation and the Scriptures'
6. F. C. Burkitt, 'The Reformation and Divine Worship'
7. W. R. Matthews, 'Private Judgment and Church Tradition'
8. R. B. Mowat, 'The Social and Economic Effects of the Reformation'
9. Ernest Barker, 'The Reformation and Nationality'
10. E. W. Barnes, 'The Reformation and the Scientific Movement of To-day'
11. R. S. Franks (Congregationalist), 'The Protestant Scholasticism and the Counter-Reformation'
12. Norman Sykes, 'Later Protestant Movements in the Church of England since the Reformation'
13. C. C. J. Webb, 'The Reformation and the Oxford Movement'
14. B. H. Streeter, 'The Basis of Church Unity'
15. H. D. A. Major, 'The New Reformation'

The papers were published in *The Modern Churchman* (August, September and October 1932), vol. xxii, Nos. 5, 6 and 7.

20. Cambridge (Girton College). 21–3 August 1933

The Christian Church and the Modern World

1. W. R. Inge, 'The Church of the New Testament'
2. Samuel McComb, 'The Christian Church as a Divine Fellowship'
3. Harold Anson, 'Creative Worship'
4. J. S. Bezzant, 'The Authority of the Christian Church; its Basis and Justification'
5. J. M. Creed, 'The Authority of the Christian Church in Doctrine'
6. G. L. H. Harvey, 'The Authority of the Christian Church in Ethics'
7. M. T. Dunlop, 'The Authority of the Christian Church in Economics, Industrial and Political Problems'
8. M. V. C. Jeffreys, 'The Christian Church and Education in the Day Schools'
9. C. F. Russell, 'The Christian Church and Education in the Public Schools'
10. J. P. Hodges, 'The Christian Church and Education in the Parish'
11. W. W. Longford, 'The Character and Call of the Church of England in relation to Roman Catholicism'
12. R. D. Richardson, 'The Character and Call of the Church of England in relation to Modernism'
13. Norman Sykes, 'The Character and Call of the Church of England in relation to the State'

The papers were published in *The Modern Churchman* (August, September and October 1933), vol. xxiii, Nos. 5, 6 and 7.

21.   Selly Oak, Birmingham. 3-8 September 1934

The Bible and the Modern Man

1.   W. R. Inge, 'The Use and Misuse of the Bible'
2.   W. R. Lofthouse, 'The Old Testament in relation to the origin and evolution of the Religion of Israel'
3.   T. H. W. Maxfield, 'The Evolution of Judaism in the Post-Exilic Period, with special reference to its Literature'
4.   E. W. Barnes, 'The Old Testament and the Modern Man'
5.   J. R. C. Webb, 'The New Testament in relation to the origin and evolution of the Christian Religion'
6.   L. Elliott-Binns, 'Varieties of Biblical Interpretation'
7.   F. C. Burkitt, 'The Religious Value of Biblical Criticism'
8.   J. F. Bethune-Baker, 'Scriptures, Creeds and Articles'
9.   J. S. Boys Smith, 'Myth and Miracle in the Bible'
10.   C. E. Raven, 'Inspiration and Prophecy'
11.   F. J. Foakes Jackson, 'The Origin, Growth and adequacy of the Canon of the New Testament'
12.   H. G. Wood, 'The Bible in National Life'
13.   H. D. A. Major, 'Christ and Criticism'
14.   B. H. Streeter, 'Modern Criticism and the Gospels'

The papers were published in *The Modern Churchman* (August, September and October 1934), vol. xxiv, Nos. 5, 6 and 7.

22.   Cambridge (Girton College). 26-31 August 1935

The Church of England: Its Constitution, Character and Call

1.   W. R. Matthews, 'The Church and the Living God'
2.   R. D. Richardson, 'The Doctrinal Characteristics of the Church of England'
3.   J. M. Creed, 'The Relation of the Church to the Nation'
4.   J. F. Clayton, 'Problems of Church of England Membership'
5.   Norman Sykes, 'The Anglican Tradition of the Office and Work of a Bishop'
6.   G. G. Coulton, 'The English Layman'
7.   J. S. Bezzant, 'The Training of the Clergy'

8. E. C. Ratcliff, 'The Church Assembly'
9. Robert C. Nesbitt, 'Church Courts'
10. A. C. Bouquet, 'Public Worship in the Church of England; Its Ideals and Problems'
11. L. B. Cross, 'Conflicting Ideals in the Church of England'
12. W. G. Whittingham, 'The Church of England and other Christian Churches'
13. C. G. Challenger, 'The Church of England as it might be'
14. Douglas White, 'The Modernist's Task in the Church of England'

The papers were published in *The Modern Churchman* (October 1935), vol. xxv, Nos. 6, 7 and 8.

23. Oxford (Somerville College). 17–22 August 1936

What to Believe

1. W. R. Matthews, 'The Rights of Reason in Religion'
2. G. L. H. Harvey, 'From Fact to Faith'
3. J. C. Hardwick, 'What to Believe about Man'
4. T. F. Royds, 'What to Believe about God'
5. J. R. C. Webb, 'The Historic Jesus'
6. R. D. Richardson, 'The Significance of Jesus for Faith'
7. M. T. Dunlop, 'The Spirit of God'
8. H. P. Kingdon, 'The Church in which we Believe'
9. A. C. Bouquet, 'The Bible'
10. Roy McKay, 'Sin and Forgiveness'
11. W. R. Inge, 'Prayer'
12. G. F. Woods, 'Immortality'
13. Gamaliel Milner, 'Why formulate our Beliefs?'
14. H. D. A. Major, 'How to Believe'

The papers were published in *The Modern Churchman* (September 1936), vol. xxvi, Nos. 5, 6 and 7.

24. Cambridge (Girton College). 30 August–4 September 1937

Christianity at the Cross-roads

1. E. W. Barnes, 'The Present Religious Crisis'
2. Roger Lloyd, 'Christianity and Civilisation'
3. F. R. Tennant, 'The Church and the New Science and the New Philosophy'

4. S. H. Hooke, 'The Church and Modern Historical Research and Biblical Criticism'
5. Guy Rogers, 'The Church and the Economic and Political Situation'
6. St John Ervine, 'The Church and the New Morality'
7. J. C. Hardwick, 'The Flight from Reason'
8. Joseph Needham, 'Christianity and Communism'
9. Arnold Wilson, 'Christianity and Fascism'
10. H. G. Mulliner, 'Christianity and the English Democratic Movement'
11. Laurence Edward Browne, 'The Fundamental Solution'
12. A. R. Vidler, 'The Romanist Solution'
13. G. L. H. Harvey, 'The Humanist Solution'
14. Claud Mullins, 'Christianity inside and outside the Churches'
15. L. B. Cross, 'The Opportunity and Mission of the Church of England'

The papers were published in *The Modern Churchman* (August, September and October 1937), vol. xxvii, Nos. 5, 6 and 7.

25. Loughborough. 5–10 September 1938

Modern Christian Education

1. Cyril Norwood, 'The Christian Teacher and the Modern World'
2. J. T. Christie, 'The Religious Ideal of Education'
3. Miss A. M. Ashley, 'Modern Christian Education and Democracy'
4. Basil Yeaxlee, 'The Place of Psychology in Religious Education'
5. H. G. Mulliner, 'The Church and the Child'
6. Neville V. Gorton, 'Public School Religious Education'
7. Norman Sykes, 'The English Universities and Modern Christian Education'
8. P. Gardner-Smith, 'The Teaching of the Old Testament'
9. C. J. Cadoux, 'The Educational Use of the New Testament'
10. R. D. Richardson, 'The Educational Value of Public Divine Worship'
11. T. F. Coade, 'The Relation of History and Art to Religion in Modern Christian Education'
12. J. C. Hardwick, 'Co-ordination of Science with Modern Christian Education'
13. A. C. Bouquet, 'Ecclesia Docens et Discens'
14. J. S. Boys Smith, 'Authority and Freedom in Modern Christian Education'

The papers were published in *The Modern Churchman* (October 1938), vol. xxviii, Nos. 5, 6 and 7.

26. Cambridge (Girton College). 28 August–1 September 1939

A Comprehensive Church

1. Cyril Norwood, 'The Ideal of a Comprehensive Church'
2. T. J. Wood, 'The Purpose, Scope and Practical Significance of the Doctrine Report'
3. W. R. Inge, 'Doctrinal Latitude in History'
4. R. B. Henderson, 'The Tests of Orthodoxy'
5. W. G. de Burgh, 'Discovery and Revelation'
6. S. A. Cook, 'Criticism, Scripture and Doctrine'
7. C. F. Russell, 'God and Nature – Creation and Miracle'
8. C. J. Wright, 'The Doctrine of the Incarnation and Presuppositions'
9. J. M. Creed, 'Jesus Christ in History and Experience'
10. Middleton Murry, 'The Holy Spirit and the Church'
11. W. G. Whittingham, 'The Ministry and Sacraments of a Comprehensive Church'
12. S. H. Hooke, 'Christian Eschatology – Its Origin and Validity'
13. A. G. Fraser, 'Christian Unity and World Evangelism'
14. J. S. Bezzant, 'Doctrine and Development'

The papers were published in *The Modern Churchman* (September 1939), vol. xxix, Nos. 5, 6 and 7.

27. This was due to be held at Somerville College, Oxford, 9–14 September 1940, but the War prevented it being held. These papers had been arranged.

The Church Looks Forward

1. Alfred Zimmern, 'Christian Values and Modern Civilization'
2. J. S. Bezzant, 'Essential Christianity in Faith'
3. Harold Anson, 'Essential Christianity in Practice'
4. A. C. Bouquet, 'The Other Great Historic Religions'
5. H. P. Kingdon, 'Bolshevism and Nazism'
6. Gilbert Murray, 'Humanism'
7. J. C. Hardwick, 'Indifferentism and Pessimism'
8. G. L. H. Harvey, 'Christian Obscurantism and Sectarianism'
9. L. B. Cross, 'The Bible in the Light of Modern Research'

10. H. D. A. Major, 'The National Church as it is and as it might be'
11. F. E. Compton, 'Public Worship and Sunday Observance'
12. Guy Kendall, 'The Christian Tradition in English Education'
13. Arnold Wilson, 'The Christian Spirit in English Public Life'

Six of these papers (those of Harold Anson, A. C. Bouquet, H. P. Kingdon, J. C. Hardwick, Guy Kendall and F. E. Compton), though not delivered, were published in *The Modern Churchman* (October 1940), vol. xxx, Nos. 5, 6 and 7.

27. Oxford (Somerville College and Regent's Park College). 26–9 July 1943

The National Church and National Life

1. Cyril Norwood, 'The National Church and the National Life'
2. J. C. Hardwick, 'The Function of Religion in the National Life'
3. W. R. Inge, 'The National Church as a Teacher of Christian Truth'
4. R. D. Richardson, 'The National Church and Divine Worship'
5. W. G. Fallows, 'National Christian Reunion'
6. J. S. Bezzant, 'The Relations of Church and State'
7. L. B. Cross, 'The National Church and Education'
8. Gamaliel Milner, 'The Parson as Politician and Economist'
9. Francis Fremantle, 'The Layman's Rights and Duties'
10. V. J. K. Brook (Conference Sermon), 'The Apostolic Gospel'

The ten papers were published in *The Modern Churchman*, vol. xxxiii, Nos. 4, 5 and 6. The Conference Sermon was published in *The Modern Churchman* (December 1943), vol. xxxiii, Nos. 7, 8 and 9.

28. Oxford (Somerville College). 13–18 August 1945

The Religion the World Needs

1. Cyril Norwood, 'The Religion the World Needs'
2. William Brown, 'Psychology and Religion'
3. Stanley Cook, 'The Relevance of the Science of Religion'
4. E. C. Dewick, 'Religion and World Unity'
5. W. R. Matthews, 'Religion and Ethics'
6. T. J. Wood, 'Religion and Truth'
7. S. H. Hooke, 'Christianity; its Universality and Finality'
8. J. W. Hunkin, 'Christianity and Goodness'

9. H. K. Andrews, 'Christianity and Beauty; Music in Public Worship'
10. St John Ervine, 'God and My Neighbour'
11. E. J. Strover, 'Reverence for Human Personality'
12. M. S. Gotch, 'Religion in a Grammar School'
13. H. C. Snape, 'A Christian Novum Organum'
14. J. P. Hinton, 'Eugenics and Christianity'
15. C. J. Wright, 'Christian Unity; its Nature and Method'
16. Samuel Cookey, 'Christian Education'
17. W. R. Inge, 'Retrospect and Prospect'

The papers were published in *The Modern Churchman* (September 1945), vol. xxxiv, Nos. 4, 5 and 6.

29. London (Westfield College). 16-21 September 1946

The Historic Jesus and his Gospel

1. Cyril Norwood, 'The Demand for the Historical Jesus'
2. G. L. H. Harvey, 'Jesus: Myth or History?'
3. David Scott, 'Jesus According to the Scriptures'
4. E. R. Buckley, 'The Synoptic Problem: Methods and Result'
5. C. J. Cadoux, 'The Historic Jesus in the Earliest Gospel Sources'
6. H. D. A. Major, 'Jesus; His Messianic Consciousness and Office'
7. P. Gardner-Smith, 'Jesus and his Gospel'
8. Norman S. Power, 'The Parables and Poetry of Jesus'
9. E. L. Allen, 'The Personal Characteristics of Jesus'
10. J. K. Nettlefold, 'Jesus and his Passion'
11. L. B. Cross, 'Jesus: his Resurrection and Ascension'
12. L. B. Cross, 'The Jesus of St. Paul'
13. C. J. Wright, 'The Jesus of St. John'
14. R. D. Richardson, 'Jesus and Christian Institutions'
15. A. W. Adams, 'Jesus and the Creeds'
16. Denys Whiteley, 'The Historic Jesus and Modern Evangelism'
17. Marcus Knight, The Conference Sermon

The papers were published in *The Modern Churchman* (September 1946), vol. xxxvi, Nos. 4, 5 and 6.

30. London (Westfield College). 22–7 September 1947

Problems of Christian Faith and Practice

1. Henry Self, 'The Christian Religion To-day. Its Tasks and Prospects'
2. T. Wigley, 'Can we be Religious to-day'
3. C. J. Wright, 'The Problems of Providence'
4. J. S. Bezzant, 'The Scheme of Salvation'
5. A. C. Bouquet, 'The Value of the Bible'
6. R. Gladstone Griffith, 'How to teach the Bible'
7. Ian Ramsey, 'Love and Equality'
8. C. F. Russell, 'Love and Force'
9. Eric W. Brewin, 'Love and Wealth'
10. Royden Shaw, 'Ordination of Women'
11. G. L. H. Harvey, 'Marriage and Divorce'
12. T. J. Wood, 'Re-union and Re-establishment'
13. H. D. A. Major, 'English Canon Law'
14. W. G. Fallows, 'Church Administration'
15. G. F. Townley, 'Church Finance'
16. F. W. Moyle, 'Imagination in Religion'

The papers were published in *The Modern Churchman* (December 1947), vol. xxxvii, Nos. 7–12.

31. Oxford (Somerville College and Regent's Park College). 26–31 July 1948

The Necessity for a Christian Modernism

1. Henry Self, 'The Necessity for a Christian Modernism'
2. S. A. Cook, 'The Causes of Christian Modernism'
3. W. R. Inge, 'Modernism True and False'
4. R. B. Henderson, 'The Faith of a Modernist Layman'
5. Martin Davidson, 'Modern Science and Christian Modernism'
6. J. S. Boys Smith, 'Christian Modernism and Barthianism'
7. Cyril Norwood, 'Christian Modernism and Education'
8. Alice Ashley, 'Christian Modernism and Education'
9. F. E. Compton, 'Christian Modernism in Pastoral Work'
10. A. C. Bouquet, 'World Evangelism and Christian Modernism'
11. Denys E. H. Whiteley, 'Christian Modernism and Church Unity'
12. E. Graham Howe, 'Psycho-Therapy and the Experience of Conversion'

13. D. L. Scott, 'Hastings Rashdall'
14. J. S. Bezzant, 'B. H. Streeter'
15. W. Richardson, 'Christian Modernism and Philosophical Theology'
16. J. W. Hunkin, 'The Charter of Christian Modernism'
17. W. M. Browne, 'Via Veritas Vita!'

The papers were published in *The Modern Churchman* (September 1948), vol. xxxviii, No. 3.

32. Bristol (The Wills Hall). 6–9 September 1949

The Flight from Reason

1. Henry Self, 'The Flight from reason'
2. L. W. Grensted, 'The Non-Rational Element in Religion'
3. H. C. Snape, 'Reason and Rationalism'
4. L. B. Cross, 'The Flight from Reason in the Interpretation of the Bible'
5. Geddes MacGregor, 'Reason and Aesthetics'
6. St John Ervine, 'Reason and Authority'
7. J. D. Pearce-Higgins, 'Beyond Reason – the Occult and the Psychic'
8. S. G. F. Brandon, 'Modern Interpretations of History and their Challenge'
9. Denys E. H. Whiteley, 'Return to Reason'
10. J. L. Wilson, 'What lack I yet?'
11. E. W. Barnes, 'Old Beliefs and New Knowledge'
12. Humphrey Paul, 'The Victorian Persecution and its Revival'

The papers were published in *The Modern Churchman* (September 1949), vol. xxxix, No. 3.

33. Cambridge (Girton College). 14–18 August 1950

Towards Christian Reformation: Reassessment and Re-Statement

1. Henry Self, 'Towards Christian Reformation'
2. A. D. Ritchie, 'The Christian Religion and Contemporary Thought'
3. C. A. Coulson, 'The Christian Religion and Contemporary Science'
4. S. H. Hooke, 'The Legacy of Hebrew-Jewish Religion'
5. Denys E. H. Whiteley, 'The Religion of the New Testament Writers'

6. W. L. Sperry, 'The Place of Jesus Christ in the Christian Religion'
7. T. F. Glasson, 'Jesus and his Gospel, since Schweitzer'
8. A. C. Bouquet, 'Jesus Christ and the Religion of Mankind: the Wider Christology'
9. L. B. Cross, 'The Trinity: Meaning or Mystery'
10. C. J. Wright, 'Dogmatic Reform in the Light of To-day'
11. R. D. Richardson, 'Christian Worship in the New Reformation'
12. E. C. Dewick, 'The Church; its Office and Function'
13. T. Wigley, 'The Outlook for Christianity'
14. W. R. Inge, Conference Sermon

The papers were published in *The Modern Churchman* (September 1950), vol. xl, No. 3.

34. Oxford (Somerville College). 13-17 August 1951

The Church: Past, Present, and Future

1. Henry Self, 'A Layman looks at the Church'
2. S. G. F. Brandon, 'The Primitive Church in its Relation to Judaism'
3. G. W. H. Lampe, 'The Early Church and the Ministry'
4. P. Gardner-Smith, 'Factors in the Development and Expansion of the Early Church'
5. T. J. Wood, 'Jesus and the Church'
6. M. T. Dunlop, 'The Church and Public Education'
7. Marcel Simon, 'The Church of England as seen by a Continental Layman'
8. William Gordon Fallows, 'Authority and Discipline in the Church'
9. Norman Power, 'The Church in the Parish'
10. H. C. Snape, 'The Holy Spirit and the Church'
11. A. W. Adams, 'Christian Reunion'
12. T. Guy Rogers, 'The Church and the Nation'
13. E. F. Carpenter, 'Diversity in Unity'

The papers were published in *The Modern Churchman* (September 1951), vol. xli, No. 3.

35. Bristol (The Wills Hall). 8-12 September 1952

Christianity To-day: Challenge and Response

1. Henry Self, 'Christianity To-day: Challenge and Opportunity'

227

2. E. F. Carpenter, 'The Contemporary Social Environment of Christianity'
3. L. W. Grensted, 'Dogmatic Religion and the Climate of our Time'
4. Francis House, 'Christianity To-day: Challenge and Response'
5. C. D. Curling, 'The Christian Challenge to Science'
6. S. G. F. Brandon, 'The Present State of Biblical Studies'
7. M. B. Foster, 'Religion in the Universities'
8. F. A. Piachaud, 'Christian Moral Standards and Contemporary Life'
9. C. S. Milford, 'Christian Strategy To-day and To-morrow'
10. H. D. Lewis, 'Revelation, Inspiration and Faith'
11. I. T. Ramsey, 'The Challenge of Contemporary Philosophy'
12. Howard E. Root, 'The Christian Vocabulary; the Problem of Communication'
13. H. H. Walsh, 'Signs of Revival'

The papers were published in *The Modern Churchman* (September 1952), vol. xlii, No. 3.

36.   Oxford (St Anne's College). 14–18 September 1953

Liberal Christianity in the Twentieth Century

1. Henry Self, 'The Permanent Values of Liberalism'
2. W. D. L. Greer, 'Liberal Christianity in an Established Church'
3. J. S. Bezzant, 'The Continuing Task of Liberal Theology'
4. W. R. Matthews, 'Liberal Protestantism'
5. D. J. W. Bradley, 'Liberal Catholicism'
6. E. L. Allen, 'Liberal Nonconformity'
7. J. W. Parkes, 'Progressive Judaism'
8. Marcel Simon, 'Continental Theology, Protestant and Catholic'
9. R. S. Lee, 'Freedom in Religion; the Psychological Basis'
10. H. C. Snape, 'The Moral Foundations of Liberalism'
11. Gilbert Murray, 'The Future of Religion'

The papers were published in *The Modern Churchman* (September 1953), vol. xliii, No. 3.

37.   London (Westfield College). 6–10 September 1954

Christian Living in Modern Society

1. Henry Self, 'Christian Living in Modern Society'

2. John Marsh, 'Work, Leisure and Religion'
3. Gerald Steel, 'The Human Factor in Business'
4. William P. Hildred, 'Has the Church failed Society?'
5. Wilfrid Garrett, 'Present Trends and Temper of Society'
6. L. G. Tyler, 'The Church and Industry'
7. Walter Reaburn, 'Casting the first stone – Crime and the Moral Outlook'
8. John Drewett, 'Christians and the Race Question'
9. M. T. Dunlop, 'The Church and the Welfare State'
10. Denys E. H. Whiteley, 'Re-mythologization: The Gospel in Contemporary Terms'
11. E. F. Carpenter, 'Marriage in the Church of England'
12. William Gordon Fallows, 'Christian Life in the Modern World'

This was the first Conference which Major had been unable to attend. The papers were published in *The Modern Churchman* (September 1954), vol. xliv, No. 3. Major appended an old article of his own on 'The Church and Economic, Social and Political Problems'.

38. Oxford (Somerville College). 25–9 July 1955

Man: His Nature and Destiny

1. Leslie S. Hunter, Conference Sermon
2. Henry Self, 'Man: his Nature and Destiny'
3. Alasdair C. McIntyre, 'The Nature and Destiny of Man: on getting the question clear'
4. G. F. Allen, 'Man's need of God'
5. L. B. Cross, 'The Bible and the Understanding of Man'
6. S. G. F. Brandon, 'The Concept of Man in the Non-Christian Religions'
7. W. H. C. Frend, 'The Doctrine of Man in the Early Church: an historical Approach'
8. H. D. Lewis, 'The Moral Status of Man'
9. J. A. Hadfield, 'The Sociological and Psychological Basis of Morality'
10. H. H. Price, 'The Implications of Psychical Research'
11. F. W. Dillistone, 'The Salvation of Man'
12. J. S. Bezzant, 'The Christian Hope for Man'

The papers were published in *The Modern Churchman* (September 1955), vol. xlv, No. 3.

39.   Cambridge (Girton College). 23–7 July 1956

Present Trends in English Religion

1.   Henry Self, 'The Fundamentalist Heresy'
2.   S. G. F. Brandon, 'Present Trends in Old Testament Studies'
3.   A. R. C. Leaney, 'Present Trends in New Testament Studies'
4.   L. John Collins, 'The Christian in Contemporary Society'
5.   C. O. Rhodes, 'The Prospects before Liberal Christianity'
6.   R. P. C. Hanson, 'The Dangers and Weakness of Roman Catholic Propaganda Today'
7.   Mervyn Stockwood, 'Religion in the University'
8.   George Every, 'Present Trends in the Anglo-Catholic Movement'
9.   H. C. Snape, 'America and the Future of Christianity'
10.   Norman Sykes, 'The Anglican Ideal and the Future'
11.   John Wren Lewis, 'The Restatement of Christianity for the Modern Educated Man'
12.   R. S. Dawson, Conference Sermon

The papers were published in *The Modern Churchman* (September 1956), vol. xlvi, No. 2.

40.   Cambridge (Girton College). 22–6 July 1957

The Sacred and the Secular

1.   H. C. Snape, Conference Sermon
2.   E. O. James, 'The Sacred and the Secular in Primitive Religions'
3.   T. A. Roberts, 'The Sacred and the Secular in the Bible'
4.   D. J. B. Hawkins (Roman Catholic), 'The Mediaeval Synthesis of the Sacred and the Secular'
5.   E. W. Hunt, 'The Renaissance, the Reformation, and After'
6.   S. F. Linsley, 'The Disintegration of the Sacred and the Secular – the contemporay situation'
7.   L. A. Garrard (Unitarian), 'The Re-integration of the Sacred and the Secular in the Life of the Church'
8.   Joseph McCulloch, 'The Re-integration of the Sacred and the Secular in the Life of the Parish'

The papers were published in *The Modern Churchman* (October 1957), vol. 1, New Series No. 2.

41. Oxford (St Peter's Hall). 8–12 September 1958

Christianity: a Faith for the World

1. G. F. Allen, 'Christianity: a Faith for the World'
2. F. W. Dillistone, 'Christian Theology and the Great Religions'
3. D. Howard Smith, 'A Critique of Foreign Missions'
4. George Appleton, 'The Challenge of Buddhism'
5. Victor E. King, 'African Reactions to Christianity'
6. S. G. F. Brandon, 'A Faith for the Present Age'
7. O. Fielding Clarke, 'Marxism; A Competitor'
8. C. K. Sansbury, 'Present Progress and Future Prospects'

The papers were published in *The Modern Churchman* (October 1958), vol. 2, New Series No. 2.

42. London (Froebel Institution, Roehampton). 31 August– 4 September 1959

Life and Death

1. T. Fish, Conference Sermon
2. A. John Drewett, 'Immortality and Ethics'
3. E. G. Parrinder, 'Immortality in Non-Christian Religions'
4. John D. Pearce-Higgins, 'Contemporary Attitudes towards Death'
5. J. Heywood Thomas, 'Immortality and Humanism'
6. Leslie Paul, 'Natural Intimations of Immortality'
7. W. H. C. Frend, 'Some Aspects of the Christian View of Immortality'
8. F. H. Cleobury, 'Immortality and Purpose'
9. C. O. Rhodes, 'Eschatology and its Validity To-day'
10. H. E. Root, 'The Logic of Eschatology'
11. S. G. F. Brandon, 'Death and the Relevance of the Christian Conception of God'

The papers were published in *The Modern Churchman* (December 1959), vol. 3, New Series.

43. Cambridge (Newnham College). 2–6 August 1960

Jesus Christ. His World and Ours

1. J. L. Wilson, Conference Sermon

2. S. G. F. Brandon, 'The Gnostics and their Problem'
3. A. R. Peacocke, 'The Christian Faith in a Scientific Culture'
4. James Parkes, 'The Jewish Background in the Incarnation'
5. F. F. Bruce, 'The Dead Sea Scrolls'
6. D. Howard Smith, 'Modern Racial Problems'
7. William Gordon Fallows, 'The Anglican Tradition of Sound Learning'
8. Charles E. Raven, 'Christianity and Biology'

The papers were published in *The Modern Churchman* (October 1960), vol. 4, New Series No. 1.

44. Oxford (St Hilda's College). 25–9 July 1961

Christ and Human Need

1. W. Norman Pittenger, 'The Christian View of Human Nature'
2. L. J. Barnes, 'The Meaning of Social Health'
3. J. T. Christie, 'Moral and Religious Values in Education'
4. R. S. O. Stevens, 'Man in an Industrial Society'
5. F. W. Dillistone, 'Liturgy and Community'
6. Michael Argyle, 'Psychological Research into the Origins of the Conscience'
7. D. Sherwin Bailey, 'Christianity and Sexual Ethics'
8. Frank Lake, 'The Resources of Christ in the Healing of Mental Pain'
9. A. O. Dyson, 'Personal History and Christian Preaching'
10. E. F. Carpenter, 'Truth and Christianity'
11. G. R. Dunstan, 'Christ and Human Need'

The papers were published in *The Modern Churchman* (October 1961), vol. 5, New Series.

45. Oxford (Somerville College). 7–11 August 1962

The Church in our contemporary World

1. M. T. Dunlop, 'The Church, the World and the Kingdom of God'
2. S. G. F. Brandon, 'Did the Roman world need Christianity?'
3. W. H. C. Frend, 'Constantine's Settlement with the Church and its Legacy'
4. E. F. Carpenter, 'The Essence and Accidents of Anglicanism'
5. David L. Edwards, 'Church and State Today and Tomorrow'

6. D. M. Paton, 'New Delhi and Rome: the Vatican Council and the Non-Roman Churches'
7. T. A. Roberts, 'Sociology and the Christian Church: the Contemporary Challenge'
8. A. John Drewett, 'England – a Field for Mission'
9. D. Howard Smith, 'The Church and the Non-Christian Religions. Existence and/or Conflict'
10. Gordon S. Wakefield, 'The Englishman's Piety'

The papers were published in *The Modern Churchman* (October 1962), vol. 6, New Series No. 1.

46. Cambridge (Girton College). 6–10 August 1963

Religion in a Scientific Age

1. C. E. Raven, 'Religion in an Age of Science'
2. Paul W. Kent, 'A Biochemical View of the Human Condition'
3. C. L. Gough, 'The Human Mind'
4. R. S. Lee, 'The Human Mind – in the light of Modern Psychology and Psychiatry'
5. John Beloff, 'The Body-Mind relationship'
6. A. O. Dyson, 'The Status of Theology in a Scientific World-View'
7. F. H. Cleobury, 'National Selection in the light of Personalist Philosophy'
8. F. A. Piachaud, 'Humanism – Scientific or Christian?'
9. J. D. Pearce-Higgins, 'The Bible in an Age of Science'
10. H. C. Snape, 'Man's future on earth and beyond. The Christian Hope Today'

The papers were published in *The Modern Churchman* (October 1963), vol. 7, New Series No. 1.

47. Oxford (St Hilda's College). 4–8 August 1964

Symbols for the Sixties

1. Alan Dunstan, Conference Sermon
2. F. W. Dillistone, 'The Quest for a New Symbolism'
3. Donald O. Soper, 'The people to whom the Symbols Speak'
4. John Heath-Stubbs, 'The Use of Contemporary English'
5. David Anderson, 'Images of Man in Sartre and Camus'
6. Ian T. Ramsey, 'Towards the Relevant in Theological Language'

7. Eric James, 'Towards the Relevant in Liturgy'
8. Gilbert Cope, 'Towards the Relevant in Church Buildings'
9. Allan Wicks, 'Towards the Relevant in Church Music'
10. Michael Forrer, 'Symbols of Renewal – Coventry Cathedral'

The papers were published in *The Modern Churchman* (October 1964), vol. 8, New Series No. 1.

48. Oxford (Somerville College). 20–30 July 1965

Christianity in Education Today

1. Denys E. H. Whiteley, 'The Age of the Amateur is over. Technique is not enough'
2. David E. Jenkins, 'Theological Education'
3. A. Chevenix-Trench, 'The Contribution of the Independent Schools'
4. John V. Barnett, 'Church Schools – Should we fight to retain them?'
5. C. G. Ludlow, 'Church Training Colleges – Are they worth the money?'
6. G. Youell, 'Christianity in the New Universities'
7. L. J. Lewis, 'The Challenge of Education in Tropical Areas'
8. Charles Taylor, 'Christianity and Students of Technology'
9. Timothy Newell Price, 'What may we expect from the Non-Church Schools?'
10. Harold Loukes, 'The Needs and Potentialities of the Less able pupil'
11. Alan M. G. Stephenson, 'Theology in the Theological College'

The papers were published in *The Modern Churchman* (October 1965), vol. 9, New Series No. 1.

49. London (Southlands College). 1–5 August 1966

Honest Religion

1. J. L. Wilson, Conference Sermon
2. F. H. Cleobury, 'God, Creation and Evolution'
3. D. Howard Smith, 'Is the Old Testament Necessary?'
4. J. S. Bezzant, 'The Doctrine of Salvation Restated'
5. Alan M. G. Stephenson, 'Is the New Testament Reliable?'
6. Edward Carpenter, 'Integrity in Thought and Life'
7. W. R. Matthews, 'The Person of Christ'

8. Monica Furlong, 'What is the Church for?'
9. Stephen Neill, 'The Church of the Future, Reunion and the Ecumenical Movement'
10. A. C. Bouquet, 'The Christian Faith and Non-Christian Religions'
11. J. D. Pearce-Higgins, 'The Christian Hope – Eternal Life'

The papers were published in *The Modern Churchman* (October 1966), vol. 10, New Series No. 1.

50. Oxford (Somerville College). 24–7 July 1967

Christ for us Today

1. A. Michael Ramsey, Opening Sermon
2. E. G. Parrinder, 'The Place of Jesus Christ in World Religions'
3. Eric W. Heaton, 'The Preparation for Christ in Israel'
4. Dennis E. Nineham, 'Jesus in the Gospels'
5. G. B. Caird, 'The Development of the Doctrine of Christ in the New Testament'
6. Maurice F. Wiles, 'The Doctrine of Christ in the Patristic Age.'
7. F. W. Dillistone, 'Jesus, the Revelation of Man'
8. H. W. Montefiore, 'Jesus, the Revelation of God'
9. L. A. Reid, 'Jesus' Significance Today. One Philosopher's view'
10. G. W. H. Lampe, 'The Saving Work of Christ'
11. P. W. Hamilton, 'Some Proposals for a Modern Christology'
12. Edward Carpenter, 'Integrity in Thought and Life'

These papers were not published in *The Modern Churchman*, but in a separate publication by SCM, London 1968.

51. Cambridge (Homerton College). 5–9 August 1968

Power within a Christian Context

1. A. J. Drewett, Conference Sermon
2. Joseph McCulloch, 'Persons in Relation'
3. H. C. Snape, 'The Biblical Background'
4. John Rae, 'Education'
5. Mollie Batten, 'The New Industrial State'
6. Donald McLachan, 'Mass Communication'
7. John Bevan, 'Government'
8. Paul Oestreicher, 'International Relations'

9. Valerie Pitt, 'Creative Imagination'
10. Leslie Paul, 'The Church of England'
11. Edward Carpenter, 'In Context'

The papers were published in *The Modern Churchman* (October 1968), vol. 12, New Series No. 1.

52. Abingdon (Culham College). 28 July–1 August 1969

Liberal Christianity in History

1. Ian T. Ramsey, Conference Sermon
2. Denys E. H. Whiteley, 'Liberal Christianity in the New Testament'
3. W. H. C. Frend, 'Liberal Christianity in the Early Church'
4. G. V. Bennett, 'Erasmus and the Reformation'
5. L. W. Cowie, 'Liberal Christians in the Seventeenth and Eighteenth Centuries'
6. Bernard M. G. Reardon, 'Liberal Protestantism and Roman Catholic Modernism'
7. Alan M. G. Stephenson, 'Liberal Anglicanism in the Nineteenth Century'
8. Norman Pittenger, 'Modernism in America'
9. Michael Richards (Roman Catholic), 'Present Liberal Trends in the Roman Catholic Church'
10. David Edwards, 'The Future of the Church of England'

The papers were published in *The Modern Churchman* (September 1969), vol. 13, New Series No. 1.

53. Abingdon (Culham College). 27–31 July 1970

Nature, Man and God

This conference was less formal

1. Nature

   Speakers: W. H. Thorpe, Edwin Barker, F. W. Dillistone

2. Man

   Speakers: Lord Wells-Pestell, Malcolm Goldsmith, Martin Israel

3. God

   Speakers: Trevor Ling, William Strawson, Stephen W. Sykes, John Drewett

236

Others who spoke were Edward F. Carpenter, Terry Thomas, Philippa Hughes, Peter N. Hamilton and H. C. Snape.

Much of the discussion is set out in *The Modern Churchman* (October 1970), vol. 14, New Series No. 1.

54. London (Digby Stuart College, Roehampton). 26–30 July 1971

Freedom and Responsibility. Man's Dilemma in a World of Change and Revolution

1. Eric Jay, 'Freedom and Responsibility in the Third World' (Eric Jay replaced Colin Morris who was ill.)
2. David Head, 'Freedom and Responsibility in a World of Science and Technology'
3. Sebastian Charles, 'Freedom and Responsibility in Britain Today'
4. F. W. Dillistone, Modern Churchmen's Union Annual Sermon
5. A. O. Dyson, 'Freedom and Responsibility in Modern Theology'
6. A. C. Bouquet, 'Freedom and Responsibility in Christian Commitment'

Dr Martin Cole, the sexologist, also spoke but his paper was not published with the above papers in *The Modern Churchman* (October 1971) vol. 15, New Series No. 1. In this number there were also reports on seminars by Ken Hills (Industrial Relations, Freedom and Responsibility), Kerry Holroyd (The Futurist Orientation of Faith) and Rex Ambler (Camilo Torres and Colombia).

55. Hertford (Balls Park College). 24–8 July 1972

Search for Meaning. Man's Quest for Faith in an Unstable World

1. Lady Kathleen Oldfield, Conference Sermon
2. H. C. Snape, 'Bleak House and the View Beyond'
3. F. A. Piachaud, 'The Christian Tradition in the Melting Pot'
4. F. H. Cleobury, 'Personal Religion and Social Responsibility'
5. Derek Bryan, 'The Ferment in China: Social and Spiritual'
6. Leslie Paul, 'The Church: Aid or Obstacle?'
7. S. W. Sykes, 'Transcendence and Christology'
8. Michael Perry and G. S. Whitby, 'The Quest for the Transcendent through the Paranormal'
9. Kenneth Leech, 'The "Hippies" and Beyond'
10. Alistair Kee, 'Christian Aims and Today's Perspectives'
11. John Collins, 'Personal Religion and Social Responsibility'

All these papers except that of John Collins were published in *The Modern Churchman* (October 1972), vol. 16, New Series No. 1.

56. Abingdon (Culham College). 23–7 July 1973

Scientific and Christian Humanism

1. Sir Hermann Bondi, 'Cosmology and the Philosophy of Scientific Progress'
2. H. C. Longuet-Higgins, 'The Scientific Study of Man'
3. A. R. Peacocke, 'Chance, Potentiality and God'
4. E. LaB. Cherbonnier, 'Biblical Contributions to the Development of the Scientific Method'
5. M. W. Thring, 'How can we Harness Science for the real Benefit of Mankind?'
6. Ted Bastin, 'The Challenge of a Non-Common Sense World-View seen as a Religious Opportunity'
7. Sherlaw Johnson, 'Mythology and Symbolism in Messiaen's Music'
8. John Ferguson, 'Faith for our Time' (Conference Sermon)

The papers were published in *The Modern Churchman* (October 1973), vol. 17, New Series No. 1.
In addition to these papers there were two sets of Seminars.
The first was on Men of Science:

Albert Einstein (led by P. N. Hamilton)
Charles Raven (led by F. W. Dillistone)
George Stapledon (led by R. Waller)
The second was on:

The Student Christian Movement (Paraic Reamonn)
Adult Education (J. Ferguson)
The Wrekin Trust (Sir George Trevelyan)
Society for Social Responsibility in Science (Hugh Sadler).

57. Hertfordshire (High Leigh, Hoddesdon). 29 July–2 August 1974

Religions and the Future of Religion

1. John Hick, 'Whatever path men choose is mine'
2. Ursula King, 'The Death of God – the Rebirth of God'. A Study in the thought of Teilhard de Chardin

3. Dow Marmur, 'Judaism today'
4. Freda West, 'The Idea of Salvation in Buddhism'
5. Wilfrid Stibbs (ex-Roman Catholic), 'Towards a Theology of Reconciliation'

Only these papers were published in *The Modern Churchman* (Winter 1974), vol. 18, Nos. 1 and 2; but there were others delivered, i.e. Homer Jack on 'Religion for Peace: What World Religions have done and can do', and a Conference Sermon by Edward Carpenter.

58. Abingdon (Culham College). 28 July–1 August 1975

Church and Society

1. Sir John Barnes, 'From Protocol to Progress'
2. Sir John Hunt
3. David Basnett
4. R. R. Osborne, 'Grounds of Hope. Power and the Church'
5. Edward Carpenter

Of these papers only those of Sir John Barnes and the Rev. R. R. Osborne were published in *The Modern Churchman*.

59. Hertfordshire (High Leigh, Hoddesdon). 19–23 July 1976

Integrity in the Religious Quest

1. Margaret Masterman
2. David Divall, 'Science and Scientific Method'
3. A. C. Adcock, 'History'
4. D. E. H. Whiteley, 'Theology'
5. Colin Thompson, 'Traditional Christian Mysticism'
6. Edward Robinson, 'Religious Experience and how to Assess it'
7. Hugh Jones, 'Christianity and Depth Psychology'
8. Gillian Mottram, 'Existential Honesty'
9. J. D. Pearce-Higgins, 'The Religious relevance of the Psychical, the Occult and the Paranormal'
10. John Drury, 'The Bible and Doctrine Today'
11. A. H. M. McClatchey, 'Religious Studies in Education Today'
12. Edward Carpenter, Closing Address

None of these papers was published in *The Modern Churchman*.

60. Abingdon (Culham College). 25–9 July 1977

Whither? A Study of the Shape of the Future

1. Allan H. Cook, 'Whither the National Sciences?'
2. Raymond Plant, 'Whither the Social Sciences?'
3. Ray Niblett, 'Whither Education?'
4. David Pailin, 'Whither Philosophy?'
5. Wilfred Mellers, 'Whither the Arts?'
6. Maurice Wiles, 'Whither Theology?'
7. Don Cupitt, 'Whither Personal Ethics?'
8. Ronald Preston, 'Whither Social Ethics?'
9. Norman Pittenger, Closing Address

All these papers were published in *The Modern Churchman* (Summer 1978), vol. 21, New Series Nos. 2 and 3.

61. Abingdon (Culham College). 17–20 July 1978

Germany and England: Prospects for a Theological Common Market

1. Stephen W. Sykes, 'Is the Anglican Church Reformed?'
2. Ingolf U. Dalferth, 'How relevant is Luther?'
3. A. O. Dyson, 'Theological Legacies of the Enlightenment'
4. J. W. Rogerson, 'Philosophy and Biblical Criticism'
5. R. C. Morgan, 'Germany and England: Historical Scepticism and Christology?'
6. Edward Carpenter, Conference Sermon
7. Dietrich Ritschol, 'How I see German Theology'

None of these papers were published in *The Modern Churchman*. But according to *The Modern Churchman*, vol. 22, No. 1, they were to be published in *Studien zur interkulturellen Geschichte des Christentums*.

62. Hertford (Balls Park College). 23–7 July 1979

Liberal Christianity in Practice

1. Edward Carpenter, 'The Spirit of Liberal Christianity'
2. James Hemming, 'The Quest of Modern Man'
3. Edward Compton, 'On being a Broad Churchman'
4. P. B. Godfrey (Unitarian), George Gorman (Quaker) and Peter Cadogan (South Place Ethical Society), 'How others practise Liberal Christianity'

5. Tom Baker, 'Present Day Insights in Worship'
6. John Mann, R. J. Stephenson and Peter Abbs, 'The Liberal Spirit in Education'
7. Alan Webster, 'The Church in the 80's'

63. Swanwick, Derbyshire (Hayes Conference Centre). 21–5 July 1980

Non-Western Theologies and their Significance for the English Church

1. Martin Conway, 'The World Church'
2. Malcolm Goldsmith, 'The World Council of Churches'
3. Andrew Kirk, 'South America and Liberation Theology'
4. Sebastian Charles, 'Black Communities and the expression of their faith'
5. John Davies, 'Can we speak of an African Theology?'
6. Ezra Tiswani, 'The Life and Theology of the English Churches'

64. Swanwick, Derbyshire (Hayes Conference Centre). 20–4 July 1981

Womanhood and Christianity

Chairman. Deaconess Diana McClatchey

65. Swanwick, Derbyshire (Hayes Conference Centre). 19–23 July 1982

Technology and Human Values

Chairman. Edgar Boyes

66. Hertfordshire (High Leigh, Hoddesdon). 18–22 July 1983

Belief in God, A Faith for Today

67. Hertfordshire (High Leigh, Hoddesdon). 23–7 July 1984

The Church in Politics

Chairman. The Rev. Dr R. John Elford

241

B. *The Churchmen's Union, later the Modern Churchmen's Union. The objects of the society as they were set out at various dates.*

1. The objects as first proposed. These are given in *The Church Gazette* (19 November 1898), p.117.

2. Objects as given at the first annual meeting. *The Church Gazette* (14 October 1899), p.703.

3. An enlarged list of objects, given in *The Church Gazette* (4 November 1899), p.68.

4. Objects as given in *The Church of England Pulpit and Ecclesiastical Review* (3 November 1900), p.212.

5. Objects as given in 1902. These are taken from the published text of Percy Gardner's *The Translation of Christian Doctrine*. These remained the objects until 1918.

6. Objects of the Churchmen's Union as given in *The Modern Churchman*, May 1919.

7. The objects of the Modern Churchmen's Union as given in *The Modern Churchman*, November 1931.

8. The objects and constitution of the Modern Churchmen's Union as given in *The Modern Churchmen's Bulletin*, No. 12 (April 1957), p.5.

9. The aims and objects of the Modern Churchmen's Union as given in a pamphlet issued in the 1960s.

10. The constitution and rules of the Modern Churchmen's Union as issued in July 1977.

11. The principles and aims of the Modern Churchmen's Union as issued in a pamphlet, February 1978.

B1. The objects as first proposed. These are given in *The Church Gazette* (19 November 1898), p.117.

THE CHURCHMEN'S UNION FOR THE ADVANCEMENT OF LIBERAL RELIGIOUS THOUGHT

Objects.

1. To unite Churchmen who consider that dogma is capable of reinterpretation and restatement in accordance with the clearer perception of truth attained by discovery and research.

2. To take such steps for the advancement of legislation in matters of doctrine, discipline, and dogma as may seem to conduce to the safety, welfare, and progress of the Church.
    The immediate action of the Union will be directed towards:
    a. *Enforcing the rights of laymen to an adequate share in Church Government.*
    b. *Making the use of the Athanasian Creed optional.*
    c. *Patronage Reform.*
    d. *Mutual Defence.*

3. To promote a conciliatory attitude towards Nonconformists, with a view to making the Church inclusive and truly national.

Rules.

1. That the Executive consist of seven clergymen and seven laymen, to be elected annually at the general meeting of members, together with the hon. treasurer and the hon. secretaries, *ex officio.*

2. That membership be open to such clergy and laity as are in sympathy with the objects of the Union, the subscription being not less than 2s. 6d. per annum.
    The minimum subscription is put at 2s. 6d., so as to place membership within the reach of ALL Churchmen and Churchwomen. We confidently look to our wealthier members for liberal support.

Note.

The official organ of the Union is THE CHURCH GAZETTE (price 2d.), which is published at 18–20, Temple House, Temple Avenue, London, E.C., where, by the courteous permission of "The Editor," are the temporary offices of "The Churchmen's Union." All letters should be addressed there to the "Hon. Secs. of The Churchmen's Union," and all cheques made payable to "The Hon. Treas. of The Churchmen's Union," and crossed "The City Bank."

B2.   Objects as given at the first annual meeting. *The Church Gazette* (14 October 1899), p.703.

"1.   To defend and maintain the teaching of the Church of England as the

243

Historic Church of the country, and as being Apostolic and Reformed.

"2.   To uphold the Historic Comprehensiveness and Corporate Life of the Church of England and her Christian Spirit of Tolerance in all things non-essential.

"3.   To give all support in their power to those who are honestly and loyally endeavouring to vindicate the truths of Christianity by the light of scholarship and research, and, while paying regard to continuity, to work for such changes in the formularies and practices in the Church of England as from time to time are made necessary by the needs and knowledge of the day.

"4.   To work for the restoration to the laity of an effective voice in all Church matters.

"5.   To encourage friendly relations between the Church of England and all other Christian bodies."

B3.   An enlarged list of objects, given in *The Church Gazette* (4 November 1899), p.68.

THE CHURCHMEN'S UNION
In necessariis unitas, in dubiis libertas, in omnibus caritas.

Its Aims and Objects.

1.   The Churchmen's Union is a society of members of the Church of England who are neither High Churchmen only, nor Low Churchmen only, nor Broad Churchmen only, but Catholics in the sense of endeavouring to combine all that is good and true in each of these three parties.

2.   As "Ritualists" have their organisations which give them self-expression and the means of propagating their distinctive principles, and as "Anti-Ritualists" are similarly organised, so the Churchmen's Union is an attempt to organise the great majority of members of the English Church who do not ally themselves with either of these extremes, that so it may be able to speak for all "sober, peaceable and truly conscientious sons of the Church of England."

3.   The Churchmen's Union, therefore, seeks to include in its organisation all those who, by an inexact but well-understood term, are known as "Moderate Churchmen," whether these are found among the historic High Church Party, or the so-called old-fashioned Evangelicals, as well as those who do not identify themselves with either of these two parties.

244

4.   It strives to set forth and maintain the doctrine and discipline of the Church of England as expressed in the Book of Common Prayer and the Thirty-nine Articles, giving due weight, where necessary in their interpretation, to the historical circumstances which have produced and continued them.

5.   The Churchmen's Union accepts, therefore, the teaching of the present formularies of the Church of England as to the authority of the Episcopate and the place of the ministry in the Church's life, while at the same time insisting on the rights of the laity to an effective voice in all Church matters; rights which are involved in their very membership in the Body of Christ, and are witnessed to unmistakably by the practice of the Primitive Church.

6.   The Churchmen's Union endeavours in every loyal way to promote a better understanding between members of the Church of England and of the Free Churches in this country.

7.   It asserts an essential continuity of life and doctrine in the Church of England, and discourages all ill-considered attempts to sever the historic connection between Church and State.

8.   While recognising the fact that the Church of Christ is and cannot but be one, though planted in many lands, yet the Churchman's Union endeavours in every way to maintain that historical setting of the Christian religion which has been found, by the experience of many generations, to be adapted to the needs and genius of the English-speaking peoples.

9.   The Churchmen's Union insists on the duty of recognising any truths reached by the research and scholarship of to-day, mindful of the fact that the revelation of God in the past cannot be contradicted by His revelation in the present; but is often illustrated by it, and often, too, cleared of misconceptions which act as obstacles in the path of honest and earnest seekers after truth.   .

10.   The Churchmen's Union deprecates all attempts to lift matters of ceremonial into a position of primary importance; holding as it does that the laws of the Church, and the general feeling of the whole community, should be allowed to determine all disputes concerning them.

11.   It upholds the historical comprehensiveness of the English Church, and her spirit of tolerance in all things indifferent.

12.   It insists on the paramount importance of maintaining the ethical teaching of Jesus Christ as the rule of Christian living, and the standard to which the national life should be urged to conform.

13.   The Churchmen's Union, in short, adopts Bishop Ken's famous description of his faith as that of "the Holy Catholick and Apostolick Faith, professed by the whole Church before the disunion of East and West"; and, moreover, it adopts from the same author its belief in the "COMMUNION OF THE CHURCH OF ENGLAND as it stands distinguished from all Papal and Puritan Innovations."

For forms of nomination or any further information apply to the Organising Secretary of the Churchmen's Union, 18, Temple House, Temple-avenue, E.C. [These aims were written by Dr W. F. Cobb and were a temporary alteration.]

B4.   Objects as given in *The Church of England Pulpit and Ecclesiastical Review* (3 November 1900), p.212.

THE CHURCHMEN'S UNION

The objects of the Churchmen's Union are – to defend the Church of England; to uphold her comprehensiveness; to support all loyal and honest attempts to elucidate the truths of Christianity by the light of scholarship and research; to assert the rights of the laity; and to encourage friendly relations with other Christian bodies.

Further information may be obtained from the Secretary, Churchmen's Union, 160, Fleet Street, E.C.

B5.   Objects as given in 1902. These are taken from the published text of Percy Gardner's *The Translation of Christian Doctrine*. These remained the objects until 1918.

OBJECTS

The objects of the Churchmen's Union are:

1.   To maintain the right and duty of the Church to restate her belief from time to time as required by the progressive revelation of the Holy Spirit.

2.   To uphold the historic comprehensiveness and corporate life of the Church of England, and her Christian spirit of tolerance in all things non-essential.

3.   To give all support in their power to those who are honestly and loyally endeavouring to vindicate the truths of Christianity by the

light of scholarship and research, and while paying due regard to continuity, to work for such changes in the formularies and practices in the Church of England as from time to time are made necessary by the needs and knowledge of the day.

4. To assert the rights and duties of the laity as constituent members of the Body of Christ.

5. To encourage friendly relations between the Church of England and all other Christian bodies.

B6. Objects of the Churchmen's Union as given in *The Modern Churchman*, May 1919.

AIMS OF THE CHURCHMEN'S UNION.

1. To affirm the continuous and progressive character of the revelation given by the Holy Spirit in the spheres of knowledge and of conduct.

2. To maintain the right and duty of the Church of England to restate her doctrines from time to time in accordance with this revelation.

3. To uphold the historic comprehensiveness of the Church of England.

4. To defend the freedom of responsible students, clerical as well as lay, in their work of criticism and research.

5. To promote the adaptation of the Church services to the needs and knowledge of the time.

6. To assert the claim of the laity to a larger share in the government and responsible work of the Church.

7. To foster co-operation and fellowship between the Church of England and other Christian Churches.

8. To study the application of Christian principles and ideals to the whole of our social life.

Annual Subscription. – Members at least 7/6; Associates, 1/-; Life Membership, £10. Cheques should be made payable to the Hon. Secretary of the Churchmen's Union.

All changes of address of C.U. members, C.U. subscriptions, and letters dealing with C.U. business, should be sent to the Hon. Secretary of the Churchmen's Union, 32 George Street, Hanover Square, W.1.

B7. The objects of the Modern Churchmen's Union as given in *The Modern Churchman*, November 1931.

AIMS OF THE MODERN CHURCHMEN'S UNION
(*Revised 28th October, 1931.*)

1. To affirm the progressive character of God's self-revelation, and the certainty that no truth can lead away from Him.

2. To proclaim Christ and His Gospel in the light of modern knowledge, endeavouring to give a clear meaning to all phrases which are open to ambiguous treatment.

3. To maintain the right and duty of the Church of England to reject what is false and to restate what is true in her traditional dogmas.

4. To defend the freedom of responsible students, clerical as well as lay, in their work of criticism and research.

5. To promote the study of the Bible according to modern critical methods, and to interpret its message in the light of such study.

6. To secure more regard for beauty and truth in Church Services and the use of language and customs in harmony with modern thought.

7. To promote the application of Christian principles in public as well as in private life.

8. To assert the right and duty of the laity to take a due share in the government and work of the Church.

9. To maintain the historic comprehensiveness of the Church of England and to foster fellowship and co-operation with other Christian Societies.

Annual Subscription. – Members, at least 10/-; Associates, 1/-, payable in January; Life Membership, £10. Cheques should be made payable to The Modern Churchmen's Union, and crossed 'Midland Bank, Wesleyan Hall, S.W.1.'

All communications as to membership, subscriptions, changes of address, and business matters should be sent to – The Organizing Secretary, Modern Churchmen's Union, Church House, Westminster, S.W.1.

The *Modern Churchman* is sent free to all full members of the Modern Churchmen's Union.

B8. The objects and constitution of the Modern Churchmen's Union as given in *The Modern Churchmen's Bulletin*, No. 12 (April 1957), p.5.

THE MODERN CHURCHMEN'S UNION
CONSTITUTION

I. The objects of the Modern Churchmen's Union are:

1. To affirm the progressive character of God's self-revelation, and the certainty that no truth can lead away from Him.

2. To proclaim Christ and His Gospel in the light of modern knowledge, endeavouring to give a clear meaning to all phrases which are open to ambiguous treatment.

3. To maintain the right and duty of the Church of England to reject what is false and to restate what is true in her traditional dogmas.

4. To defend the freedom of responsible students, clerical as well as lay, in their work of criticism and research.

5. To promote the study of the Bible according to modern critical methods, and to interpret its message in the light of such study.

6. To secure more regard for beauty and truth in Church Services and the use of language and customs in harmony with modern thought.

7. To promote the application of Christian principles in public as well as in private life.

8. To assert the right and duty of the laity to take a due share in the government and work of the Church.

9. To maintain the historic comprehensiveness of the Church of England and to foster fellowship and co-operation both in Word and Sacrament with other Christian Societies.

II. The means which the Union shall employ for effecting its objects are:

1. Holding meetings of the Union and its branches.

2. Circulating books, pamphlets and leaflets.

3. Arranging for the delivery of lectures.

249

4. Preparation and presentation of Addresses to persons in authority.

5. Making grants of money in furtherance of the objects of the Union.

6. Taking such other steps as shall appear from time to time to be conducive to the interests of the Union.

III. Members are elected by the Council, when application has been duly made. Membership is open to all members of the Church of England who declare themselves desirous of promoting the objects of the Union, and who promise to pay an annual subscription of not less than fifteen shillings.

Other persons, not being members of the Church of England, but in sympathy with the objects of the Union, may be elected as "Affiliated subscribers." Their minimum subscription is fifteen shillings.

IV. The affairs of the Union shall be administered by a President and Council in accordance with its rules and its objects.

V. The Council shall consist of:

1. Thirty elected members of the Union.

2. The President, Vice-Presidents, and the Hon. Treasurer.

3. Not more than nine members who may be co-opted by the Council to serve till the next Annual General Meeting. In appointing four of these members the special claims of the Branches should be considered.

RULES

MEMBERSHIP

1. All members whose subscriptions are not in arrear shall have the right:

a. To receive free copies of the recognised organs of the Modern Churchmen's Union.
b. To receive notices of all Meetings of the Union.
c. To nominate candidates for the Council.
d. To vote at all meetings of the Union and for the election of the Council.

2. Affiliated Subscribers shall have the rights of members under Rule 1 (a) and (b), and be entitled to attend all meetings of the Union, but shall not have the rights of members under Rule 1 (c) and (d).

3. Any Member or Affiliated Subscriber who, after receiving two notices that his or her subscription is in arrear, fails to reply, shall be deemed to have resigned.

THE COUNCIL

a. ELECTION

4. Of the thirty *elected* members, ten shall retire each year on the day of the Annual General Meeting, and shall not be re-eligible till the following year.

5. Ten members shall be elected each year at the time of the Annual General Meeting to serve on the Council for three years.

6. Any member may nominate one or more (up to four) candidates for election to the Council. The nominations must be seconded by a member of the Union and reach the Secretary four weeks before the Annual Meeting.

7. The Council shall appoint two Returning Officers, who shall draw up a list of the nominations made under the above rules, and send a copy to each member of the Union with the notice of the Annual General Meeting.

8. With the above mentioned notice there shall be sent a voting paper, so that every member of the Union (whose subscription is not in arrear) may vote by post for the election of the Council. Such voting papers shall be valid if they are returned, signed and dated, to the Secretary a week before the Annual General Meeting, at which the result of the voting shall be announced. It shall be an instruction to the Returning Officers, to regard the signatures on the voting papers as confidential.

b. POWERS AND DUTIES

9. It shall be the duty of the Council:

    a. To fix the times of meeting for the Council, for the Annual General Meeting, and for any special meetings of the Union.

b. To make bye-laws for their own regulation.

c. To deal with all applications for protection or assistance.

d. Generally to conduct the business of the Union in accordance with Sections I, II and III of the Constitution.

e. To report their proceedings to the Union at such times as they may deem expedient.

f. To appoint the Secretary of the Union and to determine his duties and stipend, and to arrange for such other assistance as may be necessary.

10. The Council shall have power to fill up casual vacancies in its own body, and to appoint Vice-Presidents, who shall be members of the Council *ex-officio*.

11. The Council shall, at its first meeting after the Annual General Meeting in each year, appoint a Chairman and Vice-Chairman who shall hold office until the corresponding meeting in the next year.

12. The President of the Union shall be elected for five years, and shall be entitled to take the chair at all meetings of the Union, of the Council, and of Committees. Failing the President, the Chairman of the Council shall preside. In the absence of a President his functions devolve upon the Chairman, and failing him, upon the Vice-Chairman.

13. At meetings of the Council seven shall form a quorum.

14. The Chairman and Secretary may summon a special meeting of the Council, and must do so at the requisition of not less than ten members of the Council.

15. If, for any reason, there should be a vacancy among the officers during the year, the Council shall have power to fill such vacancy until the expiration of the year.

ANNUAL SERVICE OF THE UNION

16. An Annual Service for members and friends of the Union shall be held in some central church on the morning of the day for which the Annual General Meeting shall be summoned.

MEETINGS OF THE UNION

17. The Annual General Meeting of the Union shall be held at such date after May 10th as may be determined each year by the Council.

18. The business of the Annual General Meeting shall be:

    a. To receive the report of the Council.

    b. To elect the President, the Council (as provided above), and the Hon. Treasurer.

    c. To discuss such business as may be brought forward.

Any member who wishes to have a resolution put upon the Agenda must give notice to the Secretary at least a fortnight before the Meeting.

Other questions may, subject to the ruling of the Chairman, be introduced, discussed, and decided at the Annual Meeting. But no question shall have precedence over those on the Agenda.

19. On the joint request in writing of twenty members of the Union, the President shall have power to summon a special meeting of the Union to discuss any matters of urgent importance. At such a special meeting, no business shall be discussed except that for which it is summoned.

BRANCHES

20. The members of the Union in any district may, with the sanction of the Council, form themselves into a Branch.

21. Every Branch recognised by the Council shall have power:

    a. To elect its own officers.

    b. To hold meetings and to take such other action within its own area as shall be consistent with I and II of the Constitution.

    c. To make rules for the government of its affairs, provided that such rules are in harmony with the constitution, aims, and rules of the Modern Churchmen's Union.

    d. To raise a special subscription from its members for local purposes, provided that such subscriptions shall not affect the subscriptions of such members to the Union.

22. Every Branch shall annually send a report of its proceedings to the Council at least a month before the Annual General Meeting. Application for membership should be made to:

THE DIRECTOR AND SECRETARY,
THE MODERN CHURCHMEN'S UNION,
9 IRONMONGER LANE,
LONDON, E.C.2.

B9. The aims and objects of the Modern Churchmen's Union as given
in a pamphlet issued in the 1960s.

ITS AIMS AND OBJECTS

The Modern Churchmen's Union is a society within the Church of
England for the advancement of liberal Christian thought.

It was founded in 1898 as a group of scholars, students and clergy who
were convinced that the findings of historical and critical study in their
application to the Bible – particularly to the New Testament – were in
conflict with some traditional presentations of Christian doctrine and
that a new approach was necessary. Furthermore they considered that, if
the Church of England was to remain distinguished by sound learning, it
was urgent that people should be free within the Church to view
orthodox tradition in this new light.

Their labours came to a head in the Modern Churchmen's Conference
at Girton in 1921. Its theme was *Christ and the Creeds*. As a result of the
keen discussion which followed, extending beyond academic and Church
circles, a commission was set up by the Archbishop of Canterbury to
investigate the extent of existing doctrinal agreement within the Church
of England. The commission issued its report in 1938. This revealed that
all its authors acknowledged that the liberal view of Christian doctrine
was held by a large number of distinguished and respected scholars within
the Church, and that to hold such views was not inconsistent with loyalty
to Christ and His Church. It seemed therefore to many as if the Modern
Churchmen's Union had fulfilled its purpose.

This, however, has not proved to be the case. The Doctrinal Report
was quietly shelved, and in many quarters in the Church the work of
liberal scholars was disparaged or neglected. Moreover, in the wider life
of the nation there had developed deep spiritual unsettlement and
insecurity. Some people have taken refuge in various types of dogmatism,
others have sought artificial reconciliation between traditional religious
beliefs and modern knowledge, others finding that no Church helps them
have abandoned organised religion altogether. These last see the
Churches as opponents of free creative endeavour and intellectual
honesty, and regard their outlooks as irrelevant to their own experience
in life.

The Modern Churchmen's Union accepts the challenge of this
situation. It believes that all true knowledge leads to God. It upholds the
progressive character of God's self-revelation to man. Hence it preaches
the Christian Gospel in the light of the truths scientific and historical
which we know today, and in terms consonant with the reason and
conscience of thoughtful men. It strives to bring the insights of the New

Testament to bear upon the whole range of human relationships. It stands for learning and critical study within the Church. In the service of Christ, it seeks to restate what is true in traditional doctrine, and to reject what has become outdated.

On particular issues, the Modern Churchmen's Union supports advances towards Christian unity, such as that manifested by the Oecumenical Movement. It believes that the historic comprehensiveness of the Church of England is a powerful factor in these advances.

It approaches discussions of Prayer Book revision in the same way. Revision of Services should aim at simplicity, and should blend modern knowledge and Biblical scholarship with the traditional symbolism and action.

In an age of rapidly shifting human relationships, it seeks to create possibilities for enlightenment and reconciliation, so that mankind may realise Christ's promise to have life and have it more abundantly.

It believes, therefore, in a comprehensive Church of England, true interpreter of the spiritual life of this country, the Church of the English people.

B10. The constitution and rules of the Modern Churchmen's Union as issued in July 1977.

CONSTITUTION

I. The objects of the Modern Churchmen's Union are:

1. To affirm the progressive character of God's self-revelation, and the certainty that no truth can lead away from Him.

2. To proclaim Christ and His Gospel in the light of modern knowledge, endeavouring to give a clear meaning of all phrases which are open to ambiguous treatment.

3. To maintain the right and duty of the Church of England to reject what is false and to restate what is true in her traditional dogmas.

4. To defend the freedom of responsible students, clerical as well as lay, in their work of criticism and research.

5. To promote the study of the Bible according to modern critical methods, and to interpret its message in the light of such study.

6. To secure more regard for beauty and truth in Church Services

and the use of language and customs in harmony with modern thought.

7.   To promote the application of Christian principles in public as well as in private life.

8.   To assert the right and duty of the laity to take a due share in the government and work of the Church.

9.   To maintain the historic comprehensiveness of the Church of England and to foster fellowship and co-operation both in Word and Sacrament with other Christian Societies.

II.   The means which the Union shall employ for effecting its objects are:

1.   Holding meetings of the Union and its branches.

2.   Circulating books, pamphlets and leaflets.

3.   Arranging for the delivery of lectures.

4.   Preparation and presentation of Addresses to persons in authority.

5.   Making grants of money in furtherance of the objects of the Union.

6.   Taking such other steps as shall appear from time to time to be conducive to the interests of the Union.

III.   Members are elected by the Council, when application has been duly made. Membership is open to all members of the Church of England and Churches in communion with it who declare themselves desirous of promoting the objects of the Union, and who promise to pay an annual subscription of not less than
Other persons, not being members of the Church of England, but in sympathy with the objects of the Union, may be elected as 'Affiliated subscribers'.

IV.   The affairs of the Union shall be administered by a President and Council in accordance with its rules and its objects.

V.   The Council shall consist of:

1.   Thirty elected members of the Union.

2.   The President, Vice-Presidents, and the Hon. Treasurer.

3. Not more than three members who may be co-opted by the Council, and not more than six Affiliated Subscribers who may be nominated at the Annual Meeting for co-option by the Council. All co-opted members serve till the next Annual Meeting.

RULES

MEMBERSHIP

1. All members whose subscriptions are not in arrear shall have the right:
   a. To receive free copies of the recognized organs of the Modern Churchmen's Union.
   b. To receive notices of all Meetings of the Union.
   c. To nominate candidates for the Council.
   d. To vote at all meetings of the Union and for the election of the Council.

2. Affiliated Subscribers shall have the rights of members under Rule 1.

3. Any Member or Affiliated Subscriber who, after receiving two notices that his or her subscription is in arrears, fails to reply, shall be deemed to have resigned.

THE COUNCIL

a. ELECTION

4. Of the thirty elected members, ten shall retire each year on the day of the Annual General Meeting.

5. Ten members shall be elected each year at the time of the Annual General Meeting to serve on the Council for three years.

6. Any member may nominate one or more (up to four) candidates for election to the Council. The nominations must be seconded by a member of the Union before the Annual Meeting.

b. POWERS AND DUTIES

7. It shall be the duty of the Council:

    a. To fix the times of meeting for the Council, for the Annual General Meeting, and for any special meetings of the Union.

    b. To make bye-laws for their own regulation.

    c. To deal with all applications for protection or assistance.

    d. Generally to conduct the business of the Union in accordance with Sections I, II and III of the Constitution.

    e. To report their proceedings to the Union at such times as they may deem expedient.

    f. To appoint the Secretary of the Union and to determine his duties and stipend, and to arrange for such other assistance as may be necessary.

8. The Council shall have power to fill up casual vacancies in its own body, and to appoint Vice-Presidents, who shall be members of the Council ex-officio.

9. The Council shall, at its first meeting after the Annual General Meeting in each year, appoint a Chairman and Vice-Chairman who shall hold office until the corresponding meeting in the next year.

10. The President of the Union shall be elected for five years, and shall be entitled to take the chair at all meetings of the Union, of the Council, and of Committees. Failing the President, the Chairman of the Council shall preside. In the absence of a President his functions devolve upon the Chairman, and failing him, upon the Vice-Chairman.

11. At meetings of the Council seven shall form a quorum.

12. The Chairman and Secretary may summon a special meeting of the Council, and must do so at the requisition of not less than ten members of the Council.

13. If, for any reason, there should be a vacancy among the officers during the year, the Council shall have power to fill such vacancy until the expiration of the year.

MEETINGS OF THE UNION

14. The Annual General Meeting of the Union shall be held at such date after 10 May as may be determined each year by the Council.

258

15. The business of the Annual General Meeting shall be:
   a. To receive the report of the Council.
   b. To elect the President, the Council (as provided above), and the Hon. Treasurer.
   c. To discuss such business as may be brought forward.

   Any member who wishes to have a resolution put upon the Agenda must give notice to the Secretary at least a fortnight before the Meeting.
   Other questions may, subject to the ruling of the Chairman, be introduced, discussed, and decided at the Annual Meeting. But no question shall have precedence over those on the Agenda.

16. On the joint request in writing of twenty members of the Union, the President shall have power to summon a special meeting of the Union to discuss any matters of urgent importance. At such a special meeting, no business shall be discussed except that for which it is summoned.

BRANCHES

17. The members of the Union in any district may, with the sanction of the Council, form themselves into a Branch.

18. Every Branch recognized by the Council shall have power:
   a. To elect its own officers.
   b. To hold meetings and to take such other action within its own area as shall be consistent with I and II of the Constitution.
   c. To make rules for the government of its affairs, provided that such rules are in harmony with the constitution, aims, and rules of the Modern Churchman's Union.
   d. To raise a special subscription from its members for local purposes, provided that such subscriptions shall not affect the subscriptions of such members to the Union.

19. Every Branch shall annually send a report of its proceedings to the Council at least a month before the Annual General Meeting.

B11. The Principles and Aims of the Modern Churchmen's Union as issued in a pamphlet, February 1978.

PRINCIPLES AND AIMS

MCU seeks to approach all aspects of religion both inside and outside the Church in a spirit of freedom and informed inquiry.

> The membership therefore includes people with a wide range of outlook and concern.

MCU, believing that Christian faith in one of its aspects is a truth-seeking activity, holds that the study of religion should not be isolated from other fields of present day thought and enquiry.

> If the Christian religion is to have any appeal and influence it has to be seen mainly to be concerned with the world as it is understood today and not only as in the past.

MCU holds then that the Church should have freedom to re-interpret and re-state its traditional doctrines, since their form is determined by the outlook of their times.

> No issues of Church Order or of morality may be settled only by reference to tradition.
> Equally, no finality should be claimed for the latest style of theological thinking. Sound scholarship helps to keep a sense of proportion.

MCU believes that the historical comprehensiveness of the Church of England is a part of its strength. It has been a source of freedom and of a vital relationship between church and people.

> MCU is therefore opposed to any narrowing of the Church that would make it an inward-looking sect which offers the easy comfort of separation from the ways and thought of the world at large.

MCU supports the ecumenical movement because it respects the traditions and work of other Churches.

> It believes that the comprehensiveness of the Church of England gives it an important role in movements towards unity and in determining its pattern.

MCU also seeks a wider ecumenical outlook in which there is a willingness to learn from other world religions and from such viewpoints as Humanism.

MCU believes that the Christian faith has implications for the whole of life, and that its own breadth of outlook enables it to appreciate and contribute to many of the ethical, social and political issues of today.

C. A List of the Dramatis Personae of English Modernism

List of Modernists

This list of English Modernists is comprehensive but hardly exhaustive. It has been drawn up through a reading of the *Liberal Churchman, The Modern Churchman, The Churchmen's Union Newsletter*, 1922–36, *The Modern Churchmen's Bulletin*, 1956–80, programmes of the Modern Churchmen's Conference, and printed lists of the members of the Churchmen's Union (which exist for 1908 and 1918) and of the Modern Churchmen's Union (which exist for 1938, 1950 and 1956).

Abbott, Edwin Abbott, Rev.

Acland, Sir Thomas Dyke

Adams, Mrs Adela Marion

Adams, Arthur White, Rev.

Adderley, James Granville, Rev.

Addis, William Edward, Rev.

Addison, William George Clibbens, Rev.

Allen, Geoffrey Francis, Rt Rev.

Allen, Ronald Edward Taylor, Rev.

Anson, Harold, Rev.

Antrobus, Sir Reginald

Ashley, Alice

Ashley, Sir William J.

Astley, Hugh John Dunkinfield, Rev.

Atkinson, Arthur George Brecks, Rev.

Avebury, Lord

Bagenal, Philip Henry

Bailey, Harry, Rev.

Bainbridge-Bell, Waldegrave Dent, Rev.

Bannister, Arthur Thomas, Rev.

Barnes, Ernest William, Rt Rev.

Barnett, Samuel Augustus, Rev. Canon

Barran, Henry

Barran, Sir John Nicholson

Bass, Charles, Rev.

Bax, Arthur Nesham, Rev.

Beeby, Charles Evans, Rev.

Beet, J. Agar, Rev.

Bentley, John Henry, Rev.

Bethune-Baker, James Franklin, Professor

Bevan, Henry Edward James, Rev.

Bezzant, James Stanley, Rev. Canon

Bieneman, Gustavus Adolphus, Rev.

Boden-Worsley, John Francis Worsley, Rev.

Bouquet, Alan Coates, Rev.

Boyd Carpenter, Archibald, Rev.

Boys-Smith, Edward Percy, Rev.

Boys Smith, John Sandwith, Rev.

Brandon, Samuel George Frederick, Rev. Professor

Bren, Robert, Rev.

Brocklehurst, Theodore Percy, Rev.

Brodie, Alastair George, Rev.

Brook, Victor John Knight, Rev.

Buckley, Eric Rede, Venerable

Budd, Kenneth George, Rev.

Burdekin, Arthur Edward, Rev.

Burkitt, Francis Crawford, Professor

Burroughs, Edward Arthur, Rt Rev.

Butterworth, George William, Rev.

Caldecott, Alfred, Rev. Professor

Canney, Edward, Rev.

Canney, Maurice Arthur

Carlyle, Alexander James, Rev.

Carpenter, Edward Frederick, Very Rev.

Channing, F. C.

Charles, Robert Henry, Venerable

Charnwood, Lord Godfrey Rathbone Benson

Cheyne, Thomas Kelly, Rev. Professor

Chillingworth, Richard Henry, Rev.

Christie, Sir John Traill

Clarke, Oliver Fielding, Rev.
Clayton, John Francis, Rev.
Cleobury, Frank Harold, Rev.
Clutton-Brock, Arthur
Cohn, John Rougier, Rev.
Coleridge, Gilbert
Compton, Frank Edward, Rev.
Cook, Stanley Arthur, Professor
Cooke, Alfred Gordon, Rev.
Cope, Gilbert Frederick, Rev.
Coulton, George Gordon
Coupland, Sir Reginald
Cowie, Leonard Wallace, Rev.
Craig, William Alban Cunningham, Rev.
Cratchley, William Joseph, Rev.
Creed, John Martin, Rev. Professor
Cremer, Frederick Daustini, Rev. Canon
Cross, Frank Leslie, Rev. Canon
Cross, Leslie Basil, Rev.
Cruickshank, Alfred Hamilton, Rev. Canon
Cummins, Alexander Griswold, Rev.
Danks, William, Rev. Canon
Davies, James Arthur, Rev.
Dearmer, Percy, Rev. Canon
Dewick, Edward Chisholm, Rev.
Diggle, John William, Rt Rev.
Dillistone, Frederick William, Rev. Canon
Dixon, John Henry Sladden, Rev.
Dodd, John Alfred, Rev.
Dougall, Miss Lily
Dowding, Alexander Theodore Woodman, Rev.
Dowell, Miss Edith
Dowson, Miss Mary Emily
Drewett, Alfred John, Rev.
Ducker, Eric Neilson, Rev.
Dunlop, Max Tulloch, Venerable

Dunstan, Alan Leonard, Rev. Canon
Du Vernet, Frederick Herbert, Most Rev.
Dyson, Anthony Oakley, Rev. Professor
Ede, William Moore, Very Rev.
Edgehill, Ernest Arthur, Rev.
Edwards, William Alfred, Rev.
Elliott, Wallace Harold, Rev. Canon
Elliott-Binns, Leonard Elliott, Rev.
Emmet, Cyril William, Rev.
Emmet, Dorothy, Professor
Emmet, William Edward, Rev.
Ervine, St John Greer
Fallows, William Gordon, Rt Rev.
Fawkes, Alfred, Rev.
Fisher, Frederick Victor
Fitz-Maurice, Sir Henry, Rev.
Fremantle, Sir Francis Edward
Fremantle, William Henry, Very Rev.
Frend, William Hugh Clifford, Professor
Furneaux, William Mordaunt, Very Rev.
Gale, Courtenay, Rev.
Galton, Arthur, Rev.
Gamble, John, Rev.
Gardner, Miss Alice
Gardner, Percy, Professor
Gardner-Smith, Percival, Rev.
Garnsey, Arthur Henry, Rev.
Garnsey, David Arthur, Rt Rev.
Geikie-Cobb, William Frederick, Rev.
Given-Wilson, Frederick George, Rev.
Glazebrook, Michael George, Rev. Canon
Goldsmith, Malcolm, Rev.
Gordon, Alan Bacchus, Rev.
Gorton, Neville Vincent, Rt Rev.
Grane, William Leighton, Rev.
Gray, Arthur

Green, Bryan Stuart Westmacott, Rev.
Greer, William Derrick Lindsay, Rt Rev.
Grensted, Laurence William, Professor
Grey, Earl
Griffith, Robert Gladstone, Rev.
Gwatkin, Henry Melvill, Rev. Professor
Haldane, John Scott, Dr
Hamilton, Peter Napier, Rev.
Handley, Hubert, Rev.
Handley-Page, Sir Frederick
Hankey, Donald
Hardwick, John Charlton, Rev. Dr
Hart, Arthur Tindal, Rev.
Hart, Henry St John, Rev.
Hart, Miss Mary Harvey
Harvey, George Leonard Hunton, Rev. Canon
Henderson, Ralph Bushill, Dr
Henslow, George, Rev. Professor
Hitchcock, Aldous Edward North, Rev.
Hodges, Joseph Percy, Rev.
Hoernlé, Edward Frederick, Rev.
Hooke, Samuel Henry, Professor
Horan, Frederick Seymour, Rev.
Hort, Sir Arthur
Hubbard, Miss Hilda
Hunkin, Joseph Wellington, Rt Rev.
Hunt, Ernest William, Rev. Professor
Hunter, Leslie Stannard, Rt Rev.
Hutchinson, Francis Ernest, Rev.
Hutton, Arthur Wollaston, Rev.
Inge, William Ralph, Very Rev.
Ingolby, Roger H., Rev.
Jackson, Henry Latimer, Rev.
Jeakes, James Malcolm, Rev.
Jenkinson, Charles, Rev.
Jennings, Arthur Charles, Rev.

Jephson, Arthur William, Rev. Canon
Jones, Sir Lawrence
Kelsall, John Edward, Rev.
Kendall, Guy
Kennedy, Geoffrey Anketell Studdert, Rev.
King, Colin, Rev.
Kingdon, Henry Paul, Rev.
Kirkby, Paul Jerome, Rev.
Knight, Marcus, Very Rev.
Lake, Kirsopp, Professor
Lampe, Geoffrey William Hugh, Rev. Professor
Leaney, Alfred Robert Clare, Rev. Professor
Lee, Roy Stuart, Rev.
Lewis, John Wren
Lilley, Alfred Leslie, Venerable
Lloyd-Baker, Miss Mary Ruth Lloyd
Longford, William Wingfield, Rev.
Lovell, George Wilfred Lechmere Stanhope, Rev.
Luce, Harry Kenneth, Rev.
Lynam, Alfred Edmund
Macan, Reginald Walter, Dr
McCallum, James Ramsey, Rev.
McComb, Samuel, Rev.
McCullock, Joseph, Rev.
McKay, Roy, Rev.
Major, Henry Dewsbury Alves, Rev. Dr
Mann, William James, Rev.
Manning, William, Rev.
Matthews, Charles Henry Selfe
Matthews, Walter Robert, Very Rev.
Maude, Joseph Hooper
Mercer, John Edward, Rt Rev.
Micklewright, Frederick Henry Amphlett, Rev.
Milner, Gamaliel, Rev.
Morgan, Conwy Lloyd, Dr
Morrison, William Douglas, Rev. Dr

Moxon, Cavendish, Rev.
Moyle, Francis (Frank) Walter, Rev.
Mulliner, Harold George, Rev.
Mullins, Claud
Nankivell, James Walter Herbert, Rev.
Nettlefold, John Kenrick, Rev.
Norwood, Sir Cyril
Nussey, Miss Dora
Nuttall, Enos, Most Rev.
Page, Arnold Henry, Very Rev.
Page-Roberts, William, Very Rev.
Palmer, Abram Smythe, Rev.
Papillon, Thomas Leslie, Rev. Canon
Parez, Claude Hubert, Rev.
Parkes, James William, Rev.
Parrish, Arthur Geoffrey, Rev.
Parsons, Richard Godfrey, Rt Rev.
Patterson, Leonard, Rev.
Pavey, James Charles John, Rev.
Payton, Wilfrid Ernest Granville, Rev.
Peacocke, Arthur Robert, Rev.
Pearce-Higgins, John Denis, Rev. Canon
Pearson, Arthur Astley
Percival, John, Rt Rev.
Perry, Michael, Venerable
Philpot, William Thomas Archibald, Rev.
Piachaud, François Allen, Rev.
Picton-Turberville, Miss Edith
Pittenger, William Norman, Rev. Professor
Plumptre, Henry Pemberton, Rev.
Povah, John Walter, Rev.
Powell, Francis Edward, Rev.
Power, Norman Sandeford, Rev.
Preece, W. Llewellyn, Rev.
Preston, Ronald Hadyn, Rev. Professor
Pryke, William Maurice, Rev.

Raimes, Lancelot, Rev.

Ramsey, Ian Thomas, Rt Rev.

Rashdall, Hastings, Very Rev.

Ratcliff, Edward Craddock, Rev. Professor

Raven, Charles Earle, Rev. Canon

Rees, Frederick Ivon Lewis, Rev.

Reiland, Karl, Rev.

Rendall, Gerald Henry, Rev.

Rhodes, Clifford Oswald, Rev.

Richardson, Alan, Rev. Professor

Richardson, Robert Douglas, Rev. Canon

Richardson, William, Rev.

Roberts, Tom Aerwyn, Professor

Robson, Archibald Francis, Rev.

Rogers, Travers Guy, Rev. Canon

Rogerson, John William, Rev. Professor

Root, Howard Eugene, Rev. Professor

Rose, Alaric Pearson, Rev.

Rose, Christopher Philip Godwin, Rev.

Rosedale, Honyel Gough, Rev.

Routh, William, Rev.

Royden, Miss Maude

Royds, Thomas Fletcher, Rev.

Russell, Charles Frank, Rev.

Russell, Edward (Lord Russell)

Ryan, William Richard Fenwick, Rev.

Sanday, William, Rev. Professor

Saunders, Kenneth, Rev.

Schomberg, Edward St George, Rev.

Scott, David Lamplough, Rev.

Scott, Frank Norman, Rev.

Seamer, Charles Ernest, Rev.

Self, Sir Henry

Sharp, Charles James, Rev.

Shebbeare, Charles John, Rev.

Shelford, Leonard Edmund, Rev.

Shen, Tzu Kao, Rt Rev.
Sheppard, Hugh Richard Lawrie ('Dick'), Rev. Canon
Sibley, George Victor Warry, Rev.
Simms, Albert Ernest Nicholas, Rev.
Skrine, John Huntley, Rev.
Slater, Edward Tillet, Rev.
Smith, D. Howard, Rev.
Smith, Nowell
Smythe, Paul Rodney, Rev.
Snape, Henry Currie, Rev.
Sorley, William Ritchie, Professor
Sparkes, Hedley Frederick Davis, Rev. Professor
Stanway, Alfred Henry, Rev.
Stapley, Annie E. (Lady Stapley)
Stapley, Sir Richard
Stead, William Force, Rev.
Stevens, Ralph Samuel Osborn, Rev. Canon
Stewart, Charles Robert Shaw, Rev.
Stone, Edward Daniel, Rev.
Storr, Vernon Faithful, Rev. Canon
Streeten, Arthur Herbert, Rev.
Streeter, Burnett Hillman, Rev. Canon
Sykes, Norman, Very Rev.
Sykes, Stephen, Rev. Professor
Symes, John Elliotson, Rev.
Symonds, Herbert, Rev.
Temple, William, Most Rev.
Tennant, Frederick Robert, Rev.
Thompson, James Matthew, Rev.
Todd, John, Rev.
Tollinton, Richard Bertram, Rev.
Townley, George Frederick, Rt Rev.
Trueman, Henry Joseph, Rev.
Turner, Arthur Charlewood, Rev.
Verschoyle, John Stuart, Rev.
Walker, Miss A. Katharine

Walker, John William
Wallbank, Newell Eddius, Rev.
Ward, Miss Dorothy
Ward, Mrs Humphrey
Webb, Clement Charles J., Professor
Webb, James Robert Charles, Rev.
Webster, Alan Brunskill, Very Rev.
Whethan, William Cecil Dampier
White, Douglas, Dr
Whiteley, Denys Edward Hugh, Rev.
Whittingham, Walter Godfrey, Rt Rev.
Wigley, Thomas
Wilkinson, John Richard, Rev.
Wilson, Sir Arnold
Wilson, Henry Albert, Rt Rev.
Wilson, James Maurice, Rev. Canon
Wilson, John Leonard, Rt Rev.
Wood, Eric Gilbert, Rev.
Wood, Fergus Henry, Rev.
Wood-Legh, Miss Kathleen M.
Woods, Edward Sydney, Rt Rev.
Woods, George Frederick, Rev. Professor
Woods, Henry George
Woodward, Clifford Salisbury, Rev.
Wright, Charles James, Rev.
Wylie, Sir Francis
Younghusband, Miss Frances M.
Younghusband, Sir Francis

D.   *The Presidents of the Churchmen's Union*
(later Modern Churchmen's Union)

1.   The Rev. Professor George Henslow, President 1898–1902.

2.   The Rev. Dr William Douglas Morrison, President 1902–1908.

3.   Sir Charles Thomas Dyke Acland, President 1908–1915.

4.   Professor Percy Gardner, President 1915–1922.

5.   The Very Rev. Hastings Rashdall, President 1923–4.

6.   The Very Rev. William Ralph Inge, President 1924–34.

7.   The Very Rev. Walter Robert Matthews, President 1934–7.

8.   Sir Cyril Norwood, President 1937–47.

9.   Sir Henry Self, President 1947–58.

10.   The Rt Rev. John Leonard Wilson, President 1958–66.

11.   The Very Rev. Edward Frederick Carpenter, President 1966–.

1.   The Rev. Professor George Henslow (1835–1925)

George Henslow was the younger son of the Rev. John Stevens Henslow, Professor of Botany at Cambridge (and friend of Charles Darwin) and his wife Harriet, daughter of the Rev. George Jenyns. He was born at Cambridge 23 March 1835. After attending school at Bury St Edmund's, he went to Christ's College, Cambridge and took his B.A. in 1858 with First Class Honours in Natural Science. He was ordained deacon in 1859 and priest in 1861 (diocese of Chichester). From 1859 to 1861 he was curate of Steyning, Sussex. He was Headmaster of Hampton Lucy Grammar School, 1861–4, and then of the Grammar School, Stove Street, London, 1865–72. He was Lecturer in Botany at St Bartholomew's Hospital, 1866–80 and also at Birkbeck and Queen's Colleges, London. He also held the office of Hon. Professor of Botany in the Royal Horticultural Society. His further clerical offices were as curate of St John's Wood Chapel, 1868–70 and of St James, Marylebone, 1870–87 (where he served under the notable liberal, R. H. Haweis). We find him resident at Ealing, 1882–1904 (where he was President of the Natural

History Society), then at Drayton House, Leamington and finally at Bournemouth, where he died 30 December 1925. See *The Times* obituary, 2 January 1926.

He seems to have died as a professed spiritualist and his early connection with Modernism was by then forgotten, but he was on the Council of the Churchmen's Union in the early years of the century after he had ceased to be President. There are articles by him in the first few volumes of *The Modern Churchman*. Major, however, did not realize that he was the first President of the Churchmen's Union and gave that honour to W. D. Morrison, who was in fact the second President. He was a Fellow of the Linnaean Society and a Fellow of the Geographical Society. His father is recorded in the *Dictionary of National Biography*.

My conclusion that he ended a spiritualist comes from the existence in the Bodleian of his work, *The Religion of the Spirit World*. Written by the Spirits themselves by the Rev. Professor George Henslow, Author of *The Proofs of the Truths of Spiritualism* (London, Kegan Paul, 1920).

2. The Rev. Dr William Douglas Morrison (1852-1943)

Morrison was a Scotsman educated at Trinity College, Glenalmond. He was ordained deacon by the Bishop of Ripon in 1877 and priest in 1878. He was curate of Sandall Magna, Wakefield, 1877-8, and then of St. John's, Wakefield, 1883-7. He then became Assistant Chaplain at the Wakefield Prison, and then from 1887 to 1898 Chaplain at Wandsworth. Major wrote, 'In this sphere he did most valuable work which led to important reforms in our prison system, especially in the treatment of young criminals, and earned for him public commendation by Lord Haldane.' He wrote *Crime and its Causes* (1890) and *Juvenile Offenders* (1896), works based not only upon his own experience but also his profound studies in criminology. In a different sphere he contributed one of the volumes in the series *The Story of the Nations*. For some years he acted as Editor of the Theological Translation Library, published by T. and T. Clark, and did very useful work himself in translating German Theology.

In 1908 he was appointed by the Crown Rector of Marylebone, where he remained until his death. Major says that he 'did much to make his parish schools the most efficient of their kind in the London Diocese. A forcible speaker, calm and dignified in manner, a sound administrator, he was an ideal rector of a great metropolitan parish: an active, practical, judicial philanthropist, without cant, without fads, without self-seeking' (*Modern Churchman* [December 1956] p.196).

His special claim to fame in the Modernist Movement is his editing of

The Liberal Churchman (1904–8), the predecessor of *The Modern Churchman* which Major started in 1911.

His doctorate was an honorary LL.D. of St Andrews, 1898.

3. Sir Charles Thomas Dyke Acland (1842–1922)

The first layman to be President of the Churchmen's Union, he was a West country landowner, with seats at Killerton (Devon) and Holnecote (Somerset). He was educated at Eton and Christ Church. He was a Member of Parliament in the '80s and '90s. Major says that 'he took no little interest in the material, religious and moral condition of the cottagers and labourers of his tenantry. A patron of a number of livings, he gave that conscientious consideration to the appointment of suitable incumbents which so often enables the lay patron, at any rate, when he is resident, to make better appointments than those which are made by overworked bishops or partisan ecclesiastical boards. He also served in the responsible position of an Ecclesiastical Commissioner.' In 1908 he contributed to *Anglican Liberalism* an essay on 'Political Liberalism'. His creed can be summed up in a sentence from that work, 'The English Churchman feels, at the bottom of his heart, that the Church exists for the Glory of God, as manifested in the good of all mankind; that, as a member of that Church, it is his duty, as in him lies, to promote the good of all men within his reach.'

When the idea of a liberal church magazine was mooted in 1911, Dyke Acland felt that the *Hibbert Journal* was sufficient. Major obviously felt that he was too preoccupied in the West country to be an efficient President.

He was the 12th Baronet, succeeding his father in 1898. His wife was Gertrude, daughter of Sir John Walrond of Bradfield. They had no children. His father was the 11th Baronet who had married Mary eldest daughter of Sir Charles Mordaunt. Both his father and grandfather are recorded in the *Dictionary of National Biography*. There is a privately printed biography of his father, *Memoir and Letters of the Rt. Hon. Sir Thomas Dyke Acland* by his son Arthur H. Dyke Acland (London 1902).

4. Percy Gardner (1846–1937)

Percy Gardner was the son of Thomas Gardner, of the Stock Exchange, by his wife Ann, daughter of Peter Pearse. He was educated at the City of London School, where he was taught by Seeley, and then at Christ's

College, Cambridge, where he attended the lectures of and was influenced by Maurice. He read Classics and studied Philosophy in his spare time and obtained firsts in both the Philosophy and the Moral Science Triposes (1869). In 1871 he became an assistant in the Department of Coins and Medals at the British Museum, and so began what became his life's work – the study of Greek coins and art in relation to Greek History. His works on numismatics were numerous. In 1874 Christ's College elected him a Fellow, but he had to forfeit it when he married Agnes, daughter of John Reid. He edited the *Journal of Hellenic Studies* from 1880 to 1896 when he was appointed Disney Professor of Archaeology at Cambridge. In 1887 he moved to Oxford when he was appointed Lincoln and Merton Professor of Classical Archaeology. He struggled for the recognition of archaeology as part of the Classical Schools.

In his early years he had been attracted to positivism and claimed to have read all the works of Auguste Comte but later (to quote Major), 'Positivism was unable to provide what Gardner's spiritual nature demanded. As the result, not simply of his studies, but of his own inner experience, he was becoming increasingly convinced that not only does man's social and political welfare demand religion, but that it is also a necessity of his personal life. He became equally convinced that the highest form of religion is alone to be found, in evolutional, not static, Christianity.' Under the influence of William James and the French Modernists he became a pragmatist. He wrote many Modernist works, of which the longest was his *Exploratio Evangelica* and frequently contributed to *The Modern Churchman*.

Major adds, 'Like Dr. Samuel Johnson, he did not appreciate jocularity, whether in clergymen or in dons. He complained of a striking episcopal portrait that it was "too lively". Life for him was dominantly a matter of duty to be done, without haste and without rest . . . he was not attracted by American culture. He did not believe in democracy or in feminism. He was a Conservative in politics, a puritan in morals, and in manner a don of the old type.' There are some interesting pictures of him in Carola Oman, *An Oxford Childhood*. His sister Alice Gardner was also a well-known Modernist. Percy Gardner wrote an autobiography, *Autobiographica*.

5.   Hastings Rashdall (1858–1924)

Elder son of the Rev. John Rashdall, incumbent of Eaton Chapel, Eaton Square, London, previously Vicar of the Priory Church, Malvern, and afterwards of Dawlish, by his wife Emily, daughter of Thomas Hankey, banker. His mother died in the year before he himself died (1923). In 1871 he went to Harrow under Montague Butler and in 1877 to New College, Oxford and gained seconds in Classical Moderations and Literae Humaniores. He then taught first at St David's College, Lampeter, then at University College, Durham and then at Hertford College, Oxford where he was elected to a fellowship in 1888. In 1895 he accepted a fellowship as tutor in philosophy at New College where he remained until appointed Dean of Carlisle in 1917, though latterly (1909–17) he combined his Oxford post with a canonry of Hereford, to which Bishop Percival appointed him. His first great work was historical, *The Universities of Europe in the Middle Ages* (1895), his second philosophical, *The Theory of Good and Evil* (1907), his third theological, *The Idea of Atonement in Christian Theology* (Bampton Lectures for 1915) (1919). His liberal outlook in theology can be seen in his *Doctrine and Development* (1898) and *Christus in Ecclesia* (1904). See P. E. Matheson, *The Life of Hastings Rashdall D.D.* (OUP, London, 1928); also P. J. Kirkby in *The Modern Churchman*, October 1927 and D. L. Scott, in *The Modern Churchman*, September 1948. His wife was Constance, daughter of Henry Francis Makins, who long survived him. There were no children.

6. William Ralph Inge (1860–1954)

He was born at Crayke, Yorkshire, the elder son of William Inge, then curate there, and later Provost of Worcester College, Oxford, and his wife, Susanna Mary, daughter of Edward Churton, Archdeacon of Cleveland. Brought up under Tractarian influence, he went to Eton and then to King's College, Cambridge, where he took firsts in both parts of the Classical Tripos and many prizes. Leaving Cambridge, he became a master at Eton but found the work uncongenial and in 1889 became a fellow at Hertford College, Oxford. In 1899 he made a name for himself by his Bampton Lectures on Christian Mysticism.

In 1905 he became Vicar of All Saints, Ennismore Gardens, and in the same year married Mary Catherine, daughter of Henry Maxwell Spooner, Archdeacon of Maidstone. In 1907 he was elected Lady Margaret Professor of Divinity at Cambridge and became a fellow of Jesus College. In 1911 he became Dean of St Paul's from which office he retired in 1934 to Brightwell Manor, near Wallingford. He was essentially a Cambridge Platonist. His most notable work was his Gifford Lectures on Plotinus. See his *Vale* (1934), his *Dairy of a Dean* (n.d.), and Adam Fox, *Dean Inge* (1960).

7. Walter Robert Matthews (1881–1973)

He was born in Camberwell, London, the son of Philip Walter Matthews (a London bank clerk) and his wife Alice. He went to Wilson's School, Camberwell, and at sixteen like his father became a bank clerk. Becoming dissatisfied, he enrolled as a student at King's College, London, and studied theology. He was ordained to a part-time curacy at St Mary Abbotts, Kensington, combining it with lecturing at King's College. He then became incumbent of Christ Church, Crouch End, in succession to C. J. Sharp. In 1918 he became Dean of King's College, London and Professor of the Philosophy of Religion. For four years 1931–4 he was Dean of Exeter and then returned to London to become Dean of St Paul's in succession to Dean Inge, from 1934 to 1967. During the period 1930–60 his theological works were widely read and very popular. Well known were *God in Christian Thought and Experience* and *The Problem of Christ in the Twentieth Century*. He resigned as President of the Modern Churchmen's Union because of a difference over policy but that did not end his connection with the Union. See his autobiography, *Memories and Meanings* (1969). He married in 1912 Margaret Bryan. They had a son (killed in action 1940) and a daughter.

8. Sir Cyril Norwood (1875–1954)

He was born in 1875 at Whalley, Lancashire, the only son of the Rev. Samuel Norwood, headmaster of the local Grammar School, by his second wife, Elizabeth Emma Sparks. His father's intemperance made him a lifelong adherent of teetotalism. He went to Merchant Taylors School in 1888 and from there won a scholarship to St John's College, Oxford, where he gained firsts in Classical Moderations and Literae Humaniores. In 1899 he headed the list of entrants to the Civil Service and was posted to the Admiralty. However in 1901 he left the service and went as Sixth Form Master at Leeds Grammar School. There he married Catherine Margaret, daughter of Walter John Kilner, a doctor of Kensington. In 1906 he was appointed Headmaster of Bristol Grammar School. Ten years later he was made Master of Marlborough. Ten years after that he was persuaded to leave Marlborough for Harrow. In 1934 he was elected Head of his old college, St John's, Oxford.

He was regarded as an outstanding authority on education. His best known work was *The English Tradition of Education* (1929). Many of the suggestions of the famous Norwood Report (1943) were incorporated in the Butler Education Act of 1944. He retired from Oxford in 1946 to live at Iwerne Minster, Dorset. His wife died in 1951 and he in 1954. He was Chairman of the Governors of Ripon Hall in succession to R. W. Macan. See *Dictionary of National Biography* and *The Modern Churchman* (December 1956), pp.234–7.

9. Sir Henry Self (1891–1975)

Sir Henry Self joined the Civil Service at the age of seventeen. His early years were spent in the Foreign Office, War Office and other departments. In 1914–18 he worked in the Ministry of Munitions. In 1919 he went to the recently formed Air Ministry. In 1936 he was Principal Assistant Secretary and a year later Deputy Under-Secretary of State. His work was strenuous because of the threat from the air by Hitler and the need to meet it. In 1938 he was employed on a mission to the United States and Canada, which had as its object the placing of orders for military aircraft. In 1940 after the outbreak of the war he again went to the U.S.A. and Canada as Head of the special mission which led to the establishment of the British Air Commission in Washington. Subsequently he was attached to the British Joint Staffs Mission and the Combined Chiefs of Staffs Organization. In 1942 he was appointed Permanent Secretary to the Ministry of Production and within a few months was back in Washington as the Minister's deputy on the Combined Production and Resources Board. When the British Supply Council was formed in Washington he became its Deputy Chairman. After the War he was appointed Permanent Secretary to the Ministry of Civil Aviation, but left this post in 1947 to become Chairman of the Central Electricity Authority, from which he retired in 1959.

His academic achievements were remarkable, especially as they were obtained as a sideline: B.Sc. (Gen.), B.Sc. (Maths.), M.Sc., B.A. (Classics), B.D., Barrister-at-Law (Lincoln's Inn) and Ph.D. He was a K.C.B., a K.C.M.G. and a K.B.E. Clifford Rhodes wrote of him, 'As President of the M.C.U. he felt that the Union had fulfilled its historical function, which had been to assist in cultivating a more rational and critical approach to the fundamentals of the Christian religion and that the relevant theme for the next phase would be to study how the values of industry could be assimilated to those of the Christian Ethic.' (*The Modern Churchman* [Summer 1975], p.144).

He married in 1918 Rosalind Audrey, daughter of the late Sir John Lonsdale Otter and had two sons. He died 15 January 1975.

Just before he died he was engaged in writing a book, *The Divine Indwelling*, but this has not yet been published.

10. John Leonard Wilson (1897–1970)

John Leonard Wilson was born in 1897, the son of the Rev. John Wilson, curate of Gateshead Fell, and his wife Mary Adelaide Halliday. He began his schooling at the Gateshead School for Girls and then for a short time went to Newcastle Grammar School, but this was not a success, and in 1908 he went to St John's School, Leatherhead, where he was not popular. In 1915 he attempted to join the army but was found to be under age. However in May 1916 he joined the training battalion of the Durham Light Infantry. He was made a sergeant and later commissioned in the 13th Battalion The Bantams and served with them in France towards the end of the War. In 1919 he went to the famous Knutsford Test School and there came under the liberal influence of F. R. Barry and Mervyn Haigh. From there he went up to Queen's College, Oxford, where among his contemporaries were Max Dunlop, Harold Mulliner and Oliver Fielding Clarke, and where he was greatly influenced by Streeter.

In 1922 he left England to join the staff of the Stuart Memorial College, Isfahan. But in May of 1923 he resigned and left Persia, travelling overland to Cairo. He returned to England and in 1924 went to Wycliffe Hall to prepare for ordination, Bishop Henson of Durham securing him a grant from the diocese of Durham. From 1924 to 1928 he was curate of Coventry Cathedral. Then came a year at Cairo as a CMS missionary but he fell out with Bishop Gwynne. He returned to a curacy at St Margaret's, Durham (in charge of St John's, Neville Cross). In 1930 he married Mary Phillips whom he had met in Cairo. He was Vicar of Eighton Banks 1930–5, and then of Roker (St Andrew's, Bishopwearmouth) 1935–8.

In 1938 he became Dean and Archdeacon of Hongkong. Then in 1941 he was appointed Bishop of Singapore. The story of his torture at the hands of the Japanese is well known. He returned to England after the War in 1948 for the Lambeth Conference and was appointed Dean of Manchester, an office he held until 1953 when he succeeded E. W. Barnes as Bishop of Birmingham. In 1969 he retired and lived at Brush House, Bainbridge, Yorks until his death in 1970. He was a Governor of Ripon Hall. See Roy McKay, *John Leonard Wilson Confessor for the Faith* (1973).

11. Edward Frederick Carpenter (1910–)

Carpenter was a student of King's College, London, where he took first class honours in History in his B.A. in 1932. He took his B.D. in 1935 and Ph.D. in 1943. He was ordained deacon in 1935 and priest in 1936. He served as a curate first at Holy Trinity, Marylebone, 1935–41, and then of St Mary, Harrow. From 1945 to 1951 he was Rector of Great Stanmore.

In 1951 began his long association with Westminster Abbey, when he became a canon there. He became Archdeacon of Westminster in 1963. The Modern Churchmen's Union Newsletter No. 13 (July 1967), wrote 'All members will be disappointed that this Newsletter does not contain a paragraph of congratulation to the President on his expected appointment to a position previously held by two other distinguished Presidents.' The reference was to the Deanery of St Paul's vacated by Matthews and held by Inge before that. However Carpenter succeeded Eric Abbott as Dean of Westminster in 1974.

Carpenter is renowned as a historian of the eighteenth-century church, having written lives of Thomas Sherlock, Thomas Tennison and Henry Compton. He also wrote *Cantuar*, a history of the Archbishops of Canterbury. The Modern Churchmen's Union Newsletter, No. 10 (October 1966) remarks, 'His warm sympathies and practical common-sense may, perhaps, be ascribed to the fact that, although a scholar of high order, he has never been cloistered in a University . . . (His) long period of parochial service is, I believe, the secret of his understanding of the practical needs and issues of the Church and of the clergy. He has also had his own troubles with his eyesight, against which he has battled courageously, and we hope successfully. It may be that he peers through somewhat thick glasses, but behind these are shrewd and benevolent eyes, and as keen an intellect as any in the Church of England.'

E. *The Secretaries of the Churchmen's Union* (later Modern Churchmen's Union)

1. The Rev. William Frederick Cobb (later Geikie-Cobb), 1899–1900.
2. The Rev. William Manning, 1900–1916.
3. The Rev. Cavendish Moxon, 1916–1919.
   Moxon had previously acted as Assistant Secretary to Manning. Miss Dora Nussey and the Rev. J. M. Jeakes acted with Moxon as Hon. Assistant Secretaries. Later Mr Llewelyn Preece took the place of Jeakes.
4. Mr Phillip Henry Bagenal, 1920–1923.
5. The Rev. John Henry Bentley, 1923–1927.
6. The Rev. Thomas John Wood, 1927–1942.
7. The Rev. Robert Gladstone Griffith, 1942–1950.
8. The Rev. Thomas John Wood, 1950–1954.
9. The Rev. Clifford Oswald Rhodes, 1954–1960.
10. The Rev. Frank Edward Compton, 1960–
    At present (1984) the Rev. F. E. Compton is Membership Secretary; the Rev. Peter Croft is General Secretary; the Rev. John Guttridge is Conference Secretary.

1. The Rev. William Frederick Cobb (later Geikie-Cobb)

William Frederick Cobb was a member of Trinity College, Dublin, where he took his B.A. in 1882, his B.D. in 1890 and his D.D. in 1895. He was curate of Send, 1882–4, Second Master of Woking College, 1882–4, curate of Addlestone, 1884–7, curate of Holy Trinity, Winchester, 1887–90, curate of St Luke, Kentish Town, 1890–4. From 1892 to 1899 he was Assistant Secretary of the English Church Union. He was curate of St Ethelburga's, Bishopsgate, 1898–1900, and was then appointed Rector by Bishop Mandell Creighton. Major wrote of him, 'The new rector's position at St Ethelburga's was not at first an easy one. There had been ceremonial scandals at the church which had ended in violent conflict, and the new rector's delicate task was to keep the mean between two extremes. This Geikie-Cobb succeeded in doing, not because he was timid, but just the reverse. He possessed sound principles and acted on them with consistency and courage. In his early days a strong High Churchman, he steadily became more liberal in his sympathies and enlightened in outlook. He was a firm believer in women's rights, and it was this, no doubt, which had not a little to do with his vigorous endeavours to secure reform in our marriage and divorce laws. (*The Modern Churchman* [December 1956], p.314). He died in 1942. He translated the letters of St Bernard and Cornelius à Lapide on 1 and 2 Corinthians. In 1914 he wrote *Mysticism and the Creed*. His most recent work was *The Humanist's Horn Book*.

2.   The Rev. William Manning

William Manning was a student of Christ's College, Cambridge. He was made deacon (1881) and ordained priest (1882) in the diocese of St Alban's. He was curate of All Saints, Woodford Wells, 1881–5 and then Vicar of St Andrew's, Leytonstone, 1885–1910. In 1910 he became Rector of Chipping Barnet (a Crown living). He departed from the Modernist cause after the famous Girton Conference. He published a volume of sermons, *Some Elements of Religion* (1908).

3.   The Rev. Cavendish Moxon

Cavendish Moxon took his B.A. at Christ Church in 1904 and in that year went to Ripon College. He was curate of St Andrew, Stourton, diocese of Ripon, from 1906 to 1908, curate of Eccles, 1908–9, curate of All Saints, Pontefract, 1909–11, St Peter, Croydon, 1911–12 and St Marylebone, 1912–14. He was Rector of Marske, 1914–18. He then became curate of Christ Church, Westminster, 1918–21. After that he went to the United States. In the early sixties he wrote from 79 Harrison Avenue, Sausalito, California, 'I'm an old man! Maybe I was at Ripon Hall; but I have no memory of being there! I do have clear and happy memories of being the Rector of Marske – a tiny place, from Ripon about 5 miles or so. I used to cycle into Ripon to do shopping that I could not do in Marske. The only memory of Oxford I have was the happy days when I was studying at Christ Church College for my degree of M.A. . . I was not happy in the pulpit, so I gave up my Church work and went to Vienna and Berlin where I studied to become a Consulting Psychologist. Now I'm happy in my work.' He was still in Crockford in 1970.

4. Phillip Henry Bagenal

According to Major (*The Modern Churchman* [December 1956], p.194) Bagenal was an O.B.E. and a barrister and journalist. He had been a private secretary to a Victorian Cabinet Minister. He was a descendant of Sir Ralph Bagenal, the only member of Parliament who in Queen Mary's reign refused to kneel to receive the Papal Absolution pronounced by Cardinal Pole on those who confessed their penitence for having supported her father's renunciation of the Papal supremacy in his dominions. He wrote about his ancestors in his *Vicissitudes of an Anglo-Irish Family, 1530–1800* (1925). One of his writings was his *The Priest in Politics* (1893). When Major joined the Churchmen's Union Bagenal was living in Kent Row, Harrogate, and they saw much of each other. Bagenal was Government Inspector of the Old Local Government Board (later the Ministry of Health) from 1896 till his retirement in 1918. During the Great War he was responsible for Belgian refugees in Yorkshire. He lived latterly in Wimbledon and died 7 August 1927. See *The Times*, (August 12). It is remarkable that there is no obituary of him in *The Modern Churchman*, especially when he had written a short history of the Union.

5. The Rev. John Henry Bentley

He was an Exhibitioner and Scholar of St John's College, Cambridge, and took a first in Oriental Languages, and won many prizes. He was made deacon in 1907 and priest in 1908 in the diocese of York and became curate of St Mark's, Broomhall, Sheffield. Then he went to Lichfield as Lecturer and Librarian at the Theological College, 1910–16. He was Vicar of Milnsbridge, 1916–18, and then Rector of Souldern (diocese of Oxford), 1918–29. He went to be Rector of Layham in the diocese of Bury St Edmund's in 1929. He left there in 1949 and went to live at Gorleston-on-Sea.

6 and 8. The Rev. Thomas John Wood

Wood was of Selwyn College, Cambridge where he took a first in the Theological Tripos. Later he took a London B.D. He was ordained at Southwark, deacon in 1913 and priest in 1914. From 1913 to 1917 he was curate of St Saviour's, Southwark (the Cathedral). He went to East Africa as a Chaplain to the Forces. After the War he became Tutor and Chaplain of St Aidan's College, Birkenhead. There the Vice-Principal (Alexander Theodore Woodman Dowding) won him over to Modernism. In 1924 he became Vicar of St John's, Clapham Rise, until 1940 when he moved to Oxfordshire to become Vicar of Charlbury. He retired to live at Burford in 1962 and died in 1973.

7. The Rev. Robert Gladstone Griffith

Griffith was ordained deacon in 1909 and priest in 1910 in the diocese of Southwark, after attending Wells Theological College. Before that he was at Emmanuel College, Cambridge. After a number of curacies he was Perpetual Curate of Pill and then Rector and Vicar of Farnborough, 1927–39. From 1939 he was Vicar of Steeple Claydon, Oxfordshire. He died as a result of a motoring accident 17 October 1950. He wrote a number of Modernist works of which the most notable was *The Necessity of Modernism* (1932).

9. The Rev. Clifford Oswald Rhodes

Rhodes took a second in Modern Greats in 1934. He went to Wycliffe Hall in 1938 and was ordained deacon at Manchester, 1938, and priest in 1939. He was curate of St Luke, Benchill, and then from 1940 to 1945 a Chaplain to the Forces. He was Editor of the *Record*, 1946–9 and then of the *Church of England Newspaper* 1949–59. He was curate of St Margaret's, Lothbury, 1954–8, and since 1958 he has been Rector of Somerton, near Oxford. He wrote *The New Church in the New Age* (1958). He has combined journalism with parochial work.

10. The Rev. Frank Edward Compton

Compton obtained a B.Sc. at Durham (St John's College) in 1934. He studied Theology at St Catherine's College, Oxford, and was at Ripon Hall under H. D. A. Major. He was curate of Acock's Green, Birmingham, 1936–9, and then (under R. D. Richardson) at Harborne, 1939–44. He was Rector of The Quinton, Birmingham, 1948–60, and then Vicar of Caynham, Herefordshire, from 1960. He now teaches and resides at The School House, Leysters, Leominster.

F.   A Memorandum of the Rev. H. C. Snape about the future of
     the Modern Churchmen's Union, issued 1979

THE FUTURE OF THE M.C.U.

The following facts seem to show that the M.C.U. *in its present form* is in
decline.

1.   The number of members over the past few years have been steadily
     declining. Losses by death and resignation have not been made up by
     the accession of new members.

2.   Largely as a consequence of (1) and also because of its irregularity in
     appearance as well as the quality of its contents the number of
     subscribers to the journal has been declining. Publishers are no longer
     sending in review copies of books for review. Increased costs of
     printing which will probably take another leap forward in the near
     future are making it impossible to produce a journal of such style and
     quality as suit a review which is of some permanent value. Today
     such a journal either has to be for specialists or heavily subsidised.

3.   The annual conference which has been a regular feature of M.C.U.'s
     activities shows signs of losing its popularity largely because of
     increasing costs.

Those who have been responsible for maintaining the work of the union
cannot be held responsible for this decline. Edward Compton has over the
years often in the face of indifference without sparing himself given of
himself to the work of the union. There does not seem as if anyone will be
found in the future ready to serve with the same devotion.

     The decline springs from the changes in the general theological and
ecclesiastical climate of the last twenty years. The framework in which
the union operates was created as a means of expressing and
communication for the highly educated churchman whose outlook
socially and politically was conservative, who was positive in his beliefs
as a Christian but critical of dogmatic traditionalism and extremes in
churchmanship. The conference has provided an opportunity for leading
liberal theologians to publish articles written in a style comprehensible to
the educated layman and the liberal minded parochial clergy fit for
subsequent publication and reference. The Modern Churchman may be
said to be the last of those quarterlies such as the Hibbert Journal which

belong to what the French happily call *haute vulgarisation*. In recent years it has been difficult to obtain articles of such calibre as command attention outside the union, while the comments on current ecclesiastical affairs are likely to appear after interest in the topic concerned has died down. Theology has declined in interest among the laity. Critical theologians no longer find it necessary to defend themselves against charges of heresy because by and large they are treated with indifference.

Young men and women for the most part are either indifferent to the claims of Christianity particularly in any traditional or institutional form or else are drawn to an extreme dogmatic position. The demand among liberally minded churchmen today is not so much for the presentation of a liberal theology as for liberal action in the fields of practical religion grounded in religious experience, Christian moral ideals which take into account the findings of biology and psychology. The Union could meet this demand within the terms of its aims and use all its resources in support of

1. affirming and maintaining the right of divorced persons to have a second marriage solemnised in the established church.

2. the admission of women to holy orders.

3. the promotion of spiritual unity without aiming at organic union between the churches.

4. the recognition of the other world religions including Judaism as valid expressions of the religious spirit.

5. All those who seek the advancement of justice between classes and nations.

In effect the M.C.U. could in my estimation fulfil its aims by becoming the clearing house for all the movements and societies within the church which are pursuing the cause of progressive Christianity in specialised fields such as:

a. The Society for the Ministry of Women in the Church
b. The Congress of Faiths
c. The Church's Fellowship for Psychical & Spiritual Studies
d. The Religious Experience Research Unit at Manchester College, Oxford.

There are probably other societies and movements to be suggested

Sir Alister Hardy pointed out in an address to the I.A.R.F. meeting in Oxford last year that the differences between *The Myth of God Incarnate* and *The Truth of God Incarnate* which was the traditionalist's reply to the former are not only greater than that between Catholics and Protestants but are as great as those which separate Christianity and Judaism or Christianity and Islam. If this is true then M.C.U. still has a part to play as a witness to a progressive faith within the C. of E. Today I would suggest that it will be best done by supporting liberal Christian action and thought wherever it is to be found.

I would suggest as a programme of action:

Circulating the societies previously mentioned and asking them to affiliate with M.C.U. sharing information etc.

Publication of bi-monthly news letter or bulletin in a cheap form to include one or two reviews, notices of forthcoming events, contributions from members.

Issues of occasional statements, paper, and pamphlets as may be called for.

Organisation of conferences when and where the demand may arise.

Subsidising the publication of books by publishers of repute which could not otherwise see the light of day.

The administration of the Union for these purposes might be organised as follows.

The main work to be done by an executive committee consisting of the President, Hon. Secretary, Hon. Treasurer, Bulletin Editor, Conference and Literature Organiser; the bulletin editor to be situated in London, Oxford or Cambridge if possible.

The Council to elect the committee for a period of five years?

The annual general meeting to be held if possible by rota in London, Birmingham and Manchester or other urban centres with a 48 hour conference held either before or after the A.G.M.

Three trustees to be appointed to hold the M.C.U.'s assets, the income to be at the disposal of the Council.

Bibliographies

1. The Complete List of all the Hulsean Lecturers

Christopher Benson   1819 and 1821

Hulsean Lectures for 1820. Twenty Discourses preached before the University of Cambridge in the year 1820 at the Lecture founded by the Rev. John Hulse. Cambridge, J. Smith; London, Baldwin, Cradock and Joy, 1820.

On Scripture Difficulties. Twenty Discourses preached before the University of Cambridge in the year 1822 at the Lecture founded by the Rev. John Hulse, M.A. Cambridge, J. Smith; London, Baldwin, Cradock and Joy, 1822.

James Clarke Franks   1821 and 1823

On the Evidences of Christianity as they were stated and enforced in the Discourses of our Lord. Comprising a connected view of the claims which Jesus advanced, of the argument by which He supported them, and of His Statements respecting the causes, progress, and consequences of Infidelity by James Clarke Franks, Chaplain of Trinity College. Cambridge, J. Smith Printer to the University, 1821.

Hulsean Lectures for 1823 on the Apostolical Preaching and Vindication of the Gospel to the Jews, Samaritans, and Devout Gentiles, as exhibited in the Acts of the Apostles, the Epistles of St Peter, and the Epistle to the Hebrews. Cambridge, J. Smith; London, C. & J. Rivington, 1823.

Temple Chevallier   1826 and 1827

On the Historical Types Contained in the Old Testament. Twenty Discourses preached before the University of Cambridge in the year 1826. At the Lecture founded by the Rev. John Hulse. Cambridge, J. & J. J. Deighton, 1826.

Hulsean Lectures for 1827 on the Proofs of Divine Power and Wisdom derived from the study of Astronomy and on the Evidence, Doctrines

288

and Precepts of Revealed Religion. Cambridge, J. & J. J. Deighton; London, C. & J. Rivington, 1827.

John James Blunt   1831

Hulsean Lectures for the year 1831. *The Veracity of the Historical Books of the Old Testament,* from the Conclusion of the Pentateuch to the opening of the Prophets, argued from the Undersigned Coincidences to be found in them, when Compared in their several parts being a Continuation of the Argument from the Veracity of the Five Books of Moses. London, John Murray, 1832.

Hulsean Lectures for the year 1832. *Principles for the Proper Understanding of the Mosaic Writings stated and applied; together with An Incidental Argument for the Truth of the Resurrection of Our Lord,* by the Rev. J. J. Blunt, Fellow of St John's College, Cambridge. London, John Murray, 1833.

Henry John Rose   1833

The Law of Moses viewed in Connexion with the history and character of the Jews with a defence of the Book of Joshua against Professor Leo of Berlin. Being the Hulsean Lectures for 1833. An Appendix containing remarks on the arrangement of the Historical Scriptures adopted by Gesenius, De Wette, etc. Cambridge, The Pitt Press, 1834.

Henry Howarth   1834

The Truth and Obligation of revealed religions, Considered with reference to prevailing opinions. Eight discourses. Cambridge 1836.

Jesus of Nazareth, the Christ of God. Eight Discourses preached (1836) before the University of Cambridge at the Lecture founded by John Hulse. London; Cambridge 1837.

Richard Parkinson   1836

Rationalism and Revelation; or the Testimony of Moral Philosophy, the System of Nature, and the Constitution of Man to the Truth of the Doctrines of Scripture; in eight discourses preached before the University of Cambridge in the year 1837. By the Rev. Richard Parkinson B.D. J. G. and F. Rivington 1838.

The Constitution of the Visible Church of Christ, considered under the heads of Authority and Inspiration of Scripture; Creeds (Tradition); Articles of Religion; Heresy and Schism; State-Alliance, preaching and National Education in Eight discourses preached before the

University of Cambridge in the year 1838 at the Lecture founded by the Rev. John Hulse. Cambridge, J. & J. J. Deighton; Oxford, J. Parker; Manchester, Bancks & Co., 1839.

Theyre Townsend Smith   1838

Hulsean Lectures for the year 1839. *Man's Responsibility in reference to his Religious Belief.* Explained and Applied. London, B. Fellowes, 1840.

Hulsean Lectures for the year 1840. *The Christian Religion in Connexion with the Principles of Morality* by the Rev. Theyre T. Smith, M.A., of Queen's College, Cambridge and Assistant Preacher at the Temple Church. London, B. Fellowes, Ludgate Street, 1841.

Henry Alford   1841

The Consistency of the Divine Conduct in revealing the Doctrines of Redemption. By the Hulsean Lecturer for the year 1841. Henry Alford, Vicar of Wymeswold. Cambridge, J. & J. J. Deighton; London, Rivington, 1842.

The Consistency of the Divine Conduct in revealing the Doctrines of Redemption. Part the Second. Being the Hulsean Lectures for the year 1842. Cambridge, J. & J. J. Deighton; London, G. F. & J. Rivington, 1843.

John Howard Marsden   1843

An Examination of Certain Passages in our Lord's Conversation with Nicodemus. Eight Discourses preached before the University of Cambridge in the year MDCCCXLIII at the Lecture founded by the Rev. John Hulse M.A. London, William Pickering, 1844.

The Evils which have resulted at Various Times from a Misapprehension of our Lord's Miracles. Eight Discourses preached before the University of Cambridge in the year MDCCCXLIV at the Lecture founded by the Rev. John Hulse, M.A. by the Rev. John Howard Marsden, B.D. Rector of Great Oakley, Essex and late Fellow of St John's College. London, William Pickering, 1845.

Richard Chevenix Trench   1845

The Fitness of Scripture for unfolding the Spiritual Life of Men: being the Hulsean Lectures for the year 1845. Cambridge, Macmillan, Barclay and Macmillan, 1845.

Christ, the Desire of All Nations or the Unconscious Prophecies of Heathendom, being the Hulsean Lectures for the year MDCCCXLVI. Cambridge, Macmillan, Barclay and Macmillan; London, John W. Parker, 1846.

Christopher Wordsworth   1846

On the Canon of Scriptures of the Old and New Testament and the Apocrypha. Eleven discourses preached before the University of Cambridge for the year 1847 by Christopher Wordsworth, D.D., Canon of Westminster. London, Francis and John Rivington, 1848.

William Gilson Humphry   1848

The Doctrine of a Future State in Nine Sermons preached before the University of Cambridge in the year 1849 at the Lecture founded by the Rev. John Hulse. London, John W. Parker; Cambridge, John Deighton; Macmillan, Barclay and Macmillan.

The Early Progress of the Gospel: in Eight Sermons preached before the University of Cambridge in the year MDCCCL. At the Lecture founded by the Rev. John Hulse, M.A., by William Gilson Humphry, Fellow of Trinity College. London, John W. Parker; Cambridge, John Deighton; Macmillan & Co., 1851.

George Currey   1850

The Confirmation of Faith by Reason and Authority. The Hulsean Lectures, preached before the University of Cambridge in 1852 by the Rev. George Currey, Preacher at the Charterhouse. Cambridge, John Deighton; Macmillan & Co.; London, F. & J. Rivington, 1853.

The Explanation of the Gospel, as exhibited in the History of the Israelites. The Hulsean Lectures preached before the University of Cambridge in 1851. Cambridge, John Deighton; Macmillan & Co.; London, F. & J. Rivington, 1852.

Benjamin Morgan Cowie   1852

Scripture Difficulties. Four Sermons preached before the University of Cambridge in April 1853, at the Lecture founded by the Rev. John Hulse to which is added a sermon preached before the University on Ascension Day 1852. London, F. & J. Rivington; Cambridge, J. Deighton, 1853.

Scripture Difficulties. Sermons preached before the University of Cambridge including the Hulsean Lectures for 1854; and three other sermons, by the Rev. Morgan Cowie, M.A. late Fellow of St John's College. London, Rivingtons, 1855.

Harvey Goodwin   1855

The Doctrines and Difficulties of the Christian Faith contemplated from the standing ground afforded by the Catholic doctrine of the being of our Lord Jesus Christ. Being the Hulsean Lectures for the year 1855. Cambridge 1856.

Charles Anthony Swainson   1857

The Creeds and the Church in their Relation to the Word of God and to the Conscience of the Christian. The Hulsean Lectures for the year 1857. By Charles Anthony Swainson, Principal of the Theological College and Prebendary of Chichester. Formerly Fellow and Tutor of Christ's College, Cambridge. Cambridge, Macmillan & Co., 1858.

The Authority of the New Testament; the Conviction of Righteousness; and the Ministry of Reconciliation. Three Series of Lectures delivered before the University of Cambridge in 1848 and 1858. Cambridge and London, Macmillan & Co., 1859.

Charles John Ellicott   1859

Historical Lectures on the Life of Our Lord Jesus Christ. Being the Hulsean Lectures for the Year 1859. C. J. Ellicott, D.D., Bishop of Gloucester and Bristol. London, John W. Parker and Son, 1860.

John Lamb   1860

The Seven Words Spoken against the Lord Jesus or An Investigation of the Motives which led his Contemporaries to reject him. Being the Hulsean Lectures for the year 1860. Rev. John Lamb, Senior Fellow of Gonville and Caius College and Minister of St Edward's, Cambridge. 1861.

Charles Merivale   1861

Not published.

John Saul Howson   1862

The Character of St. Paul. Being the Cambridge Hulsean Lectures for 1862.
3rd edition, London, Strahan & Co., 1873.

Francis Morse   1863

Not published.

Daniel Moore   1864

The Age and the Gospel. Four Sermons preached before the University of Cambridge at the Hulsean Lecture, 1864, to which is added A Discourse on Final Retribution, by Daniel Moore, M.A., Incumbent of Camden Town, Camberwell. London, Oxford and Cambridge, Rivingtons, 1865.

James Moorhouse   1865

Our Lord Jesus Christ. The Subject of Growth in Wisdom. Four Sermons. Being the Hulsean Lectures for 1865. Preached before the University of Cambridge. The Rev. J. Moorhouse, St John's College. London and Cambridge, Macmillan & Co., 1866.

Edward Henry Perowne   1866

The Godhead of Jesus: Four Sermons (Being the Hulsean Lectures for 1866). Preached before the University of Cambridge: to which are added Two Sermons preached before the University on Good Friday and Easter Day 1866. Cambridge, Deighton, Bell & Daldy, 1867.

Charles Pritchard   1867

Analogies in the Progress of Nature and Grace. Four Sermons preached before the University of Cambridge (Being the Hulsean Lectures for 1867) to which are added two sermons preached before the British Association in 1866 and 1867 by the Rev. C. Pritchard, M.A., F.R.S., President of the Royal Astronomical Society. Cambridge, Deighton, Bell & Co., 1868.

John James Stewart Perowne   1868

Immortality. Four Sermons Preached before the University of Cambridge, being the Hulsean Lectures for 1868. By J. J. Stewart Perowne, Vice-Principal and Professor of Hebrew in St David's College, Lampeter. Cambridge, Deighton, Bell & Co; London, Bell and Daldy, 1869.

John Venn   1869

On Some of the Characteristics of Belief Scientific and Religious. Being the

293

Hulsean Lectures for 1869, by J. Venn, M.A., Fellow and Lecturer of Gonville and Caius College, Cambridge. London and Cambridge, Macmillan & Co., 1870.

Frederick William Farrar   1870

The Witness of History to Christ. Five Sermons preached before the University of Cambridge. Being the Hulsean Lectures for the Year 1870. By the Rev. F. W. Farrar, D.D., F.R.S., Canon of Westminster. London, Macmillan & Co., 1880.

Fenton John Anthony Hort   1871

The Way the Truth the Life. The Hulsean Lectures for 1871. By Fenton John Anthony Hort, D.D. Some time Hulsean Professor and Lady Margaret's Reader in Divinity in the University of Cambridge. London, Macmillan & Co., 1893.

Josiah Brown Pearson   1872

Not published.

Stanley Leathes   1873

The Gospel its own Witness. The Hulsean Lectures for 1873 by the Rev. Stanley Leathes, M.A., Minister of St Philip's, Regent Street, Professor of Hebrew, King's College, London. London, Henry S. King & Co., 1874.

George Martin Straffen   1874

Sin, as set forth in Holy Scripture. The Hulsean Lectures for 1874 by George M. Straffen, M.A., Vicar of Clifton, York. London & Edinburgh, Williams & Norgate, 1875.

Edward Thomas Vaughan   1875

Some Reasons of our Christian Hope: Being the Hulsean Lectures for 1875. By Edward T. Vaughan, Rector of Harpenden, Hon. Canon of Peterborough and formerly Fellow of Christ's College, Cambridge. London, Macmillan & Co., 1876.

Edwin Abbott Abbott   1876

Not published.

George Smith Drew   1877

The Human Life of Christ revealing the order of the Universe. Being the Hulsean Lectures for 1877. G. S. Drew, M.A., Vicar of Holy Trinity, Lambeth. London, Longmans, Green, Reader & Dyer, 1878.

William Boyd Carpenter   1878

The Witness of the Heart to Christ. Being the Hulsean Lectures preached before the University of Cambridge in the year 1878. By the Right Rev. W. Boyd Carpenter, D.D., Lord Bishop of Ripon. London, SPCK, 1879.

Vincent Henry Stanton   1879

Not published.

Thomas Thomason Perowne   1880

Not published.

Joseph Foxley   1881

Secularism, Scepticism, Ritualism, Liberationism. The Hulsean Lectures preached before the University of Cambridge on the Four Sundays in Advent 1881. By Joseph Foxley, M.A., Vicar of Market Weighton. Formerly Fellow of St John's College. London, Longmans, Green & Co., n.d.

Frederick Watson   1882

The Law and the Prophets. The Hulsean Lectures for 1882. Preached before the University of Cambridge. Revised and enlarged. Cambridge, Fabb & Tyler, 1883.

John James Lias   1883

The Atonement viewed in the light of certain Difficulties. Being the Hulsean Lectures for 1883, 1884 by the Rev. J. J. Lias, Vicar of St Edward's, Cambridge. Cambridge, Deighton, Bell & Co., 1884.

Thomas George Bonney   1884

The Influence of Science and Theology. The Hulsean Lectures for the year 1884. Cambridge, Deighton, Bell & Co., 1885.

William Cunningham   1885

S. Austin and His Place in the History of Christian Thought. By W. Cunningham, B.D., Chaplain and Birkbeck Lecturer, Trinity College, Cambridge. London, C. J. Clay & Sons; Cambridge University Press Warehouse, 1886.

John de Soyres   1886

Christian Reunion. The Hulsean Lectures for 1886. London, J. & A. Macmillan, 1888.

Joseph Hirst Lupton   1887

Not published.

Henry Major Stephenson   1888

Christ the Life of Men. The Hulsean Lectures for 1888. By the Rev. H. M. Stephenson, M.A., Vicar of Bourn, Camb., Late Head Master of St Peter's School, York, formerly Fellow of Christ's College, Cambridge. Cambridge University Press 1890.

Edward George King   1889

The 'Asaph' Psalms in their Connexion with the early religion of Babylonia. The Hulsean Lectures for the year 1889. Cambridge, Deighton, Bell & Co.; London, G. Bell and Sons, 1890.

John Llewelyn Davies   1890

Order and Growth, as involved in the Spiritual Constitution of Human Society. By the Rev. J. Llewelyn Davies, M.A., Chaplain to the Queen; Vicar of Kirkby Lonsdale; formerly Fellow of Trinity College, Cambridge. London, Macmillan & Co., 1891.

Arthur Temple Lyttelton   1891

The Place of Miracles in Religion. The Hulsean Lectures for 1891. By the Right Rev. the Hon. A. T. Lyttelton, D.D., Bishop of Southampton. London, John Murray, 1899.

John Bickford Heard   1892

Alexandrian and Carthaginian Theology Contrasted. The Hulsean Lectures 1892–3. Edinburgh, T. & T. Clark, 1893.

296

Mandell Creighton   1893

Persecution and Tolerance. Being the Hulsean Lectures preached before the University of Cambridge in 1893–4. London, Longmans, Green & Co., 1895.

Alfred Barry   1894

The Ecclesiastical Expansion of England in the Growth of the Anglican Communion. The Hulsean Lectures for 1894–5, by Alfred Barry, D.D., D.C.L. London, Macmillan & Co., 1895.

William Moore Ede   1895

The Attitude of the Church to some of the Social Problems of Town Life. By W. Moore Ede, Rector of Gateshead; Hon. Canon of Durham. With a Preface by the Right Rev. the Lord Bishop of Durham. Cambridge University Press 1896.

Samuel Cheetham   1896

The Mysteries Pagan and Christian. Being the Hulsean Lectures for 1896–7. By S. Cheetham, D.D., F.S.A., Archdeacon and Canon of Rochester. London, Macmillan & Co., 1897.

James Edward Cowell Welldon   1897

The Hope of Immortality. By the Rev. J. E. C. Welldon, Head Master of Harrow School. New York, The Macmillan Co.; London, Macmillan & Co., 1898.

James Maurice Wilson   1898

The Gospel of the Atonement. Being the Hulsean Lectures for 1898–9. By James M. Wilson, Vicar of Rochdale, Archdeacon of Manchester, and Late Headmaster of Clifton College. London, Macmillan & Co., 1899.

Arthur James Mason   1899

Not published.

Frederic Henry Chase   1900

The Credibility of the Book of the Acts of the Apostles. Being the Hulsean Lectures for 1900–1. By Frederic Henry Chase, D.D., President of

Queens' College, and Norrisian Professor of Divinity, Cambridge. London, Macmillan & Co., 1902.

Frederick Robert Tennant   1901

The Origin and Propagation of Sin. Being the Hulsean Lectures delivered before the University of Cambridge in 1901–2. By F. R. Tennant, M.A. (Camb.), B.Sc. (Lond.). London, Cambridge University Press, 1902.

Frederick John Foakes-Jackson   1902

Christian Difficulties in the Second and Twentieth Centuries. A Study of Marcion and his Relation to Modern Thought. The Hulsean Lectures 1902–3. By F. J. Foakes-Jackson, B.D., Fellow of Jesus College, Cambridge and Hon. Canon of Peterborough. Cambridge, W. Heffer and Sons; London, Edward Arnold, 1903.

William Allen Whitworth   1903

Not published.

Charles William Stubbs   1904

The Christ of English Poetry. The Hulsean Lectures delivered in the University of Cambridge 1905. Charles William Stubbs, Dean of Ely. London, J. M. Dent & Co., 1906.

Henry Joseph Corbett Knight   1905

The Temptation of our Lord Considered as related to the Ministry and as a Revelation of His Person. The Hulsean Lectures 1905–6. London, Longmans, Green & Co., 1907.

James Pounder Whitney   1906

Episcopate and the Reformation. Our Outlook. London, Robert Scott; Milwaukee, Wis., The Young Churchmen Co., 1917. The Lectures appeared originally in *English Church Review*, Dec. 1915–Mar. 1916.

John Howard Bertram Masterman   1907

The Rights and Responsibilities of National Churches. The Hulsean Lectures 1907–8. Cambridge University Press 1908.

John Neville Figgis   1908

The Gospel and Human Needs. **Being the Hulsean Lectures delivered**
before the University of Cambridge, 1908–9. With additions. By John
Neville Figgis, Litt.D., Of the Community of the Resurrection, Hon.
Fellow of S. Catharine's College, Cambridge. London, Longmans,
Green and Co., 1909.

William Edward Chadwick   1909

Social Relationships in the light of Christianity. The Hulsean Lectures for
1909–10. London, Longmans, Green & Co., 1910.

Ernest Arthur Edghill   1910

The Revelation of the Son of God. Some Questions and Considerations
arising out of a study of Second Century Christianity. Being the
Hulsean Lectures for 1910–11. By Ernest Arthur Edghill. Subwarden
of the College of St Saviour, Southwark and Wilberforce Missioner,
Lecturer in Ecclesiastical History at King's College, London. London,
Macmillan & Co., 1911.

Reginald James Fletcher   1911

Dei Christus Dei Verbum. The Hulsean Lectures for 1911–12. London,
G. Bell & Sons, 1913.

Henry Latimer Jackson   1912

Not published.

William Leighton Grane   1913

Hulsean Lectures not published, but *Church Divisions and Christianity*
(London, Macmillan & Co., 1916) was developed from them.

Hugh Fraser Stewart   1914

The Holiness of Pascal. The Hulsean Lectures 1914–15. Cambridge
University Press 1915.

Herbert Armstrong Watson   1915

Mysticism of St. John's Gospel. Being the Hulsean Lectures delivered
before the University of Cambridge 1915–16. Revised and enlarged.
London, Robert Scott, 1916.

Arthur Stuart Duncan-Jones   1916

Ordered Liberty or **An** Englishman's Belief in his Church. Being the Hulsean Lectures delivered before the University of Cambridge for 1916–17. London, Longmans, Green & Co., 1917.

John Owen Farquhar Murray   1917

The Goodness and Severity of God. Hulsean Lectures (1917–18). By the Rev. J. O. F. Murray, D.D., Master of Selwyn College, Cambridge. London, SCM, 1924.

Francis Ernest Hutchinson   1918

Christian Freedom. Hulsean Lectures, 1918–19. By Francis E. Hutchinson, M.A., Oxon and Cantab. Formerly Chaplain of King's College, and Lecturer of Magdalene College, Cambridge. London, Macmillan & Co., 1920.

Alexander Nairne   1919

The Faith of the New Testament. London, Longmans, Green & Co., 1920.

Philip Napier Waggett   1920

Knowledge and Virtue. The Hulsean Lectures for 1920–21. By P. N. Waggett, M.A., Oxon and Cantab., Hon. D.D. Oxon. Society of St John the Evangelist. Oxford, Clarendon Press, 1924.

Leonard Elliott-Binns   1921

Erasmus the Reformer. A Study in Restatement. Being the Hulsean Lectures delivered before the University of Cambridge for 1921–22. London, Methuen & Co., 1923.

Charles Frank Russell   1922

Religion and Natural Law. The Hulsean Lectures, 1922–3. By C. F. Russell, M.A., Headmaster of King Edward VI School, Southampton. Formerly Fellow of Pembroke College, Cambridge. Oxford, Basil Blackwell, 1923.

Stewart Andrew McDowall   1923

Evolution, Knowledge and Revelation. Being the Hulsean Lectures delivered before the University of Cambridge, 1923–4. Cambridge University Press 1924.

Alan Coates Bouquet   1924

The Christian Religion and its Competitors To-day. Being the Hulsean Lectures for 1924–5. Delivered before the University of Cambridge by the Rev. A. C. Bouquet, D.D., Hon. C.F. Formerly a Scholar of Trinity College and a Lady Kay Scholar of Jesus College, Vicar of All Saints, Cambridge. Cambridge University Press 1925.

William Ralph Inge   1925

The Platonic Tradition in English Religious Thought. The Hulsean Lectures at Cambridge 1925–26. By William Ralph Inge, C.V.O., D.D. Dean of St Paul's, Fellow of the British Academy. London, Longmans, Green & Co., 1926.

Charles Earle Raven   1926

The Creator Spirit. A Survey of Christian Doctrine in the light of Biology, Psychology and Mysticism. The Hulsean Lectures, Cambridge, 1926–7. The Noble Lectures, Harvard, 1926. By Charles E. Raven, D.D. Canon of Liverpool and Chaplain to the King. With an Appendix on Biochemistry and Mental Phenomena by Joseph Needham, M.A., Ph.D. London, Martin Hopkinson & Co., 1927.

Edmund Gough de Salis Wood   1927

Not published.

Charles Archibald Anderson Scott   1929

New Testament Ethics. An Introduction. The Hulsean Lectures, 1929. By C. A. Anderson Scott, formerly Naden Divinity Student, St John's College, Cambridge. Hulsean Prizeman. Cambridge University Press 1930.

Allan John M. Macdonald   1931

Authority and Reason in the Early Middle Ages. The Hulsean Lectures, 1931–2. Delivered in the University of Cambridge in Michaelmas Term, 1931. London, Oxford University Press, 1933.

Herbert George Wood   1933

Christianity and the Nature of History. The Hulsean Lectures, 1933–4. London, Cambridge University Press, 1934.

John Martin Creed   1935

> *The Divinity of Jesus Christ.* A Study in the History of Christian Doctrine since Kant. By John Martin Creed, D.D., Ely Professor of Divinity in the University of Cambridge, Fellow of St John's College. Cambridge University Press 1938.

John Burnaby   1937

> *Amor Dei. A Study of the Religion of St. Augustine.* The Hulsean Lectures for 1938. By John Burnaby, Fellow of Trinity College, Cambridge. London, Hodder and Stoughton, 1938.

Stephen Charles Neill   1939 and 1940

> Not published. Subject: *The Trinity.*

Edward Chisholm Dewick   1947

> *The Christian Attitude to other Religions.* By E. C. Dewick, D.D. Cambridge University Press 1953.

William Owen Chadwick   1949

> *The Early Medieval Doctrine of the Church.* Not yet published.

Robert Henry Thouless   1950

> *Authority and Freedom.* Some Psychological Problems of Religious Belief. By Robert H. Thouless, Sc.D., Fellow of Corpus Christi College, Cambridge, Reader in Educational Psychology in the University of Cambridge. London, Hodder & Stoughton, 1954.

Laurence Edward Browne   1952

> *The Quickening Word. A Theological Answer to the Challenge of Islam.* The Hulsean Lectures, 1954. Cambridge, W. Heffer & Sons, 1955.

Henry Chadwick   1954

> *Origen.* The greater part of these lectures, in one form or another, were published in *Early Christian Thought and the Classical Tradition* (Oxford, Clarendon Press, 1966).

Hendrik Kraemer   1956

A Theology of the Laity. By Hendrik Kraemer. Sometime Professor of the History of Religions in the University of Leiden; late Director of the Ecumenical Institute, Bossey, Switzerland. London, Lutterworth Press, 1958.

Clifford William Dugmore   1958

The Doctrine of Grace in the English Reformers. Not published.

Peter Runham Ackroyd   1960

Exile and Restoration. A Study of Hebrew Thought of the Sixth Century B.C. London, SCM, 1968.

George Frederick Woods   1962

A Defence of Theological Ethics. The Hulsean Lectures, 1964. Cambridge 1966.

Peter Richard Baelz   1964

Prayer and Providence. A Background Study. By P. R. Baelz, Fellow and Dean of Jesus College, Cambridge. London, SCM, 1968.

David Lawrence Edwards   1966

Religion and Change. By David Edwards, Fellow and Dean of King's College, Cambridge. London, Hodder & Stoughton, 1969.

John Arthur Thomas Robinson   1968

The Human Face of God. London, SCM, 1973.

Kathleen Louise Wood-Legh   1970

Not published. Subject: *Reward*.

Maurice Frank Wiles   1973
The Remaking of Christian Doctrine. The Hulsean Lectures, 1973. London, SCM, 1974.

Peter Bingham Hinchliff   1975

The Relationship between Mission and Empire in the Nineteenth Century. Not yet published.

Alan Malcolm George Stephenson   1979

The Rise and Decline of English Modernism.

Gordon McGregor Kendal   1981

The Problem of Pleasure: A Christian Analysis. Not published.

a. *MS Sources*

b. *Periodicals*

c. *Printed volumes, pamphlets and articles*

a. *MS Sources*

Major papers now present at Ripon College, Cuddesdon.
Ripon Hall papers present at Ripon College, Cuddesdon.
Papers and letters on Modernism in the possession of the author.
Lambeth Conference Papers at Lambeth Palace.

b. *Periodicals*

Birmingham Diocesan Bulletin
The Broad Churchman
Cambridge Review
The Challenge
Church Gazette (*The Church Gazette. A Review of Liberal Religious Thought.* Vols. 1–6, 12 March 1898–29 Dec. 1900).
The Church of England Newspaper
Church of England Pulpit and Ecclesiastical Review
The Church Quarterly Review
The Daily Express
Daily Telegraph
Hibbert Journal
Guardian
Impetus
The Interpreter
The Liberal Churchman
Manchester Guardian
The Modern Churchman
The New Christian
The Observer

Parson and Parish
Prism
Spectator
The Sunday Pictorial
The Sunday Times
Tablet
Theology
The Times
The Universe
The Way
Western Morning News and Mercury
York Quarterly.

c. *Printed volumes, pamphlets and articles*

Abbott, Edwin A., *Through Nature to Christ or The Ascent of Worship through Illusion to Truth*. London, Macmillan & Co., 1877.
—*Onesimus*. London, Macmillan & Co., 1882.
—*The Kernel and the Husk*. Letters on Spiritual Christianity. By the author of 'Philochristus' and 'Onesimus'. London, Macmillan & Co., 1886.
—*The Spirit on the Waters*. The Evolution of the Divine from the Human. London, Macmillan & Co.; New York, Macmillan Co., 1897.
—*Silanus the Christian*. London, Adam & Charles Black, 1906.
—*Johannine Grammar*. London, Adam & Charles Black, 1906.
—*Philochristus. Memoirs of a disciple of the Lord*. London, Macmillan & Co., 1916.

Acland, Richard, *We teach them wrong: Religion and the Young*. London, Victor Gollancz, 1963.

Adams, Arthur W., 'The Christian Platonists of Cambridge' in *Modern Churchman*, vol. xxix, No. 1, April 1939.

Allen, Alexander V. G., *The Continuity of Christian Thought: A Study of Modern Theology in the Light of its History*. London and New York, Ward, Lock, 1884.
—*Christian Institutions* (International Theological Library). Edinburgh, T. & T. Clark, 1898.
—*Freedom in the Church or The Doctrine of Christ* as the Lord hath commanded, and as this Church hath received the same according to the commandments of God. New York, Macmillan Co., 1907.

Allen, Geoffrey, *Law with Liberty*. London, SCM, 1942.

Allen, Willoughby C., *A Critical and Exegetical Commentary on the Gospel according to S. Matthew* (The International Critical Commentary). Edinburgh, T. & T. Clark, 1912.

Angus, Samuel, *Alms for Oblivion. Chapters from a Heretic's Life*. Sydney and London, Angus and Robertson, 1943.
—*Forgiveness and Life*. Chapters from an uncompleted book *The Historical Approach to Jesus*. Edited by Ernest H. Vines. Introduction by H.D.A. Major. (Date Dec. 1946). Sydney, London, Melbourne, Wellington, Angus and Robertson, 1962.

Anson, Harold, *Looking Forward*. London, William Heinemann, 1938.
—*T. B. Strong. Bishop, Musician, Dean, Vice-Chancellor*. London, SPCK, 1949.

Arnold, Matthew, *God and the Bible. A Review of Objections to 'Literature and Dogma'*. London, Smith, Elder & Co., 1875.
—*Last Essays on Church and Religion*. London, Smith, Elder & Co., 1877.
—*Literature and Dogma*. An Essay towards a better apprehension of the Bible. London, Smith, Elder & Co., 1883.
—*St. Paul and Protestantism* with other essays. London, Smith, Elder & Co., 1889.

Asher, Felix, 'Robertson of Brighton, 1816–1853' in *The Modern Churchman*, vol. v, No. 12 (March 1916), pp.602–9.

Avebury, Lord, Address to the Churchmen's Union on moving the adoption of the report, 1903 in Occasional Papers, No. VI, The Churchmen's Union.

Ayer, Alfred J., *Language, Truth and Logic*. London, Victor Gollancz, 1936.

Bagenal, Philip H., 'The Origin of the Churchmen's Union', in *The Modern Churchman* (December 1920), pp.490–4.
—'The Modern Movement in the Church of England' in the *Hibbert Journal* (January 1922), pp.220–35.
—*The Modern Movement in the Church of England*. Churchmen's Union Pamphlets No. 3. The Churchmen's Union, The Church House, Westminster. n.d., probably 1923. The pamphlet was republished in *The Modern Churchman* (April 1937), pp.10–22.

Baker, John Austin, *The Foolishness of God*. London, Darton, Longman & Todd, 1970.

Barnes, Ernest William, 'English Modernism. III The Father of English Modernism', in *The Challenge* (8 June 1923), p.203.

—*Should such a Faith offend? Sermons and Addresses*. London, Hodder & Stoughton, 1927.
—*Scientific Theory and Religion*. The World described by Science and its Spiritual Interpretation. Cambridge University Press 1933.
—*The Rise of Christianity*. London, New York, Toronto, Longmans, Green, 1947.

Barnett, Henrietta O., *Canon Barnett. His Life, Work, and Friends*. By his wife. 2 vols. London, John Murray, 1918.

Barr, James, *The Semantics of Biblical Language*. London, Oxford University Press, 1961.

Barry, F. R., *Period of My Life*. London, Sydney, Auckland, Toronto, Hodder and Stoughton, 1970.

Bartsch, Hans Werner, ed., *Kerygma and Myth. A Theological Debate*. With Contributions by Rudolf Bultmann, Ernst Lohmeyer, Julius Schniewind, Friedrich Schumann, Helmut Thieliecke, and Austin Farrer. E. trans. Reginald H. Fuller. London, SPCK, 1953.

Beeby, C. E., *Creed and Life*. A Critical Enquiry concerning the Ancient Orthodox Creed and a Declaration of its Contents in proof of its capacity to meet the needs of modern life. London, Simpkin, Marshall, Hamilton, Kent & Co.; Birmingham and Leicester, The Midland Educational Co., 1897.
—*Doctrine and Principles. Popular Lectures on Primary Questions*. London, Edinburgh and Oxford, Williams & Norgate, 1900.
—'Doctrinal Significance of a Miraculous Birth', in *Hibbert Journal*, October 1903.

Bennett, G. V., 'Erasmus and the Reformation', in *The Modern Churchman*, vol. xiii (N.S.) No. 1 (October 1969), pp.41–55.

Benson, Arthur Christopher, *The Life of Edward White Benson Sometime Archbishop of Canterbury*. 2 vols. London, Macmillan, 1899.

Bethune-Baker, James Franklin, *An Introduction to the Early History of Christian Doctrine*. London, Methuen, 1903.
—*The Miracle of Christianity*. A Plea for the Critical School in regard to the use of the Creed. A Letter to the Rt. Rev. Charles Gore. London, 1914.
—*The Faith of the Apostles' Creed*. An Essay in adjustment of Belief and Faith. London, Macmillan & Co., 1918.
—*The Way of Modernism & Other Essays*. Cambridge University Press 1927.

Bezzant, J. S., 'Bishop Barnes and the Diocese of Birmingham' in *Theology*, vol. 68, No. 535 (January 1965), pp.14–20.

The Bible in Basic English. Cambridge University Press in association with Evans Brothers 1949.

Birch, A. H., 'Creed and Conscience', in *The Hibbert Journal*, vol. 46, No. 3 (April 1948), pp.198–204.

Blakeney, E. H., 'Defenders of the Faith in the Second Century', in *The Modern Churchman*, vol. xxxi, No. 4, July 1941.

Blunt, A. W. F., 'My Reply to Bishop Barnes', in *Sunday Pictorial*, 14 December 1947.

Blythe, Ronald, *The Age of Illusion. England in the Twenties and Thirties 1919–40.* Harmondsworth, Middlesex, Penguin Books, 1964.

Blytheway, M. E., *Index of Contributors, Subjects and Titles. The Modern Churchman 1931–1941. vols. xxi–xxx.* Oxford, Basil Blackwell, 1941.

Boden-Worsley, J. F. W., 'Memories of Modernists and others', in *Theology*, vol. xli, No. 243 (September 1940), pp.151–9.

Boman, Thorlief, *Hebrew Thought compared with Greek.* London, SCM, 1960.

Braley, Evelyn Foley, ed., *Letters of Herbert Hensley Henson.* Chosen and edited by Evelyn Foley Braley. London, SPCK, 1951.

Brown, William Adams, *The Essence of Christianity. A Study in the History of Definition.* New York, Charles Scribner's Sons, 1902.

Budd, K. G., *The Story of Donald Hankey. A Student in Arms.* London, SCM, 1931.

Burdekin, Arthur Edward. *Index of Articles in The Modern Churchman 1911–1931. Volumes I–XX.* Oxford, Basil Blackwell, 1931.

Buren, Paul van, *The Secular Meaning of the Gospel.* Based on an Analysis of its Language. London, SCM, 1963.

Burge, H. M., *The Doctrine of the Resurrection of the Body.* Documents relating to the Question of Heresy raised against the Rev. H. D. A. Major, Ripon Hall, Oxford. London and Oxford, A. R. Mowbray & Co.; Milwaukee, U.S.A., The Morehouse Publishing Co., 1922.

Burkitt, F. C., *'The Failure of Liberal Christianity' and Some Thoughts on the Athanasian Creed.* Two Addresses. Cambridge, Bowes and Bowes, 1910.

309

Cadbury, H. J., *The Peril of Modernizing Jesus*. London, Macmillan, 1937; SPCK, 1962.

Cadoux, Cecil John, *The Case for Evangelical Modernism*. A Study of the Relation between Christian Faith and Traditional Theology. London, Hodder & Stoughton, 1938.

Campbell, R. J., *The New Theology*. London, Chapman & Hall, 1907.
—*A Spiritual Pilgrimage*. London, Williams & Norgate, 1916.

Carpenter, William Boyd, 'The Education of a Minister of God', in *Hibbert Journal*, vol. iii (1905), pp.433–51.

Case, Shirley Jackson, *The Historicity of Jesus*. A Criticism of the contention that Jesus never lived, a statement of the evidence for his existence, an estimate of his relation to Christianity. Chicago, Illinois, The University of Chicago Press, 1912.

Casserley, J. V. Langmead, *The Retreat from Christianity in the Modern World*. The Maurice Lectures for 1951. London, New York, Toronto, Longmans, Green, 1952.

Chadwick, Owen, *The Victorian Church*. Part 1, London, Adam & Charles Black, 1966. Part 2, 1970.

Champneys, Arthur C., 'A Different Gospel which is not Another Gospel'. Examined by Arthur C. Champneys. Foreword on Science and Miracles by F. A. Dixey, M.D., F.R.S. London, G. Bell & Sons, 1922.

Chardin, Pierre Teilhard de, *The Phenomenon of Man*. London, Collins Fontana Books, 1965.

Chase, F. H., *Belief and Creed*. Being an Examination of Portions of 'The Faith of a Modern Churchman' dealing with the Apostles' Creed. London, Macmillan & Co., 1918.

Cheyne, T. K., *Bible Problems and the New Material for their Solution. A Plea for Thoroughness of Investigation addressed to Churchmen and Scholars*. London, Williams & Norgate; New York, G. P. Putnam's Sons, 1904.

Cheyne, T. K. and J. Sutherland Black, *Encyclopaedia Biblica*. A Critical Dictionary of the Literary Political and Religious History, the Archaeology, Geography and Natural History of the Bible. London, Adam & Charles Black, 4 vols., 1899–1903.

Chillingworth, H. R. 'Archbishop Whately', in *The Modern Churchman*, vol. xxxix, No. 2 (June 1949), pp.105–13.

The Churches of England and South India. A Joint Statement by the Anglican Evangelical Group Movement, the Church Society, and the Modern Churchmen's Union. London, The Modern Churchmen's Union, 1955.

Churchmen's Union. List of Members. Women's Printing Society Ltd., 66 & 68 Whitcomb St., W.C. n.d., but almost certainly 1909.

Clarke, O. Fielding, *For Christ's Sake*. A Reply to the Bishop of Woolwich's book, *Honest to God*, and a positive continuation of the discussion. Wallington, Surrey, The Religious Education Press, 1953.
—*Unfinished Conflict. An Autobiography*. Derby, The Citadel Press, 1970.

Cleobury, F. H., *The Armour of Saul. A Reconsideration of the Easter Faith*. London, James Clarke, 1957.
—*Christian Rationalism and Philosophical Analysis*. London, James Clarke, 1959.
—*A Study in Christian Apologetic*. Supplement to Faith and Thought, vol. 100. London, The Victorian Institute, 1972.
—*From Clerk to Cleric*. Cambridge, James Clarke, 1976.

Cobb, William Frederick, *Theology Old and New*. (The Church's Outlook for the Twentieth Century. A Series of Handbooks on Ecclesiastical Problems edited by John Henry Burn.) London, Elliot Stock, 1902.
—*Mysticism and the Creed*. London, Macmillan, 1914.

Cohu, J. R., *The Evolution of the Christian Ministry*. The Modern Churchmen's Library, No. 111. London, John Murray, 1918.

Coleman, A. M., 'The Jubilee of Mark Pattison's Memoirs', in *The Modern Churchman*, vol. xxv, No. 10, pp.566–73. Republished in his *Six Liberal Thinkers* (Oxford, Basil Blackwell, 1936), pp.35–43.

Coleridge, Samuel Taylor, *Aids to Reflection and The Confessions of an Inquiring Spirit*. To which are added his Essays on Faith and the Book of Common Prayer etc. (Bohn's Libraries). London, George Bell & Sons, 1893.
—*Confessions of an Inquiring Spirit*. Reprinted from the third edition 1853 with the Introduction by Joseph Henry Green and the note by Sara Coleridge. Edited with an Introductory Note by H. St J. Hart. London, Adam & Charles Black, 1956.

Contentio Veritatis. Essays in Constrictive Theology by Six Oxford Tutors. London, John Murray, 1902.

Conybeare, William John, 'Church Parties' in *Edinburgh Review*, XCVIII (October 1853), pp.273–342.

Cratchley, W. J., 'Richard Whately: Archbishop of Dublin', in *The Modern Churchman*, vol. xxvi, No. 10, January 1937.

Creed, John Martin, *The Gospel according to St. Luke*. The Greek Text with Introduction, Notes, and Indices. London, Macmillan, 1930.

Cunningham-Craig, W. A., 'Broad Churchmen of the Nineteenth Century. (I) Renn Dickson Hampden', in *The Modern Churchman*, vol. ii, No. 7 (October 1912), pp.332–8.
—'Broad Churchmen of the Nineteenth Century. (II) Thomas Arnold', in *The Modern Churchman*, vol. ii, No. 12 (March 1913), pp.556–62.
—'Broad Churchmen of the Nineteenth Century. (III) Frederick Denison Maurice', in *The Modern Churchman*, vol. iii, No. 3 (July 1913), pp.142–7.

Cupitt, Don, *The Debate about Christ*. London, SCM, 1979.

Danks, William, *The Gospel of Consolation. University and Cathedral Sermons*. Preface by the Dean of Canterbury (H. Wace) and an Appreciation by the Right Rev. Bishop Boyd Carpenter. London, Longmans, Green, 1917.

Davidson, Randall T., *The Six Lambeth Conferences 1867–1920*. Compiled under the direction of the Most Reverend Lord Davidson of Lambeth, Archbishop of Canterbury 1903–1928. London, SPCK, 1929.

Davidson, Randall Thomas and William Benham, *Life of Archibald Campbell Tait, Archbishop of Canterbury*. 3rd edn, 2 vols. London, Macmillan, 1891.

Davies, Charles M., *Orthodox London* or *Phases of Religious Life in the Church of England*. London, Tinsley Brothers, Strand, 1874. Second Series, 1875.

Davies, D. R., *In Search of Myself*. The Autobiography of D. R. Davies. London, Geoffrey Bles, 1961.

Dictionary of National Biography. Oxford University Press.

Dillistone, F. W., *Charles Raven. Naturalist, Historian, Theologian*. London, Sydney, Auckland, Toronto, Hodder & Stoughton, 1975.

Doctrine in the Church of England. The Report of the Commission on Christian Doctrine appointed by the Archbishops of Canterbury and York in 1922. London, SPCK, 1938.

Dodd, C. H., *Christian Beginnings*. A Reply to Dr Barnes' 'The Rise of Christianity'. London, Epworth Press, n.d. (Reprinted from the *London and Holborn Quarterly Review*, July 1947).

Dougall, Lily and Cyril W. Emmet, *The Lord of Thought*. A Study of the Problems which confronted Jesus Christ and the Solution He offered. London, SCM, 1922.

Douglas, C. E., *The Redemption of the Body*. Four Lectures on the Resurrection. With an examination of the Bishop of Oxford's pamphlet by Hakluyt Egerton. London, The Faith Press, 1922.
—*The Appeal to His Grace the Archbishop of Canterbury concerning the refusal of the Lord Bishop of Oxford to hear an accusation brought against the Rev. H. D. A. Major of professing disbelief in the Truth of the Creeds*. London, The Faith Press, 1922.

Draper, W. H., *Recollections of Dean Fremantle. Chiefly by Himself*. Edited by the Master of the Temple. London, Cassell, 1921.

Driver, S. R., *An Introduction to the Literature of the Old Testament*. (International Theological Library). 8th edn revised. Edinburgh, T. & T. Clark, 1909.

Ede, W. Moore, 'What we owe to Frederick Denison Maurice and his disciples', in *The Modern Churchman*, vol. xxiii, No. 9 (December 1933), pp.527–34.

Edwards, David L., *Ian Ramsey Bishop of Durham. A Memoir*. London, New York, Toronto, Oxford University Press, 1973.

Emmet, Cyril W., *Conscience, Creeds and Critics*. A Plea for Liberty of Criticism within the Church of England. London, Macmillan, 1918.

Essays and Reviews. 7th edn. London, Longman, Green, Longman and Roberts, 1961.

Fallows, William Gordon, 'A Modern Priscilla and Aquila'. Retirement of Canon H. D. A. Major, D.D., F.S.A., 30 June 1960. Merton Vicarage, Bicester, Oxford.
—*Mandell Creighton and the English Church*. London, Oxford University Press, 1964.

Farrar, Frederic W., *The Life of Christ*. London, Paris and Melbourne, Cassell, 1894.
—*The Life and Work of St. Paul*. London, Paris, New York and Melbourne, Cassell, n.d.

Fawkes, Alfred, *The Genius of the English Church*. London, John Murray, 1917.
—*The Church a Necessary Evil and other Sermons*. Oxford, Basil Blackwell, 1932.

Fitzgerald, Maurice H., *A Memoir of Herbert Edward Ryle, K.C.V.O., D.D., sometime Bishop of Winchester and Dean of Westminster*. London, Macmillan, 1928.

Fitzgerald, Penelope, *The Knox Brothers*. Edmund (Evoe) 1881–1971, Dillwyn 1883–1943, Wilfred 1886–1950, Ronald, 1888–1957. London, Macmillan, 1977.

Fitzroy, A. I., *Dogma and the Church of England*. Edinburgh and London, William Blackwood & Sons, 1891.

Foakes-Jackson, F. J., 'Christ in the Church: the Testimony of History', in *Essays on Some Theological Questions of the Day* by Members of the University of Cambridge. Edited by Henry Barclay Swete. London, Macmillan, 1905.
—'The Cambridge Conference of the Churchmen's Union', in *Hibbert Journal*, vol. xx, No. 2 (January 1922), pp.193–207.
—ed., *The Faith and the War*. A Series of Essays by members of the Churchmen's Union and others on the Religious Difficulties aroused by the present condition of the world. London, Macmillan, 1916.

Foakes-Jackson, F. J. and Kirsopp Lake, *The Beginnings of Christianity*. Part I. The Acts of the Apostles. vol. I Prolegomena I The Jewish, Gentile and Christian Backgrounds. London, Macmillan, 1920.

Forman, R. S., ed., *Great Christians*. London, Ivor Nicholson & Watson, 1933.

Fosdick, Harry Emerson, *The Living of These Days. An Autobiography*. London, SCM, 1957.

Fox, Adam, *Dean Inge*. London, John Murray, 1960.

Fremantle, W. H., *The Gospel of the Secular Life*. Sermons preached at Oxford, with a Prefatory Essay. London, Paris, New York, Cassell, Petter, Galpin & Co., 1882.
—*The World as the Subject of Redemption* being an attempt to set forth the functions of the Church as designed to embrace the whole race of mankind. Eight lectures delivered before the University of Oxford in the year 1883 on the foundation of the late Rev. John Bampton. London, Rivingtons, 1885.
—'The Religious Influence of Benjamin Jowett', in *The Modern Churchman*, vol. v, No. 2 (May 1915), pp.69–75.

Frend, W. H. C., 'Liberalism in the Early Church', in *The Modern Churchman*, vol. xiii (N. S.) (October 1969), pp.28–40.

Gamble, John, *Baptism Confirmation and the Eucharist*. Together with a brief

exposition of the Church Catechism. London, John Murray, 1918. The
Modern Churchman's Library, No. IV.

Gardner, Alice, *Synesius of Cyrene* (in the Series The Fathers for English
Readers). London, SPCK, 1886.
—*The Conflict of Duties and other Essays*. London, T. Fisher Unwin, 1903.
—*Within Our Limits. Essays on Questions Moral Religious, and Historical.*
London, T. Fisher Unwin, 1913.
—*Our Outlook as Changed by the War.* A Paper read in Newnham College
on Sunday, 25th October 1914. Cambridge, W. Heffer & Sons;
London, Simpkin, Marshall, 1914.

Gardner, Percy, *Exploratio Evangelica. A Survey of the Foundations of
Christianity.* London, Adam & Charles Black, 1907.
—*Evolution in Christian Doctrine.* London, Williams & Norgate; New
York, G. P. Putnam's Sons, 1918.
—*The Translation of Christian Doctrine.* A Paper read before the members of
the Churchmen's Union at St. Martin's Vestry Hall, Charing Cross,
on Wednesday, April 23rd, 1902. (The Churchmen's Union, St.
Andrew's Vicarage, Leytonstone, N.E.).
—*Modernism in the English Church.* London, Methuen, 1926.
—*Autobiographica.* Oxford, Basil Blackwell, 1933.

Gardner-Smith, Percival, *The Christ of the Gospels. A Study of the Gospel
Records in the light of Critical Research.* With a Foreword by F. J. Foakes-
Jackson. Cambridge, W. Heffer & Sons, 1938.
—'Synesius of Cyrene' in *The Modern Churchman*, vol. xxx, No. 12 (March
1941). pp.500–10.

—'Left Wing Criticism' (a review of E. W. Barnes' *The Rise of
Christianity*) in *The Modern Churchman*, vol. xxxvii, No. 2 (July 1947),
pp.166–72.

Geikie-Cobb, W. F., *The Humanists Horn Book.* Bishopsgate, Press of St
Ethelburga's Church, n.d.

Glazebrook, M. G., *The Letter and the Spirit.* A Reply to the Bishop of Ely's
Criticisms on *The Faith of a Modern Churchman.* London, John Murray,
1920.
—*The Faith of a Modern Churchman.* London, John Murray, 1925.

Glover, T. R., *The Jesus of History.* With a Foreword by the Archbishop of
Canterbury. London, SCM, 1918.

Gore, Charles, *The Basis of Anglican Fellowship in Faith and Organization.* An
Open Letter to the Clergy of the Diocese of Oxford. London, A. R.
Mowbray; Milwaukee, U.S.A., The Young Churchman Co., 1914.

—*The Reconstruction of Belief. Belief in God. Belief in Christ The Holy Spirit and the Church*. New Edition in One Volume. London, John Murray, 1926.

—ed., *Lux Mundi*. A Series of Studies in the Religion of the Incarnation. 7th edn. London, John Murray, 1890.

Goudge, H. L., 'Catholicism and Liberal Christianity', in *Church Quarterly Review*, vol. xciii (January 1922), pp.205ff.

Green, Michael, ed., *The Truth of God Incarnate*. London, Sydney, Auckland, Toronto, Hodder & Stoughton, 1977.

[Grierson, Walter], *Modernism: And what it did for me* by The Enquiring Layman. London, George Newnes, 1929.

Griffith, R. Gladstone, *The Necessity of Modernism*. London, Skeffington & Son, 1932.

Gwatkin, H. M., *The Bishop of Oxford's Open Letter. An Open Letter in Reply*. London, New York, Bombay, Calcutta and Madras, Longmans, Green, 1914.

Hadham, John (James Parkes), *Good God. A Study of His Character and Activities*. (A Penguin Special). Harmondsworth, Allen Lane, Penguin Books, 1940.

Hall, A. Clifford, *Modernism and Youth—An Attempt at Interpretation*. Modernist Pamphlets on Religious Life and Thought. No. 2. London, Union of Modern Free Churchmen, 1943.

Hall, Francis J., *Christianity and Modernism*. U.S.A., Edwin S. Goreham, 1924.

Hammerton, H. J., *This Turbulent Priest. The Story of Charles Jenkinson, Parish Priest and Housing Reformer*. With a Foreword by His Grace the Archbishop of York (Cyril Garbett). London, Lutterworth Press, 1952.

Handley, Hubert, *The Fatal Opulence of Bishops. An Essay on a Neglected Ingredient of Church Reform*. London, Adam & Charles Black, 1901.

—*Theological Room. Gathered Papers*. London, Constable, 1914.

—*A Visit to Ripon Hall*. London, Williams & Norgate, 1925.

—ed., *A Declaration of Biblical Criticism by some 1725 Clergy of the Anglican Communion*. London, Adam & Charles Black, 1906.

Hardwick, J. C., 'Ecclesiae Gubernator' (Connop Thirlwall) in *The Modern Churchman*, vol. vii, No. 2 (May 1917), pp.59–65.

—'John Colet' in *The Modern Churchman*, vol. xv, No. 4, July 1925.

—*Freedom and Authority in Religion*. London, Skeffington & Son, n.d.

—*A Professional Christian*. London, Jonathan Cape, 1932.

Harnack, Adolf, *What is Christianity?* Sixteen Lectures. Delivered in the University of Berlin during the Winter Term, 1899–1900. E. trans. by Thomas Bailey Saunders. London, Williams & Norgate; New York, G. P. Putnam's Sons, 1904.

Harris, Charles, *Creeds or No Creeds?* A Critical Examination of the Basis of Modernism. With Forewords by the Right Rev. the Lord Bishop of Lichfield and the Warden of Wadham College, Oxford. London, John Murray, 1922.

Harvey, G. L. H. ed., *The Church and the Twentieth Century.* London, Macmillan, 1936.

Hatch, Edwin, *The Influence of Greek Ideas and Usages on the Christian Church.* London, Williams & Norgate, 1907.

Haweis, H. R., *The Dead Pulpit.* London, Bliss, Sands, 1896.

Headlam, A. C., 'The Modernist Christology', in *Church Quarterly Review*, vol. 93, pp.201–32, January 1922.

Hebert, A. G., *Liturgy and Society. The Function of the Church in the Modern World.* London, Faber & Faber, 1935.
—*Memorandum on the Report of the Archbishops' Commission on Christian Doctrine.* London, published for the Church Union by SPCK, 1939.

Hecht, Isobel FitzRoy, 'Robertson of Brighton', in *The Modern Churchman*, vol. iii, No. 6 (September 1913), pp.294–302.
—*Alfred Williams Momerie—A Victorian Preacher. Modern Churchman*, vol. iii, No. 11 (February 1914), pp.630–42.

Henslow, George, *Genesis and Geology. A Plea for the Doctrine of Evolution, being a sermon preached November 5th, 1871, at St. John's Church, Marylebone.* London, Robert Hardwicke, 1871.
—*What was the Fall? A Sermon.* Reprinted from *The Church of England Pulpit.* London, Church of England Pulpit Office, n.d.

Henson, H. Hensley, *Sincerity and Subscription.* A Plea for Toleration in the Church of England. London and New York, Macmillan, 1903.
—*The Creed in the Pulpit.* London, New York, Toronto, Hodder & Stoughton, 1912.
—*Retrospect of an Unimportant Life.* Volume I 1863–1920, Volume II 1920–1939. London, New York, Toronto, Oxford University Press, 1943.

Herrmann, Willibald (*sic*), *The Communion of the Christian with God*: A Discussion in agreement with the view of Luther. E. trans. by J.

Sandys Stanyon. Willibald a mistake for Wilhelm. London, Edinburgh and Oxford, Williams & Norgate, 1895.

Hick, John, ed., *The Myth of God Incarnate*. London, SCM, 1977.

Hickin, L., 'Liberal Evangelicals in the Church of England', in *Church Quarterly Review*, Jan. to Mar. 1968.

Holland, Henry Scott, *A Bundle of Memories*. London, Wells Gardner, Darton & Co., 1915.

Hort, Arthur Fenton, *Life and Letters of Fenton John Anthony Hort*. 2 Vols. London, Macmillan & Co., 1896.

Hunkin, J. W. (Bishop of Truro), *The Gospel for Tomorrow*. (A Penguin Special). Harmondsworth, Penguin Books, 1941.

Hunt, John, *Religious Thought in England in the Nineteenth Century*. London, Gibbings & Co., 1896.

Hutton, Arthur Wollaston, *Ecclesia Discens*. Occasional Sermons and Addresses. London, Francis Griffiths, 1904.

Inge, W. R., *Faith and Knowledge*. Sermons. Edinburgh, T. & T. Clark, 1905.
—*Truth and Falsehood in Religion*. Six Lectures delivered at Cambridge to undergraduates in the Lent Term 1906. London, John Murray, 1906.
—*Christian Mysticism*. Considered in eight lectures delivered before the University of Oxford. London, Methuen, 1918.
—*Outspoken Essays* (First Series). London, New York, Toronto, Bombay, Calcutta and Madras, Longmans, Green, 1919.
—*Outspoken Essays* (Second Series). London, New York, Toronto, Bombay, Calcutta, Madras, Longmans, Green, 1922.
—*Diary of a Dean. St. Paul's 1911–1934*. London, New York, Melbourne, Sydney, Cape Town, Hutchinson, n.d.
—*Our Present Discontents*. London, Putnam, 1938.

Jagger, Peter J., *A History of the Parish and People Movement*. Leighton Buzzard, The Faith Press, 1978.

Jasper, Ronald, *Arthur Cayley Headlam*. Life and Letters of a Bishop. With a Foreword by the Dean of St Paul's (W. R. Matthews). London, Faith Press, 1960.

Jesus or Christ? Essays by G. Tyrrell, E. S. Talbot, H. Weinel, Percy Gardner, Paul Wilh. Schmiedel, Henry Jones, Richard Morris, Oliver Lodge, Henry Scott Holland, Joseph Rickaby, Nathan Söderblom, A. E. Garvie, R. J. Campbell, James Drummand, Benjamin W. Bacon, J.

E. Carpenter, James Collier, R. Roberts. Being the Hibbert Journal Supplement for 1909. London, Williams & Norgate, 1909.

Johnson, Hewlett, *Searching for Light. An Autobiography.* London, Michael Joseph, 1968.

Jones, Harry, *Fifty Years or Dead Leaves and Living Seeds.* London, Smith, Elder, 1895.

Kee, Alistair, *The Way of Transcendence. Christian Faith without Belief in God.* Harmondsworth, Penguin Books, 1971.

Kenyon, Frederic G., *The Bible and Modern Scholarship.* London, John Murray, 1948.

Kirk, Kenneth E., ed., *The Apostolic Ministry.* Essays on the History and Doctrine of Episcopacy. Prepared under the direction of Kenneth E. Kirk, London, Hodder & Stoughton, 1946.

Knox, R. A., *Some Loose Stones. Being a Consideration of Certain Tendencies in Modern Theology illustrated by reference to the book called 'Foundations'.* London, New York, Bombay and Calcutta, Longmans, Green, 1914.

Lake, Kirsopp, *The Historical Evidence for the Resurrection of Jesus Christ.* London, Williams & Norgate; New York, G.P. Putnams, 1912.
—*The Earlier Epistles of St. Paul.* Their Motive and Origin. London, Rivingtons, 1914.
—*The Stewardship of Faith.* Our Heritage from Early Christianity. London, Christophers, 1915.
—*Landmarks in the History of Early Christianity.* London, Macmillan, 1920.
—*Paul: his Heritage and Legacy.* London, Christophers, 1934.

Lambert, Brooke, *Sermons and Lectures* by the late Brooke Lambert (Vicar of Greenwich), edited by Ronald Bayne. With a Memoir by J. E. G. de Montmorency. Greenwich, Henry Richardson, 1902.

Lambeth Conference 1878. Report of Committee on Subject V. Order of Reference – To consider and draw up a Report on prevailing Infidelity, and on the best practical remedies. Copy at Lambeth Palace Library, unpublished.

Lambeth Conference 1888. Committee No. I On Definite Teaching of the Faith to various classes and the means thereto. There are two versions of this, both never published, in Lambeth Palace Library.

The Lambeth Conference 1958. The Encyclical Letter from the Bishops together with the Resolutions and Reports. London, SPCK; Connecticut, The Seabury Press, 1958.

319

Lambeth Occasional Reports 1931–8. With a Foreword by the Bishop of Winchester (Mervyn Haigh). London, SPCK, 1948.

Lewis, John Wren, *Return to the Roots. A Study in the meaning of the word 'God'.* The Modern Churchmen's Union, 1955.

Lightfoot, Robert Henry, *History and Interpretation in the Gospels.* The Bampton Lectures 1934. London, Hodder & Stoughton, 1935.

Lloyd, Roger, *The Church of England 1900–1965.* London, SCM, 1966.

Lockhart, J. G., *Charles Lindley, Viscount Halifax. Part 1, 1839–1885. Part 2, 1885–1934.* London, Geoffrey Bles, The Centenary Press, 1935 and 1936.

Luce, H. K., *The Gospel according to S. Luke.* With Introduction and Notes. Cambridge University Press 1949.

Macan, Reginald W., *The Resurrection of Jesus Christ.* An Essay in Three Chapters. Published for the Hibbert Trustees. London and Edinburgh, Williams & Norgate, 1977.

McCallum, James Ramsay, *Abelard's Ethics.* Oxford, Basil Blackwell, 1935.
—*Abelard's Christian Theology.* Oxford, Basil Blackwell, 1948.
—'Peter Abelard', in *The Modern Churchman,* vol. xxxii, Nos. 4, 5 and 6, September 1942.

Mackarness, E. D., 'Benjamin Jowett: Preacher and Prophet', in *The Modern Churchman,* vol. xlv, No. 4 (December 1955), pp.319–26.

McKay, Roy, *John Leonard Wilson Confessor for the Faith.* London, Sydney, Auckland, Toronto, Hodder & Stoughton, 1973.

Mackay, R. W., *The Tubingen School and its Antecedents.* A Review of the History and Present Condition of Modern Theology. London and Edinburgh, Williams & Norgate, 1863.

McNabb, Vincent, *From a Friar's Cell.* Oxford, Basil Blackwell, 1923.

Macquarrie, John, *Principles of Christian Theology.* London, SCM, 1966.

Major, Henry D. A., 'The Creed as Ethical Stimulus' in *The Modern Churchman,* vol. i, No. 6 (September 1911), pp.300f.
—'Theological Colleges', in *The Modern Churchman,* vol. i, No. 8 (November 1911), pp.441–7, and No. 9 (December 1911), p.505.
—'A Modern View of the Incarnation', in *The Modern Churchman,* vol. iii, No. 9 (December 1913), pp.465–74.
—'A Fearless Father in God', in *The Modern Churchman,* vol. iii, No. 11 (February 1914), pp.579–88.

—*A Modern View of the Incarnation*. Privately printed for Conference of Anglican Fellowship, April 5–7, 1915 in the Office of the Modern Churchman. W. Parr, Knaresborough, Yorks.

—'The Problem of the Creeds', in *The Modern Churchman*, vol. vii, No. 4 (July 1917), pp.156–7.

—'Modern Churchmen or Unitarians?', in *Hibbert Journal*, vol. xx, No. 2 (1922), pp.208–19.

—*A Resurrection of Relics*. A Modern Churchman's Defence in a recent charge of heresy. Oxford, Basil Blackwell, 1922.

—*Reminiscences of Jesus by an Eye-witness*. London, John Murray, 1925.

—*English Modernism. Its Origin, Methods, Aims*. Being the William Belden Noble Lectures delivered in Harvard University 1925–6. Harvard, Harvard University Press; London, Oxford University Press, 1927.

— *Thirty Years After*. A New Zealander's Religion. Auckland, Wellington, Christchurch, Dunedin, New Zealand. Melbourne, Sydney, London, Whitcombe & Tombs Ltd; Oxford, Basil Blackwell, 1929.

—*The Roman Church and the Modern Man*. London, Eyre & Spottiswoode, 1934.

—*The Church's Creeds and the Modern Man*. London, Skeffington & Son, n.d.

—'Towards Prayer Book Revision', in *The Church and the Twentieth Century*, edited by G. L. H. Harvey. London, Macmillan, 1936.

—*Basic Christianity*. The World Religion. Oxford, Basil Blackwell, 1944.

—'Criticism and Conscience'. A Reply to Dr. Birch's article 'Creed and Conscience'. *The Hibbert Journal*, vol. 46, No. 3 (April 1948), pp.205–11.

—'A Martyr of the Miraculous', in *The Modern Churchman*, vol. 38, No. 4 (December 1948), pp.336–8.

—'The Renaissance of F. D. Maurice', in *The Modern Churchman*, vol. xli, No. 2 (June 1951), pp.99–103.

—'Agnosticism, Gnosticism, and Knowledge of God' (a review of John Wren Lewis, *Return to Roots*) in *The Modern Churchman*, vol. 45, No. 4 (1955). pp.353–4.

Major, Henry D. A., T. W. Manson and C. J. Wright, *The Mission and Message of Jesus*. An Exposition of the Gospels in the light of Modern Research. London, Ivor Nicholson & Watson, 1937.

Manning, W., *Some Elements of Religion*. London, Francis Griffiths, 1908.

Marriage and Divorce in the Church of England. Memoranda submitted to the Royal Commission on Marriage and Divorce by The Modern Churchmen's Union. The Modern Churchmen's Union 1952.

Marriage and the Church's Task. The Report of the General Synod Marriage Commission. London, Central Board of Finance, 1978.

Martin, E. J., 'Frederic William Farrar 1831–1931', in *The Modern Churchman*, vol. xx, No. 12 (March 1931), pp.667–74.

Mascall, Eric, *Up and Down in Adria. Some Considerations of Soundings.* London, The Faith Press, 1963.

—*The Secularisation of Christianity.* An Analysis and a Critique. London, Darton, Longman & Todd, 1965.

Masterman, C. F. G., *The Life of Frederick Denison Maurice* (Leaders of the Church, 1800–1900. Ed. by George W. E. Russell). London and Oxford, A. R. Mowbray, 1907.

Matheson, P. E., *The Life of Hastings Rashdall D.D.,* Dean of Carlisle, Fellow of the British Academy, Honorary Fellow of New College. London, Oxford University Press, 1928.

Mathews, Shailer, *The Faith of Modernism.* New York, Macmillan Co., 1925.

Matthews, W. R., *Studies in Christian Philosophy. Being the Boyle Lectures, 1920.* London, Macmillan, 1921.

—*The Purpose of God.* London, Nisbet, 1935.

—*God in Christian Thought and Experience.* London, Nisbet, 1939.

—*The Thirty-Nine Articles.* A Plea for a New Statement of the Christian Faith as understood by the Church of England. (An Expanded version of a lecture given at Sion College) London, Hodder & Stoughton, 1961.

—*Memories and Meanings.* London, Hodder & Stoughton, 1969.

Maurier, Daphne du, *Vanishing Cornwall. The Spirit and History of Cornwall.* Harmondsworth, Middlesex, Penguin Books, 1972.

Meiklejohn, R., 'The Churchmanship of Thomas Arnold', in *The Modern Churchman*, vol. ix, No. 1 (April 1919), pp.34–9.

Mendieta, Emmanuel Amand de, *Anglican Vision.* London, SPCK, 1971.

Michaelhouse, John (i.e. Joseph McCulloch), *Charming Manners.* London, J. M. Dent & Sons, 1932.

Micklem, Nathaniel, *The Box and the Puppets (1888–1953).* London, Geoffrey Bles, 1957.

Milner, Gamaliel, 'John Hales and his Friends', in *The Modern Churchman*, vol. v, No. 4, July 1915.

Momerie, Alfred Williams, *Inspiration* and other sermons preached in the

Chapel of the Foundling Hospital. Edinburgh and London, William Blackwood & Sons, 1890.

—*Church and Creed.* Sermons preached in the Chapel of the Foundling Hospital. Edinburgh and London, William Blackwood & Sons, 1890.

—*The Origin of Evil* and other sermons, preached in St Peter's, Cranley Gardens. Edinburgh and London, William Blackwood & Sons, 1891.

—*Personality.* The Beginning and End of Metaphysics and a necessary assumption in all positive philosophy. (Fifth edition revised.) Edinburgh and London, Blackwood & Sons, 1895.

—*Immortality and other Sermons.* Edinburgh and London, William Blackwood & Sons, 1901.

Momerie, Vehia, *Dr. Momerie. His Life and Work.* Written and edited by his wife. Edinburgh and London, Blackwood & Sons, 1905.

Montefiore, Claude G., *The Origin and Growth of Religion as illustrated by the religion of the Ancient Hebrews.* London and Edinburgh, Williams & Norgate, 1892.

Montefiore, Hugh, *Truth to Tell.* A Radical Restatement of Christian Truth. London, Collins (Fontana Books), 1966.

Morgan, Dewi, ed., *They Became Anglicans.* Personal Statements of Sixteen Converts to the Anglican Communion. London, A. R. Mowbray, 1959.

Morison, E. F., 'The Message of Charles Kingsley', in *The Modern Churchman,* vol. xv, Nos. 1 and 2 (April and May 1925), pp.22–6.

Morris, Colin, *Include Me Out.* Confessions of an Ecclesiastical Coward. London, Epworth Press, 1968.

—*Unyoung, Uncoloured, Unpoor.* London, Epworth Press, 1969.

Morrison, William Douglas, *Crime and its Causes.* London, Sonnenschein, 1890.

—*The Jews under Roman Rule* (The Story of the Nations). London, T. Fisher Unwin; New York, G. P. Putnam's Sons, 1890.

—*Juvenile Offenders.* London, Unwin, 1896.

—*The Liberal Churchman.* A Quarterly Review. London, Williams & Norgate, 1904–8.

Moule, C. F. D., ed., *Miracles.* Cambridge Studies in their Philosophy and History. London, A. R. Mowbray, 1965.

Moyle, Frank W., *Neville Gorton, Bishop of Coventry 1943–55.* Reminiscences by Some of his friends. Edited and arranged by Frank W. Moyle. London, SPCK, 1957.

Mulliner, H. G., 'John Frederick Denison Maurice' in *The Modern Churchman*, vol. xvii, Nos. 6, 7 and 8 (October 1927), pp.474–80.

Nineham, Dennis, *The Gospel of St. Mark.* (The Pelican Gospel Commentaries). Harmondsworth, Penguin Books, 1963.
—ed., *The Church's Use of the Bible. Past and Present.* London, SPCK, 1963.

Nunn, H. P. V., *What is Modernism?* London, SPCK, 1932.

Oman, John, *Honest Religion.* With an Introduction by Frank H. Ballard and a Memoir of the Author by George Alexander and H. H. Farmer. Cambridge University Press 1942.

Page, Robert J., *New Directions in Anglican Theology. A Survey from Temple to Robinson.* London, A. R. Mowbray, 1967.

Paley, William, *A View of the Evidences of Christianity.* In Three Parts. A New Edition, with Notes, Appendix, and Preface, by the Rev. E. A. Litton. London, SPCK, n.d.

Palmer, William Scott (i.e. Mary Emily Dowson), *The Diary of a Modernist.* London, Edward Arnold, 1910.

Parkes, James, *Voyage of Discoveries* by James Parkes (John Hadham). London, Victor Gollancz, 1969.

Parks, Leighton, *What is Modernism?* New York and London, Charles Scribner's Sons, 1924.

Paul, C. Kegan, *Memories.* London, Routledge & Kegan Paul, 1971.

Peart-Binns, John S., *Blunt.* Queensbury, Yorkshire, Mountain Press, n.d.

Pelz, Werner and Lotte, *God is No More.* London, Victor Gollancz, 1963; Harmondsworth, Penguin Books, 1968.

Pittenger, W. Norman, *The Word Incarnate.* A Study of the Doctrine of the Person of Christ. Welwyn, Herts., James Nisbet, 1959.
—*The Christian Understanding of Human Nature.* Welwyn, Herts., James Nisbet, 1964.
—*Time for Consent? A Christian's Approach to Homosexuality.* London, SCM, 1967, enlarged edition, 1970.
—*Christology Reconsidered.* London, SCM, 1970.
—ed., *Christ for Us Today.* Papers read at the Conference of Modern Churchmen, Somerville College, Oxford, July 1967 with an appended essay by Edward Carpenter, President of the Modern Churchmen's Union. London, SCM, 1968.

Pringle-Pattison, A. Seth, *The Idea of God in the Light of Recent Philosophy.* The Gifford Lectures, delivered in the University of Aberdeen in the years 1912 and 1913. New York, London, Toronto, Melbourne and Bombay, Oxford University Press, 1920.

Pryke, W. Maurice, *Modernism as a Working Faith*. Cambridge, W. Heffer & Sons, 1925.

Purcell, William, *Woodbine Willie*. An Anglican Incident. Being some account of the life and times of Geoffrey Anketell Studdert Kennedy, poet, prophet, seeker after truth, 1883–1929. London, Hodder & Stoughton, 1962.

Quick, Oliver Chase, *The Christian Sacraments*. London, Nisbet, 1927.
—*Doctrines of the Creed*. Their Basis in Scripture and their Meaning Today. London, Nisbet, 1938.

Ramsey, Arthur Michael, *The Gospel and the Catholic Church*. London, New York, Toronto, Longmans, Green, 1936.
—*Jesus Christ in Faith and History*. An Inaugural Lecture in the University of Durham, October 25, 1940. Theology Occasional Papers, New Series, No. 3. London, SPCK, n.d.
—*The Resurrection of Christ. An Essay in Biblical Theology*. London, Geoffrey Bles, 1946.
—*The Glory of God and the Transfiguration of Christ*. London, New York, Toronto, Longmans, Green, 1949.
—'Modernism Past and Present', in *The York Quarterly* (May 1957), New Series No. 3, pp.2f.
—*From Gore to Temple*. The Development of Anglican Theology between Lux Mundi and the Second World War 1889–1939. The Hale Memorial Lectures of Seabury-Western Theological Seminary, 1959. London, Longmans, Green, 1960.
—*Image Old and New*. London, SPCK, 1963.

Ramsey, Ian T., *Religious Language: an Empirical Placing of Theological Phrases*. London, SCM, 1957.
—ed., *Biology and Personality. A Symposium*. Frontier Problems in Science, Philosophy and Religion. Oxford, Basil Blackwell, 1965.

Ranchetti, Michele, *The Catholic Modernists. A Study of the Religious Reform Movement 1864–1907*. London, Oxford University Press, 1969.

Rashdall, Hastings, 'Professor Sidgwick on the Ethics of Religious Conformity: a Reply', in *International Journal of Ethics*, vol. vii, No. 2 (January 1897), pp.137–68.
—*Doctrine and Development*. University Sermons. London, Methuen, 1898.
—'In what sense was Christ the Son of God', in Occasional Paper No. VI, The Churchmen's Union.

—*Christus in Ecclesia.* Sermons on the Church and its Institutions. Edinburgh, T. & T. Clark, 1904.

—'Clerical Liberalism' in *Anglican Liberalism* by Twelve Churchmen. London, Williams & Norgate; New York, G. P. Putnam's Sons, 1908.

—*Conscience and Christ.* Six Lectures on Christian Ethics. London, Duckworth, 1916.

—*The Idea of Atonement in Christian Theology.* Being the Bampton Lectures for 1915. London, Macmillan, 1919.

—*Jesus Human and Divine.* Three Sermons together with a Theological Essay. London and New York, Andrew Melrose, 1922.

—*God and Man.* Selected and edited by H. D. A. Major and F. L. Cross, Oxford, Basil Blackwell, 1930.

Raven, Charles E., 'A Fore-runner' (F. D. Maurice), in *The Modern Churchman,* vol. xviii, No. 10 (January 1929), pp.582–6.

—*Natural Religion and Christian Theology.* The Gifford Lectures 1951. First Series: Science and Religion. Cambridge University Press 1953.

—'E. W. B. – The Man for the Moment' in *The Modern Churchman,* vol. 45, No. 1 (March 1955), pp.11–24.

Reardon, Bernard M. G., *Liberal Protestantism.* Edited and Introduced. London, Adam & Charles Black, 1968.

Relton, Herbert M., *A Study in Christology. The Problem of the Relation of the Two Natures in the Person of Christ.* With a Preface by Arthur C. Headlam. London, SPCK, 1917.

Report of a Meeting held at Lambeth Palace in support of the claims of Lightfoot Hall, His Grace the Archbishop of Canterbury in the Chair on Saturday, 18 January 1902.

Reville, Jean, *Liberal Christianity. Its Origin, Nature, and Mission.* Translated and edited by Victor Leuliette. London, Williams & Norgate; New York, G. P. Putnams, 1903. (Crown Theological Library).

Rhymes, Douglas, *No New Morality. Christian Personal Values and Sexual Morality.* London, Constable, 1964.

Richardson, Alan, *The Redemption of Modernism.* London, Skeffington & Son, 1933.

—*The Miracle-Stories of the Gospels.* London, SCM, 1941.

—*Christian Apologetics.* London, SCM, 1955.

—*An Introduction to the Theology of the New Testament.* London, SCM, 1958.

—ed., *Four Anchors from the Stern.* Nottingham Reactions to recent Cambridge Essays. (Alan Richardson, A. R. C. Leanery, Stuart G. Hall, James Richmond). London, SCM, 1963.

Richardson, R. D., *The Gospel of Modernism.* New edn with Appendices. London, Skeffington & Son, 1935.

Rickards, Edith C., *Bishop Moorhouse of Melbourne and Manchester.* London, John Murray, 1920.

Robertson, F. W., 'An Unpublished Lenten Sermon' by Robertson of Brighton (taken down in shorthand by Miss K. Lowndes, in *the Modern Churchman*, vol. vi, No. 12 (March 1917) pp.572–9.

Robinson, J. Armitage, *Some Thoughts on the Incarnation.* With a Prefatory Letter to the Archbishop of Canterbury. London, Longmans, Green, 1905.

Robinson, John A. T., *The Body. A Study in Pauline Theology.* Studies in Biblical Theology. London, SCM, 1952.
—*Jesus and His Coming.* The Emergence of a Doctrine. London, SCM, 1957.
—*Honest to God.* London, SCM, 1963.
—*The New Reformation.* London, SCM, 1965.
—*Exploration into God.* London, SCM, 1967.
—*But that I can't believe!* London, Collins, Fontana Books, 1967.
—*In the end, God . . . A Study of the Christian Doctrine of the Last Things.* (Theology for Modern Men, No. 4) London, James Clarke, 1950, republished by Collins (Fontana Books), 1968.

Robinson, John A. T. and David L. Edwards, *The Honest to God Debate.* Some reactions to the book 'Honest to God' edited by David L. Edwards with a new chapter by its author John A. T. Robinson. London, SCM, 1963.

Rogers, T. Guy, ed., *Liberal Evangelicalism. An Interpretation* by Members of the Church of England. London, Hodder & Stoughton, 1923.
—ed., *The Inner Life. Essays in Liberal Evangelicalism* by Members of the Church of England. London, Hodder & Stoughton, n.d.

Root, Howard, ed., *Marriage, Divorce and the Church.* The Report of the Commission on the Christian Doctrine of Marriage. London, SPCK, 1971.

Rowell, Geoffrey. *Hell and the Victorians.* A Study of the nineteenth-century theological controversies concerning eternal punishment and the future life. Oxford, Clarendon Press, 1974.

Rowse, A. L., *A Cornishman at Oxford.* The Education of a Cornishman. London, Jonathan Cape, 1965.

Royds, T. F., 'Parties and Party Spirit: their use and abuse', in *The Modern Churchman*, vol. xix, No. 1 (April 1929), pp.7–15.

—*Sorrow Sin and Suffering.* London, Skeffington & Son, 1932.

—*Haughton Rectory or Four Country Parsons.* Shrewsbury, Wilding & Son, 1953.

Ryle, Herbert Edward, *The Canon of the Old Testament. An Essay on the Gradual Growth and Formation of the Hebrew Canon of Scripture.* London, Macmillan, 1904.

—*Early Narratives of Genesis. A Brief Introduction to the Study of Genesis I – XI.* London, Macmillan, 1904.

Sabatier, Auguste, *Outlines of a Philosophy of Religion, based on Psychology and History.* Authorized translation by Rev. T. A. Seed. London, Hodder & Stoughton, 1897.

—*The Religions of Authority and the Religion of the Spirit.* With a Memoir of the author by Jean Reville and a note by Madame Sabatier. London, Williams & Norgate, 1904. (Theological Translation Library)

Sanday, William, *Inspiration. Eight Lectures on the Early History and Origin of the Doctrine of Biblical Inspiration.* Being the Bampton Lectures for 1893. London, New York, Bombay, Calcutta and Madras, Longmans, Green, 1893.

—*Bishop Gore's Challenge to Criticism.* A Reply to the Bishop of Oxford's Open Letter on the Basis of Anglican Fellowship. London, Longmans, Green, 1914.

—*Divine Overruling.* Edinburgh, T. & T. Clark, 1920.

—'Edwin Hatch 1835 – 1889', in *The Modern Churchman,* vol. x, Nos. 6 & 7 (September 1920), pp.378 – 85.

—*The Position of Liberal Theology.* A Friendly Examination of the Bishop of Zanzibar's Open Letter entitled 'The Christ and His Critics'. London and Manchester, The Faith Press, 1920.

Sanday, William and N. P. Williams, *Form and Content in the Christian Tradition.* A Friendly Discussion between W. Sanday and N. P. Williams. London, New York, Bombay and Calcutta, Longmans, Green, 1916.

Sanders, Charles Richard, *Coleridge and the Broad Church Movement.* Studies in S. T. Coleridge, Dr. Arnold of Rugby, J. C. Hare, Thomas Carlyle and F. D. Maurice. Durham, North Carolina, Duke University Press, 1942.

Sanders, J. N., *The Foundations of the Christian Faith. A Study of the Teaching of the New Testament in the Light of Historical Criticism.* London, A. & C. Black, 1950.

Sandford, E. G., ed., *Memoirs of Archbishop Temple,* by Seven Friends. 2 vols. London, Macmillan, 1906.

Schweitzer, Albert, *The Quest of the Historical Jesus. A Critical Study of its Progress from Reimarus to Wrede.* Translated by W. Montgomery. With a Preface by F. C. Burkitt. London, A. & C. Black, 1922.

Scott, D. L., 'South Africa's Greatest Bishop', in *The Modern Churchman*, vol. xxxvii, No. 1 (April 1947), pp.52–61.

—'F. D. Maurice: a Prophet of the Kingdom', in *The Modern Churchman*, vol. xxxix, No. 1, pp.58–63. (A review of A. R. Vidler, *The Theology of F. D. Maurice*, London, SCM, 1948).

—'Some Reflections on Robertson of Brighton. Died August 15th 1853', in *The Modern Churchman*, vol. xliii, No. 4 (December 1953), pp.284–92.

—'Rowland Williams, 1817–1870', in *The Modern Churchman*, vol. xlv, No. 2 (June 1955), pp.118–25.

—'The Enigma of Charles Kingsley', in *The Modern Churchman*, vol. 4, (N. S.), No. 2 (January 1961), pp.131–2. (A review of R. B. Martin, *The Dust of Combat. A Life of Charles Kingsley,* London, Faber & Faber, 1959).

Seeley, J. R., *Ecce Homo. A Survey of the Life and Work of Jesus Christ.* London, Macmillan, 1903.

—*Natural Religion* by the author of 'Ecce Homo'. London, Macmillan, 1882.

Self, Henry, 'Bishop Barnes', by Sir Henry Self, in *The Modern Churchman*, vol. 44, No. 1 (March 1954), pp.14–24.

—The Divine Indwelling. A Reconciliation of Science, Religion, and Philosophy. The typescript of Chapter 14 of a proposed book, 1969.

Selwyn, Edward Gordon, *Essays Catholic & Critical* by Members of the Anglican Communion. London, SPCK, 1926.

Shannon, R. T., 'John Robert Seeley and the Idea of a National Church. A Study in Churchmanship, Historiography and Politics', in *Ideas and Institutions of the Victorians*, ed. Robert Robson. London, G. Bell & Sons, 1967.

Sidgwick, A. and E. M., *Henry Sidgwick.* London, Macmillan, 1906.

Sidgwick, Henry, 'The Ethics of Religious Conformity', in *International Journal of Ethics* (April 1896), vol. vi, No. 3, pp.273–90.

Simpson, D. C., *Pentateuchal Criticism.* With an Introduction by the Right Rev. H. E. Ryle. London, New York, Toronto, Hodder & Stoughton, 1914.

Simpson, W. J. Sparrow, *Broad Church Theology.* London, Robert Scott; Milwaukee, U.S.A., The Morehouse Publishing Co., 1919.

Smith, J. S. Boys, *Christian Doctrine and the Idea of Evolution*. Cambridge, Bowes & Bowes, 1930.

Smith, Nowell Charles, ed. *Letters of Sydney Smith*. 2 vols. Oxford, Clarendon Press, 1953.

Stanley, A. P., *Christian Institutions. Essays on Ecclesiastical Subjects*. London, John Murray, 1882.
—*Essays chiefly on Questions of Church and State from 1850–1870*. London, John Murray, 1884.

Stephenson, Alan M. G., 'William Sanday', in *The Modern Churchman*, vol. 9, No. 4 (N. S.) (July 1966), pp.257–72.
—*Anglicanism and the Lambeth Conferences*. London, SPCK, 1978.

Sterrett, J. Macbride, *Modernism in Religion*. New York, Macmillan Co., 1922.

Stewart, Herbert Leslie, *Modernism. Past and Present*. London, John Murray, 1932.

Strauss, David Friedrich, *The Life of Jesus Critically Examined*. Translated from the Fourth German Edition by George Eliot. Fifth Edition in one volume. London, Swan Sonnenschein, 1906.

Streeter, B. H., *Reality. A New Correlation of Science & Religion*. London, Macmillan, 1926.
—ed. *Foundations*. A Statement of Christian Belief in terms of Modern Thought by Seven Oxford Men. London, Macmillan, 1912.

Sykes, S. W., *The Integrity of Anglicanism*. London and Oxford, A. R. Mowbray, 1978.

Sykes, S. W. and J. P. Clayton, ed., *Christ Faith and History*. Cambridge Studies in Christology. Cambridge University Press 1972.

Symes, J. E., *Broad Church*. London, Methuen, 1913.

Temple, Frederick, *The Relations between Religion and Science*. Eight Lectures preached before the University of Oxford in the year 1884 on the foundation of the late Rev. John Bampton, M.A. London, Macmillan, 1884.

Thompson, James Matthew, *Miracles in the New Testament*. London, Edward Arnold, 1911.
—*My Apologia* by J. M. T. Printed for Private Circulation Only (at the Alden Press, Oxford).

Thornhill, Alan, *One Fight More*. London, Frederick Muller, 1943.

Til, Cornelius van, *The New Modernism. An Appraisal of the Theology of Barth and Brunner.* London, James Clarke & Co., 1946.

Tollinton, R. B., *Clement of Alexandria. A Study in Christian Liberalism.* 2 vols. London, Williams & Norgate, 1914.

—'Clement of Alexandria', in *The Modern Churchman*, vol. viii (August to October 1918), pp.327–32.

Vahanian, Gabriel, *The Death of God.* The Culture of our Post-Christian Era. New York, George Braziller, 1957.

Vidler, Alexander Roper, *20th Century Defenders of the Faith.* London, SCM, 1965.

—*F. D. Maurice and Company. Nineteenth Century Studies.* London, SCM, 1966.

—*A Variety of Catholic Modernists.* Cambridge University Press 1970.

—*Scenes from a Clerical Life.* An Autobiography. London, Collins, 1977.

—'Bishop Barnes: A Centenary Retrospect' in *The Modern Churchman*, vol. 18 (N. S.) No. 3 (Spring 1975), pp.87–98.

—ed., *Soundings.* Essays concerning Christian Understanding. Cambridge University Press 1966.

—ed., *Objections to Christian Belief.* London, Constable, 1963.

Wakefield, Gordon S., 'Hoskyns and Raven. The Theological Issue', in *Theology*, vol. 78, No. 665 (November 1975), pp.568–76.

Wand, J. W. C., *Anglicanism in History and Today.* London, Weidenfeld & Nicolson, 1961.

Ward, F. W. Orde, ed., *Lux Hominum. Studies of the Living Christ in the World of To-day.* London, Francis Griffiths, 1907.

Waugh, Evelyn, *Decline and Fall.* London, Penguin Books, 1978.

Were, Peter, 'Forgotten Liberals and "Basic Christianity"', in *The Modern Churchman*, vol. 13, (N. S.), No. 3 (April 1970), pp.279–81.

Weston, Frank, *The Christ and His Critics.* An Open Pastoral Letter to the European Missionaries of his Diocese. London and Oxford, A. R. Mowbray; Milwaukee, U.S.A., The Morehouse Publishing Co., 1919.

White, Douglas, *Modern Light on Sex and Marriage.* London, Skeffington & Son, 1932.

Whiteley, D. E. H. and R. Martin, *Sociology, Theology and Conflict.* Oxford, Basil Blackwell, 1969.

Wickey, N. J. Gould, 'The Doubt of Robertson of Brighton', in *The Modern Churchman*, vol. x, No. 10 (January 1921), pp.525–30.

Wigley, T., *The Necessity of Christian Modernism*. London, James Clarke, 1939.

Wiles, Maurice, ed., *Christian Believing*. The Nature of the Christian Faith and its Expression in Holy Scripture and Creeds. A Report by the Doctrine Commission of the Church of England. London, SPCK, 1976.

Wilkinson, Alan, *The Church of England and the First World War*. London SPCK, 1978.

Wilkinson, John, ed., *Catholic Anglicans Today*. London, Darton, Longman & Todd, 1968.

Willey, Basil, 'Rector and Master: Mark Pattison and Benjamin Jowett', in *The Modern Churchman*, vol. 2, (N. S.), No. 3 (March 1959), pp.135–9.

Williams, Charles D., Annual Sermon 1908, preached in St Martins-in-the-Fields, Charing Cross. The Churchmen's Union. Women's Printing Society Ltd., 66 and 68 Whitcomb Street, W.C.

Williams, David, *Genesis and Exodus. A Portrait of the Benson Family*. London, Hamish Hamilton, 1979.

Williams, N. P., *Miracles* (Modern Oxford Tracts). London, Longmans, Green, 1914.

Wilson, Arnold T. and J. S. Wilson, *James M. Wilson: an Autobiography. 1836–1931*. London, Sidgwick & Jackson, 1932.

Wilson, James M., *How Christ saves us or The Gospel of the Atonement*. Being the Hulsean Lectures for 1898–9. London, Macmillan, 1905.

Woodlock, Francis, *Modernism and the Christian Church*. Three Farm Street Lectures: to which is added a chapter on the Problem and the Prospects of Christian Reunion by Francis Woodlock S.J. With a Preface by G. K. Chesterton. London, Longmans, Green, 1925.

Woods, H. G., 'Past Liberalism', in *Anglican Liberalism*, by Twelve Churchmen, ed. Hubert Handley. London and New York, Williams & Norgate, 1908.

Wright, C. J., *Miracle in History and in Modern Thought or Miracle and Christian Apologetic*. New York, Henry Holt & Co., 1930.

Index of Names and Places

Abbott, Edwin A. 17, 22, 26, 43, 45, 46, 52, 53, 66, 91, 93
Abelard, Peter 40
Acland, Sir Richard 75
Acland, Sir Thomas Dyke 75, 77, 88, 97, 99, 101, 103
Adams, Arthur W. 40, 89, 162, 188
Addis, W. E. 63
Alford, Bradley 52, 53
Alford, Henry 17, 22, 53
Allen, A. V. G. 87, 140
Allen Geoffrey F. 18, 109, 154, 179, 180, 181, 189, 199
Allen, Willoughby C. 85, 133
Allington, Dean 154
Altizer, Thomas J. J. 194
Altrincham 163
Alves, Mary V. 83
Angus, Samuel 5, 20, 190, 205
Anson, Harold 4, 20, 50, 51, 113, 125, 151
Aquinas, St Thomas 118, 128
Arius 124
Arminius 124
Arnold, Matthew 47
Arnold, Thomas 24, 41, 43, 44, 47, 50, 70, 178
Ashby St Ledger 105
Asher, Felix 41
Ashley, Professor 75
Aston Clinton 106
Athanasius 69, 128
Attwood, Dr 102
Augustine, St (Canterbury) 84, 118
Augustine, St (Hippo) 18, 75, 187
Austin, W. 95
Ayer, A. J. 155

Babel 2
Baelz, Peter 17, 23, 197
Bagenal, Philip H. 28, 48, 52, 53, 58, 76, 101, 111
Bagley Wood 109, 141
Baker, John 195
Barnes, E. W. 3, 11, 12, 13, 14, 15, 19, 21, 44, 69, 101, 109, 113, 115, 116, 118, 124, 140, 141, 143, 144, 145, 146, 148, 150, 153, 162, 163, 164, 165, 166, 167, 168, 169, 170, 171, 172, 173, 174, 175, 176, 178, 179, 189, 190, 199
Barnes, Sir John 12, 145, 149, 163, 165, 167, 169, 170, 174, 176
Barnett, Mrs Henrietta 76, 107
Barnett, Samuel A. 46, 53, 75, 107
Barr, James 189

Barry, Alfred 23
Barry, F. R. 137, 160
Barth, Karl 6, 18, 154, 180, 181, 193
Baur, Ferdinand C. 31, 32
Baxter, Richard 90
Bayne, R. 76
Beatty, William 84
Bedale Grammar School 55
Beeby, Charles E. 34, 49, 69, 70
Beeching, Dean 133
Benham, William 49, 63, 77
Benigni, U. 5
Bennett, G. V. 40
Benson, A. C. 20
Benson, Christopher 15, 16, 21, 22
Benson, E. W. 4, 20, 38, 49, 163
Bentley, John R. 150
Berkeley, Lord 144, 162
Bernard, St 59
Bethune-Baker, J. F. 12, 14, 100, 105, 107, 108, 109, 111, 113, 115, 117, 118, 119, 120, 121, 123, 133, 154
Bevan, Edwyn 102
Bezzant, James S. 14, 109, 139, 140, 158, 159, 164, 165, 192
Bickersteth, E. H. 4
Bickersteth, Robert 67
Bicknell, E. J. 137, 148
Bindley, T. H. 113
Birch, A. H. 173
Bishopthorpe 136
Bithynia 1
Blackburne, Francis 40
Blakeney, E. H. 50
Blunt, A. W. F. 95, 174
Blythe, Ronald 33
Boar's Hill 144, 145, 162, 178
Boden-Worsley, J. F. W. 123
Bodleian Library 25, 97, 144
Boman, T. 189
Bond, C. J. 143
Bonhoeffer, Dietrich 6, 185, 191
Boughton, C. H. K. 95, 96
Bouquet, Alan C. 14, 17, 21, 201
Bourn 19
Bonney, Thomas G. 17, 22
Boynton 179
Bradley, Charles L. 93
Bradley, Dean 56, 57, 69
Braley, E. F. 20, 176, 204
Brandon, S. G. F. 116, 201

INDEX